Digital Signal Processing in FORTRAN

Digital Signal Processing in FORTRAN

Fred Taylor
University of Cincinnati

Steve L. Smith
Rice University

Lexington Books
D.C. Heath and Company
Lexington, Massachusetts
Toronto London

Library of Congress Cataloging in Publication Data

Taylor, Fred, 1940-
Digital signal processing in Fortran.

Bibliography: p. 397
Includes index.
1. Signal processing. 2. SPECTRUM IV (Computer program)
I. Smith, Steve L., joint author. II. Title.
TK5012.5.T34 621.38'0433'0285424 75-28940
ISBN 0-669-00330-1

Published simultaneously in Canada

Printed in the United States of America

International Standard Book Number: 0-669-00330-1

Library of Congress Catalog Card Number: 75-28940

To Lori, Robin, and Brooke Taylor
and Gerry and Marjorie Smith

Contents

Preface

Digital signal processing is receiving increased attention in science and engineering. The advent of the Fast Fourier Transform (FFT) has added new impetus to digital signal and spectral analysis. Numerous books, monographs, and papers have been written on the theory and practice of FFT and the companion topics of fast correlation, coherence, spectral power densities and so forth.[a] In addition several manufacturers have developed dedicated fast Fourier systems, which perform extremely well in the field. These systems use mini-computers or special-purpose digital hardware to perform the required transform operations. These dedicated devices are computationally fast and are engineered to be user-oriented. Here, user orientation means that a set of keyboard options is available to the user to perform selected tasks. For example, with the push of a button a user can perform a Fourier transform, an inverse transform, or any of the standard spectral operations. No prior programming experience is required to harness the power of these digital machines. If programming experience exists, then nesting these push-button options in a program will allow the user to perform complex signal analysis. However, such systems are significantly expensive (typically $30,000 for a minimum configuration).

In 1973, having no funds to acquire a dedicated FFT hardware system, we turned to the only computer system available to us: a general-purpose digital computer. A digital signal analysis software systems package did not exist at that time. In fact, the only digital-signal-processing technique available was an FFT routine resident in the system library. This program was very inflexible and did not support fast correlation, fast cross-correlation, coherence analysis, and so forth. We sensed the need for a complete, integrated, user-oriented digital signal analysis software package for general-purpose digital computers, so we embarked on a software development program that would incorporate the desirable features of the dedicated hardware systems. We labeled our software system SPECTRUM IV (spectral analysis in FORTRAN IV). The use and utility of SPECTRUM IV are documented in this book.

The highly flexible, easy-to-use spectral-analysis components of SPECTRUM IV allow it to be applied directly to problems in electrical and mechanical engineering, the biological sciences, physics, and the social sciences. Electrical engineers would find the package extremely useful in the study of linear systems, digital and continuous communications systems, stationary random processes, pattern recognition and classification, and control systems. Biologists would find the package useful in the design

[a] A partial list of publications in the area of digital-signal processing can be found in the bibliography.

and analysis of linear bioloqical models and biological signal analysis. Physicists and mechanical engineers would find the package useful in the study of acoustic and vibrational systems. Social scientists would find the fast-correlation and spectral-decomposition features of SPECTRUM IV extiemely useful in the study of the periodic behavior of social systems. In all cases the software system can be used in an educational as well as a research environment.

To understand the structure of SPECTRUM IV, one must understand the motivations and philosophy that arose during the construction of this program. The program originally consisted of Singleton's mixed radix (capable of a 1024-point transform) FFT routine, a small main program to input data, and a display of results. The desire for more flexible input-output led to the development of the initial-card-input, card-punch, and line-printer routines. The correlation routines were the next to be developed, along with routines to scale and manipulate the data. What followed was an assortment of programs, each one desired to perform a particular function (for example, matched filter, transfer function).

The final organization of SPECTRUM IV was conceived as a matter of inconvenience. The task of reprogramming SPECTRUM IV on an IBM 360 computer (originally written for a CDC 3100) prompted a complete rethink of the program. We decided to retain the overlay structure (required of the CDC 3100 due to limited memory size) while incorporating direct-access features for the more sophisticated IBMs. During this changeover, the user-diagnostic errors were revised to be more restrictive toward user-programming errors whereas other routines were written to provide the user with information about the program's internal status.

The authors bear the responsibility of maintaining and upgrading the contents of this software system. As a convenience to the user, the entire software package can be purchased from the authors at a nominal cost. Price and ordering information can be found on a special card at the end of this book. Upon authorization, SPECTRUM IV will be sent to the user on 300-foot, 800 BPI, 9-track, standard-label magnetic tape in FORTRAN IV source form. Personnel at the user's computation center can easily produce a complete source listing of SPECTRUM IV from the tape. If desired, a source listing alone can be secured. In all cases the fee for this service will be the cost of duplication plus postage. Additional information about this service can be obtained from the authors or by contacting the Computer Center of the University of Texas at El Paso, El Paso, Texas 79968 (915-747-5000).

We want to express our appreciation to the technical staff of the computation center at the University of Texas at El Paso for their support in the development of this software system. A special debt is owed to Gale and Evelyn Larson for their unselfish assistance in producing this manuscript. Finally, we voice our praise and apologies to all the students who tested the qualitative and quantitative features of SPECTRUM IV.

Digital Signal Processing in FORTRAN

1 Introduction

A. Purpose

Linear system theory is at the foci of modern system design and analysis. The advancement of science, engineering, and technology since the early 1950s has been accelerated by linear concepts. Scientists and engineers rely on linear system theory to explain observed physical behavior, thus the theory has become a widely used and accepted technical language within the technical community. Often ideas are exchanged using the analogies, models, symbolisms, and concepts unique to linear system theory. Many contemporary communication, control, and measurement devices are simply the implementation of a linear theoretic concept in terms of electromechanical hardware.

One of the most useful topics of this general theory is spectral analysis. Here linear systems are analyzed from a frequency content point of view. The familiar operational methods of Fourier fall into this classification. Correlation, convolution, and coherence also can be performed in the frequency domain. Unfortunately, except for the simplest low-dimension problem, obtaining numerical solutions in the frequency domain is nontrivial. The nature of such problems is computational rather than conceptual. Most of the computations associated with modern frequency-domain analysis are accomplished digitally. Using modern, efficient numerical methods, these individual calculations can be dispatched effectively. However, the casual user is generally unaware of the existence of these new techniques. A student of the art would be conscious of those methods but may not have the time or programming skill required to implement them. Even if a collection of spectral analysis routines were available, in general they would not be integrated into a complete software system. That is, the individual spectral analysis programs would need to be connected as subroutines are to a main program.

The purpose of this book is to acquaint the reader with the theory, utility, and basic techniques of digital signal analysis and spectral analysis. The use and structure of the numerical algorithms, supporting each theoretically developed topic, are also documented. The component methods of spectral analysis—such as the Fourier transform, co-relation, filtering, and so forth—have been integrated into a self-contained software package to allow a user to nest individual techniques together to provide for sophisticated signal analysis. In addition, because of special software design considerations, the user can perform a particular spectral analysis task through the use of a mnemonic. For example, the mnemonic representing a Fourier transform is FFT. Therefore, to perform a Fourier transform, the user need state only that an FFT operation is to be performed. However, a user needs to be concerned with input-output data rules. The input-output rules, which are common to all component parts of this software system package, are not difficult and require no a priori programming skill. The combined effect of simple input-output and mnemonic routine calls make the system extremely easy to use.

Besides offering a systematic approach to digital signal analysis, the software package described in this book contains an error-diagnostic routine. The structural and format requirements placed on the software system are tested automatically for consistency. A detected error initiates the printing of an error message, which allows the user to locate and correct programming "bugs." Finally, graphic capabilities are included in the total package. If desired, time- or frequency-domain data can be outputted on a line printer in graphic form. The entire software package and concept, as presented will be referred to as SPECTRUM IV. It is a hybrid label representing a spectral analysis package coded in FORTRAN IV.

The use of SPECTRUM IV is controlled through a sequence of commands encoded on computer cards. SPECTRUM IV operation consists of three distinct programming units:

1. *Job control language (JCL)*. The purpose of JCL is to gain entry to the user's computer. A JCL operation will supply cost accounting, job identification, priority, and resource information to the computer system, when and where required. The JCL will also specify the origin of SPECTRUM IV. SPECTRUM IV may reside on card, tape, or disk files depending on the user's preference, provided the files do not exceed any computer system constraint. Staff programmers familiar with the user's system will supply the required JCL information.
2. *SPECTRUM IV commands*. The system-supplied programs discussed in this book can be interconnected to perform spectral and time-series analysis. In this programming section, the user specifies these routines, input data records, and output requests. They may be nested to any depth—that is, a complex problem might require many SPECTRUM IV operations to achieve the desired result. Alternatively, the user may wish to perform a few operations on many signal records. The nesting is accomplished within the structural constraint of SPECTRUM IV.
3. *Termination*. The termination of a SPECTRUM IV analysis is accomplished through the four-letter mnemonic TERM. These letters appear in columns one through four of the computer card (see Figure 1-1). This

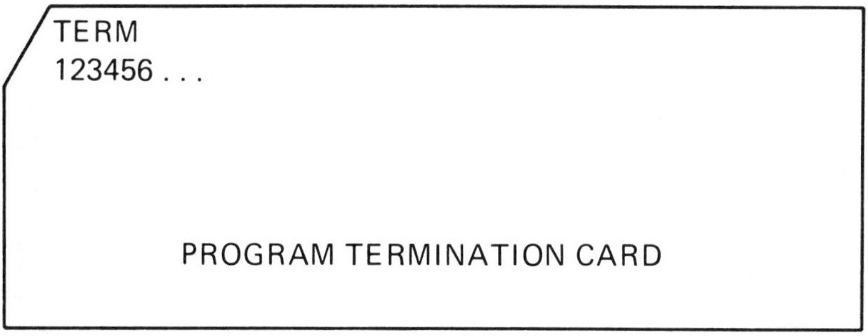

Figure 1-1. Program Termination Card.

card follows the SPECTRUM IV command card block. The execution of the TERM will cause a sign-off message to be printed. Any program-termination housekeeping cards required by the user computer system will follow the TERM card. The complete SPECTRUM IV control and command structure is diagrammed in Figure 1-2.

B. Program Structure

A potential user must be aware of certain options and restrictions associated with SPECTRUM IV program structure. Under software control, data are entered, processed, and outputted. The mathematical techniques used to process and manipulate data are developed in future chapters. These computational and functional routines are connected by a common data-storage area. Storage space is provided to the system in terms of dimensioned data arrays. In general, the user will explicitly address three SPECTRUM IV working arrays—A, B, and C. During a SPECTRUM IV execution cycle, data will be entered and removed from these arrays through a series of commands.

A management policy is used to preserve the integrity of the arrays. The arrays of SPECTRUM IV belong to one of three management categories. They are:

I. null (all zero entries);

II. free (unprotected); and

III. protected (array is protected from alteration by any input operation)

The algorithms in this book use a variety of management philosophies. When it is required, the user will be informed of any array-management restriction imposed on the use of a computational or functional routine

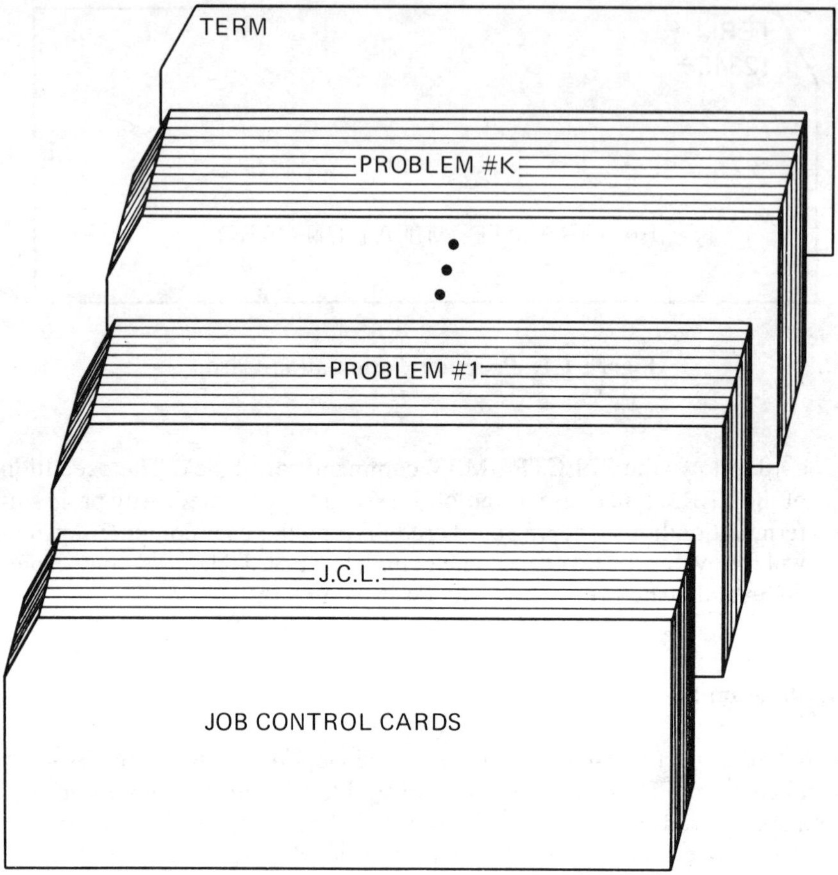

Figure 1-2. Complete SPECTRUM IV Control and Command Structure.

found in SPECTRUM IV. Some of the programs found in the software system make direct use of a Fourier operation. A Fourier operation will automatically assign the transformed array a protection code, in order to prohibit the entry of any new data into that location unless the protection code is altered. If the protected array is to be re-entered, the user should use the following guidelines to establish the removal of protection:

1. If the data in a protected array is of no use, the user is instructed to remove it through one of the SPECTRUM IV zeroing operations. These admissible operations will set the contents of the array(s) of interest to zero and simultaneously remove any protection previously established on that array.

2. To ensure future use of a data array, the user is instructed to output

that array to one of the admissible SPECTRUM IV data-storage devices. Doing so will preserve the contents of the originally protected array for future use. In addition, the memory protection associated with that array is removed.

3. To output the contents of a protected array for analysis or display, the user is instructed to use the system display options. Besides supplying the user with a hard copy of the contents of the interrogated array, these operations will remove any previously assigned memory protection.

4. To edit or alter the contents of a protected array, the user is instructed to use the array-correction capabilities of SPECTRUM IV. This operation can be applied to an array having memory protection.

The following operations are allowed on class III (protected) arrays:

1. Output: output data for display using PRINT or PLOTTER; output data for storage using PUNCH or DISK OUT
2. Zero array: null an array using ZERO OUT or null all arrays using CLEAR-AL
3. Edit array: edit the contents of an array in place using CORRECT
4. Terminate: terminate program execution using TERM

A standard set of commands allows the user to input data to and from the array structure. A user of SPECTRUM IV must be familiar with these basic operations. Since the operations are common to all the routines of SPECTRUM IV, a comprehensive analysis of their use follows.

Input Requirements

SPECTRUM IV allows the user complete versatility in the inputting of data. The user can enter data into a system array by any of the following four methods:

1. Punch cards: (read in)
2. SPECTRUM IV library: (library)
3. User-supplied programs: (user)
4. Disk input capacity: (this feature is documented in Section C of Chapter 5.)

Time-domain (TIME) or frequency-domain (FREQ) data can be loaded into an array using these options. The user must use these input options in a prespecified manner. An internal error-diagnostic routine monitors input operations, it will detect and declare errors in syntax, format, and sequencing.

READ IN. Routine READ IN allows a user to input data from punched cards. To request such an operation, the six-letter mnemonic READbIN is required ("b" denotes a blank space). In addition, a set of parameters that characterize the attributes of the input space are also requested. These parameters describe which domain (time or frequency) the data resides in, the total number of sample values to be considered, and the sample frequency. Restrictions imposed on a READ IN command are:

1. Data must be loaded into array A, B, or C.
2. The array must not belong to management category III (protected).
3. The user must specify the domain to which the data belongs. Time = TIME and frequency = FREQ.
4. The user must specify what FORTRAN IV format is to be used—E or F.
5. The total number of sample values, denoted NPOINT, must satisfy

$$1 \leq \text{NPOINT} \leq 1024$$

6. An end-of-file card is required to terminate a data read from cards. Located physically at the end of the data deck, it will initiate an error-diagnostic check against the prespecified READ IN format requirements.
7. A set of optional parameters can be used to augment the previous READ IN declarations. It is possible to define the starting and stopping data locations in an input data string. The labels NSTART and NSTOP denote these locations. They have a default value of 1 and NPOINT, respectively. A third parameter, NM, must be supplied if the NSTART-NSTOP option is to be used. It must satisfy

$$\text{NPOINT} = \text{NM} = \text{NSTOP} - \text{NSTART} + 1$$

Besides satisfying the above requirements, a READ IN operation requires an ordering of control and data cards. A READ IN operation consists of the sequencing of primary and secondary control cards followed by data and end-of-file cards. Under some conditions, such as cross-correlation, two arrays are to be loaded simultaneously. When two arrays are read, a second ensemblage of control cards is required. The sequencing and structure of the operation are treated in Table 1-1.

Data can occur in either the time or the frequency domain, with either an E or an F FORTRAN IV format. Time-domain data will be assumed to be real numbers, whereas frequency-domain data will be considered complex numbers. That is, because frequency-domain data represent gain-phase or real-imaginary behavior, a complex mathematical representation is required. Data must be treated as shown in Figure 1-3.

Time-domain data are packed six real numbers per card. The packing density in the frequency domain is three complex numbers per card. The complex numbers are listed alternately as real and imaginary numbers. An

Table 1-1
Sequencing and Structure of a READ IN Operation

Column Number	*Description*	*Format or Content*
Primary information card—one required		
1-7	Calls READ IN	READ IN
15	Array 1—1st data set	A1
20	Array 2—2nd data set (optional)	A1
27-30	Domain of Array 1	A4
37-40	Domain of Array 2	A4
50	Format	E or F
57-60	Number of sample values (NPOINT)	I4
61-72	Sampling frequency Hz (optional) default value = 1 Hz	F12.2
80	Multiple READ IN option default = 0 single array read only 1 = dual array read	0 = default or 1
Secondary information card—one/array		
20	Format	A1
27-30	Domain indicator	A4
37-40	NM (optional)	I4
47-50	NSTART (optional)	I4
57-60	NSTOP (optional)	I4
End-of-file card—one/array		
1-8	E data format or F data format	EEEEEEEE FFFFFFFF

example of the sequencing of primary, secondary, and end-of-file cards can be found in Figure 1-4. The example problem in Figure 1-4 considers the entry of two data arrays. SPECTRUM IV will automatically output all control parameters that characterize the input data set upon completion of a READ IN operation.

LIBRARY. A collection of commonly used test and evaluation functions are incorporated in SPECTRUM IV. Trigonometric functions, pulses, and noise sources reside in an addressable library. By assigning the proper option number to the seven-letter mnemonic LIBRARY, program LI-

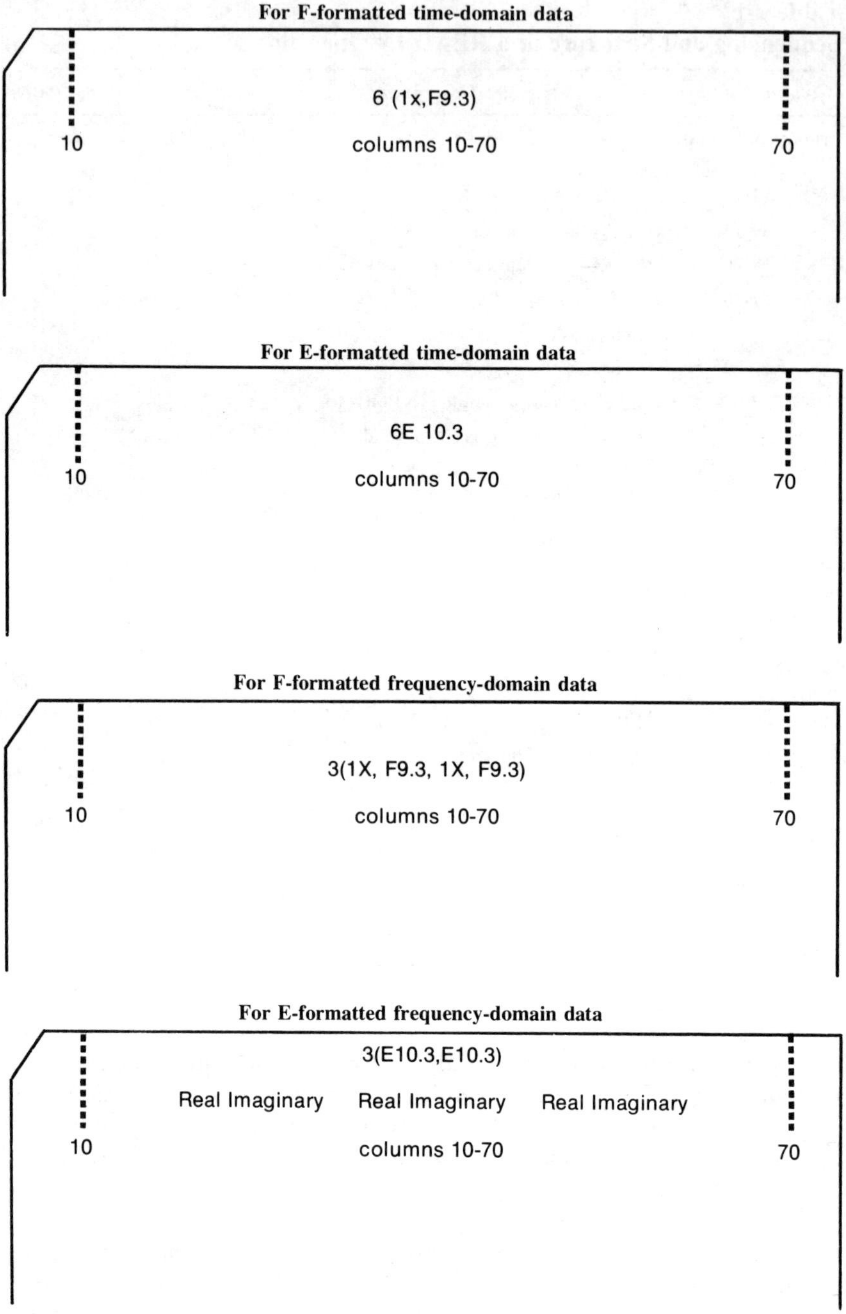

Figure 1-3. Data Format for a READ IN Operation.

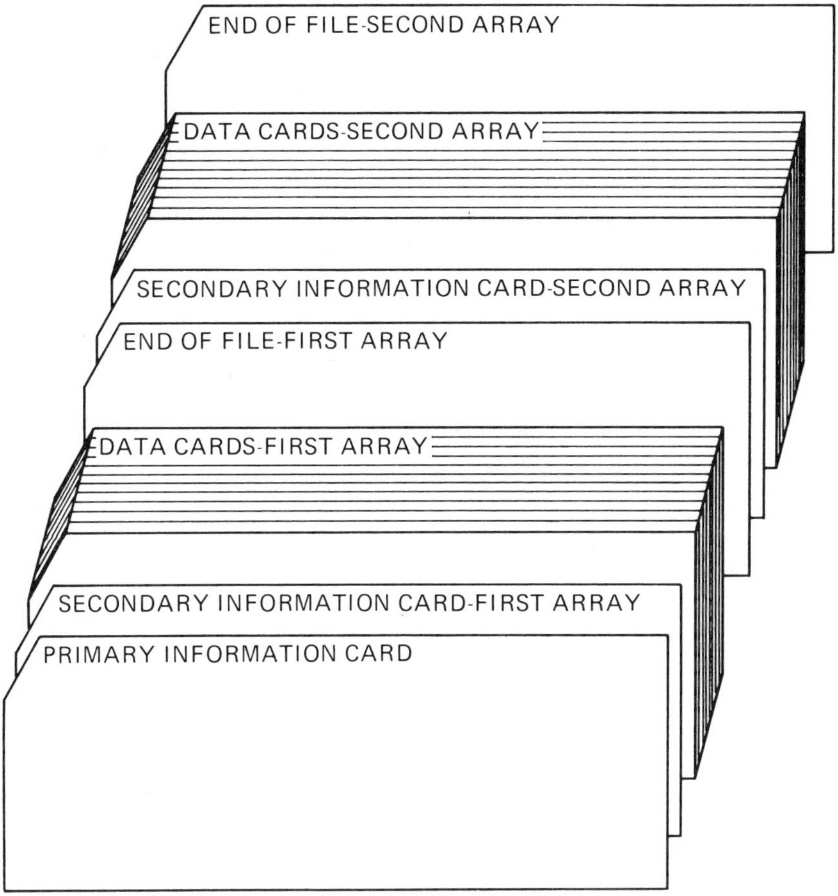

Figure 1-4. Card Control Sequence for a Dual READ IN.

BRARY will input the desired data record into a prespecified array. In particular, the signal sources available to a user are, over a prespecified sampling interval T:

Option	*Function f(t)*
1	$f(t)$ = sine wave
2	$f(t)$ = pulse centered about zero (even)
3	$f(t)$ = sine wave + uniform noise
4	$f(t)$ = pulse + uniform noise
5	$f(t)$ = uniform noise
6	$f(t)$ = cosine wave

7	$f(t)$ = cosine wave + uniform noise
8	$f(t)$ = sine wave + Gaussian noise
9	$f(t)$ = pulse + Gaussian noise
10	$f(t)$ = Gaussian noise
11	$f(t)$ = cosine wave + Gaussian noise

When the trigonometric functions are used, and amplitude AMP, a frequency TAU, and a d-c offset DCLEVEL must be specified by the user. That is, the trigonometric functions found in SPECTRUM IV satisfy

$$\text{sine wave} = \text{AMP} * \sin(2\pi \text{TAU}t) + \text{DCLEVEL}$$

$$\text{cosine wave} = \text{AMP} * \cos(2\pi \text{TAU}t) + \text{DCLEVEL}$$

Pulse trains generated in the SPECTRUM IV library are defined in terms of a duty cycle TAU, an amplitude AMP, and a d-c offset DCLEVEL (see Figure 1-5).

The resident uniform noise source produces a random process that is uniformly distributed on the interval [0, 1] multiplied by a user requested gain VARI. That is,

$$f(t) = \text{VARI} \times \text{U}[0, 1]$$

The resident noise generator also produces a normal (Gaussian) random process with mean WMEAN and variance VARI. Notationally, that is

$$f(t) = \text{N (WMEAN, VARI)}$$

The 11 optional routines give the user a very flexible test signal source. The user will find it an invaluable design and diagnostic tool. However, there are restrictions on the use of LIBRARY:

1. Data must be loaded into array A, B, or C.
2. The designated array, selected to receive the data, must not be of management class III (protected).
3. The format requirements of LIBRARY must be satisfied. These format requirements are shown in Table 1-2.

Finally, LIBRARY control parameters are echo-printed automatically by SPECTRUM IV.

USER LIB. If a requested signal is not resident in subroutine LIBRARY, the following program, USER LIB, is to be used. Program USER LIB allows the user to generate the mathematical properties of a desired test signal. The mathematical properties may be known from either the physics of a problem or a traditional acceptance of a class of test signals. The mathematical description of the test signal is encoded as a FORTRAN IV source program. This program must be labeled OWN. To use this feature of SPECTRUM IV, the eight-letter mnemonic USER LIB is used. In addi-

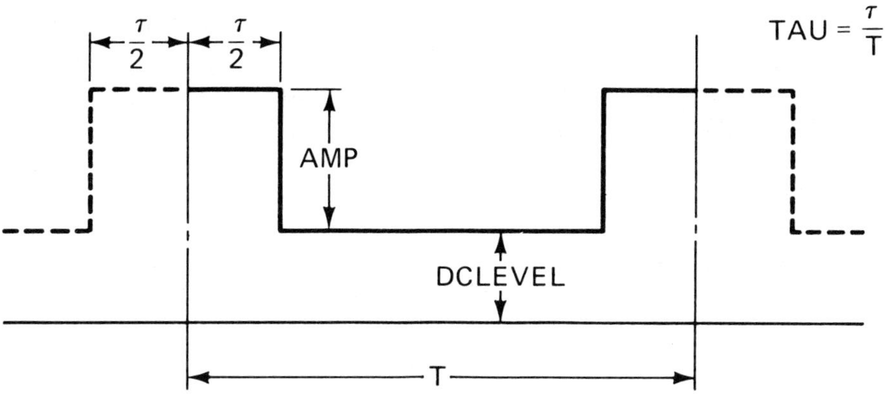

Figure 1-5. Pulse Trains in the SPECTRUM IV Library.

Table 1-2
Format Requirements of LIBRARY

Column Number	*Description*	*Format or Content*
Primary information card		
1-7	Calls LIBRARY	LIBRARY
15	Array to be loaded	A1
57-60	Number of sample values (NPOINT)	I4
61-72	Sampling frequency	F12.2
Secondary information card		
1-40	Identifying message about signal source (optional) example "THIS IS A SINE WAVE"	10A4
44-45	Option number	I2
46-50	AMP	F5.1
51-55	DCLEVEL	F5.1
56-65	TAU	F10.3
66-70	VARI	F5.3
71-75	WMEAN	F5.1

tion, other control parameters, used to facilitate a data exchange between OWN and USER LIB, must be supplied. Restrictions imposed on USER LIB are:

1. Data must be loaded into array A, B, or C.

2. The array selected to receive data must not be of management class III (protected).
3. The user-supplied subroutine used to generate the test input, in a FORTRAN IV source code, must be labeled OWN.
4. OWN must obey a prespecified COMMON statement structure in a FORTRAN IV sense. It is:

```
 SUBROUTINE OWN
 INTEGER SPL
 COMMON     REST(6148),TEMR(1024),TEMC(1024),FRN(20),
    FCN(20),FRD(20),FC
1D(20),PN(21),PD(21),REST1(82),NPOINT,
    REST2(5),SPL,REST3(2)
```

As a programming convenience, several addressable test signals may be nested into subroutine OWN. Therefore a user may choose to code several potentially useful signals into OWN, and choose one or more of them to be used during execution. The selection of a program is accomplished under SPECTRUM IV control. In addition, the test signal, composed of the sample values

$$\delta(1), \delta(2), \ldots, \delta(N)$$

where $\delta(i)$ is in general a complex number and can be generated using subroutine OWN. The user can also produce a polynomial of the form

$$H(x) = \sum_{i=1}^{C} \lambda(i)x^{i-1} \Big/ \sum_{i=1}^{D} \sigma(i)x^{i-1}$$

where $\lambda(i)$ and $\sigma(i)$ are real numbers. Subroutine OWN of SPECTRUM IV will also allow the user to define $H(x)$ in factored form as follows:

$$H(x) = \prod_{i=1}^{C}(x - \alpha_i) \Big/ \prod_{i=1}^{D}(x - \beta_i)$$

where α_i and β_i are complex numbers in general.

Thus a transfer function can be mathematically synthesized using the software options found in SPECTRUM IV. The parameters found in program USER, which is called from subprogram OWN, have been assigned the following roles:

NPOINT	number of sample values to be transferred to SPECTRUM IV. That is, NPOINT = N
TEMR	real part of $\delta(i)$, $i = 1, 2, \ldots,$ NPOINT
TEMC	imaginary part of $\delta(i)$, $i = 1, 2, \ldots,$ NPOINT
PN	numerator factors of $H(x)$. That is, $\lambda(i)$, $i = 1, 2, \ldots, C$

PD	denominator factors of $H(x)$. That is, $\sigma(i)$, $i = 1, 2, \ldots, D$
FRN	real part of $\alpha(i)$, $i = 1, 2, \ldots, C$
FRD	real part of $\beta(i)$, $i = 1, 2, \ldots, D$
FCN	imaginary part of $\alpha(i)$, $i = 1, 2, \ldots, C$
FCD	imaginary part of $\beta(i)$, $i = 1, 2, \ldots, D$
SPL	indirect address of desired subprogram of OWN

Whenever the factors of $H(x)$ appear in complex form, it is explicitly required that they be given in complex conjugate pairs.

An example of the structure of a typical OWN program is as follows:[a]

```
      SUBROUTINE OWN
      INTEGER SPL
      COMMON     REST(6148),TEMR(1024),TEMC(1024),FRN(20),
         FCN(20),FRD(20),FC-
     1D(20),PN(21),PD(21),REST1(82),NPOINT, REST2(5),SPL,RE-
         ST3(2)
      GO TO (n1, n2, n3, ..., nm), SPL
       .
n1     .                         User Program 1
       .
      GO TO 99
       .
n2     .                         User Program 2
       .
      GO TO 99
       .
n3     .
       .
      GO TO 99
       .
nm     .                         User Program m
       .
99    CONTINUE
      RETURN
      END
```

The program in subprogram OWN can be used as a self-contained description of a signal process, or as an augmentation of a routine found in LIBRARY. As a self-contained program, the user would characterize a

[a] A comprehensive analysis of the use and limitations of program OWN can be found in Chapter 6.

signal process explicitly in terms of a FORTRAN IV source code. If, however, the user wishes to add to the signal constructed in program OWN, a noise process found in LIBRARY, an augmentation process can be used. Here the noise time series found in LIBRARY routine 5 or 10 can be added algebraically to the data set produced by a USER LIB operation by using a few optional parameters.

Two cards, termed the primary information and identification cards, are used in a USER LIB generation. The structure of a primary information card is shown in Table 1-3.

The second card, the identification card, allows the user to give a written description of the requested USER LIB operation. For example, the user might state "THIS IS AN EXPONENTIAL TEST SIGNAL," or "THIS IS A LOW-PASS FILTER." If the signal process to be created is entirely self-contained in subroutine OWN, the secondary information card contains only this identification label. If the signal created in OWN is used to augment a LIBRARY signal, optional parameters are required. These parameters are identical to those found in the secondary information card of a LIBRARY call. The structure of this card is shown in Table 1-4.

The salient parameters of the primary information and identification card are echo-printed by SPECTRUM IV automatically. A comprehensive example of the USER LIB/OWN programs can be found in Chapter 4.

Output Requirements

Data produced through a spectral operation can be outputted under SPECTRUM IV control. The user has a choice of four output medias:

1. Line printer: tabular data list
2. Line printer: graphics
3. Card punch: data storage
4. Disk: data storage

A comprehensive analysis of the first three options will be discussed shortly. Use of the disk option is covered in Chapter 5.

The line printer can be used to display data in graphic as well as tabular form. The card-punch option allows the user to store data on punch cards. Current data can be conveniently formatted and stored for future use. The disk storage capability allows the user access to an efficient mass storage device. All output options are fully integrated into SPECTRUM IV.

PRINT. If data are to be displayed in tabular form, routine PRINT must be used. Program PRINT will cause data generated by SPECTRUM IV to be listed on the line printer. Program PRINT is called by the five-letter mnemonic PRINT. This option requires two control cards, called the

Table 1-3
Structure of a Primary Information Card

Column Number	Description	Format or Contents
Primary information card		
1-8	Calls USER LIB	USERbLIB
15	Designates data array to be used by USER LIB	A1
57-60	NPOINT	I4
61-72	Sampling frequency (optional; default = 1 Hz)	F12.2
78-80	Indirect address of subprogram of OWN to be used	I3

Table 1-4
Structure of an Identification Card

Column Number	Description	Format or Contents
Identification card		
1-40	Identify test	10A4
44-45	Optional parameter (Option number of LIBRARY 5 or 10)	I1
66-70	Optional parameter (VARI of LIBRARY)	F5.3
71-75	Optional parameter (WMEAN of LIBRARY)	F5.1

primary and secondary information cards. The first card calls PRINT and defines the salient features of the stored data. The second card specifies how the line printer is to interpret the stored data. A second feature of the secondary information card is that it allows the user to define the array starting and stopping location if desired. Restrictions on the use of PRINT are:

1. The data in the designated array must be in the domain specified by the primary information card.
2. The array to be listed must not be the null array (all zeros)
3. If the optional partial listing is desired, starting at location NSTART and stopping at location NSTOP, then

$$\text{NPOINT} = \text{NM} = \text{NSTOP} - \text{NSTART} + 1$$

4. The user is limited to 200 lines of print-out unless otherwise specified on the primary information card.

The structure of the PRINT card ensemble is shown in Table 1-5.

Table 1-5
Structure of the PRINT Card Ensemble

Column Number	*Description*	*Format or Contents*
Primary information card		
1-5	Calls PRINT	PRINT
15	Array to be printed: A, B, or C	A1
27-30	Domain of stored data TIME = time, FREQ = frequency	A4
50	Format of stored data (FORTRAN IV sense)	E or F
57-60	Number of data values to be listed (NPOINT)	I4
80	Optional parameter 1 = more than 200 lines desired 0 = default	I1
Secondary information card		
20	Format to be printed (FORTRAN IV sense)	E or F
27-30	Domain of printed data TIME = time, FREQ = frequency	A4
37-40	Total number of consecutive data points to be listed called NM	I4
47-50	Starting location called NSTART	I4
57-60	Stopping location called NSTOP	I4

SPECTRUM IV automatically echo-prints the array, domain, sampling frequency, number of sample points, and resolution information. Where applicable, the highest frequency component that can be processed without error (that is, Nyquist frequency) is displayed. The data is listed, point by point, in the requested format, E or F.

PLOTTER. To use the line printer's graphic capacity, routine PLOTTER must be used. Program PLOTTER is called by the seven-letter mnemonic PLOTTER. This routine has the capability to graphically display time-domain or frequency-domain data. Frequency-domain data is interpreted in terms of a magnitude and/or phase plot. Briefly, for time-domain applications, PLOTTER will produce a normalized image of the data stored in a data array. The normalized time-domain data, having values over the interval ± 1, has its true value plotted to the side. Another option allows the user to normalize the data over the interval 0 to 1: In the frequency domain, a normalized magnitude plot can be requested. The magnitude spectra will be normalized to one. The true magnitude is also printed to the side. When a phase plot is requested, a principal angle residing between $\pm\pi$ is displayed. The true phase angle is printed to the side.

Table 1-6
Structure of the PLOTTER Control Cards

Column Number	*Description*	*Format or Contents*
Primary information card		
1-7	Calls PLOTTER	PLOTTER
15	Array to be plotted (A, B, or C)	A1
57-60	Number of points to be plotted (NPOINT)	I4
80	Optional parameter to designate TIME—domain output form. Option 0 = plot normalized to −1 to 1 range. Option 1 = plot normalized to 0 to 1 range	I1
Secondary information card		
1-4	Designate domain plot	TIME or FREQ
8-15	Designate type of frequency-domain plot	MAG or PHASE
16-20	NSTART	I4
22-25	NSTOP	I4
29-80	Label (identification)	13A4

Two cards are required to use PLOTTER. The first card, the primary information card, contains the mnemonic PLOTTER array designator and number of points to be plotted. The second card, called the secondary information card, is used to designate the type of display requested, the starting array location (denoted NSTART) the stopping array location (denoted NSTOP), and up to 52 letters of message, which are used to identify the plotted data. Restrictions imposed on PLOTTER are:

1. The data in the designated array must be in the domain specified by the primary information card.
2. The array to be plotted must not be the null array (all zeros).
3. The number of points to be plotted, namely, NPOINT, must satisfy.

$$\text{NPOINT} = \text{NSTOP} - \text{NSTART} + 1$$

The structure of the PLOTTER control cards is shown in Table 1-6.

The PLOTTER output is divided into two parts. The first output is composed of an echo print of the designated array, domain, number of sample values, sample frequency, and resolution information. The second phase is the actual graph. Normalized data are plotted, as requested, with the actual values printed to the side.

PUNCH. Routine PUNCH allows the user to generate a data base on punch cards. The operation of PUNCH parallels that of routine PRINT.

Table 1-7
Structure of the PUNCH Routine

Column Number	*Description*	*Format or Contents*
Primary information card		
1-5	Calls PUNCH	PUNCH
15	Array to be punched (A, B, or C)	A1
27-30	Domain of stored data TIME = time, FREQ = frequency	A4
50	Format of stored data (FORTRAN IV sense)	E or F
57-60	Number of data values to be punched (NPOINT)	I4
80	Optional parameter 1 = more than 200 cards desired 0 = default	I1
Secondary information card		
20	Format to be punched (FORTRAN IV sense)	E or F
27-30	Domain of punched data TIME = time, FREQ = frequency	A4
37-40	NM	I4
47-50	NSTART	I4
57-60	NSTOP	I4

PUNCH is called through the five-letter mnemonic PUNCH. Two cards are required to control PUNCH. The purpose of the parameters associated with the cards is described in the PRINT section. Restrictions imposed on the use of PUNCH are identical to those imposed on PRINT. The structure of PUNCH is shown in Table 1-7.

The output of PUNCH has the quality of that found in PRINT, except the data appears on punch cards. Three types of cards can be punched. The identification card, shown in Figure 1-6a, is similar to the secondary identification card, but it contains fewer parameters. The data card (Figure 1-6b) contains actual data. The end-of-file card (Figure 1-6c) is used by SPECTRUM IV as in a READ-IN operation.

This completes the discussion of input-output protection rules of SPECTRUM IV. A table summarizing system protection philosophy, domain restrictions, and array constraints associated with each functional SPECTRUM IV operation can be found in Appendix A. The remainder of this book will be directed toward the development of these operations. The material in Appendix A underscores the restrictions and options belonging to SPECTRUM IV computational routines. Therefore the reader should become familiar with the contents of Appendix A at the earliest possible time.

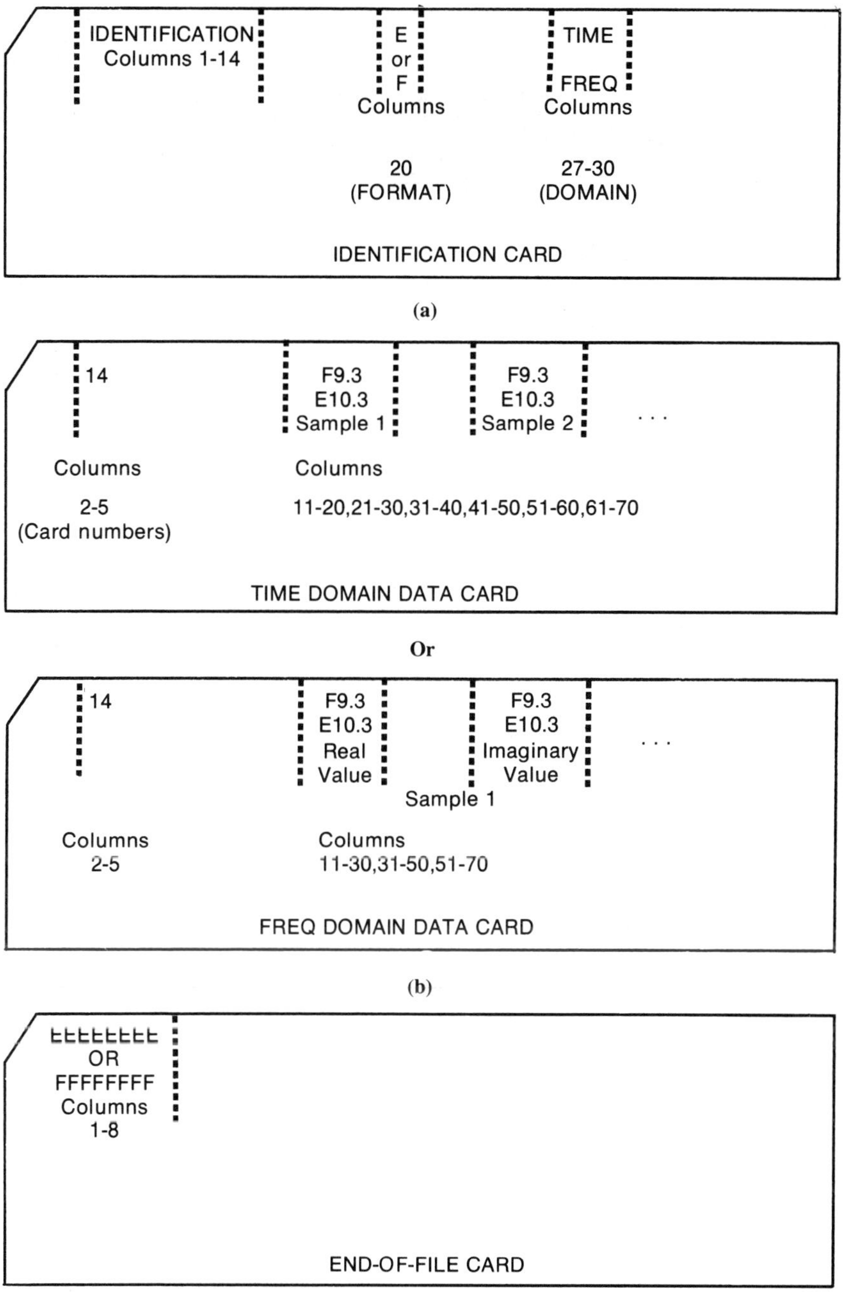

Figure 1-6. Samples of PUNCH Output: Identification Card (a); Data Card (b); and End-of-file Card (c).

2 Single-variant Spectral Analysis

The quantitative and qualitative investigation of a single signal is called single-variant analysis. If the study relates time- and frequency-domain behavior together, the study is called single-variant spectral analysis. Here the time and frequency properties of a signal are mathematically interrelated. Information about the periodic or aperiodic character of a signal can be obtained through this analysis procedure. To the engineer and physicist, spectral information is used to design and analyze vibrating and oscillating systems; electronic, mechanical, acoustic filters, and signal-conditioning systems; control, communication, sonar, and radar systems; seismology; noise, and so forth. The detection of periodic behavior in signals produced by biological, economic, societal, or ecological systems is also of major interest to the scientist.

Single-variant spectral analysis, as presented in this chapter, concentrates on Fourier transform, inverse Fourier transform, autocorrelation, and power spectral density.

Fourier transform and power-spectral density investigate the frequency-domain properties of a time-domain signal. Inverse Fourier transform generates a time-domain image of a signal characterized in the frequency domain. Autocorrelation produces a measure of the internal similarity that exists in a signal.

A. Fourier Transforms

Spectral Analysis

The decomposition of an arbitrary waveform into sinusoidal components has been known and used by the technical community for over a century. It was Fourier's 1822 study[a] that systematized such methods and that has made rich and elegant theories possible. Using transform methods, tremendous breakthroughs have been made in the study of linear systems, optics, wave propagation, biological signal processing, and random processes. The electronic age brought forth a series of analog devices that, over a limited frequency range, measured the spectral properties of an analog

[a] A brief historical background of Fourier and his contemporaries can be found in reference [4].

signal. Such devices were slow, required operator skill, and often would not yield repeated measurements. In addition, phase measurements could be accomplished only with with great difficulty. The availability of large-scale digital computers in the 1960s had little initial impact on spectral analysis. These software-based systems were slow, and they consumed large amounts of computer memory. It was not until the Cooley-Tukey algorithm was published and accepted that spectral analysis harnessed the power of the modern digital computers.[b] The Cooley-Tukey algorithm is a representative of a general class of discrete Fourier transforms; it is often called the Fast Fourier Transform (FFT).

The Discrete Fourier Transform (DFT)

The continuous Fourier transform (CFT) transforms a class of time-domain signals—say, $x(t)$—into the frequency domain. The inverse operation is called the inverse continuous Fourier transform (ICFT). These operations are mathematically defined as follows:

$$X(f) = \int_{-\infty}^{\infty} x(t) \exp(-j2\pi ft)\, dt \qquad \text{(CFT)} \qquad (2.1)$$

$$x(t) = \int_{-\infty}^{\infty} X(f) \exp(j2\pi ft)\, dt \qquad \text{(ICFT)} \qquad (2.2)$$

where $j = \sqrt{-1}$. Here $X(f)$ is called the spectrum of $x(t)$. The spectrum of $x(t)$ is a description of $x(t)$ in the frequency domain. It is characterized by a complex number representing magnitude and phase.

A special case of the Fourier transform is the Fourier series (FS). If $x(t)$ is periodic over some interval of time—say, $[-T/2, T/2]$—it is possible to express the frequency-domain behavior of $x(t)$ as a discrete, rather than a continuous series.[c] Fourier series can appear in either the trigonometric or the exponential form. The familiar trigonometric series is given by

$$x(t) = a_0 + \sum_{i=-\infty}^{\infty} a_i \cos(2\pi it/T) + b_i \sin(2\pi it/T) \qquad \text{(FS)} \qquad (2.3)$$

where

$$a_0 = \frac{1}{T}\int_{-T/2}^{T/2} x(t)\, dt$$

---

[b] A brief and interesting historical development of the discrete Fourier transform can be found in reference [4].

[c] Certain integration conditions must be satisfied also. Periodic signals generated in the real world always satisfy these signal conditions.

$$\left.\begin{aligned} a_n &= \frac{1}{T}\int_{-T/2}^{T/2} x(t)\cos(2\pi nt/T)\,dt \\ b_n &= \frac{1}{T}\int_{-T/2}^{T/2} x(t)\sin(2\pi nt/T)\,dt \end{aligned}\right\} \tag{2.4}$$

Using Euler's identity,

$$\left.\begin{aligned} \sin(a) &= [\exp(ja) - \exp(-ja)]/2j \\ \cos(a) &= [\exp(ja) + \exp(-ja)]/2 \end{aligned}\right\} \tag{2.5}$$

Equation (2.3) can be written in an exponential format. The result is that an exponential Fourier series is given by

$$x(t) = \sum_{i=-\infty}^{\infty} A_i \exp(j2\pi it/T) \tag{2.6}$$

where

$$A_o = a_o$$

$$A_i = \left\{\begin{matrix} (a_i - jb_i/2 & \text{for } i > 0 \\ (a_i + jb_i/2 & \text{for } i < 0 \end{matrix}\right\} \tag{2.7}$$

The notable difference between a general CFT and the FS is resolution.

The CFT spectra is a continuous image into the frequency domain, ranging from $-\infty$Hz to ∞Hz. The spectra generated by the Fourier series is a discrete cover of that interval. In fact, if the interval of repetition (called the fundamental period) is T, thereby defining the fundamental frequency of $x(t)$ to be f_0 where

$$f_o = \frac{1}{T} \tag{2.8}$$

the Fourier series exhibits spectral information at kf_o Hz only, $k = (\ldots, 2, -1, 0, 1, 2, \ldots)$.[d] In terms of a harmonic concept,

$|k| = 0$ implies the 0 harmonic (DC)
$|k| = 1$ implies the first harmonic (fundamental)
$|k| = 2$ implies the second harmonic

The discrete Fourier transform (DFT) is conceptually similar to both the CFT and the FS. It is like the CFT in form, except integration is replaced by

[d] It should be noted that a negative frequency can also be interpreted as a positive frequency. For example, $\cos(-2\pi ft) = \cos(2\pi ft)$ and $\sin(-2\pi ft) = -\sin(2\pi ft)$.

summation. It is like the Fourier series in that it is a transformation of a time-domain record of length T into the discrete frequency domain. However, it differs from both in that it transforms a discrete time-domain record into the frequency domain. This discrete time record is called a time series. Another difference is that the frequency spectrum of a DFT does not range from $-\infty$Hz to ∞Hz, but resides in a finite subinterval of that infinite interval. The hierarchy of Fourier transforms is diagrammed in Figure 2-1.

A time-series record of a signal $x(t)$ is generated by sampling. Let a sample be taken every Δt seconds for a total of T seconds. Then the time series record of $x(t)$ would consist of N sample values, where

$$N = T/\Delta t$$

Let the time series record

$$x(0\,\Delta t),\ x(1\,\Delta t),\ x(2\,\Delta t),\ \ldots,\ x[(N-1)\,\Delta t]$$

be denoted

$$x(10),\ x(1),\ x(2),\ \ldots,\ x(N-1) \tag{2.9}$$

Again, let the fundamental frequency (first harmonic) of $x(t)$ be denoted f_o, where

$$f_o = 1/T \text{ Hz}$$

or, in radians per second,

$$\omega_o = 2\pi f_o \text{ radians/sec.}$$

Then the discrete Fourier transform can be defined to be

$$X(i) = \frac{1}{N} \sum_{k=0}^{N-1} x(k)\, W_N^{ik} \quad (i = 0, 1, \ldots, N-1) \quad \text{(DFT)} \tag{2.10}$$

and the inverse discrete Fourier transform is given by

$$x(k) = \sum_{i=0}^{N-1} X(i)\, W_N^{-ik} \quad (i = 0, 1, \ldots, N-1) \quad \text{(IDFT)} \tag{2.11}$$

where

$$W_N^{ik} = \exp(-2\pi jik/N) \quad (j = \sqrt{-1}) \tag{2.12}$$

The frequency components of the discrete Fourier transform are located at kf_o, $k = 0, 1, 2, \ldots, N-1$. This process is characterized in block diagram form in Figure 2-2. Here the sampling is assumed to be performed by a phaser completing a cycle every T seconds. The time interval between samples is the sampling rate Δt, where $\Delta t = T/N$ seconds.

One of the interesting features of the DFT is that both the time-series

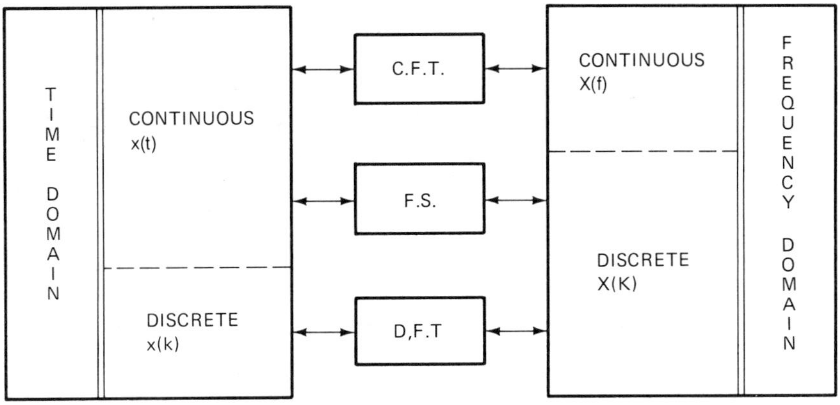

Figure 2-1. Hierarchy of Fourier Transforms.

sample values and Fourier coefficients—namely, $x(k)$ and $X(i)$—are periodic. That is, for m an integer

$$\left.\begin{aligned} x(k) &= x(mN + k) \\ X(i) &= X(mN + i) \end{aligned}\right\} \tag{2.13}$$

In addition, if $x(k)$ is a real sequence of sample values, then there is symmetry in the transformation of time series. This symmetry, in the frequency domain, is about the so-called folding frequency f_F, where

$$f_F = \frac{Nf_o}{2} \tag{2.14}$$

In addition, the real components of $X(f)$—that is, $Re[X(f)]$—have even symmetry about f_F whereas the imaginary components—that is, $Im[X(f)]$—have odd symmetry (antisymmetry). The symmetry properties of $X(f)$ allow the spectral components of $X(f)$, existing from $N/2$ to $N - 1$, to be interpreted as negative frequency locations. The periodic behavior of $X(f)$ gives rise to the relation

$$X(-k) = X(N - k) \qquad (k = 0, 1, 2, \ldots, N - 1) \tag{2.15}$$

Then it follows that $X(k)$ and $X(-k)$ form a complex conjugate pair. That is,

$$X(k) = X(-k)^* \tag{2.16}$$

where * denotes complex conjugation. The discussed symmetry properties are interpreted graphically in Figure 2-3.

The Fast Fourier Transform (FFT). The Cooley-Tukey FFT algorithm is a

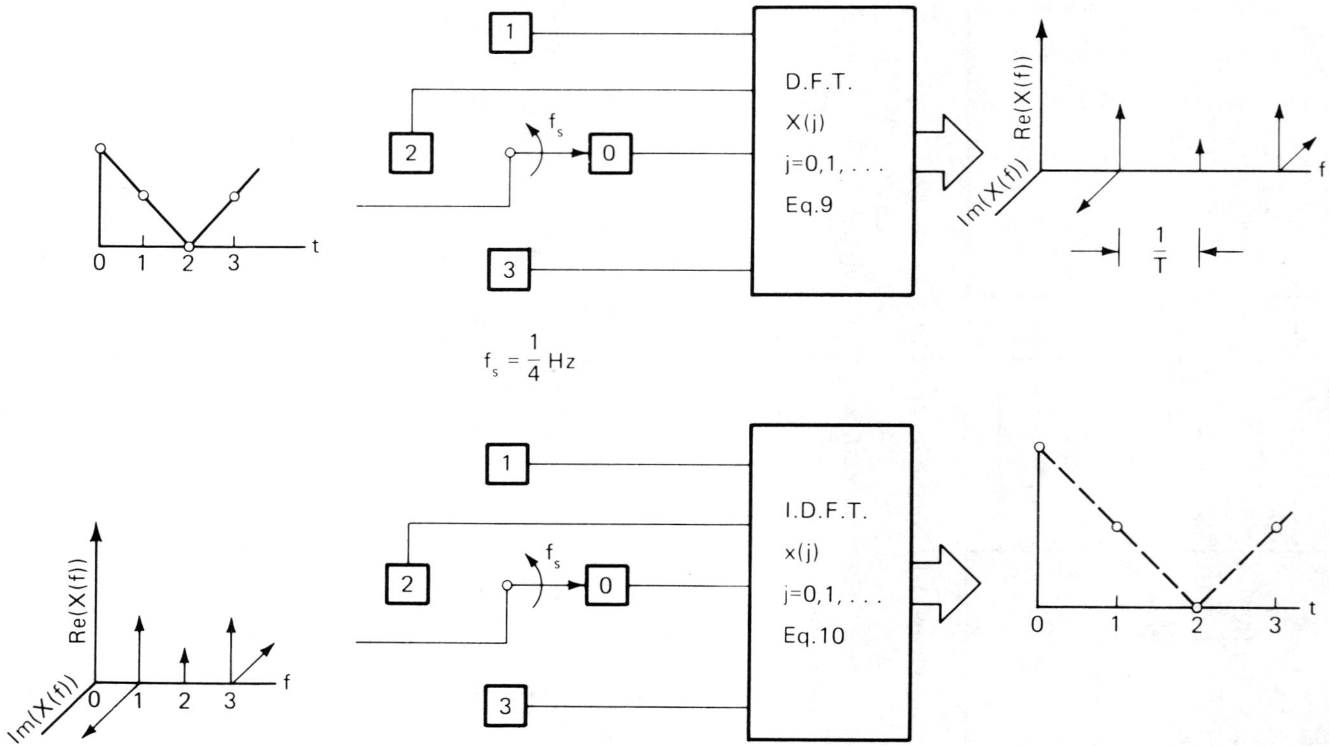

Figure 2-2. Model of a DFT and IDFT for $N = 4$

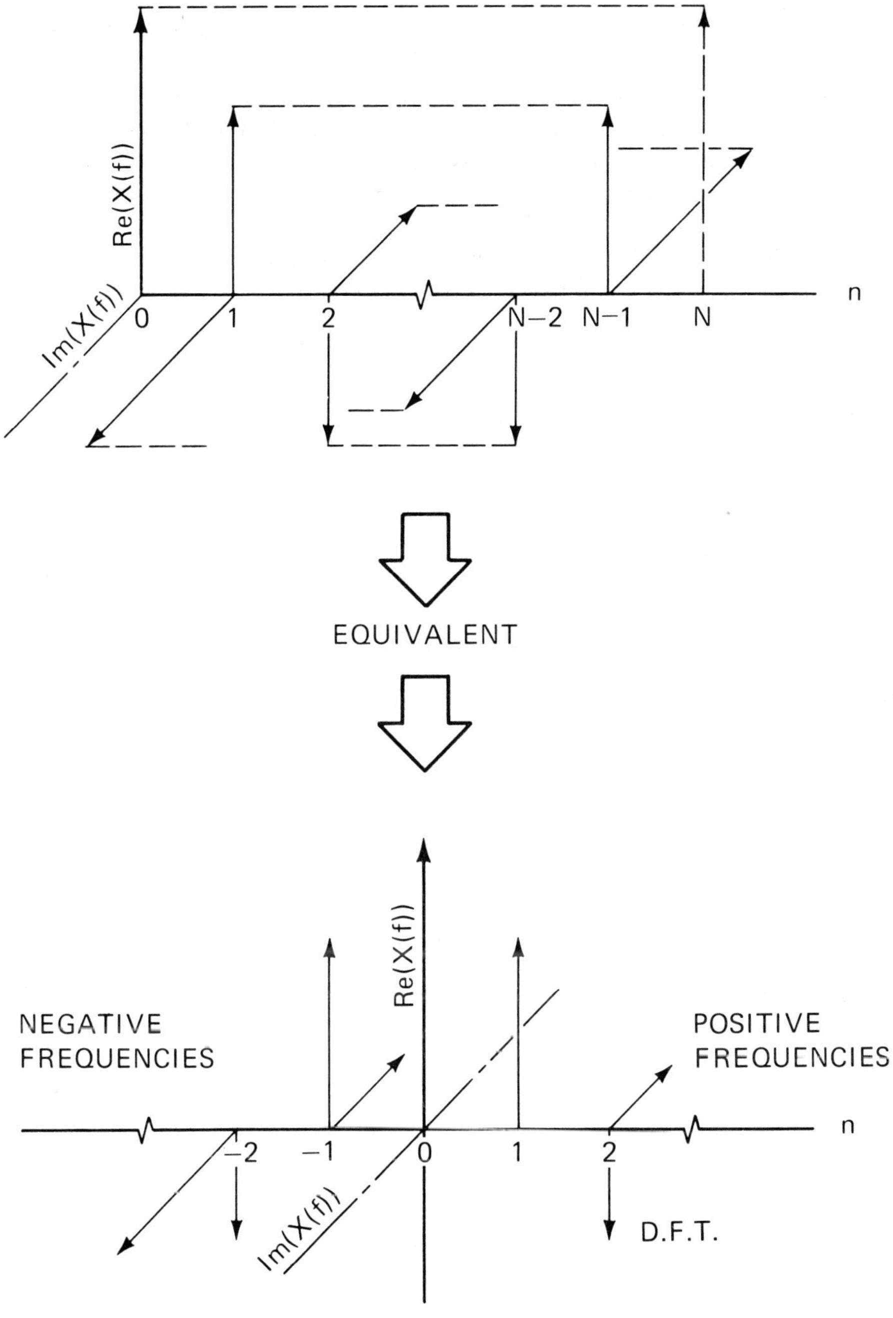

Figure 2-3. Symmetry Properties of the Discrete Fourier Transform.

numerically efficient method of producing discrete transforms. The generation of a spectra using Equation (2.10) would require approximately N^2 complex multiplications and additions. An FFT-produced spectra would require approximately $2N\log_2(N)$ complex multiply and add operations. The computational savings associated with the FFT method are shown in Figure 2-4. The increased efficiency is accomplished through the use of recursive operations on small groupings of data.

Briefly, the development of the FFT algorithm proceeds as follows:

Let a time series input be given and denoted $x(k)$ $(k = 0, 1, 2, \ldots, N - 1)$.

Let that time series be further decomposed into two disjointed sequences, say, $y(k)$ and $z(k)$, where

$$\left.\begin{aligned} y(k) &= x(2k) \\ z(k) &= x(2k + 1) \end{aligned}\right\} \left(k = 0, 1, \ldots, \frac{N}{2} - 1\right) \tag{2.17}$$

That is, the sample values of $x(k)$ are alternately loaded into the array y and z. Let a discrete Fourier representation of the time series $y(k)$ and $z(k)$ be taken and denoted $Y(i)$ and $Z(i)$, respectively. In particular, $Y(i)$ and $Z(i)$ would satisfy

$$\left.\begin{aligned} Y(i) &= \sum_{k=0}^{(N/2)-1} y(k)\, W_N^{2ik} \\ Z(i) &= \sum_{k=0}^{(N/2)-1} z(k)\, W_N^{2ik} \end{aligned}\right\} \left(i = 0, 1, \ldots, \frac{N}{2} - 1\right) \tag{2.18}$$

Noting

$$\begin{aligned} W^i Z(i) &= W^i \sum_{k=0}^{(N/2)-1} x(2k + 1) W^{2ik} \\ &= \sum_{k=0}^{(N/2)-1} x(2k + 1) W^{i(2k+1)} \end{aligned}$$

the Fourier representation of $x(k)$ can be synthesized from the disjoint transforms $Y(i)$ and $Z(i)$ as follows:

$$X(i) = \sum_{k=0}^{(N/2)-1} x(2k)\, W_N^{2ik} + x(2k + 1)\, W_N^{i(2k+1)} \tag{2.19}$$

$$(i = 0, 1, \ldots, N - 1)$$

or, in terms of Equation (2.18),

$$X(i) = Y(i) + W^i\, Z(i) \tag{2.20}$$

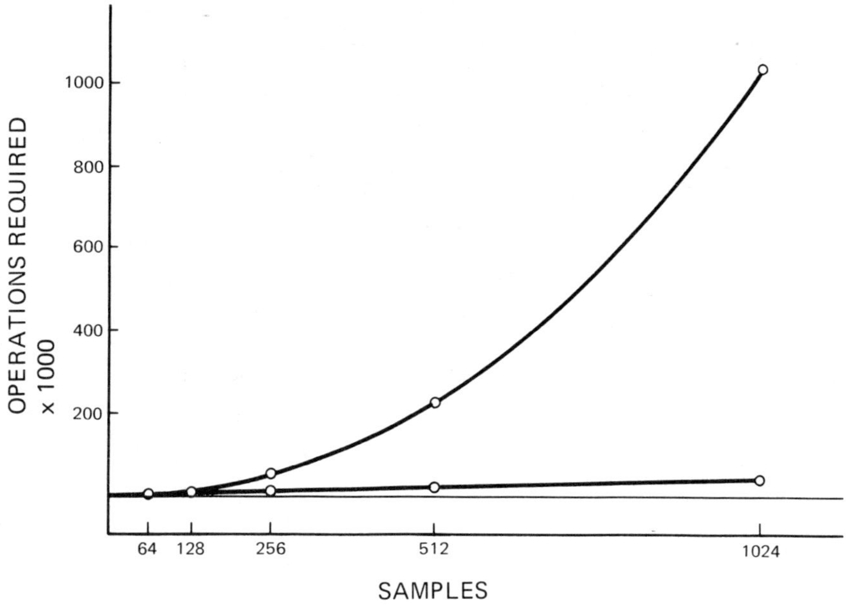

Figure 2-4. The FFT Method's Computational Savings.

A further simplification can be obtained if one recalls that $X(i)$ can be extended, using Equation (2.15), to be

$$\left.\begin{aligned} X(i) &= Y(i) + W^i Z(i) \\ X(i \quad + N/2) &= Y(i) - W^i Z(i) \end{aligned}\right\} \left(i = 0, 1, \ldots, \frac{N}{2} - 1\right) \tag{2.21}$$

Using the results of Equation (2.16), one may represent the negative frequency components as follows:

$$X(-i) = X^* \,(i) = Y^* \,(i) - W^{i*}Z^*(i) = Y(-i) - W^{-i}Z(-i) \tag{2.22}$$

where * denotes complex conjugation.

Suppose, for example, that $N = 8$. The DFT and FFT generation of the spectra of $x(k)$, for this value of N, is block diagrammed in Figure 2-5. One notes that the DFT requires $N^2 = 64$ operations to produce the required spectra, whereas the FFT approach required only $2(N/2)^2 = 32$ operations.

If such savings can be reaped by partitioning the original time series into two subseries, would a further decomposition result in additional savings? In general, yes. The optimal decomposition of N time series samples is known to satisfy the following equation:

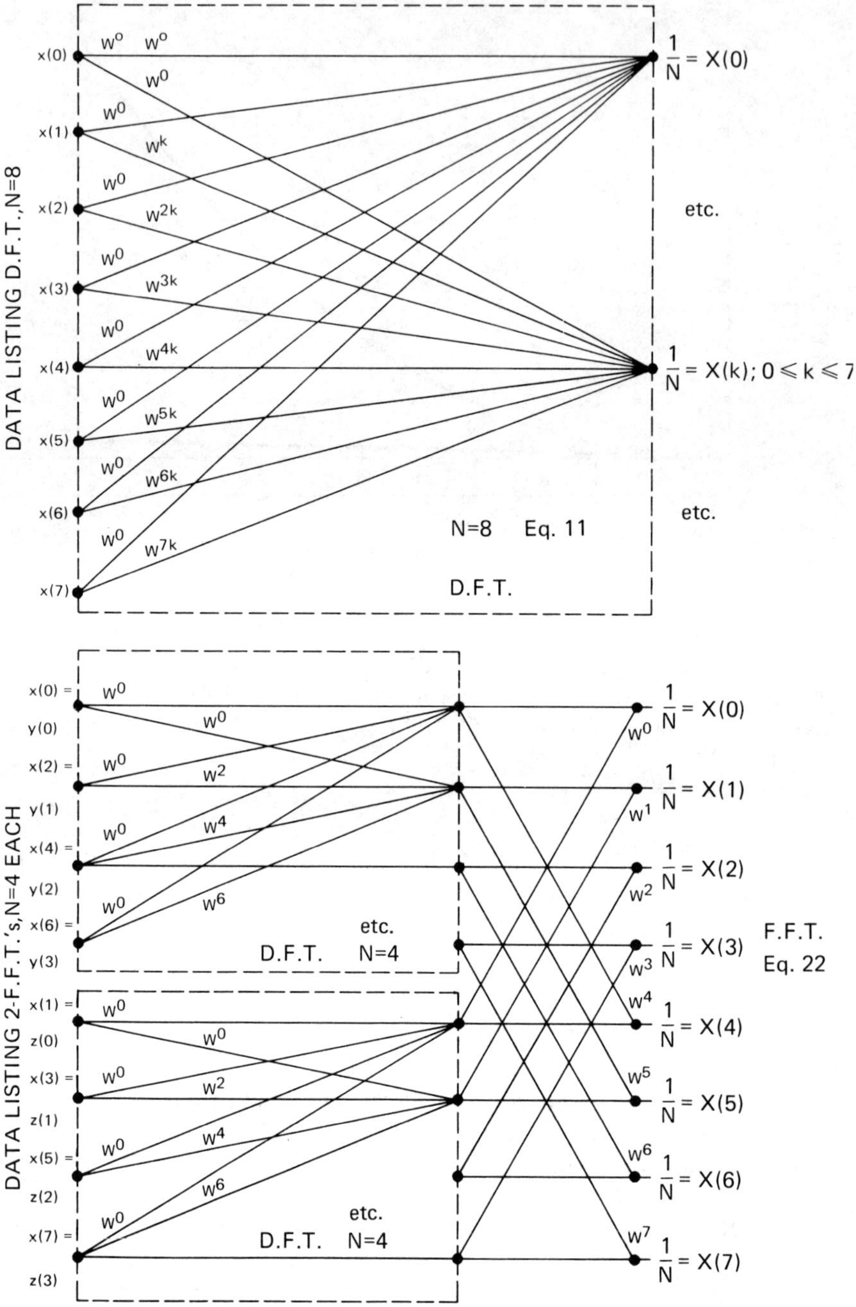

Figure 2-5. DFT and FFT Generation of the Spectra of $x(k)$ for $N = 8$.

$$N = \prod_{i=1}^{m} n_i = n_1 \times n_2 \times \ldots \times n_m \qquad (2.23)$$

where n_i is a prime number. If all the n_i's have value two (for example, $8 = 2*2*2 = 2^3$), the algorithm is said to be radix (2) (radix means "root"). The example previously considered is reinvestigated using a radix (2) approach. The resulting mechanics of this operation can be found in Figure 2-6.

Often the number of samples in a time series representing a physical process does not lend itself to radix (2) operations. For example, the sampling of a socioeconomic process on a monthly basis for a year would yield 12 samples. The number 12 cannot be factored into a radix (2) format. If a radix (2) FFT analysis is to be performed over this data set, only 8 sample values could be used. The distortion induced in the sample space may produce an unrealistic transform. Therefore it is desirable to have an FFT algorithm that will accept data in a mixed radix form. The FFT algorithm developed for this book is a mixed-radix algorithm. It would interpret the example problem in the following factored form:

$$N = 12 = 2*2*3$$

that is, $n_1 = n_2 = 2$ and $n_3 = 3$.

Error Sources. The utility of an FFT analysis is great. However, there are latent error sources inbedded in this method that the user must be aware of. These error sources fall into three categories: aliasing, leakage, and the picket fence effect.

1. Aliasing. As the name implies, a signal may be impersonated (an alias) by another—a problem exemplified in Figure 2-7. Here the chosen sample rate is too slow to completely characterize the input signal. As a consequence, a bogus low-frequency signal impersonates the higher-frequency input signal. The aliasing problem can be removed by requiring the sample rate chosen to be at least twice that of the highest frequency residing in the signal to be sampled. This condition is often called the Nyquist condition. For example, suppose a signal $x(t)$ is "bandwidth limited" to a frequency f_{max}. That is, there is a bandwidth limitation imposed on $x(t)$ in that all frequency components of $x(t)$ reside at frequencies less than or equal to f_{max} Hz. Then a nonaliasing sample rate would be f_s where f_s is greater than or equal to $2f_{max}$ Hz.

2. Leakage. Leakage is an undesirable harmonic distortion. The following example dramatizes the problem:

Suppose a signal $x(t)$ is given by

$$x(t) = \sin(2\pi f_o t)$$

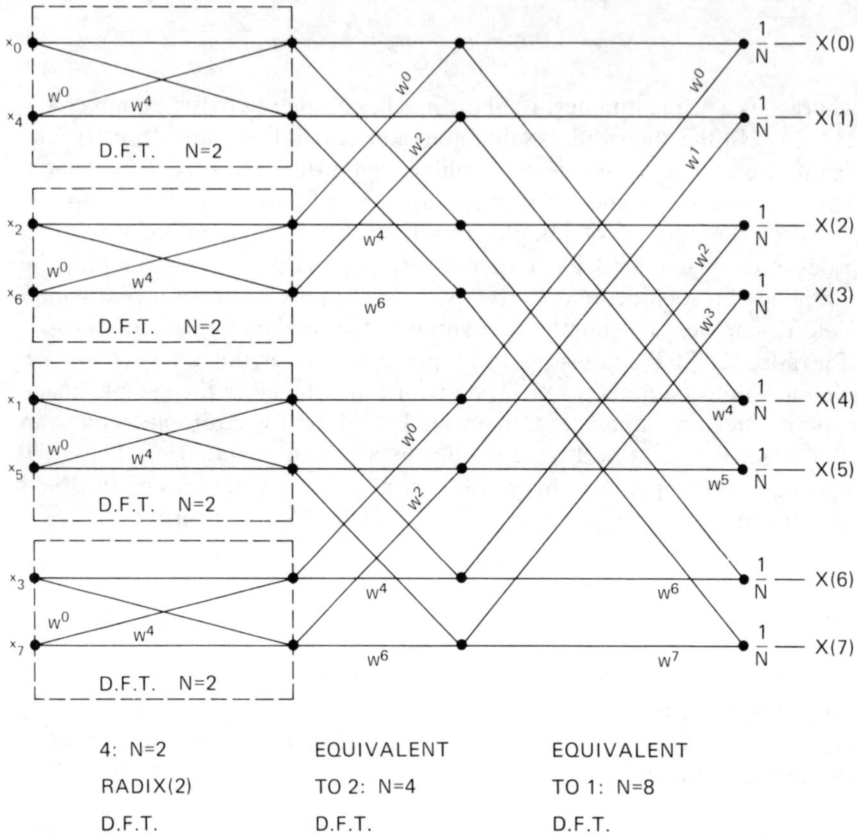

Figure 2-6. Radix 2 FFT for $N = 8$

Then the fundamental period associated with $x(t)$ is given by T_o where

$$T_o = \frac{1}{f_o}$$

Consider now $x(t)$ to be sampled above the Nyquist rate for T seconds. Suppose further that $T = T_o$. The resulting Fourier representation of $x(t)$ would have a nontrivial component at f_o Hz only. However, suppose the same sample rate is used, but the sampling continues for greater than T_o seconds. That is, $T = \alpha T_o$. Suppose further that α is a noninteger. Then the resulting Fourier representation of the new time series would have more

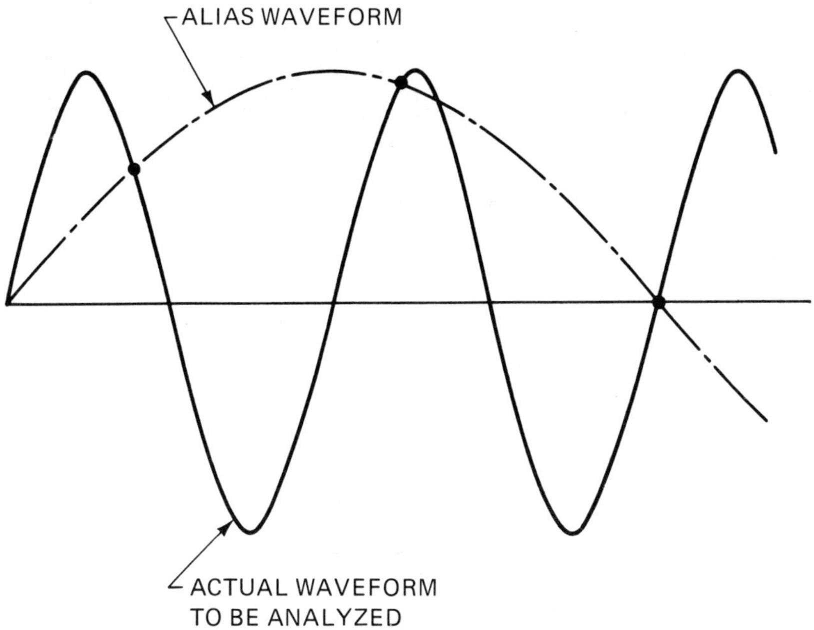

Figure 2-7. Aliasing.

than one nontrivial frequency component because the new time series is not periodic in the sampling interval. The example problem is graphically interpreted in Figure 2-8.

The leakage problem can be minimized by establishing a sampling interval that is long compared to the fundamental period of the signal to be analyzed. The problem of leakage also may be reduced by a periodicity-inducing filter. Such a filter is used to make an aperiodic time series appear "nearly" periodic. For example, a popular periodicity-inducing filter is the Hanning filter. Over a period T_o, the Hanning filter, denoted $H(t)$, satisfies

$$H(t) = \frac{1}{2} [1 - \cos(2\pi f_o t)]$$

(see Figure 2-9). The Hanning filter will alter an input process, say $x(t)$, as follows:

$$y(t) = H(t)\, x(t)$$

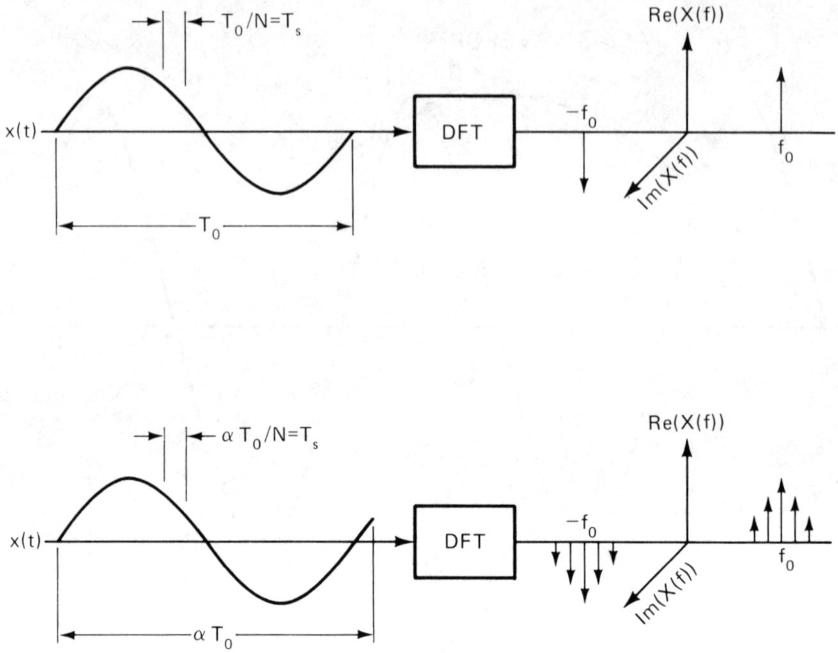

Figure 2-8. LEAKAGE

where $y(t)$ represents the filter output. Suppose the value of $x(0)$ is different from the value of $x(T_0)$. Then it is obvious that the process $x(t)$ is aperiodic. However, the output $y(t)$ will have identical end-point values, namely $y(0) = t(T_o) = 0$. In addition, $y(t)$ will appear to be generally more periodic over the interval 0 to T_o. A dramatization of a Hanning operation can be found in Figure 2-10.

3. Picket Fence Effect. A third source of error is called the picket fence effect. The DFT can be envisioned as a set of narrow bandpass filters whose center frequencies are located at k/T Hz, $k = 0, 1, 2, \ldots, N - 1$. The combined effect of these filters is graphically interpreted in Figure 2-11. The FFT filter response curve resembles a picket fence. The frequency components of an input signal $x(t)$ that reside at $k/T = kf_o$ Hz will be transformed without distortion. However, frequency components of $x(t)$ that reside at noninteger multiples of f_o are transformed with distortion.

Ensemble-averaging techniques can be used to minimize the effects of the picket fence effect. Interpolation methods, which minimize the effects of this error source, are available also.

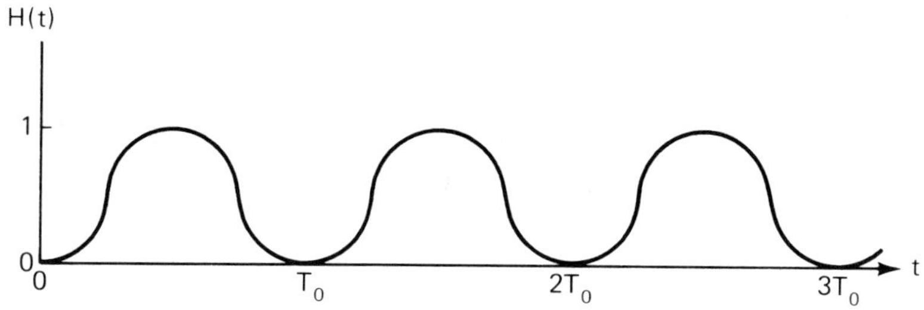

Figure 2-9. Hanning Filter.

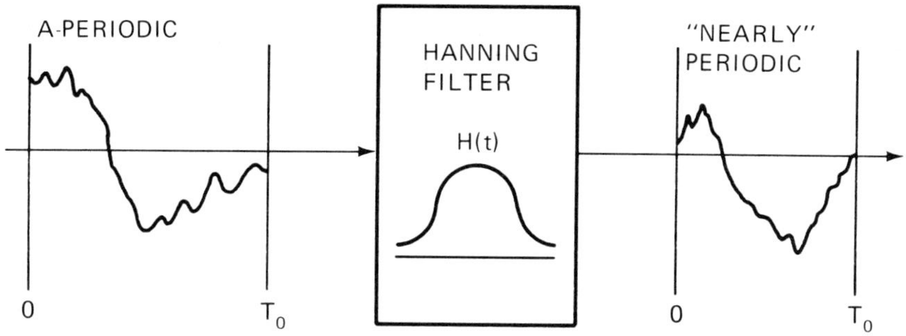

Figure 2-10. A Hanning Operation.

The Mixed-radix FFT. The mixed-radix FFT algorithm used in this book is due to Singleton [20]. A user can choose the size of the array to be transformed to be an integer number less than or equal to 1024. Exceptions are found in Table 2-1. An FFT operation on a time series is initiated with the three-letter mnemonic FFT. The data that must reside in the time domain in array A are transformed and returned to that array. Restrictions imposed on the use of the mixed radix FFT routine are:

1. The number of data points, denoted NPOINT (see Chapter 1), must conform mathematically to the following rules:
   a. The maximum prime factor contained in NPOINT must be less than or equal to 23.
   b. The maximum number of prime multiplicative factors in NPOINT is 11.
   c. The product of the square free factors of NPOINT must be less than or equal to 210.

   (A table of inadmissible values of NPOINT can be found in Table 2-1.)

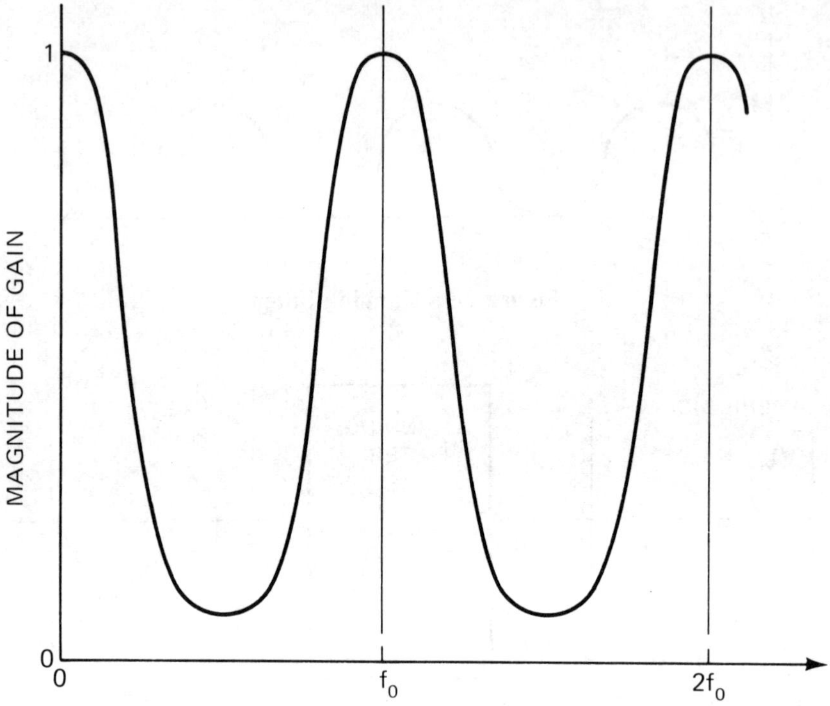

Figure 2-11. Combined Effect of Narrow Bandpass Filters.

2. The data to be transformed must reside in array A.
3. The contents of array A must be in the time (TIME) domain.

The structure of an FFT call is shown in Table 2-2.

When an FFT is performed, SPECTRUM IV will automatically output a status statement indicating the success of the operation as well as listing the array information parameters. These include sample frequencies, record size, and domain information.

The Inverse Fast Fourier Transform (IFFT): The Mixed-radix IFFT. The inverse transform is performed similarly to the FFT. An IFFT is initiated with the four-letter mnemonic IFFT. Restrictions imposed on the mixed-radix IFFT are:

1. Same as for FFT.
2. Same as for FFT.
3. The contents of array A must be in the frequency (FREQ) domain.
4. Array A cannot be a null array (that is, all zeros).

Table 2-1
Inadmissible Values of NPOINT

29	31	37	41	43	47	53	58	59	61	62
67	71	73	74	79	82	83	86	87	89	93
94	97	101	013	106	107	109	111	113	116	118
122	123	124	127	129	131	134	137	139	141	142
145	146	148	149	151	155	157	158	159	163	164
166	167	172	173	174	177	178	179	181	183	185
186	188	191	193	194	197	199	201	202	203	205
206	211	212	213	214	215	217	218	219	222	223
226	227	229	232	233	235	236	237	239	241	244
246	248	249	251	254	257	258	259	261	262	263
265	267	268	269	271	274	277	278	279	281	282
283	284	287	290	291	292	293	295	296	298	301
318	303	305	307	309	310	311	313	314	316	317
381	219	321	326	327	328	329	331	332	333	334
335	337	339	341	344	346	347	348	349	353	354
355	356	358	359	362	365	366	367	369	370	371
372	373	376	377	379	381	382	383	386	387	388
389	393	394	395	397	398	401	402	403	404	406
407	409	410	411	412	413	415	417	419	421	422
423	424	426	427	428	430	431	433	434	435	436
438	439	443	444	445	446	447	449	451	452	453
454	457	458	461	463	464	465	466	467	469	470
471	472	473	474	477	478	479	481	482	485	487
488	489	491	492	493	496	497	498	499	501	502
503	505	508	509	511	514	515	516	517	518	519
521	522	523	524	526	527	530	531	533	534	535
536	537	538	541	542	543	545	547	548	549	551
553	554	555	556	557	558	559	562	563	564	565
566	568	569	571	573	574	577	579	580	581	582
583	584	586	587	589	590	591	592	593	596	597
599	601	602	603	604	606	607	609	610	611	613
614	615	617	618	619	620	622	623	626	628	629
631	632	633	634	635	636	638	639	641	642	643
645	647	649	651	652	653	654	655	656	657	658
659	661	662	664	666	667	668	669	670	671	673
674	677	678	679	681	682	683	685	687	688	689
691	692	694	695	696	608	698	699	701	703	705
706	707	708	709	710	711	712	713	716	717	718
719	721	723	724	725	727	730	731	732	733	734
737	738	739	740	742	743	744	745	746	747	749
751	752	753	754	755	757	758	761	762	763	764
766	767	769	771	772	773	774	775	776	777	778
779	781	783	785	786	787	788	789	790	791	793
794	795	796	797	799	801	802	803	804	806	807
808	809	811	812	813	814	815	817	818	820	821
822	823	824	826	827	829	830	831	834	835	837
838	839	841	842	843	844	846	848	849	851	852
853	854	856	857	859	860	861	862	863	865	866
868	869	870	871	872	873	876	877	878	879	881
883	885	886	887	888	889	890	892	893	894	895
898	899	901	902	903	904	905	906	907	908	909
911	913	914	915	916	917	919	921	922	923	925
926	927	928	929	930	932	933	934	937	938	939

Table 2-1 (cont.)

940	941	942	943	944	946	947	948	949	951	953
954	955	956	957	958	959	961	962	963	964	965
967	970	971	973	974	976	977	978	979	981	982
983	984	985	986	987	989	991	992	993	994	995
996	997	998	999	1002	1003	1004	1005	1006	1007	1009
1010	1011	1013	1015	1016	1017	1018	1019	1021	1022	1023
1025	1027	1028	1030	1031	1032	1033	1034	1036	1037	1038

Table 2-2
Structure of an FFT Call

Column Number	*Description*	*Format or Contents*
Primary information card		
1-3	Calls FFT	FFT

The structure of an IFFT call is shown in Table 2-3. An IFFT will automatically generate the output message described in the FFT section.

The remainder of this section of the chapter is used to exemplify the use of program FFT. Several examples are offered that highlight the salient features of this routine. If an error is incurred during the execution of an FFT operation, SPECTRUM IV will detect it and automatically display a note describing the nature of the error. An FFT operation will automatically assign array A memory protection.

Example. The following example problem is designed to exhibit the salient features of the FFT routine used in SPECTRUM IV. The problem makes use of the transform methods, library call, and display options available in this book. The problem is composed of the following parts:

1. Generate 50 samples of a pure sine wave having a frequency of 100 Hz sampled at a 1000-Hz rate. This task is performed through a call to the system library. An FFT is performed on the input time series and a magnitude plot of the resulting spectra is produced.
2. Generate 50 samples of a pure sine wave having a frequency above the Nyquist (folding frequency) rate of 500 Hz. Let that frequency be 600 Hz. Perform an FFT on the time series produced by a call to the system library and generate a magnitude plot of the resulting spectra.
3. Generate 50 samples of a pure sine wave which is not periodic in the sampling interval. Let the sample rate again be 100 Hz, which gives rise to sampling interval of 50 msec. Let an FFT be taken of the library-produced time series and a magnitude plot of the resulting spectra be produced.

Table 2-3
Structure of an IFFT Call

Column Number	Description	Format or Contents
Primary information card		
1-4	Calls IFFT	IFFT

4. Generate 50 samples of a noise-corrupted pure sine wave of frequency 100 Hz, sampled at a 1000-Hz rate. Let the noise process be normal, mean value zero with unity variance. This task is accomplished through a call to the system library. Let an FFT be performed on the synthesized time series, and plot the magnitude spectra of the resulting transform.

The control card sequence used in this experiment can be found in Figure 2-12. The sinusoidal signal required for this problem came from library options one and eight. In addition, because all time series are 50 points in length, only the first 25 harmonics are plotted. The remaining 25 harmonics would represent negative-frequency harmonics. The result of the experiment can be found in Figures 2-13 through 2-16. It is interesting to note that a pure sinusoid that is periodic in the sampling interval contains spectral information at only one frequency, which is located at line 5 of Figure 2-13. Since the frequency of that plot has been specified to be 0.200E 02 Hz, line 5 represents signal energy located at 100 Hz. The amplitude of that line is equal to its theoretical value of 0.5. If a sinusoid is analyzed that has a frequency above the Nyquist sampling rate—500 Hz for this problem—aliasing will occur. The result of aliasing can be found in Figure 2-14. Here the FFT algorithm assumed the 600-Hz input sine time series to be dominated by a 400-Hz sinusoid. The 400-Hz line can be found at line 20. If an input time series is not periodic in the sampling interval, leakage will result. The synthesized 150-Hz input sinusoid is such a signal. Here the sampling interval is 50 msec in length. The 150-Hz signal has a period of 6.667 msec. Therefore the sampling interval is not an integer multiple of the signal period. The effect of leakage can be found in Figure 2-15. There is a considerable amount of spectral energy, the fundamental amount of which theoretically exists at line 7.5. When noise is added to a pure sinusoid, the resulting spectra will be enriched. The noise processes, being highly randomized, contribute many frequencies to the resulting spectra. However, the evidence of the sinusoidal component of the input series can be found at 200 Hz, equivalently line 10 (see Figure 2-16).

Example. Consider the periodic pulse train diagram shown in Figure 2-17. The Fourier representation for such a pulse train is known to be given by a

```
CARD        COLUMN                                                                      8Ø
            123456789Ø12        .         .         .         .         .         .      .
-------------------------------------------------------------------------------------------
1           LIBRARY     A                                               5Ø      1ØØØ.ØØ
2           SINE                                          1   1.          1ØØ.
3           FFT
4           PLOTTER     A                                               25
5           FREQ   MAG          1    25     SINE SPECTRA (MAGNITUDE)
6           LIBRARY     A                                               5Ø      1ØØØ.ØØ
7           SINE ALIAS                                    1   1.          6ØØ.
8           FFT
9           PLOTTER     A                                               25
1Ø          FREQ   MAG          1    25     SINE (ALIAS)
11          LIBRARY     A                                               5Ø      1ØØØ.ØØ
12          SINE LEAKAGE                                  1   1.          15Ø.
13          FFT
14          PLOTTER     A                                               25
15          FREQ   MAG          1    25     SINE (LEAKAGE)
16          LIBRARY     A                                               5Ø      1ØØØ.ØØ
17          SINE PLUS NOISE                               8   1.          2ØØ.    1.    Ø.
18          FFT
19          PLOTTER     A                                               25
2Ø          FREQ   MAG          1    25     SINE PLUS NOISE
21          TERM
                      .         .         .         .         .         .         .      .
```

Figure 2-12. Control Card Sequence for Fourier Experiment.

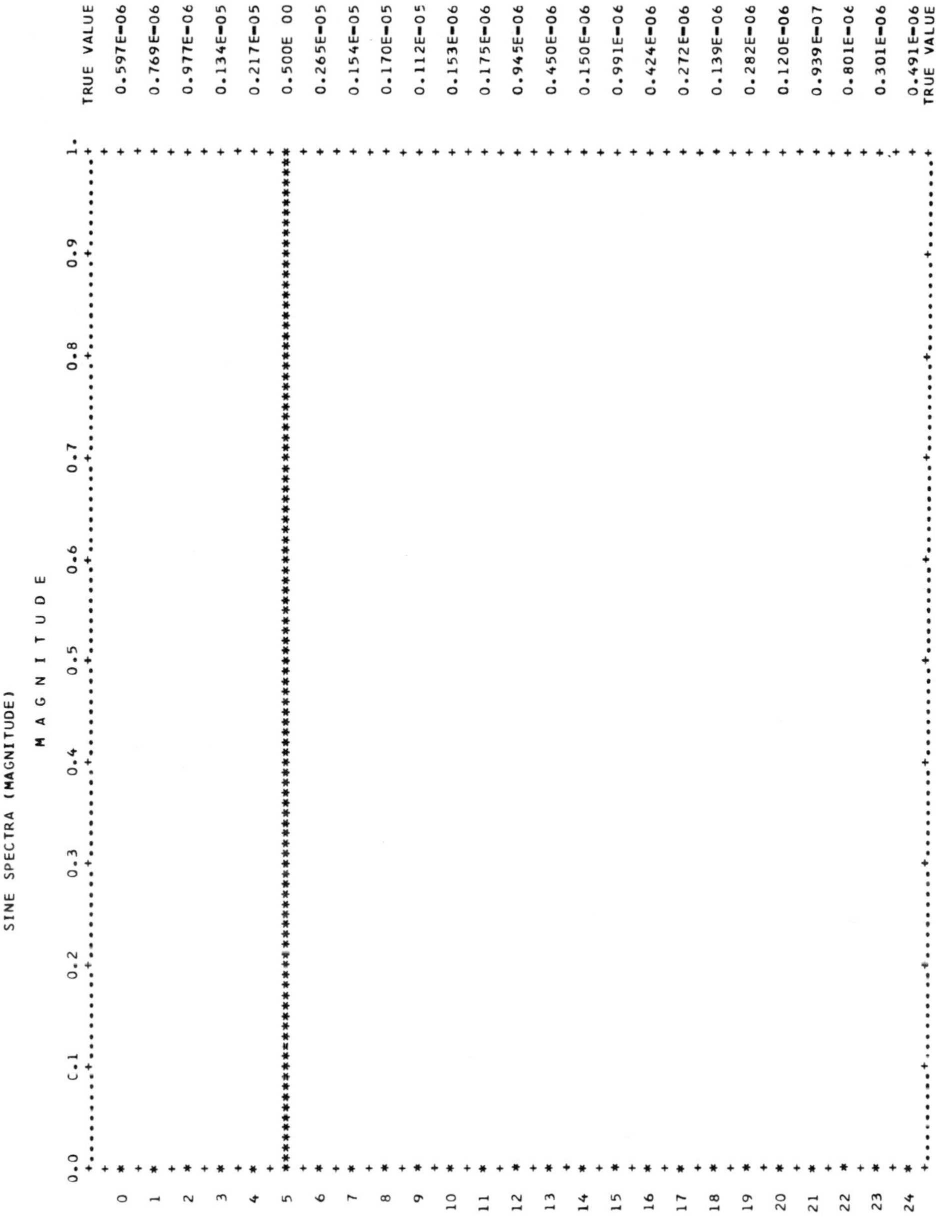

Figure 2-13. Magnitude Plot of a Pure Sine Wave (Fourier Experiment).

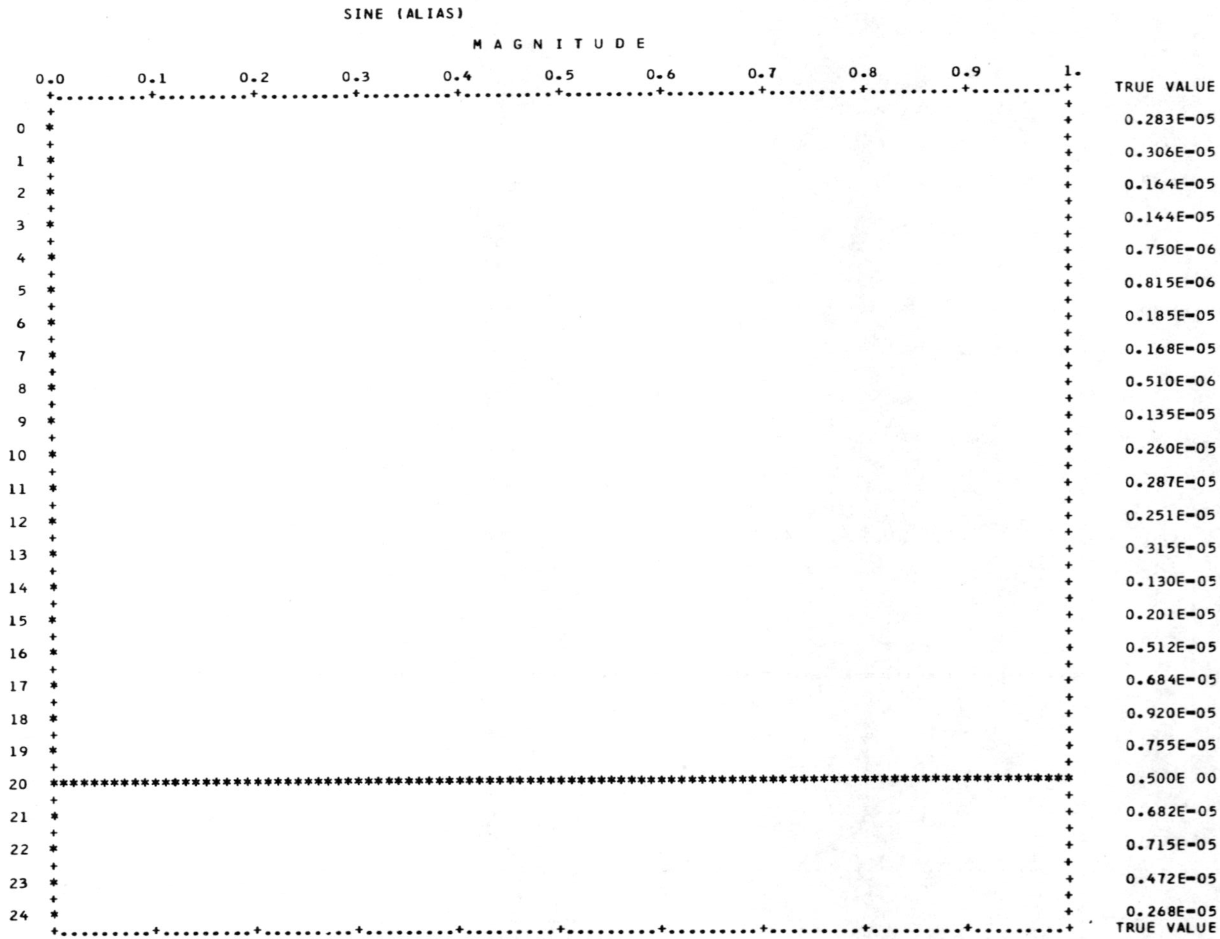

Figure 2-14. Magnitude Plot of an Alias Sine Wave. (Fourier Experiment).

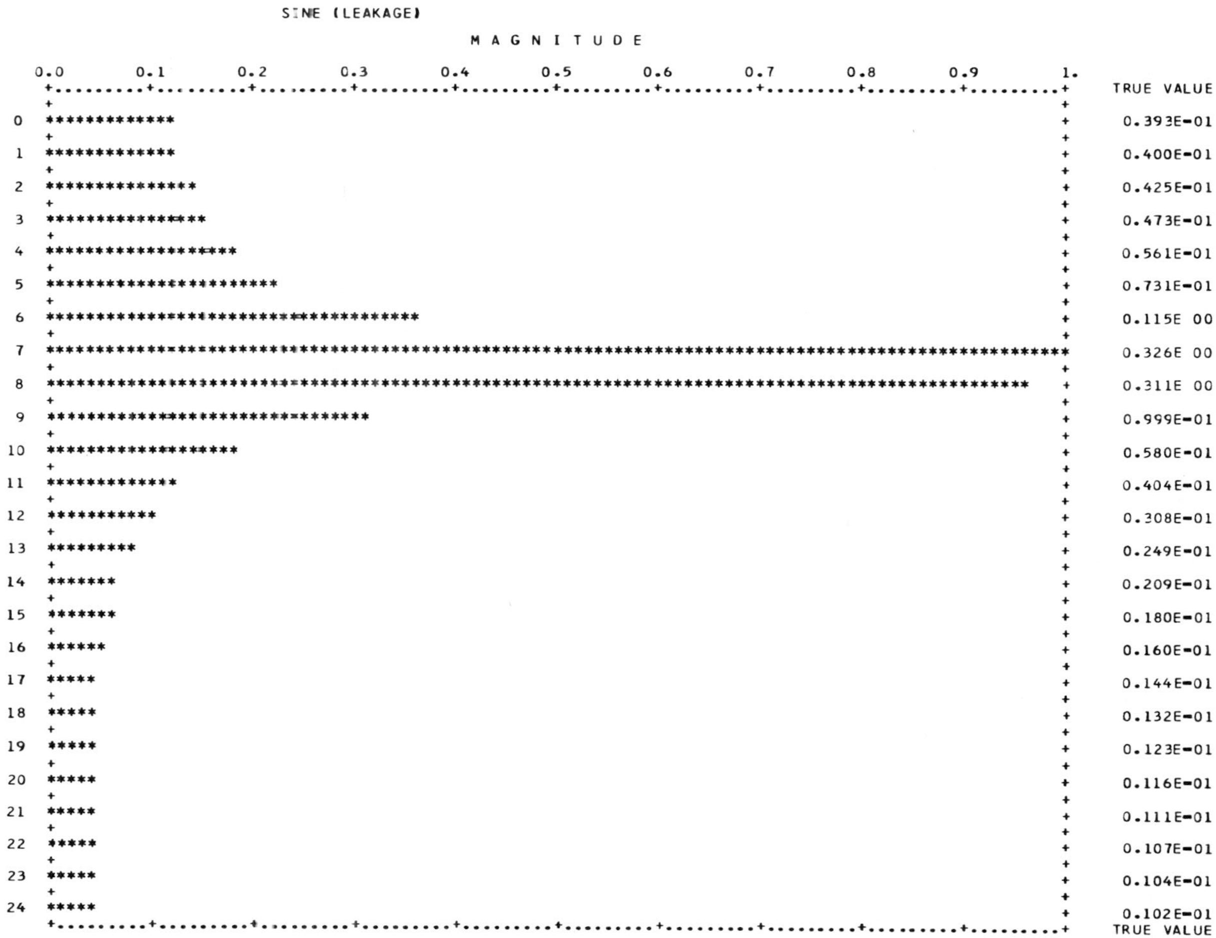

Figure 2-15. Magnitude Plot of a Leakage Test (Fourier Experiment).

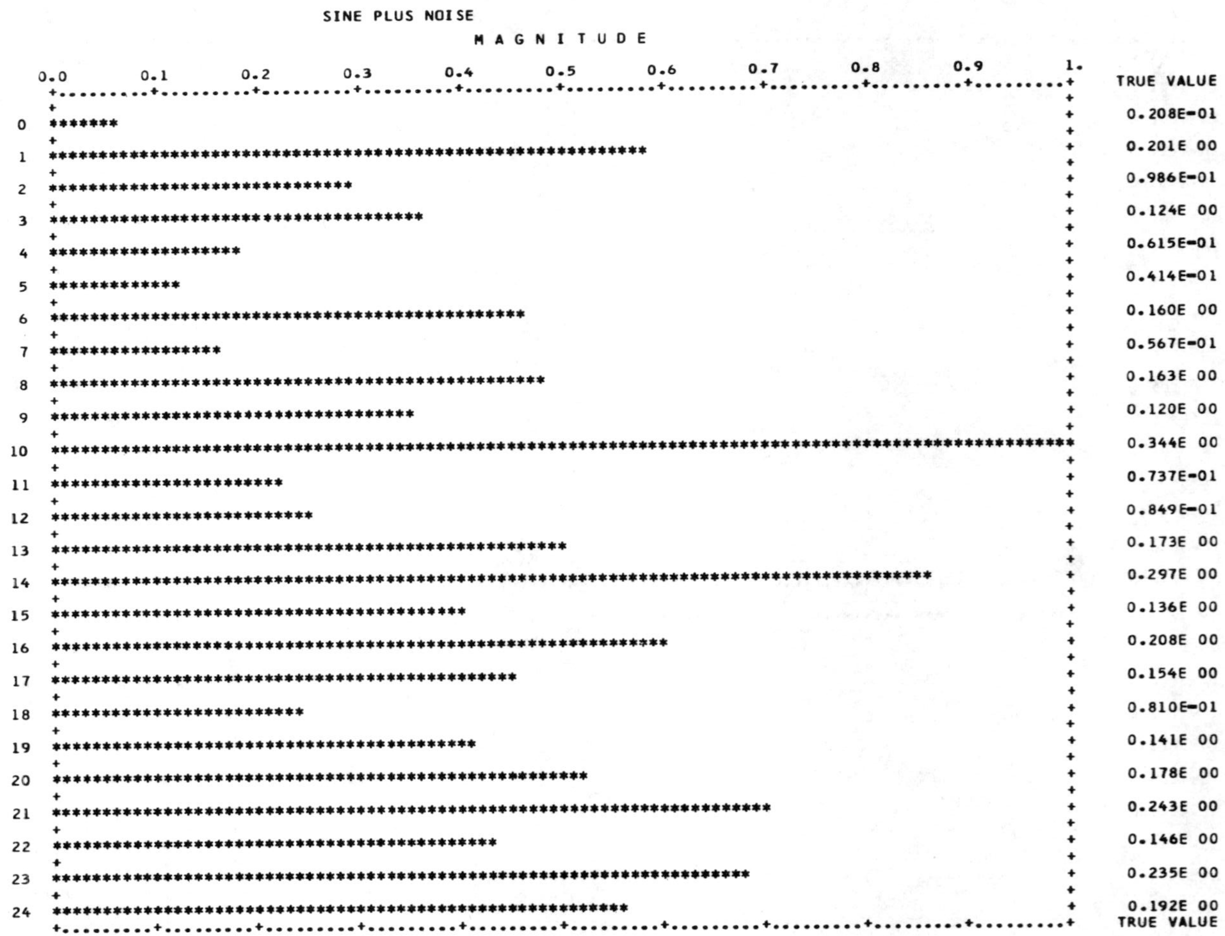

Figure 2-16. Magnitude Spectra of a Sine Wave in Noise (Fourier Experiment).

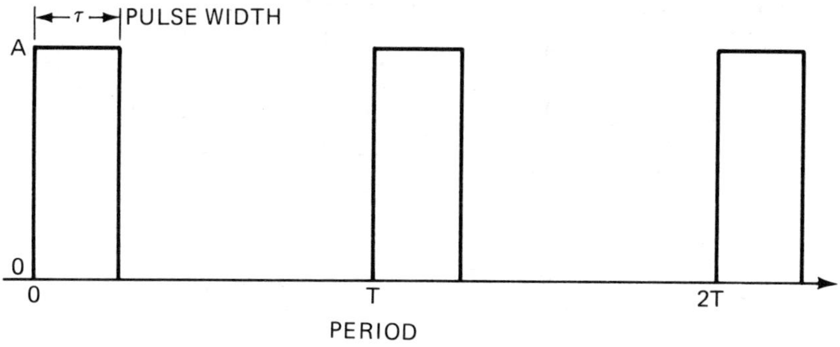

Figure 2-17. Periodic Pulse Train Diagram.

$\sin(x)/x$ relationship. If $x(t)$ is sampled over an interval T, the amplitude of the nth harmonic, denoted $X(nf)$, is given by

$$X(nf_o) = \frac{A\tau}{T} \frac{\sin(\pi f_n \tau)}{(\pi f_n \tau)} \qquad (n = 0, 1, \ldots,)$$

where $f_n = nf_o = n/T$.

It is often convenient to represent $X(nf_o)$ in terms of the pulse "duty cycle," denoted d where

$$d = \frac{\tau}{T} \text{(on time)}$$

then

$$X(nf_o) = \frac{A\tau}{T} \frac{\sin(\pi n \tau/T)}{(\pi n \tau/T)}$$

$$= Ad \frac{\sin(n\pi d)}{(n\pi d)}$$

The magnitude of $X(nf_o)$ can be found diagrammed for various duty cycles d in Figure 2-18. Small duty cycles result in a very "rich" frequency-domain representation. Similarly, the d-c component and the amplitude on a per-harmonic basis decreases at a rate of $1/\tau$.

Now consider the following specific problem. Let a pulse train $x(t)$ be defined as follows (see Figure 2-19):

$$x(t) = \begin{cases} 2 \text{ if } .005 \geq t \\ 0 \text{ if } .005 < t < .095 \\ 2 \text{ if } .095 \leq t \end{cases}$$

Let $x(t)$ be sampled at a rate of 1000 samples/sec. Let it be required that

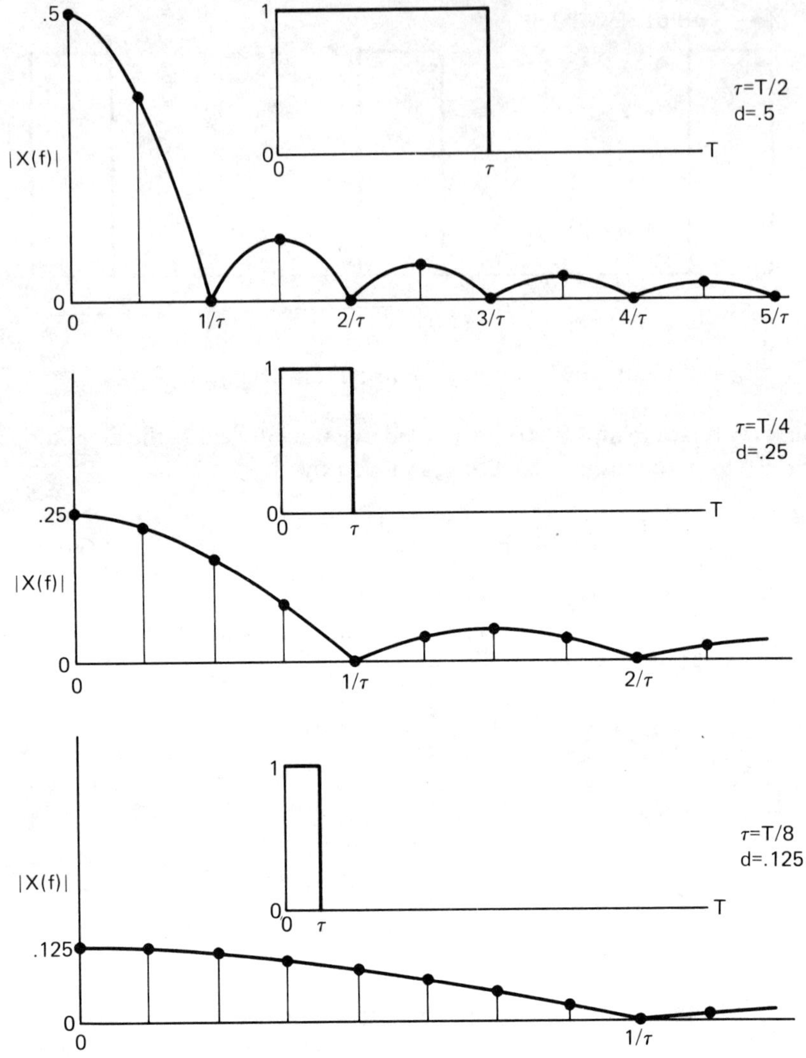

Figure 2-18. Magnitude of $X(nf_0)$ for Various Duty Cycles d.

1. the time series $x(n\ \Delta t)$ be plotted (100 points)
2. an FFT be taken
3. the magnitude spectra be plotted (50 points)
4. the phase spectra be plotted (50 points)
5. an IFFT be performed

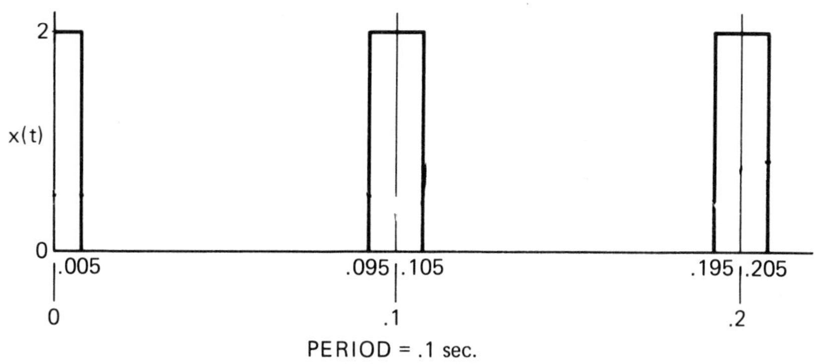

Figure 2-19. Sample Pulse

6. the resulting time series be plotted (100 points)

The control card required of such an operation can be found in Figure 2-20. All operations are performed on data resident in array A. Recall that the FFT and IFFT algorithms operate only on array A data. The card sequence shown generates a pulse train having amplitude 2, duty cycle 0.1, and a d-c level 0 by using LIBRARY option 2. The other requested operations, such as FFT, IFFT, and plotting duties, are also performed in a straightforward manner under SPECTRUM IV control. Figures 2-21 through 2-25 display the results of these actions.

B. Autocorrelation

Correlation is a measure of similarity. The correlation of a signal, say, $x(t)$ with itself is called the autocorrelation. The autocorrelation function, denoted $R_x(\tau)$, measures average similarity between $x(t)$ and its delayed version $x(t + \tau)$. For example, if $R_x(\tau)$ is a large positive number, then $x(t)$ strongly resembles $x(t + \tau)$. Therefore changes in $x(t)$ will be reflected in proportional changes in $x(t + \tau)$. Equivalently, that $R_x(\tau)$ has large negative value implies that changes in $x(t)$ are inversely related to changes in $x(t + \tau)$. Finally, $R_x(\tau)$ having a value of zero indicates that $x(t)$ and $x(t + \tau)$ have, on the average, very little in common.

There is another interpretation for correlation. If for some τ, $R_x(\tau)$ is large, $x(t)$ has a tendency to repeat itself every τ seconds. That is, $x(t)$ will exhibit periodic behavior at a frequency of $1/\tau$ Hz. Therefore there is a connection between the autocorrelation function and the frequency domain. Program AUTO-C (autocorrelation) will allow the user to generate the autocorrelation function from any inputted time- or frequency-domain signal.

```
CARD       COLUMN                                                                        80
           123456789012       .         .         .         .         .         .         .
--------------------------------------------------------------------------------------------
1          LIBRARY       A                                           40      200.
2          THIS IS A PULSE DUTY CYCLE .1               2  2.0  0.0      .100
3          PLOTTER       A                                           40
4          TIME              1   40    THIS IS A PULSE OF DUTY CYCLE      .1
5          FFT
6          PLOTTER       A                                           20
7          FREQ   MAG        1   20    SIN(X)/X MAGNITUDE      .1
8          PLOTTER       A                                           20
9          FREQ   PHASE      1   20    SIN(X)/X PHASE          .1
10         PRINT         A         FREQ                    F         40
11                           F      FREQ
12         IFFT
13         PLOTTER       A                                           40
14         TIME              1   40    RECONSTRUCTED PULSE        .1
15         TERM
                    .         .         .         .         .         .         .         .
```

Figure 2-20. Card Control Sequence for Fourier Transform Experiment.

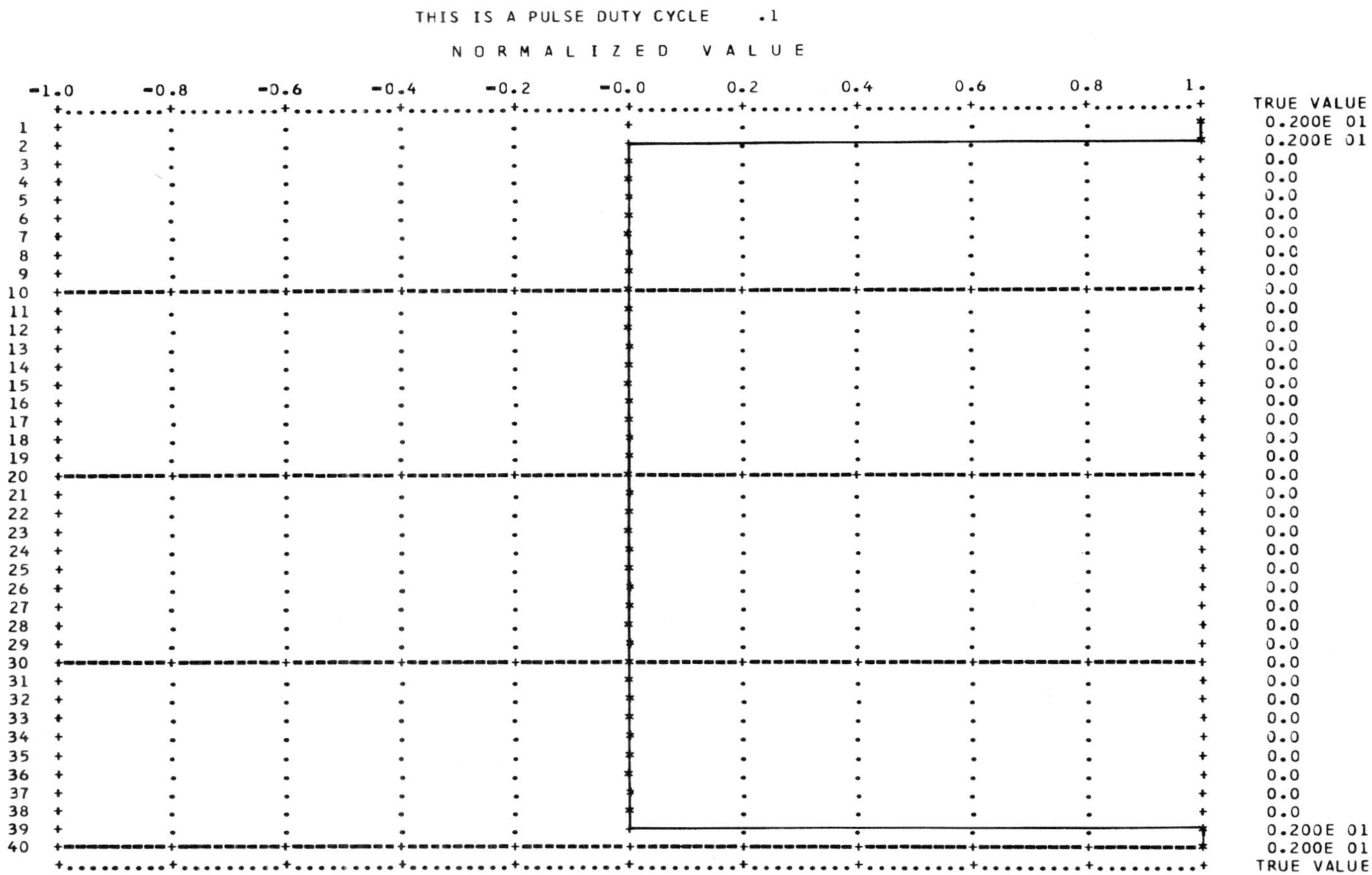

Figure 2-21. Pulse (Fourier Transform Experiment).

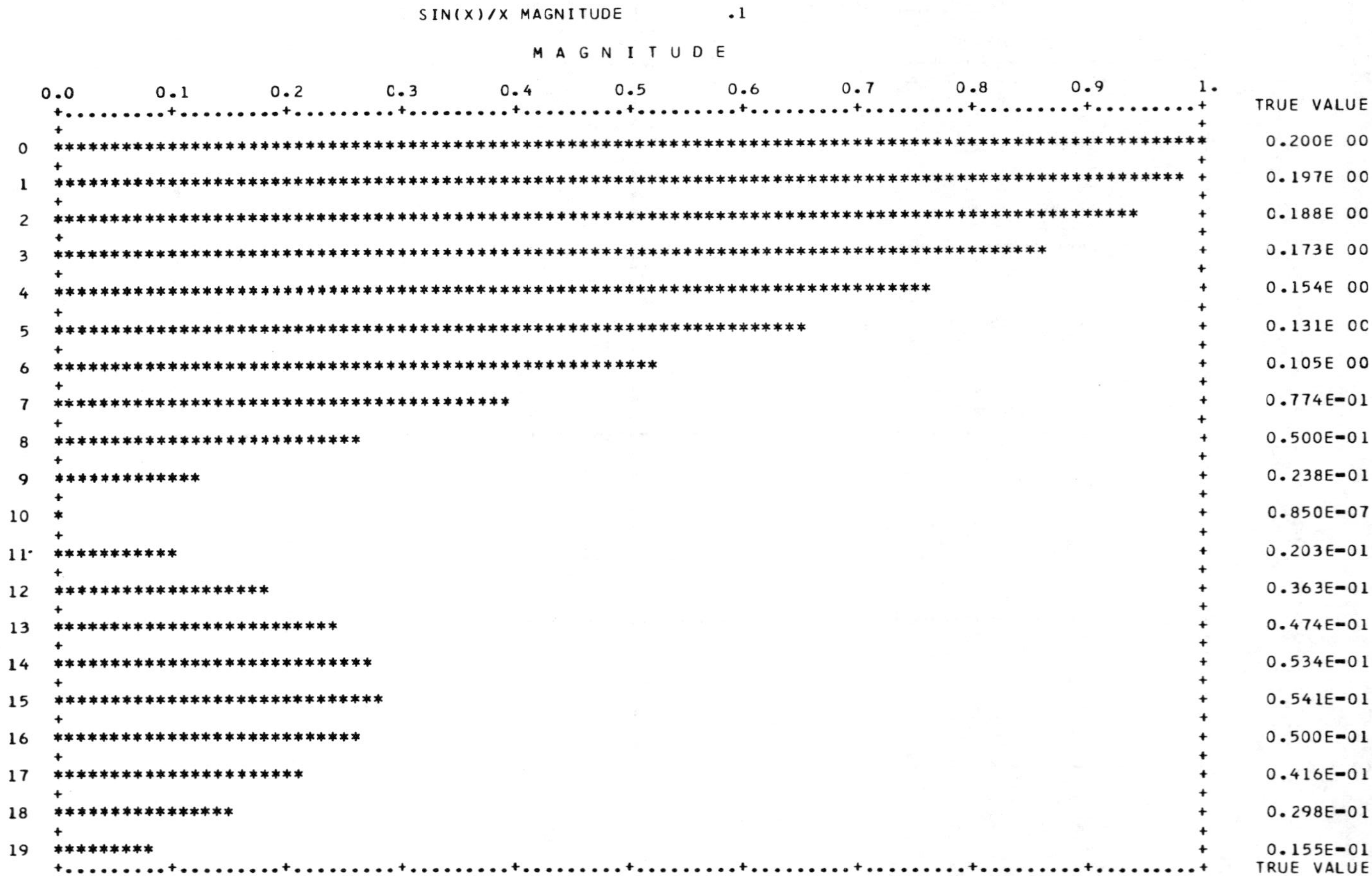

Figure 2-22. Magnitude Spectra (Fourier Transform Experiment).

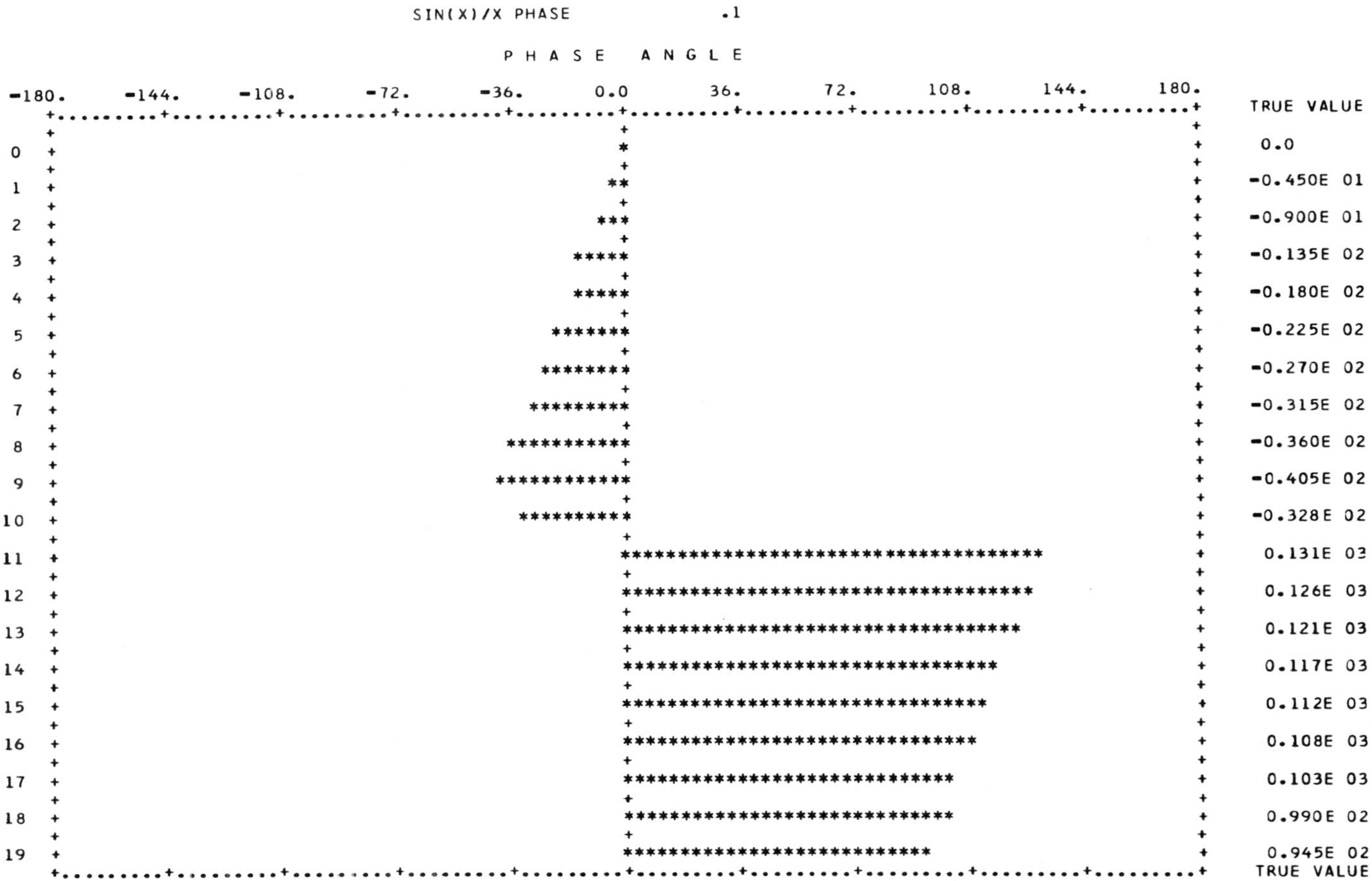

Figure 2-23. Phase Spectra (Fourier Transform Experiment).

LINE PRINTER FUNCTIONAL TASK

OUTPUT FROM ARRAY A

INFORMATION IN THE FREQUNCY DOMAIN

NUMBER OF FOURIER COEFFICIENTS 40

SAMPLING FREQUENCY OF THE DATA WAS 200.0 HZ

HIGHEST FREQUENCY COMPONENT CF DATA TO PREVENT ALIASING IS 0.1000E 03

FREQUENCY RESOLUTION OF THE SPECTRAL OUTPUT IS 5.0 HZ

HARMONIC	REAL VALUE	COMPLEX VALUE	THESE ARE THE NEGATIVE HARMONICS		
0	0.200	0.0			
1	0.196	-0.015	-19	-0.001	-0.015
2	0.186	-0.029	-18	-0.005	-0.029
3	0.168	-0.040	-17	-0.010	-0.040
4	0.146	-0.048	-16	-0.015	-0.048
5	0.121	-0.050	-15	-0.021	-0.050
6	0.093	-0.048	-14	-0.024	-0.048
7	0.066	-0.040	-13	-0.025	-0.040
8	0.040	-0.029	-12	-0.021	-0.029
9	0.018	-0.015	-11	-0.013	-0.015
10	0.000	-0.000	-10	-0.000	-0.000
11	-0.013	0.015	-9	0.018	0.015
12	-0.021	0.029	-8	0.040	0.029
13	-0.025	0.040	-7	0.066	0.040
14	-0.024	0.048	-6	0.093	0.048
15	-0.021	0.050	-5	0.121	0.050
16	-0.015	0.048	-4	0.146	0.048
17	-0.010	0.040	-3	0.168	0.040
18	-0.005	0.029	-2	0.186	0.029
19	-0.001	0.015	-1	0.196	0.015

Figure 2-24. Tabular Listing of Spectra (Fourier Transform Experiment).

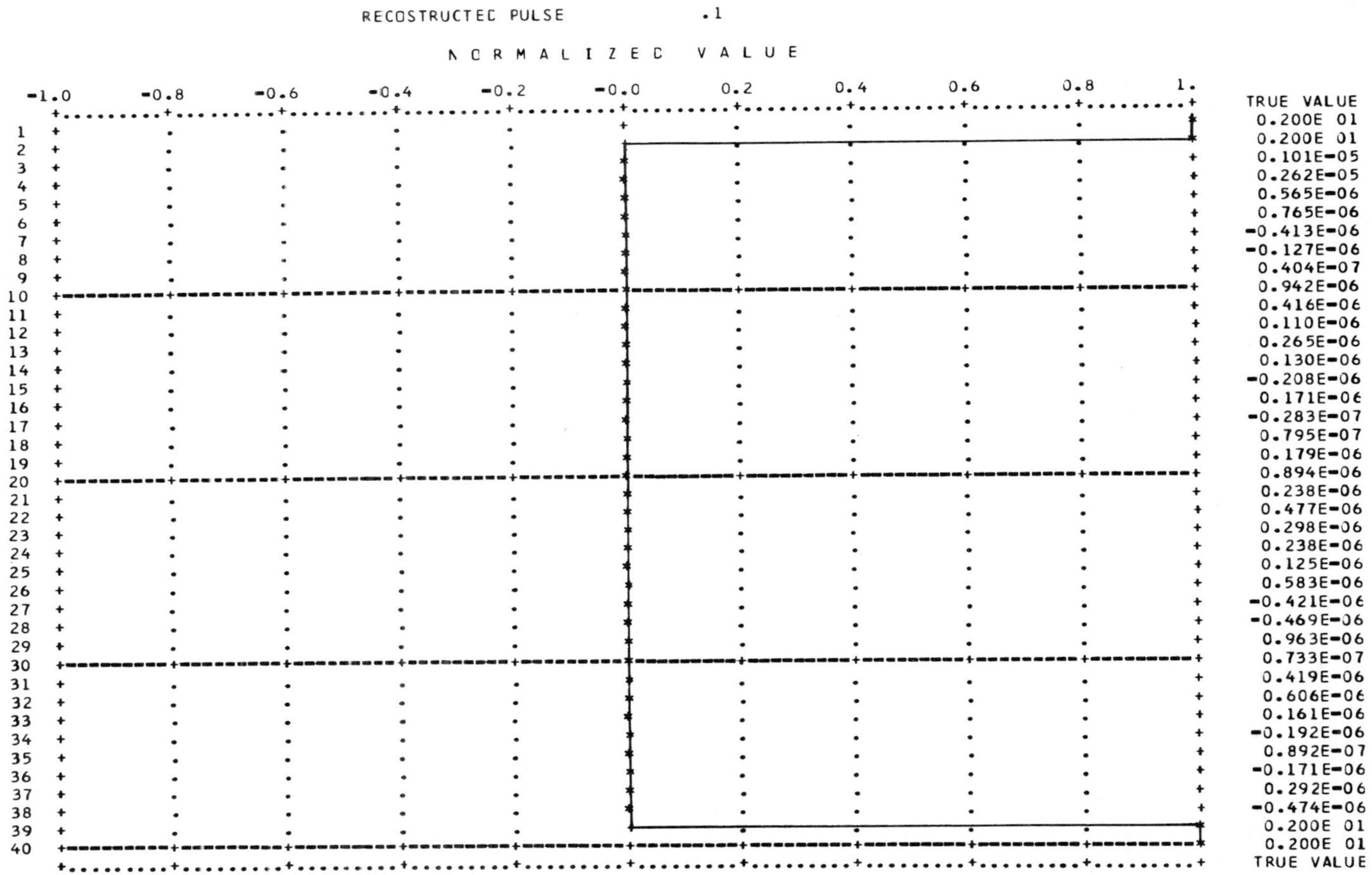

Figure 2-25. Recreated Time Series (Fourier Transform Experiment).

Theory

Let the autocorrelation function associated with the signal $x(t)$ be denoted $R_x(\tau)$, where

$$R_x(\tau) = \frac{1}{T}\int_{-T/2}^{T/2} x(t)x(t-\tau)\,dt \tag{2.24}$$

as $T \to \infty$. Therefore $R_x(\tau)$ measures the average value of $x(t)\,x(t-\tau)$. Let the following substitution of variables be defined

$$t = \gamma - \tau$$

therefore, for τ given,

$$dt = d\gamma$$

Then

$$R_x(\tau) = \frac{1}{T}\int_{-T/2}^{T/2} x(\gamma + \tau)x(\gamma)\,d\gamma = R_x(-\tau) \tag{2.25}$$

Therefore $R_x(\tau)$ is an even function of τ. The frequency-domain characteristics of $R_x(\tau)$ can be obtained through the direct application of a Fourier transform. Suppose the Fourier coefficients of $x(t)$ are c_n such that

$$x(t) = \sum_{n=-\infty}^{\infty} c_n \exp(j\omega_n t) \tag{2.26}$$

where $\omega_n = 2\pi n f_o$ and $f_o = 1/T$. Then, from Equation (2.23), for τ given

$$R_x(\tau) = \frac{1}{T}\int_{-T/2}^{T/2}\left[\sum_{m=-\infty}^{\infty} \frac{c_m \exp(j2\pi mt)}{T}\right]$$

$$\left\{\sum_{n=-\infty}^{\infty} c_n \exp\frac{[j2\pi n(t-\tau)]}{T}\right\} dt$$

$$= \frac{1}{T}\sum_{n=-\infty}^{\infty} c_n \exp\frac{(j2\pi n\tau)}{T}\sum_{m=-\infty}^{\infty} c_m$$

$$\times \int_{T-/2}^{T/2} \exp\frac{[j2\pi(m+n)\,\tau]}{T}dt$$

$$= \frac{1}{T}\sum_{n=-\infty}^{\infty} c_n \exp\frac{(j2\pi n\tau)}{T}\sum_{m=-\infty} c_m \frac{\sin[\pi(m+n)]}{\pi(m+n)/T} \tag{2.27}$$

However,

$$\frac{\sin[\pi(m+n)]}{\pi(m+n)/T} = \begin{Bmatrix} 0 \text{ if } m \neq -n \\ T \text{ otherwise} \end{Bmatrix}$$

Using this property, Equation (2.27) can be written as

$$R_x(\tau) = \sum_{n=-\infty}^{\infty} c_n c_{-n} \exp\frac{(-j\pi n\tau)}{T}$$

$$= \sum_{n=-\infty}^{\infty} |c_n|^2 \exp\frac{(-j\pi n\tau)}{T} \quad (2.28)$$

For notational brevity, let $|c_n|^2$ be denoted $G_x(f_n)$, where $G_x(f_n)$ is traditionally called the power spectral density of the process $x(t)$. Therefore

$$R_x(\tau) = \mathscr{F}^{-1}[G_x(f)] \quad (2.29)$$

And it follows that

$$G_x(f) = \mathscr{F}[R_x(\tau)] \quad (2.30)$$

where $\mathscr{F}$ denotes the Fourier operator.

Therefore the autocorrelation function of the process $x(t)$ can be obtained through a Fourier transform of the power spectral density function $G_x(f)$. Equivalently, if the autocorrelation function of a process is known, the power spectral density function can be found through an inverse transform. Program AUTO-C computes the autocorrelation function of an input time series under SPECTRUM IV control. In block diagram form, program AUTO-C is presented in Figure 2-26.

Since $R_x(\tau)$ is an even function, only the real components of $\mathscr{F}^{-1}[G_x(f)]$ are of use to the user. Therefore, there exists $N/2$ usable values of $R_x(n\tau)$, where τ equals the sampling rate. Finally, if the process to be analyzed is random, ensemble averaging should be used to statistically improve $R_x(\tau)$.

Wrap-Around Error

When a signal $x(t)$ is periodic over some sampling period T, the autocorrelation function $R_x(\tau)$ has well-defined even symmetry about $\tau = 0$. Therefore autocorrelation of an NPOINT time series can be completely characterized in NPOINT/2 sample values. For example, suppose $x(t)$ is the time series found in Figure 2-27a. The autocorrelation $R_x(\tau)$ is given in Figure2-27b. However $R_x(\tau)$ can be represented by the NPOINT/2 values displayed in Figure 2-27c.

It should be recalled that a discrete transform operates on periodic data. However, there are many nonperiodic time series records in the "real world." Take, for example, the wave form found in Figure 2-28a. Here, for any $\tau > 0$, $x_1(t + \tau)$ will overlap a portion of the nonperiodic extension $x_2(t)$. This will introduce an error in the calculation of $R_x(\tau)$. This effect is called a

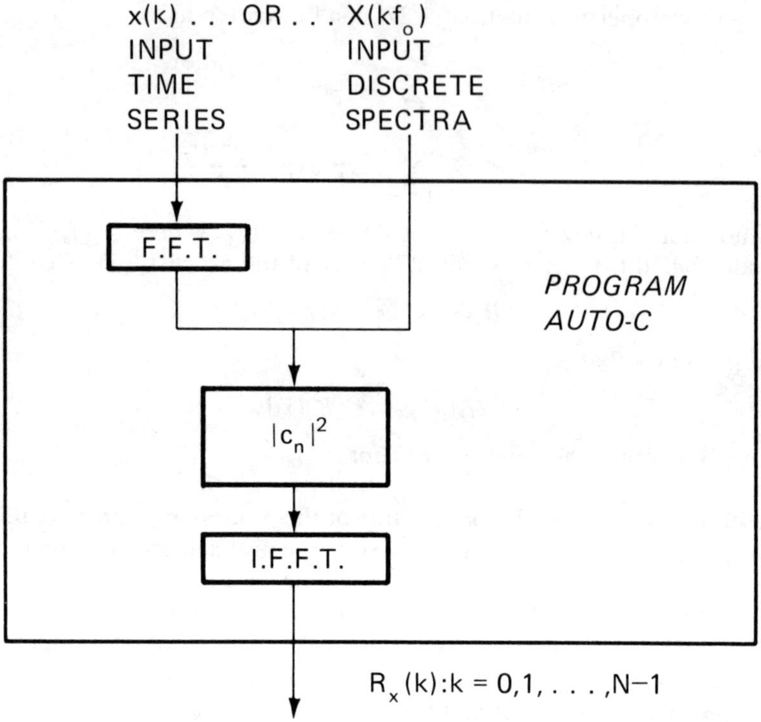

Figure 2-26. Program AUTO-C.

WRAP-AROUND ERROR. It can be partially eliminated through the use of time comprehension methods [25]. This technique will produce valid autocorrelation data over a subinterval of T. The valid subinterval is the first and fourth quarters of the interval T, a feature that is exemplified in Figure 2-28b, SPECTRUM IV will perform this operation through the use of option WRAP-AROUND.

Correlation Coefficient

The user may desire to interpret the results of an autocorrelation operation in terms of the so-called correlation coefficient. Let $\rho_x(\tau)$, the correlation coefficient, be defined as follows:

$$\rho_x(\tau) = \frac{R_x(\tau)}{R_x(0)} \tag{2.31}$$

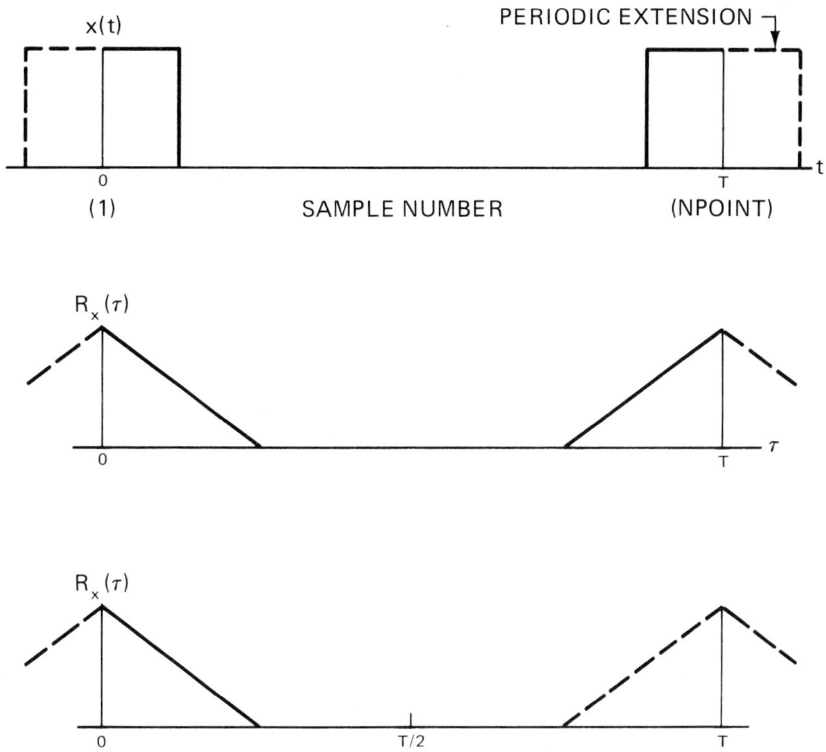

Figure 2-27. Periodic Autocorrelation.

It should be noted that $R_x(0) \geq R_x(\tau)$. That is, $x(t)$ is most similar to $x(t + \tau)$ when $\tau = 0$. Therefore

$$-1 \leq \rho_x(\tau) \leq +1$$

for all τ, when the values of $\rho_x(\tau)$ imply

$$-1 \longleftarrow 0 \longrightarrow +1$$

minimum average inverse similarity	no average similarity	maximum average similarity

The correlation coefficient can be produced from autocorrelation data through a normalization. Program NORMAL, documented in Section A of Chapter 5, can be used to accomplish this task.

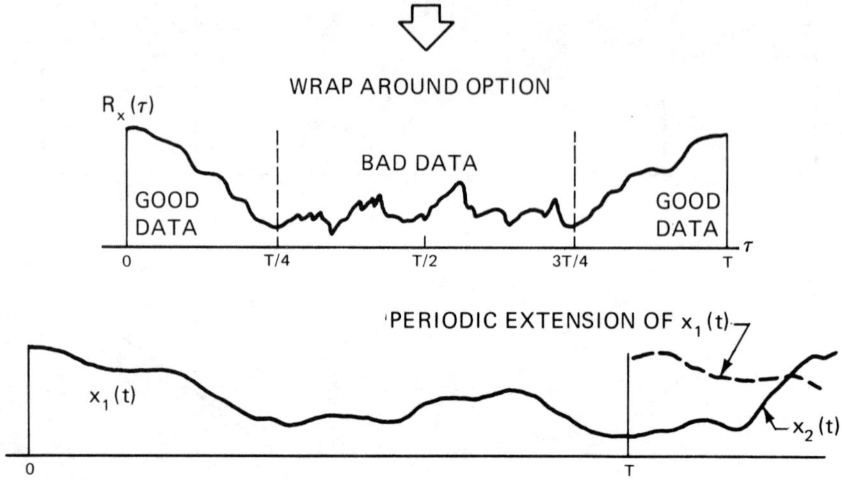

Figure 2-28. Nonperiodic Autocorrelation.

Execution of Auto-C

An autocorrelation operation can be performed on an input process by using the six-letter mnemonic AUTO-C. An autocorrelation will be performed on the data in a prespecified array, and the result of the autocorrelation is returned to the same array. If a nonperiodic time series is to be generated, the user is instructed to use the WRAP-AROUND option. The execution of this operation will remove the second and third quarters of $R_x(\tau)$. The only restriction placed on the use of AUTO-C is that the array to be analyzed cannot be the null array. It is suggested, since the output data set is quartered through the WRAP-AROUND option 1, that the user define the value of NPOINT given in an input operation as a multiple of four. See Table 2-4.

The output of AUTO-C consists of a label that designates which array contains the time domain $R_x(\tau)$. The data stored in that array must be interpreted with respect to the option used. A standard AUTO-C presents NPOINT/2 data points to the user. If the WRAP-AROUND option is used, only the first NPOINT/4 data values in the returned NPOINT/2 point array are valid data. SPECTRUM IV will assign to the autocorrelated array memory protection automatically.

Example. Consider the periodic pulse train diagrammed in Figure 2-29. Let the sample rate be $1k$ Hz and the period be 64 msec. The autocorrelation function $R_x(\tau)$ is well known and also is given in Figure 2-30.

Table 2-4
Structure of an AUTO-C Call

Column Number	Description	Format or Contents
Primary information card		
1-6	Calls AUTO-C	AUTO-C
15	Array requested A, B, or C are used to specify which array holds input data. Data may be in either the TIME or FREQ domain. SPECTRUM IV will return processed data to origin array originally automatically	A1
80	WRAP-AROUND option = 1 (default = 0)	1 or VOID

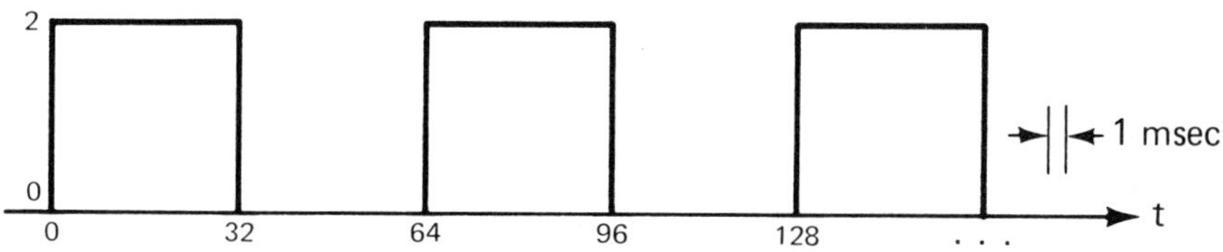

Figure 2-29. Periodic Pulse Train.

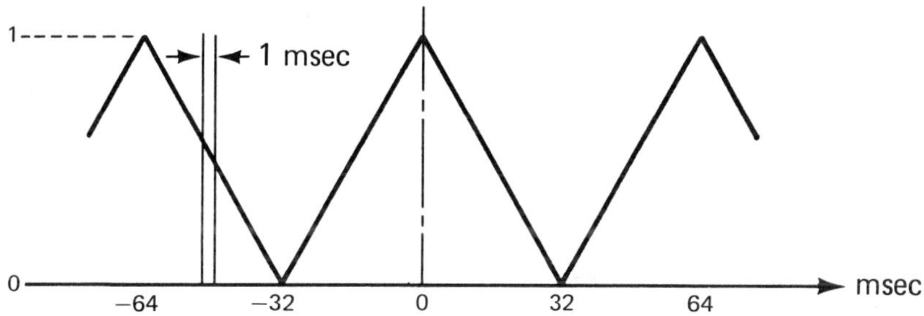

Figure 2-30. Autocorrelation Function.

The generation $R_x(\tau)$ under SPECTRUM IV control, with a graphical display of $x(t)$ and $R_x(\tau)$ without the WRAP-AROUND option, is accomplished as follows (see cards 1 through 7 of figure 2-31). The requested pulse train is generated in the SPECTRUM IV library, placed in array A, and plotted. The contents of array A are autocorrelated using no WRAP-AROUND option (that is, column 80 is void). The autocorrelated data, always located in array A, are then plotted. The τ axis is divided into 31 discrete time intervals of 0.00100E−1 msec each.

The same problem is again treated, except that the WRAP-AROUND option is used. The control cards and print-out for this problem can be found in cards 8 through 14 of Figure 2-31. It should be noted that a "1" now exists in column 80 of the AUTO-C card. Finally, it is observed that only the first and fourth quadrant data are supplied to the user by SPECTRUM IV. The card control sequence required for such an operation is found in Figure 2-31. The results of this action are found in Figures 2-32 and 2-33.

Example. It has been stated that autocorrelation is a measure of similarity. Autocorrelation can be used to test the degree of randomness in a data set as well. Noise processes, say, $n(t)$, are often classified by their degree of correlation. If a noise process has a finite correlation, as depicted in Figure 2-34, knowledge of the noise process at time t will, in a statistical sense, imply what the value of the process may be at time $t + \tau$. However, if $n(t)$ is uncorrelated with $n(t + \tau)$ for all $\tau \neq 0$, then knowledge of $n(t)$ will imply nothing about the value of $n(t + \tau)$. This is depicted in Figure 2-35.

Mathematical tests on system performance often require that a noise process have very short correlation times. Under such a hypothesis, the system cannot anticipate what the next sample value of noise will be. Therefore, for the purpose of simulation, the input is highly randomized.

Under SPECTRUM IV, such a test can be conducted. The card control sequence for this experiment can be found in Figure 2-36. A normal (Gaussian) noise record, mean value zero, and variance one are generated in the system library and plotted. An autocorrelation was performed. Since the record is random, the WRAP-AROUND option is used. The AUTO-C was then plotted. The results of the experiment can be found in Figures 2-37 and 2-38. Except for τ equal zero, the autocorrelation function has a small residual value. That is, the noise process has extremely short correlation times.

C. Power Spectral Density

Introduction

It was noted in the study of autocorrelation that there is a connection between the autocorrelation function and the frequency domain. The frequency-domain representation of the autocorrelation function was called the power spectral density, or power spectrum. The power spectrum of a signal, say, $x(t)$, is a display of the energy contained in $x(t)$ on a per-Hertz basis. Therefore a power spectral analysis can be used to locate a frequency location, or locations, where signal (or noise) energies reside. Thus filters may be designed that would have high gain at frequency

```
CARD      COLUMN                                                                    8Ø
          123456789Ø12        .         .         .         .         .         .         .
--------------------------------------------------------------------------------------------
1         LIBRARY       A                                               64       1ØØØ.
2         THIS IS A PULSE DUTY CYCLE .5                  2  2.Ø   Ø.Ø       .5ØØ
3         PLOTTER       A                                               64       1ØØØ.
4         TIME                   1   64   A PULSE OF DUTY CYCLE .5
5         AUTO-C        A
6         PLOTTER       A                                               64       1ØØØ.
7         TIME                   1   64   THE AUTO CORRELATION OF PREVIOUS PULSE
8         LIBRARY       A                                               64       1ØØØ.
9         THIS IS A PULSE OF DUTY CYCLE .5               2  2.Ø   Ø.Ø       .5ØØ
1Ø        PLOTTER       A                                               64       1ØØØ.
11        TIME                   1   64   A PULSE OF DUTY CYCLE .5
12        AUTO-C        A
13        PLOTTER       A                                               32       1ØØØ.
14        TIME                   1   32   THE AUTO CORRELATION OF PREVIOUS PULSE
15        TERM
                    .         .         .         .         .         .         .         .
```

Figure 2-31. Card Control Sequence for Autocorrelation Example.

THE AUTO CORRELATION OF PREVIOUS PULSE

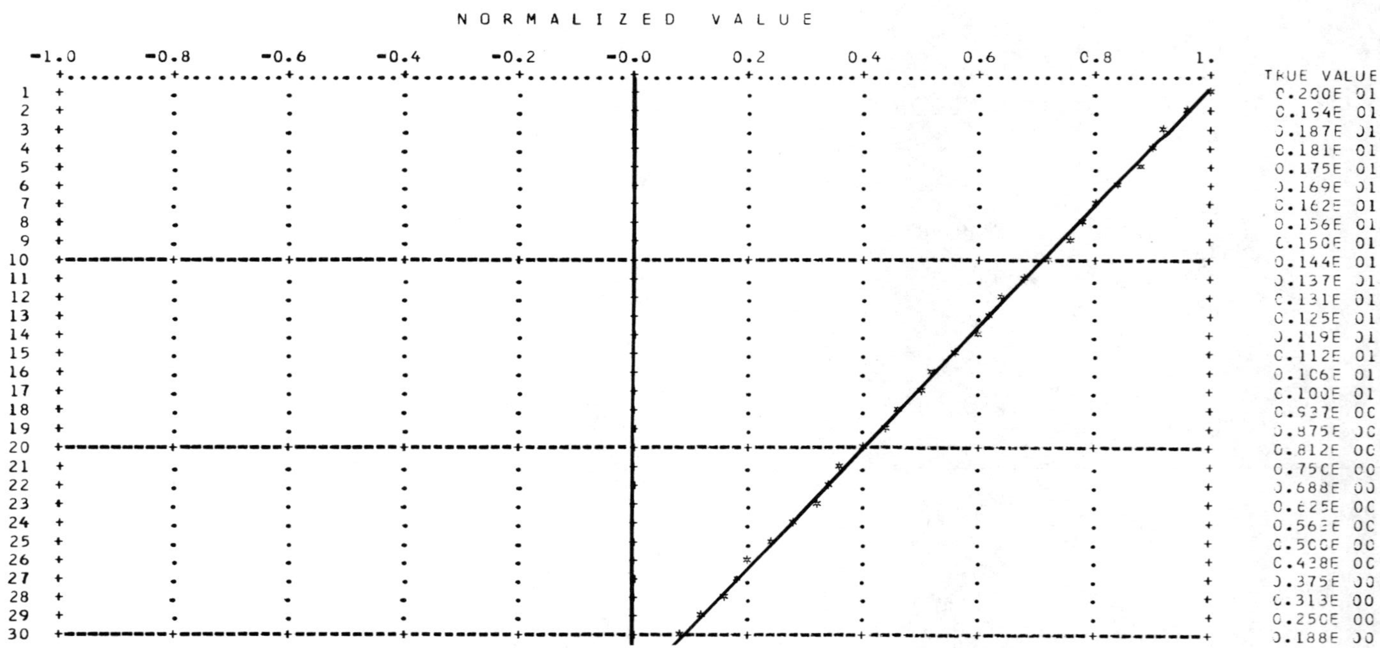

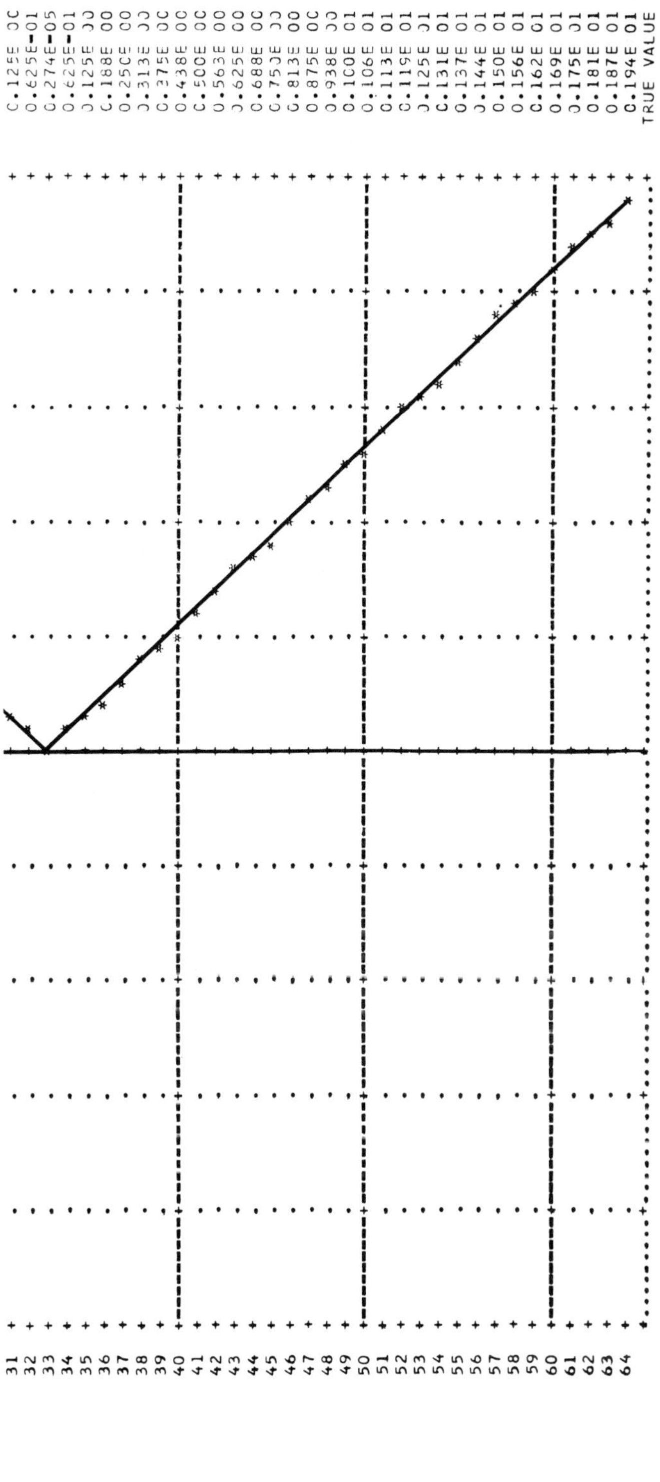

Figure 2-32. Autocorrelation of a Pulse.

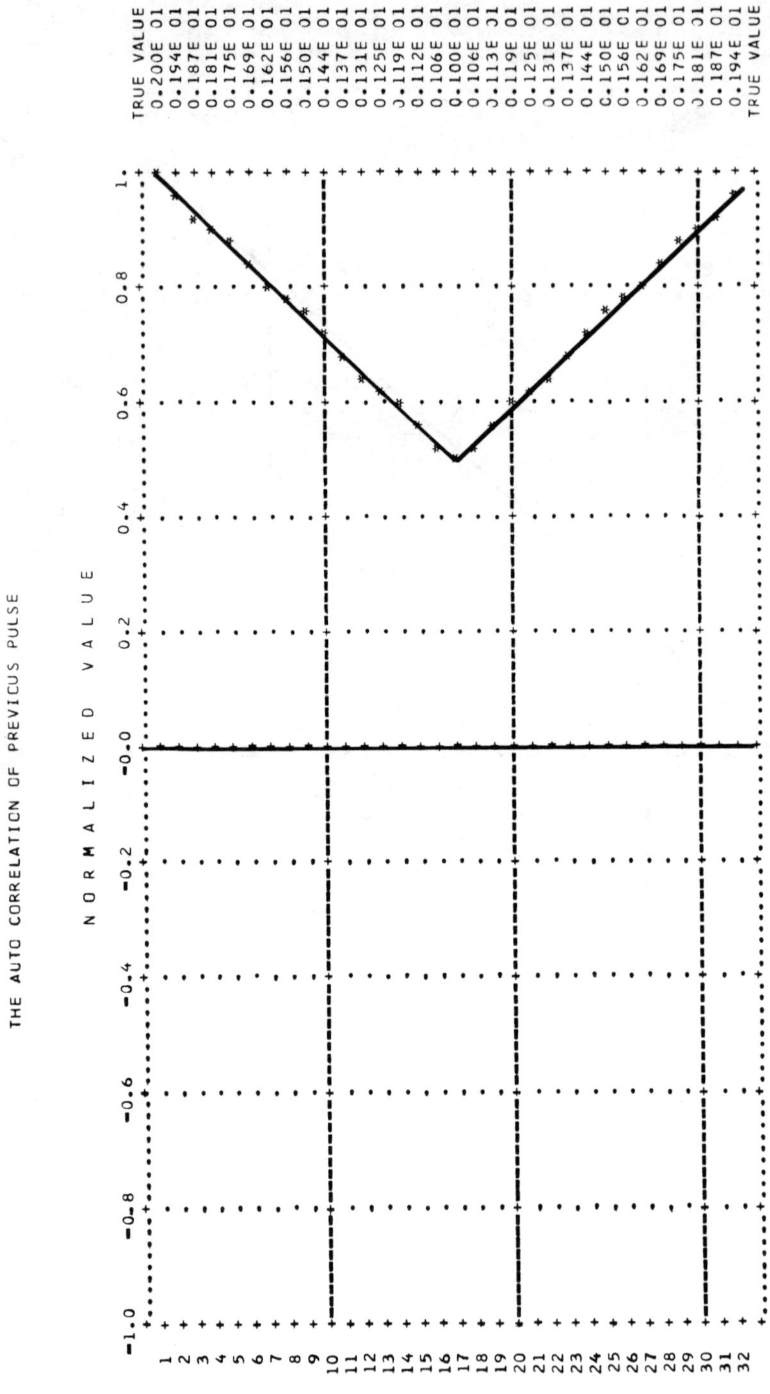

Figure 2-33. Autocorrelation of a Pulse with WRAP-AROUND Removal.

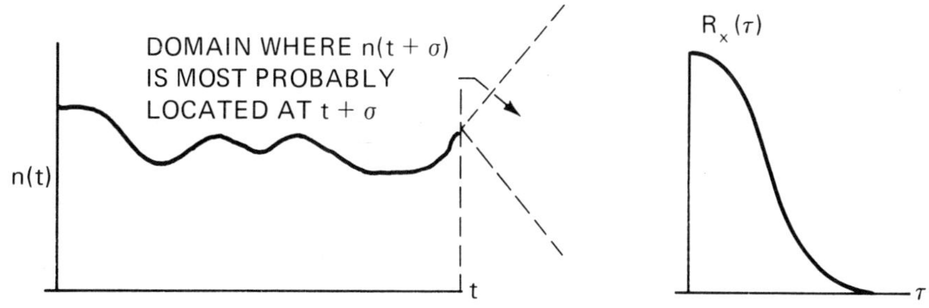

Figure 2-34. Noise Process with Finite Correlation Time.

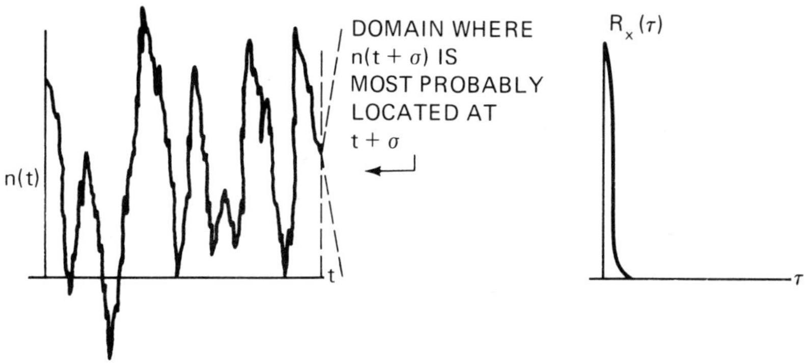

Figure 2-35. Noise Process with Short Correlation Time.

locations occupied by signal energy and low gain over any frequency range occupied only by noise energy. Therefore, the study and design of communication systems often can be accomplished through the direct application of a power spectral analysis.

The amount of periodic energy in a time series is directly measured through a power spectral density. Therefore any periodic behavior in a time series can be uncovered through a power spectral density. This mathematical tool is often found useful in the study of oscillatory or vibrational systems found in nature. Biological rhythms, for example, can be studied conveniently with a power spectral analysis. Program PSD, as supplied to the user under SPECTRUM IV, will perform power spectral operations.

Theory

Let a signal $s(t)$ be defined, and consider its Fourier representation to be

$$s(t) = \sum_{n=-\infty}^{\infty} c_n \exp(j\omega_n t) \tag{2.32}$$

```
CARD        COLUMN                                                                    8Ø
            123456789Ø12     .         .         .         .         .         .       .
----------------------------------------------------------------------------------------
1           LIBRARY      A                                          64        64.
2           GAUSSIAN NOISE WITH MEAN=Ø & VARIANCE=1    1Ø  1.Ø  Ø.Ø            1.Ø  Ø.Ø
3           PLOTTER      A                                          64
4           TIME               1   64     THIS IS GAUSSIAN NOISE WITH MEAN=Ø & VARIANCE=1
5           AUTO-C       A                                                               1
6           PLOTTER      A                                          32
7           TIME               1   32     THIS IS THE AUTOCORRELATION OF GAUSSIAN NOISE
8           TERM
                       .         .         .         .         .         .         .       .
```

Figure 2-36. Card Control Sequence for Autocorrelation Noisy Example.

The power in $s(t)$ is given by P_s, where

$$P_s = \frac{1}{T}\int_0^T s(t)^2\,dt \tag{2.33}$$

In terms of its Fourier coefficients,

$$\begin{aligned} P_s &= \frac{1}{T}\int_0^T s(t) \sum_{n=-\infty}^{\infty} c_n \exp(j\omega_n t)\,dt \\ &= \sum_{n=-\infty}^{\infty} c_n \frac{1}{T}\int_0^T s(t) \exp[-j(-\,\omega_n t)]\,dt \\ &= \sum_{n=-\infty}^{\infty} c_n c_n^* = \sum_{n=-\infty}^{\infty} |\,c_n\,|^2 = c_0^2 + 2\sum_{n=1}^{\infty} c_n^2 \end{aligned} \tag{2.34}$$

where if

$$c_n = \frac{1}{T}\int_0^T s(t) \exp(-j\omega_n t)\,dt$$

then

$$c_n^* = \frac{1}{T}\int_0^T s(t) \exp[-j(-\omega_n t)]\,dt \tag{2.35}$$

The *power spectra* of a process $s(t)$ defines how the signal power is distributed as a function of frequency. Equation (2.34) indicates how the power of $s(t)$ is decomposed into a d-c component (that is, c_0^2) and harmonic power components (that is, $2\,|c_n|^2$, $n \neq 0$). Often the power in a process is described in terms of a power spectral density denoted $G_s(f)$. The discrete power spectral density is given by

$$G_s(f_n) = \begin{Bmatrix} c_0^2 \text{ in } n = 0 \\ 2c_n^2 \text{ otherwise} \end{Bmatrix} \tag{2.36}$$

Therefore the total power in the process $s(t)$ can be given the alternative representation

$$P_s = \sum_{n=0}^{\infty} G_s(f_n) \tag{2.37}$$

Therefore, if a signal $s(t)$ has a Fourier representation, its power is easily computed through a complex conjugate multiplication. However, if $s(t)$ is nonperiodic, as in the case of a random process, it would not have an *exact* Fourier series. The power in such nonperiodic signals can be reasonably approximated through spectral averaging. Here a series of records would be Fourier analyzed individually to produce the power spectra associated

THIS IS GAUSSIAN NOISE WITH MEAN=0 & VARIANCE=1

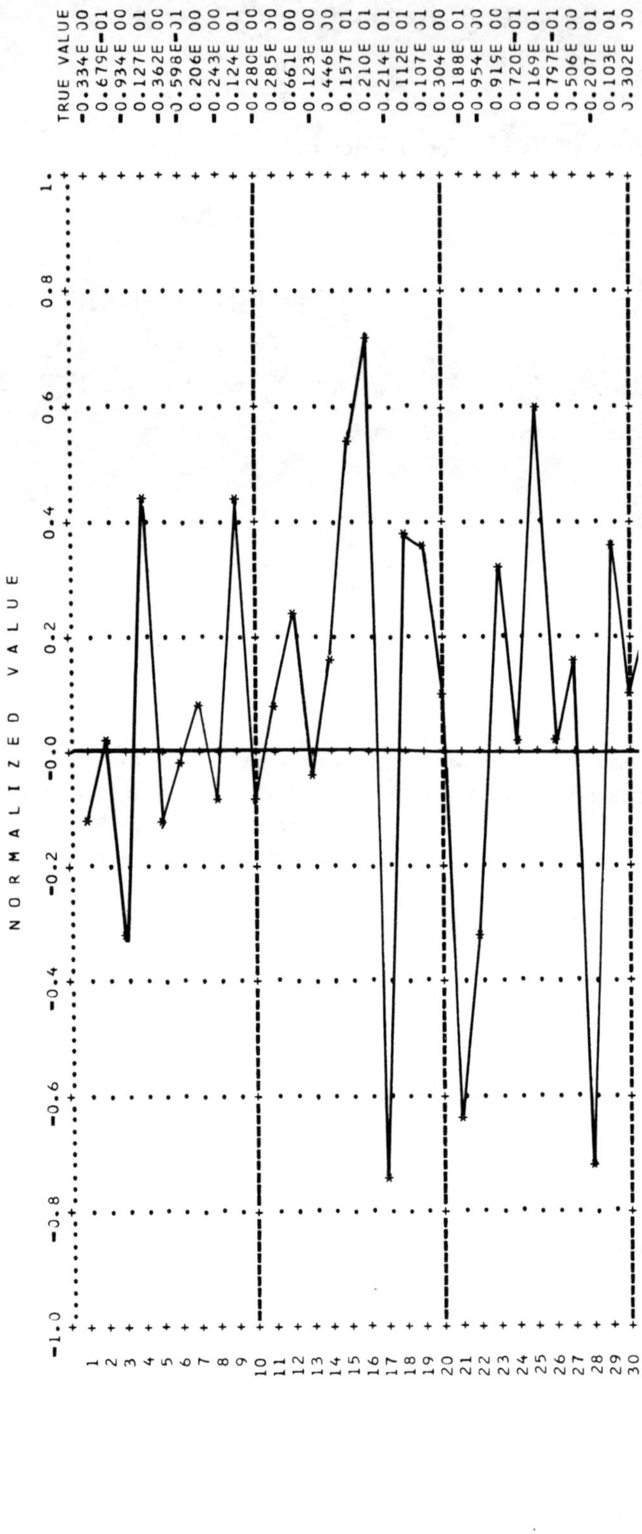

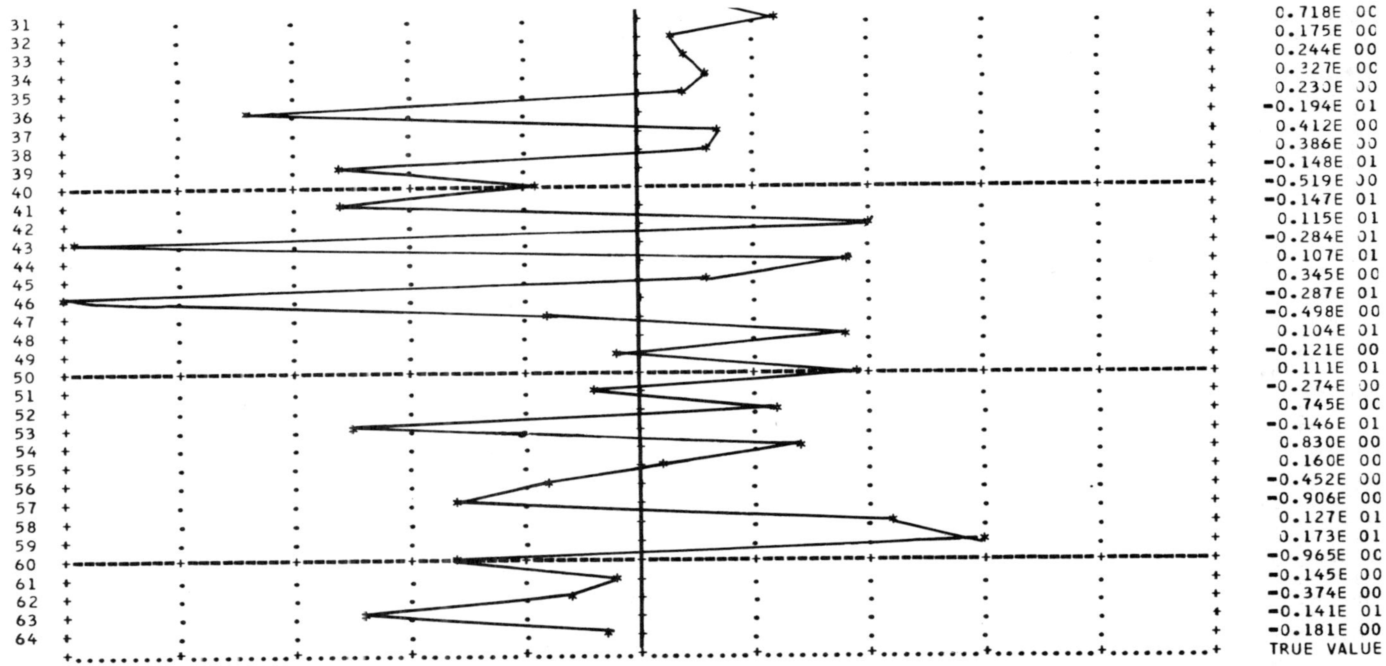

Figure 2-37. Noisy Time-series Record.

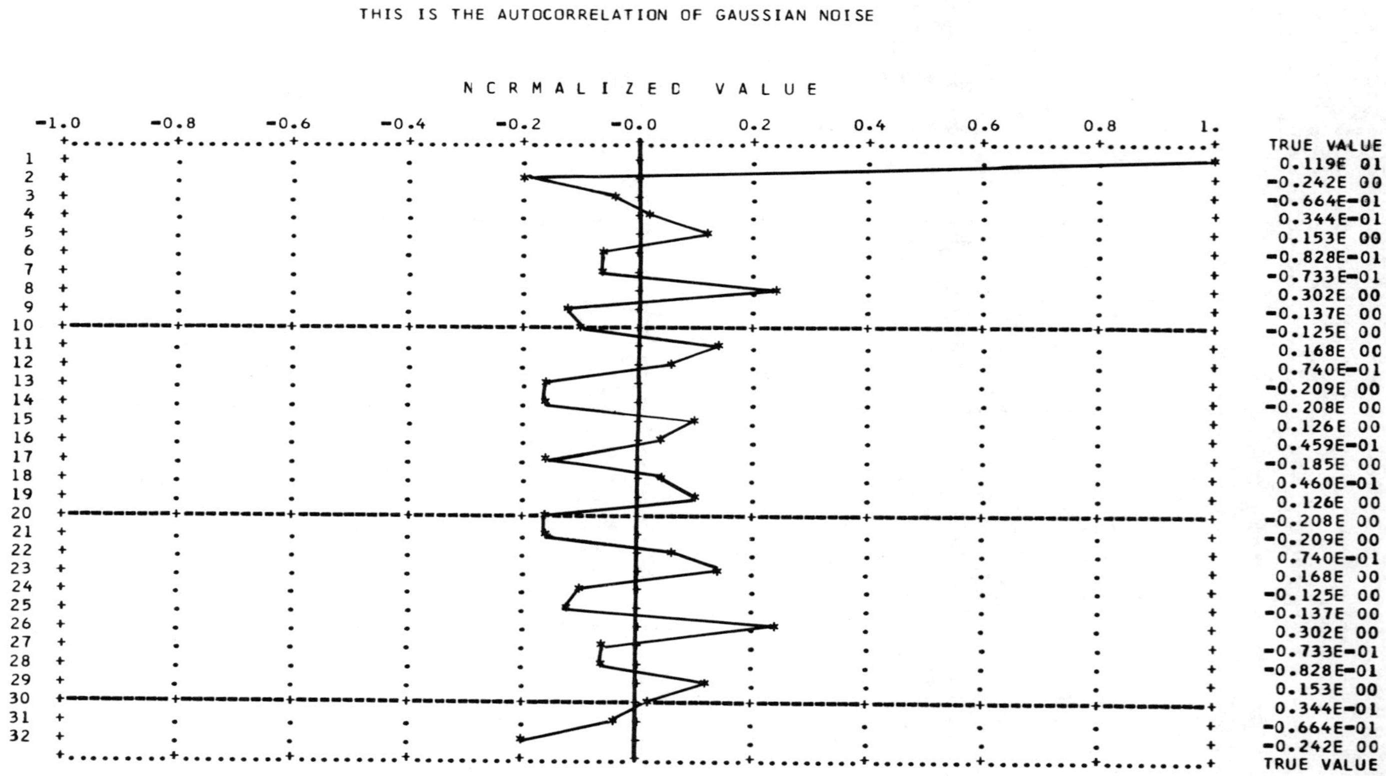

Figure 2-38. Autocorrelation of a Gaussian Noise Record with WRAP-AROUND Removal.

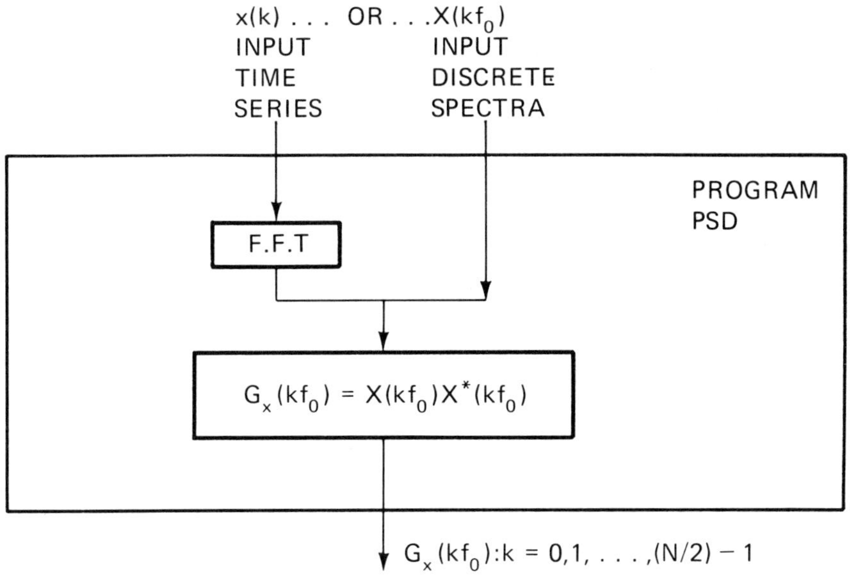

Figure 2-39. Program PSD.

with that record. These individual power spectras then would be averaged, and the average spectra would serve to represent the power spectra of the nonperiodic signal under analysis.

Program PSD computes the power spectral density of a signal $x(t)$, inputted in the time domain or $X(f)$, inputted in the frequency domain shown in Figure 2-39.

Execution of PSD

A power spectral density operation can be performed on an input time series by using the three-letter mnemonic PSD. A power spectral operation will be performed on the data in a prespecified array. The result of a PSD operation is returned to the same array in the frequency domain. The only restriction on the use of PSD is that it cannot operate on the null matrix. The control structure for PSD is shown in Table 2-5. The output of PSD consists of labels that identify the contents of the transformed array. The contents of the output array are automatically protected.

Warning: It has been experimentally observed that numerical underflows may occasionally occur when performing a PSD operation on frequency-domain data. This condition can be rectified by performing an

Table 2-5
Structure of a PSD Call

Column Number	*Description*	*Format or Contents*
Primary information card		
1-3	Calls PSD	PSD
15	Array requested (A, B, or C) is used to specify which array holds input data. The data may be entered in either the TIME or FREQ domain.	A1

IFFT on the frequency-domain data, and then by performing a PSD operation on the resulting time-domain data.

To supply the user with a more thorough understanding of the power spectral density computing capabilities of SPECTRUM IV, two examples follow. They involve the analysis of the power spectral representation of an inpulse and a pulse train. Both these experiments will be "nested" into one complete SPECTRUM IV execution.

The PSD of an Impulse. If an input exists for only one sample instant, it is called an impulse. A unit discrete impulse is denoted δ_K. Here δ_K is historically called the Kronecker delta function, and specified as follows (see Figure 2-40).[f]

$$\delta_K(i) = \begin{Bmatrix} 1 \text{ if } i = 0 \\ 0 \text{ otherwise} \end{Bmatrix}$$

The Fourier representation of $\delta_K(i)$ is unique in that it has a constant amplitude for all frequencies.[g] The real Fourier representation of $\delta_K(i)$ is diagrammed in Figure 2-41. The constant amplitude spectral often is referred to as being "white," following the physicist's definition of "white light." Here white light implies that an equal amount of light energy can be found at all frequencies of the visible spectrum. Recall that the discrete transform of $\delta_K(i)$ contained all harmonics of f_0, and that the real amplitudes of these harmonics were equal. This mathematical structure suggests that $\delta_K(i)$ may be synthesized through the additive effects of a series of pure

[f]The continuous version of the Kronecker delta function is the Dirac delta distribution $\delta_D(t)$, where

$$\int_{-\infty}^{\infty} g(t)\delta_D(t - \tau)\, dt = g(\tau)$$

[g]The continuous version of this property can be stated as follows:

$$\mathscr{F}[\delta_D(t)] = 1 \text{ for all frequencies}$$

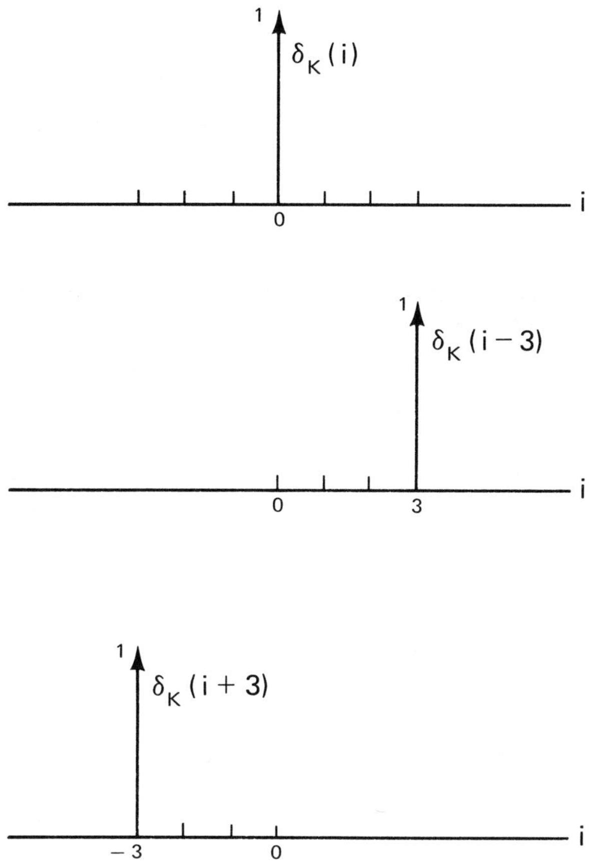

Figure 2-40. Kronecker Delta Function.

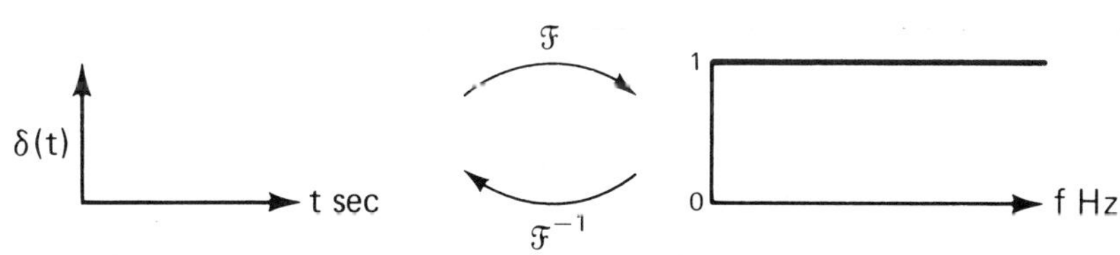

Figure 2-41. Fourier Representation of $\delta_K(i)$.

cosine generators (see Figure 2-42). The "white" property of the discrete data function is extremely useful in spectral analysis. It means that the application of an impulse can excite a given linear system simultaneously at all harmonics.

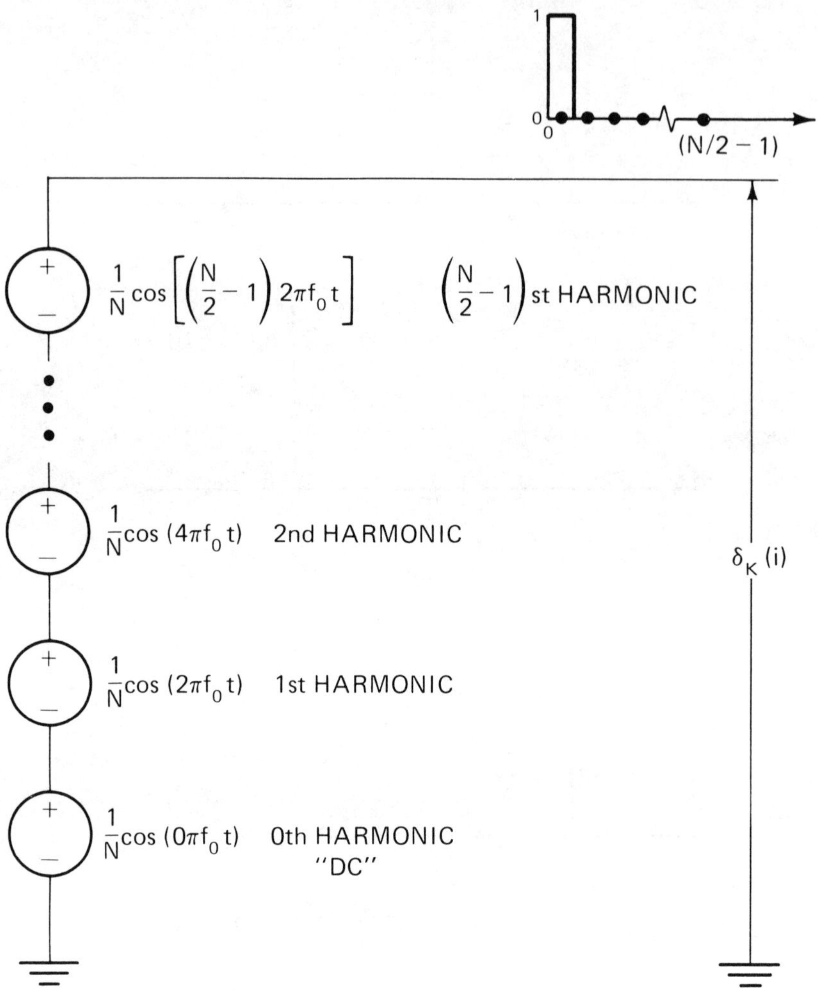

Figure 2-42. Synthesis of the Kronecker Delta

Performing a power spectral density operation on an impulse can be accomplished through the PSD operation of SPECTRUM IV. The control card structure, which generates an impulse, computes its power spectral density and graphically displays the results as shown in Figure 2-43.

The PSD of a Pulse Train. Consider again the pulse train that was introduced in the autocorrelation section. The power spectral density is given by the Fourier transform of the autocorrelation function. The autocorrelation

```
CARD    COLUMN                                                                   8Ø
        123456789Ø12      .          .          .          .          .          .          .
---------------------------------------------------------------------------------------------
1       USER LIB      B                                                   64        1.ØØ       1
2       IMPULSE
3       PLOTTER       B                                                   64
4       TIME                1    64    THIS IS THE PLOT OF AN IMPULSE
5       PSD           B
6       PLOTTER       B
7       FREQ    MAG         1    32    THIS IS THE PSD OF AN IMPULSE
8       LIBRARY       B                                                   64    1ØØØ.Ø
9       THIS IS A PULSE OF DUTY CYCLE  .5            2  2.Ø   Ø.Ø      .5ØØ
1Ø      PLOTTER       B                                                   64    1ØØØ.Ø
11      TIME                1    64    A PULSE OF DUTY CYCLE .5
12      PSD           B
13      PLOTTER       B                                                   32    1ØØØ.Ø
14      FREQ    MAG         1    32    THIS IS PSD OF A PULSE OF DUTY CYCLE .5
15      PRINT         B           FREQ                     F          32
16                          F     FREQ        32           1          32
17      TERM
                    .          .          .          .          .          .          .          .
```

Figure 2-43. Card Control Sequence for Power Spectral Density Example.

```
FORTRAN IV G LEVEL  21                  OWN                 DATE = 75156          15/48/08              PAGE 0001

0001              SUBROUTINE OWN
            C
            C  THE FOLLOWING FIVE STATEMENTS SHOULD BE INCLUDED IN ANY SUBROUTINE OWN
0002              REAL*8 BAN
0003              INTEGER DSO,E,F,TIME,FREQ,SPL
0004              COMMON REST(6148),TEMR(1024),TEMC(1024),FRN(20),FCN(20),FRD(20),
                 1FCD(20),PN(21),PD(21),REST1(82),NPOINT,REST2(5),SPL,REST3(2)
0005              COMMON /LETTER/ F,E,MAR(3),LAIS(60),TIME,FREQ,IBAN,BAN,LN,NN,NP
            C
            C
0006              WRITE(LN,3) SPL
0007            3 FORMAT(10X,'USER PROGRAM NUMBER ',I2,/)
0008              TEMR(1)=64
0009              RETURN
0010              END
```

Figure 2-44. Subroutine OWN (Power Spectral Density Example).

function associated with the pulse train has been established to be a triangular wave. The power spectral density therefore becomes the Fourier transform of a triangle wave, which is known to be characterized by a $(\sin x)^2/x^2$ relation. Through a direct application of Equation (2.33), the power spectral density can be computed through a complex conjugate multiplication. The Fourier representation of the pulse train is given by a $\sin x/x$ relationship. Therefore it follows that the power spectral density associated with a pulse train is characterized by $(\sin x)^2/x^2$.

Execution of the Example Problem

The card control sequence associated with this two-part problem can be found in Figure 2-43. Since an impulse does not reside in the system library, it must be generated. The first call in the control card sequency accomplishes that task. Here the first program of subroutine OWN is called by USER LIB. Subroutine OWN can be found in Figure 2-44. The creation of the impulse is accomplished directly by assigning the first value of the data array TEMR to be 64, and all others are defined to be zero by default. Note that the power spectral representation of an impulse (see Figure 2-45) is flat (see Figure 2-46). Since the original impulse had a sample value of 64 for its only nontrivial value, the power contained in that discrete process is 64 units. Summing the powers in the 64 positive and negative frequency components, which have a value of unity each, with result in the same power value—namely, 64 units.

The construction of the pulse train used in the second problem, of duty cycle equals 0.5, was accomplished through a LIBRARY call. The power spectral representation of that pulse train (see Figure 2-47) can be seen to agree with theory (see Figure 2-48).

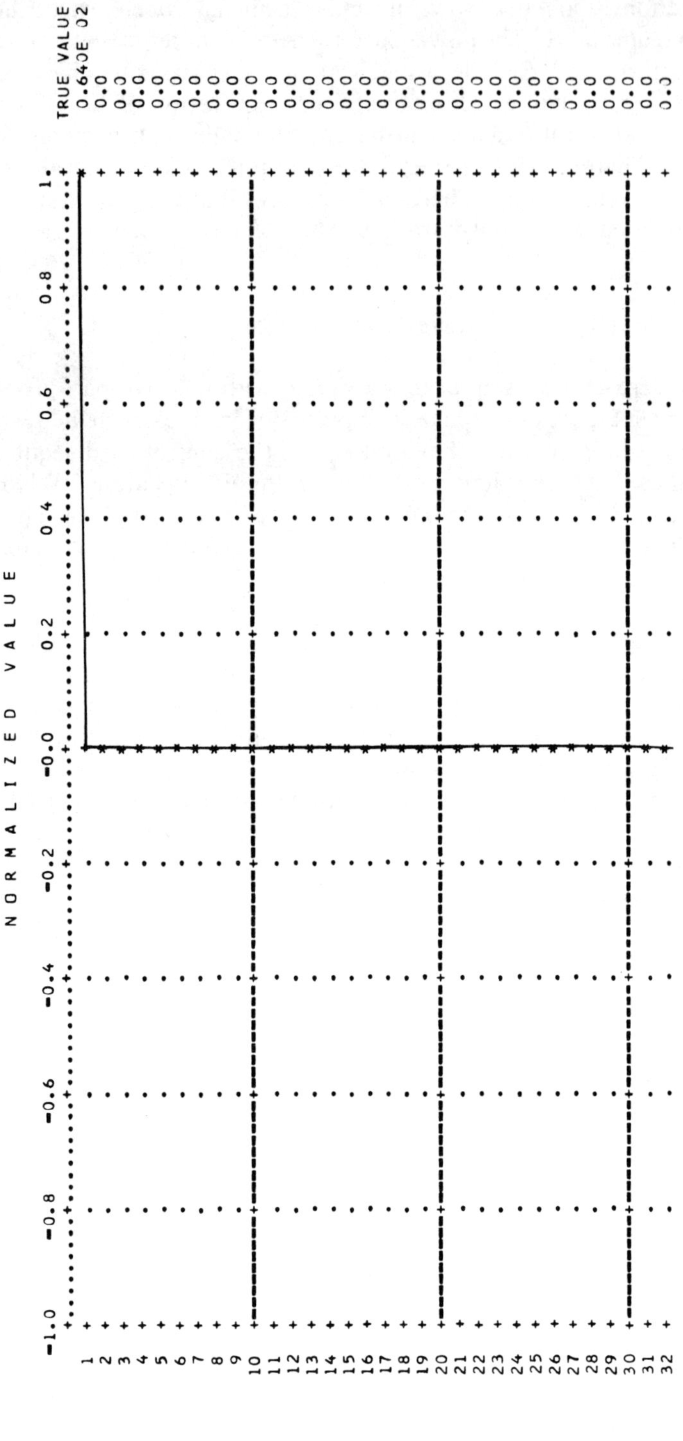

THIS IS THE PLOT OF AN IMPULSE

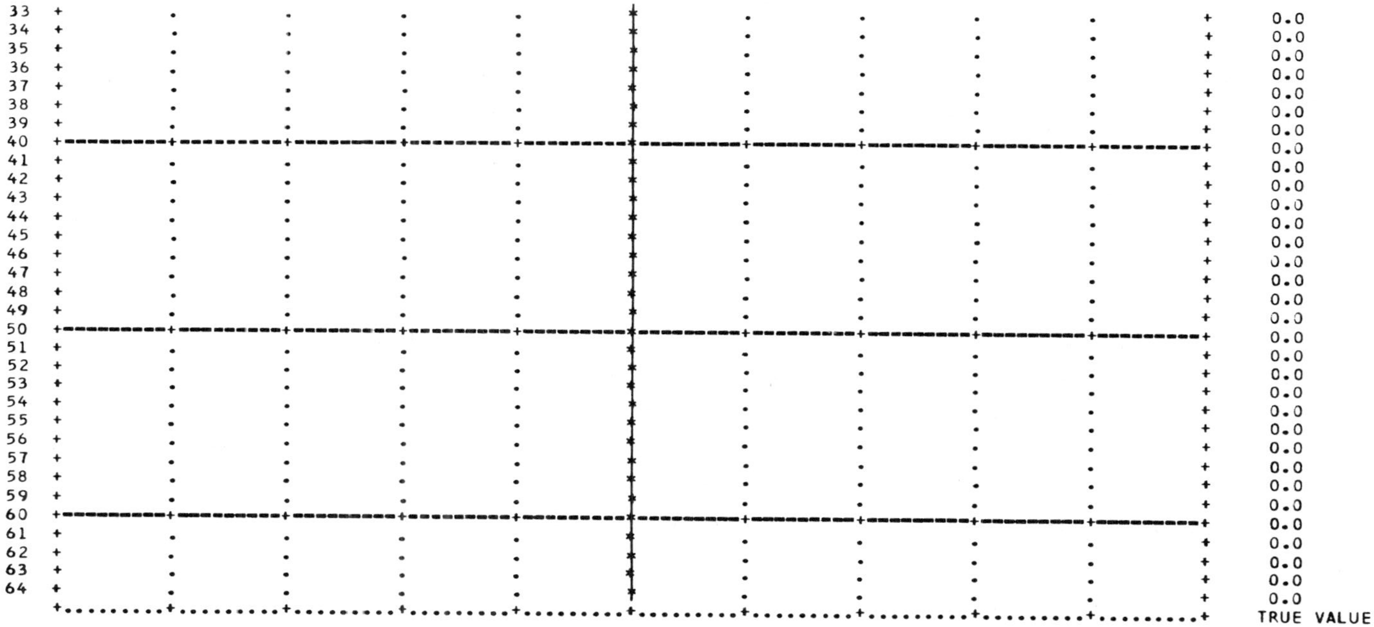

Figure 2-45. Impulse (Power Spectral Density Example).

THIS IS THE PSD PLOT OF AN IMPULSE

M A G N I T U D E

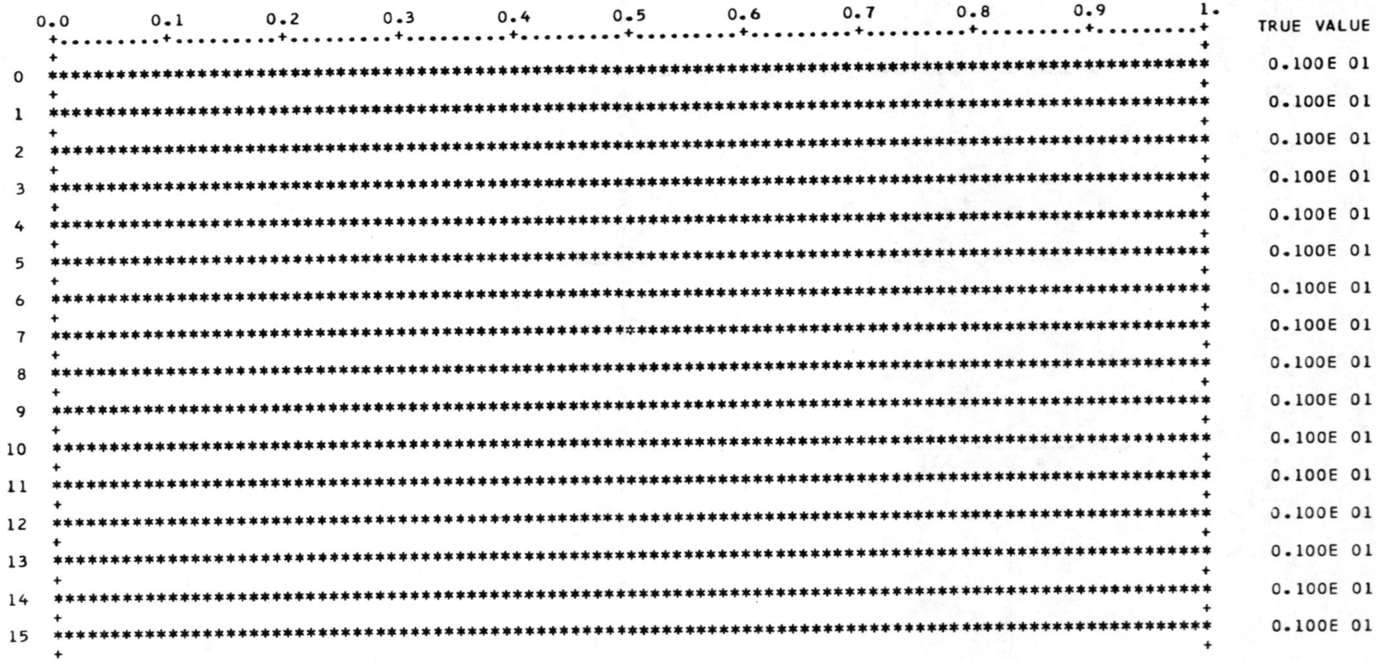

Figure 2-46. PSD of an Impulse (Power Spectral Density Example).

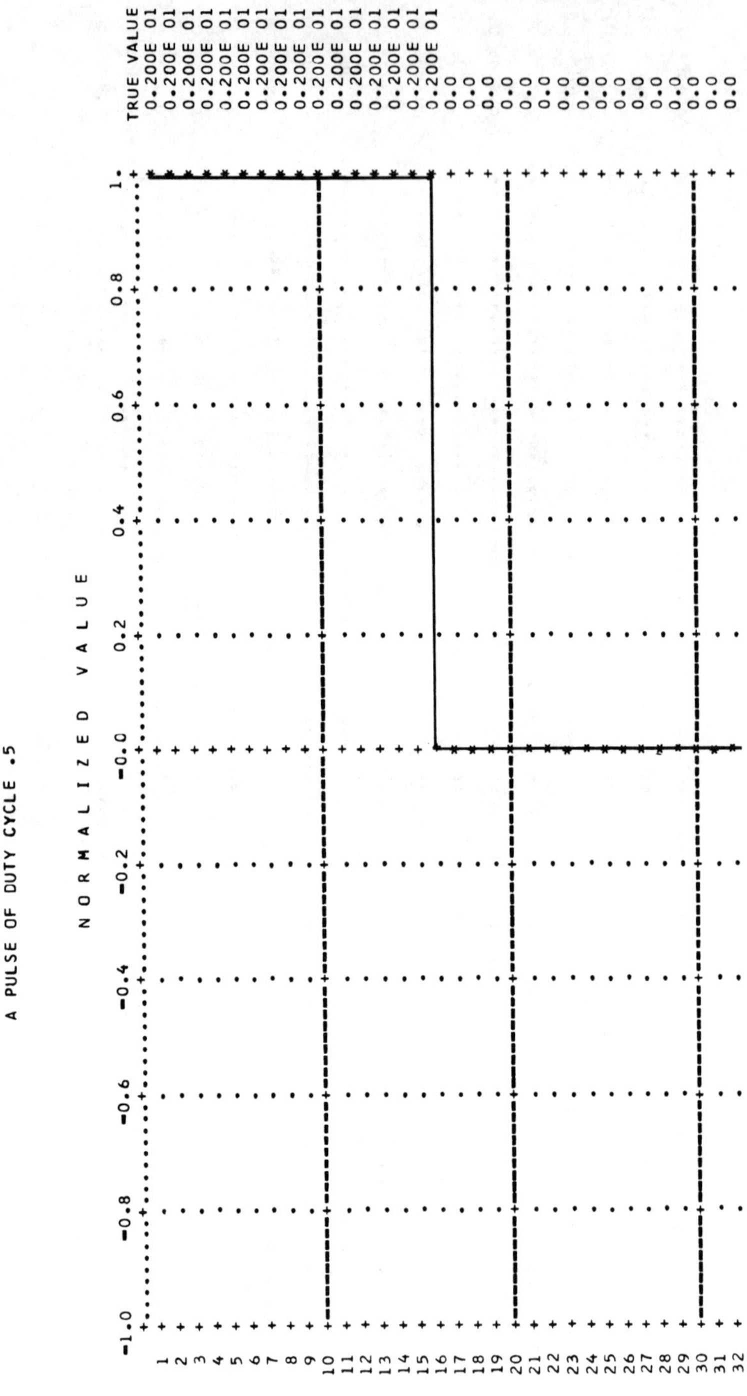
A PULSE OF DUTY CYCLE .5
N O R M A L I Z E D   V A L U E
-1.0 -0.8 -0.6 -0.4 -0.2 -0.0 0.2 0.4 0.6 0.8 1.
TRUE VALUE
0.200E 01
0.0
1 2 3 4 5 6 7 8 9 10 11 12 13 14 15 16 17 18 19 20 21 22 23 24 25 26 27 28 29 30 31 32

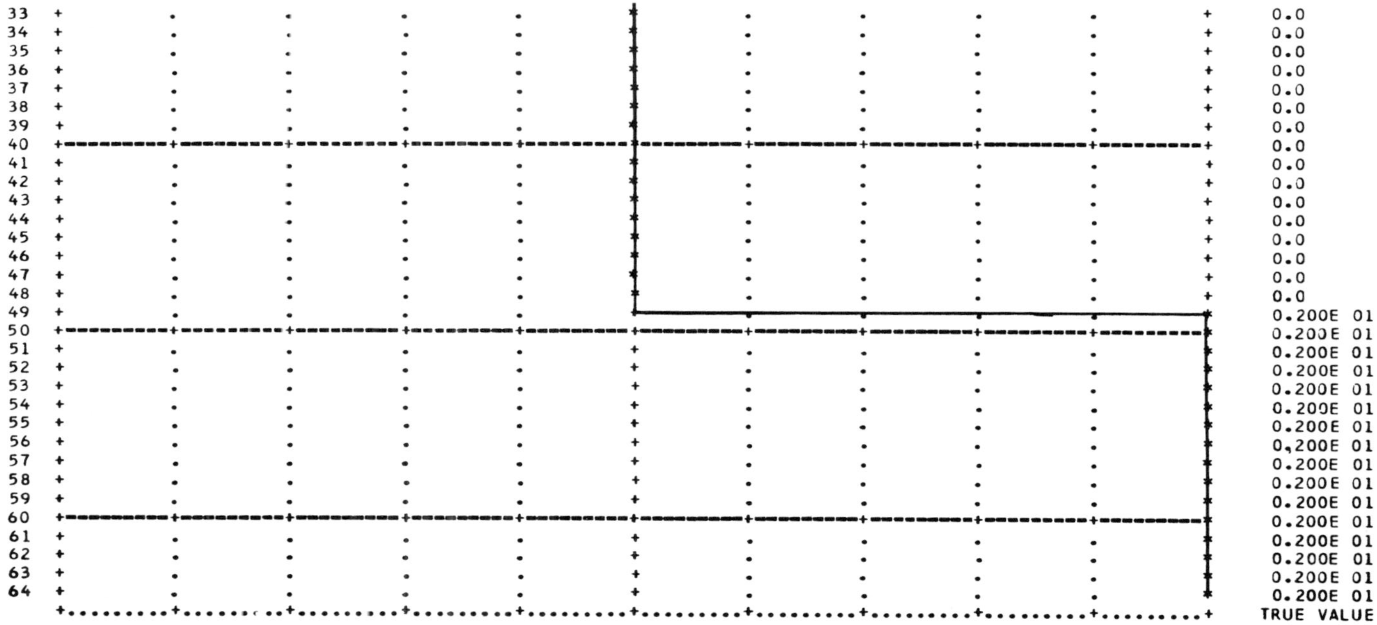

Figure 2-47. Pulse Train (Power Spectral Density Example).

THIS IS PSD PLOT OF A PULSE OF DUTY CYCLE .5

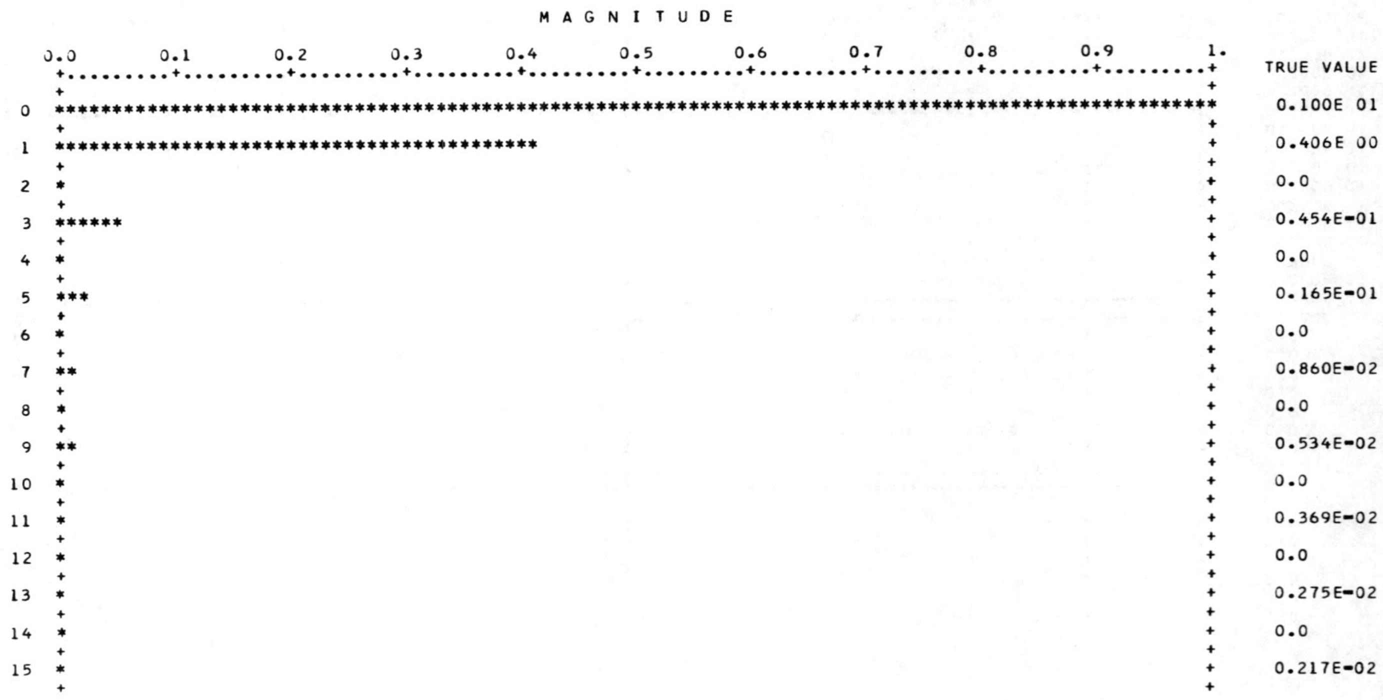

Figure 2-48. PSD of a Pulse Train (Power Spectral Density Example).

LINE PRINTER FUNCTIONAL TASK

OUTPUT FROM ARRAY A

INFORMATION IN THE FREQUNCY DCMAIN

NUMBER OF FOURIER COEFFICIENTS 64

SAMPLING FREQUENCY OF THE CATA WAS 1000.0 HZ

HIGHEST FREQUENCY COMPONENT OF DATA TO PREVENT ALIASING IS 0.5000E 03

FREQUENCY RESOLUTION OF THE SPECTRAL OUTPUT IS 15.6 HZ

HARMONIC	REAL VALUE	COMPLEX VALUE
0	1.000	0.0
1	0.406	0.0
2	0.0	0.0
3	0.045	0.0
4	0.0	0.0
5	0.017	0.0
6	0.0	0.0
7	0.009	0.0
8	0.0	0.0
9	0.005	0.0
10	0.0	0.0
11	0.004	0.0
12	0.0	0.0
13	0.003	0.0
14	0.0	0.0
15	0.002	0.0
16	0.0	0.0
17	0.002	0.0
18	0.0	0.0
19	0.002	0.0
20	0.0	0.0
21	0.001	0.0
22	0.0	0.0
23	0.001	0.0
24	0.0	0.0
25	0.001	0.0
26	0.0	0.0
27	0.001	0.0
28	0.0	0.0
29	0.001	0.0
30	0.0	0.0
31	0.001	0.0

Figure 2-49. PSD Table Listing (Power Spectral Density Example).

3 Bivariant Spectral Transforms

The quantitative and qualitative simultaneous study of two signals is called bivariant analysis. If the study relates time- and frequency-domain behavior together, it is called bivariant spectral analysis. In linear system theory and time-series analysis, bivariant analysis can be used to establish a mathematical connection between a system's input and output or to define the interrelationship between signal pairs. In conventional engineering, the design of filters (or compensators) is extremely important. A filter's performance can be deduced from its input-output characteristics, and the relation is obtained from a bivariant analysis. The analysis can be performed in the time domain (impulse response) or in the frequency domain (transfer function). As a result of a bivariant operation, linear systems can be analyzed or modeled.

Bivariant methods are applicable to both experimental and theoretical model building. The structure of a linear system model can be dictated by the physics of the problem, or it can be assumed to be known. The parameters of a theoretically developed model can be obtained experimentally or from physical considerations. A bivariant operation can be used to produce model coefficients for an experimental data or to verify the integrity of the model through simulation or numerical experimentation. Once a representative model has been constructed, the engineer or scientist can perform a series of controlled tests on the mathematical system. The results of these tests will allow the user to predict the behavior of the real system under similar stimuli.

Often the scientist is interested in uncovering similarities within signal classes. Given two signals, from, say, a biological, mechanical, or societal system, their similarity can be obtained from a bivariant transform. Such an analysis can be used to determine whether two signals are independent, dependent, or somewhere in between. The study of an engineering system often requires that certain events be independent. If signals and noise are independent, certain theoretical conjectures can be made about the overall system performance. In some natural systems, dependence is sought. The biological or ecological rhythms in a natural system are often interdependent. In all cases bivariant transforms can be used to measure these system qualities.

Finally, an engineer or scientist may be interested in measuring data confidence. System input-output measurements can be made unusable by the introduction of noise. The influence of noise, internal to a linear system, can be measured through bivariant operations. Therefore a measured input-output phenomenon can be interpreted with respect to some noise-distortion factor. This analysis is applicable to any linear systems problem that uses a measured (rather than simulated) data base.

The bilinear methods considered in this chapter are (1) convolution, (2) transfer function, (3) cross-correlation (and cross-power spectral density), and (4) coherence function. Convolution and transfer function describe system input-output behavior from a time- and frequency-domain format. Cross-correlation investigates the interdependence of signals in either the time or the frequency domain. The coherence function measures the effects of internal noise on an input-output relationship.

A. Convolution

A linear system can be considered to be a filter. A basic problem of linear system theory is defining system input-output behavior. In general, a filter's output is a distorted time- or frequency-domain version of the input process. Contemporary linear system analysis (equivalently, linear filter analysis) attempts to quantify these effects.

Linear filters can fall into one of two classes: memory devices or memoryless devices. Memoryless filters can change only the magnitude profile of the input signal; often they are found implemented as attenuation networks composed of passive (nonreactive) elements. Filters having memory, however, can alter the phase and/or amplitude profile of an input signal process. They can be modeled by either differential or difference equations.

Difference equation models are characterized by a series of time delays of length, T seconds each. For u and x representing system input and output respectively, the discrete representation of a linear filter is given by

$$x(kT) = \sum_{i=1}^{N} a_i x[(k - i)T] + \sum_{j=1}^{M} b_j u[(k - j)T] \tag{3.1}$$

The discrete filter found in Equation (3.1) also can be written in state variable form. Here the matrix-vector representation of a linear filter is

$$\mathbf{x}(kT) = \mathbf{A}\mathbf{x}[(k - 1)T] + \mathbf{B}\mathbf{u}[(k - 1)T \quad k \geq N; k \geq M \tag{3.2}$$

where

$$\mathbf{x}(kT) = \begin{bmatrix} x[(k-1)T] \\ x[(k-2)T] \\ \vdots \\ x[(k-N)T] \end{bmatrix} \quad \mathbf{u}(kT) = \begin{bmatrix} u[(k-1)T] \\ u[(k-2)T] \\ \vdots \\ u[(k-N)T] \end{bmatrix}$$

The realization of Equations (3.1) and (3.2) can be found in Figure 3-1. The filter's memory is found in the delay feedback network. That is, the system remembers what the filter's previous inputs and outputs were.

The differential equation representation of a linear filter is

$$\frac{d^n x(t)}{dt^n} = \sum_{i=0}^{N-1} a_i \frac{d^i x(t)}{dt^i} + \sum_{i=0}^{M-1} b_i \frac{du^i(t)}{dt^i} \tag{3.3}$$

or in terms of a state variable formulation,

$$\dot{\mathbf{x}}(t) = \mathbf{A}\mathbf{x}(t) + \mathbf{B}\mathbf{u}(t), \tag{3.4}$$

where · denotes a first-time derivative and where

$$\mathbf{x}(t) = \begin{bmatrix} x(t) \\ \dfrac{dx(t)}{dt} \\ \vdots \\ \dfrac{d^{N-1}x(t)}{dt^{N-1}} \end{bmatrix} \quad \mathbf{u}(t) = \begin{bmatrix} u(t) \\ \dfrac{du(t)}{dt} \\ \vdots \\ \dfrac{d^{M-1}u(t)}{dt^{M\ \ 1}} \end{bmatrix}$$

Figure 3-2 is a block diagram of the two continuous linear filter formulations. The memory of a continuous filter is found in the nature of a differential equation, which can remember past events. For example, the solution to a differential equation is known to be continuously dependent on initial conditions.

The output of a filter to an input stimuli is defined through a process

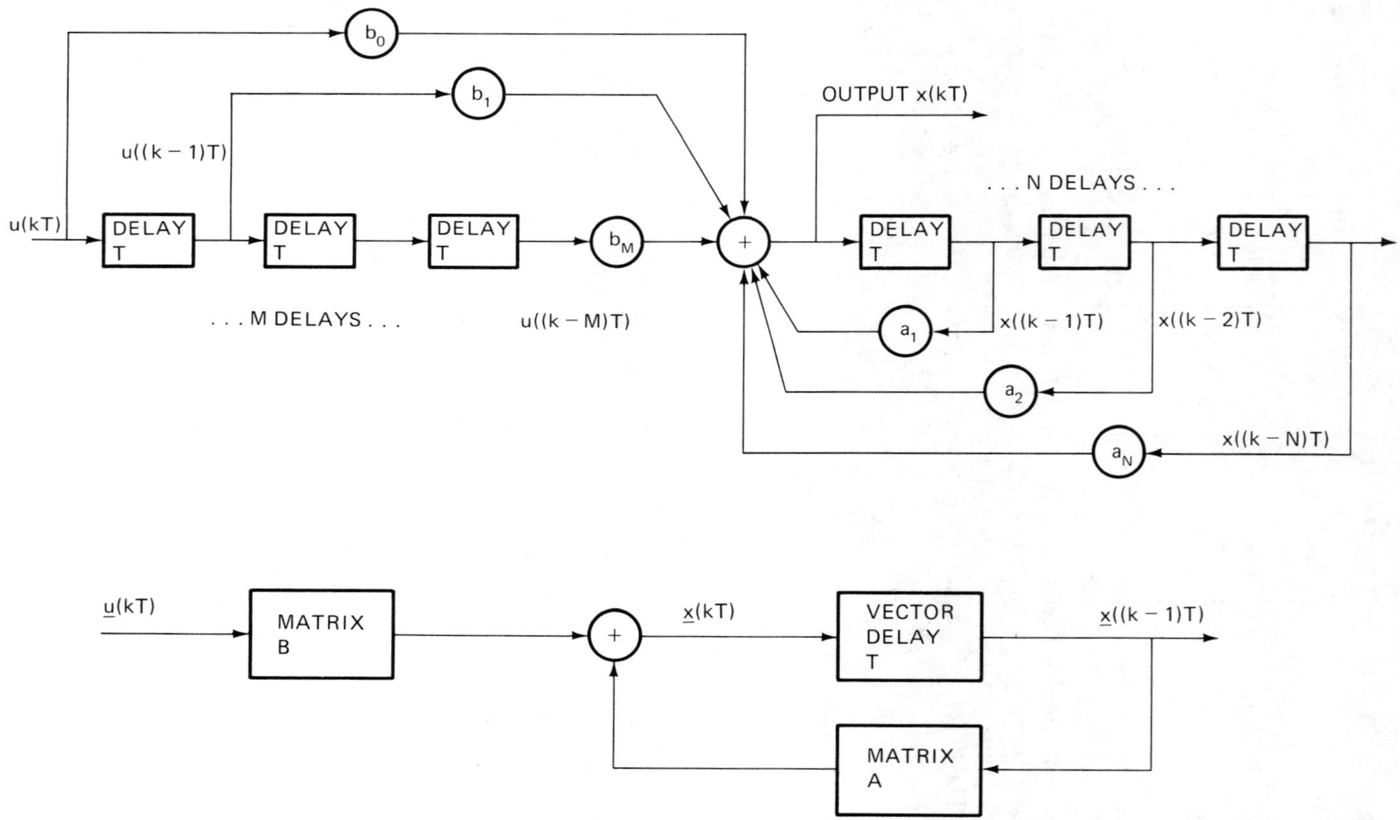

Figure 3-1. Discrete Filter Block Diagram.

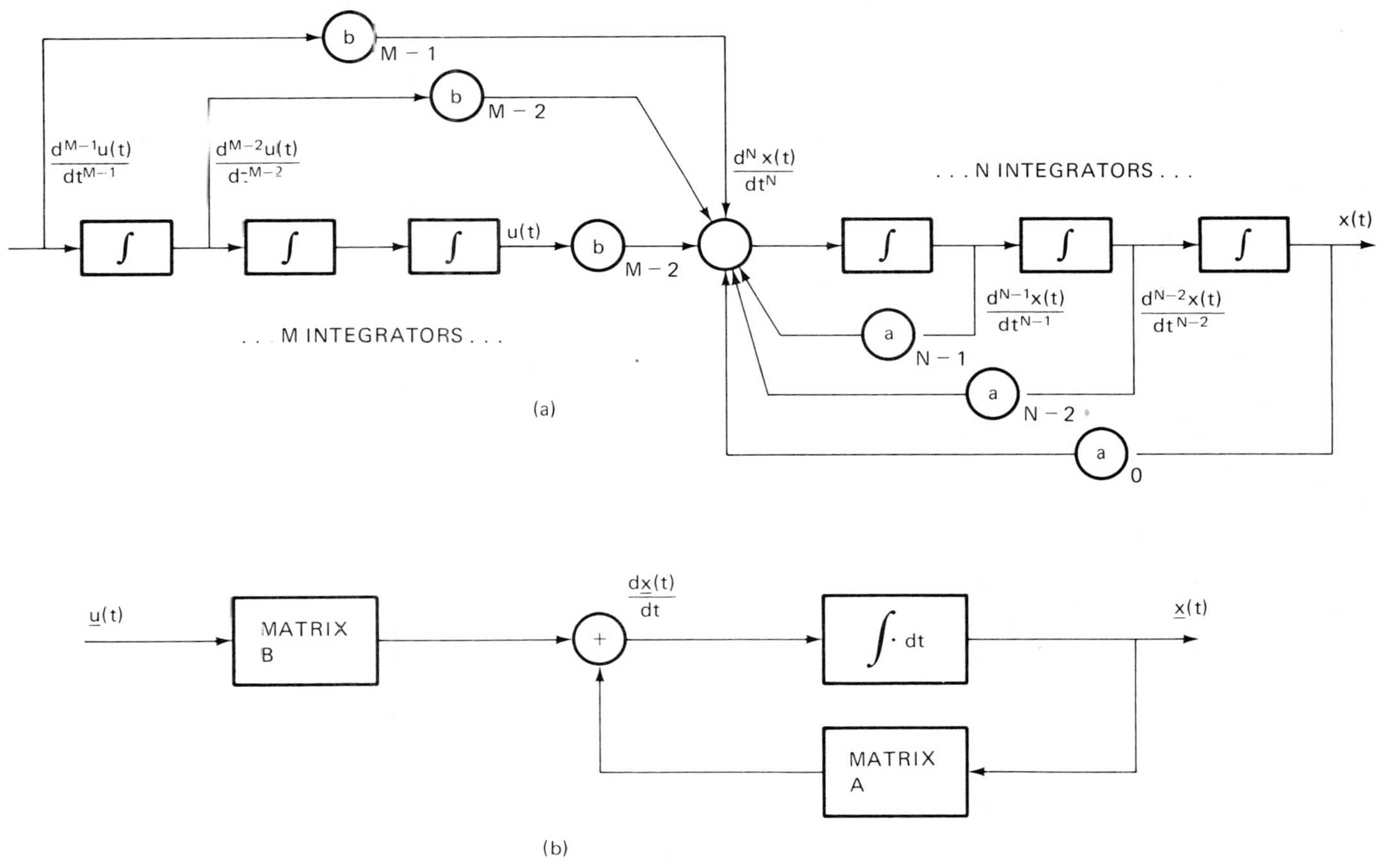

Figure 3-2. Continuous Filter Block Diagram.

called convolution. The convolution of two time-domain signals, say, $x(t)$ and $h(t)$, is denoted $x(t) * h(t)$. Here $x(t)$ will be assumed to be the input signal, and $h(t)$ represents the filter impulse response.[a] An impulse response, as the name implies, is the time-domain response of a linear filter to an impulse. You will recall that the impulse function had some unique and interesting properties; one of the most salient features was that its frequency representation was constant for all frequencies. That is, an impulse can be thought of as a series of equal-amplitude, pure sinusoidal oscillators. Therefore an inputted impulse will cause the filter to see all frequencies to appear at the input simultaneously. Therefore the filter response $h(t)$ can be envisioned as the cumulative effect of the filter interacting with each individual sinusoidal oscillator. SPECTRUM IV contains program CONVOLVE, which allows the user to convolve two input records.

Theory

Consider the system shown in Figure 3-3. The output $y(t)$ is defined as the convolution of the input $x(t)$ with the system's "impulse response" $h(t)$. The convolution of $x(t)$ and $h(t)$ is denoted

$$y(t) = ht)*x(t) \tag{3.5}$$

and it is defined to be, over an observation period T,

$$y(t) = \frac{1}{T}\int_T h(t-\sigma)x(\sigma)\,d\sigma \tag{3.6}$$

as $T \rightarrow \infty$. Solving Equation (3.6) often can pose a difficult computational problem. However, a major computational simplification can be achieved by using frequency-domain methods. Consider then the Fourier transformation of $y(t)$, denoted $Y(f)$.

$$\begin{aligned}
Y(f) &= \mathcal{F}[y(t)] \\
&= \mathcal{F}\left[\frac{1}{T}\int_T h(t-\sigma)x(\sigma)\,d\sigma\right] \\
&= \frac{1}{T}\int_T \frac{1}{T}\int_T h(t-\sigma)\,x(\sigma)\,d(\sigma)\,\exp(-j2\pi ft)\,dt \\
&= \frac{1}{T}\int_T \frac{1}{T}\int_T h(t-\sigma)\,\exp(-j2\pi ft\,dt)\,x(\sigma)\,d\sigma\,dt \qquad (3.7)
\end{aligned}$$

[a] It is implicitly assumed that all initial conditions are equal to zero when a convolution is performed.

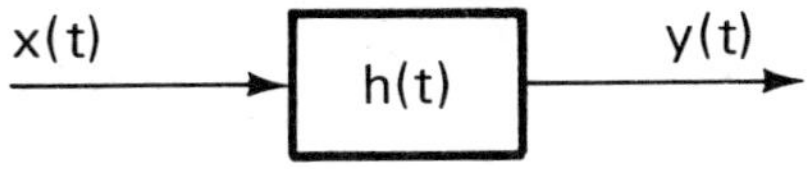

Figure 3-3. Linear System.

For $s = t - \sigma$, Equation (3.7) becomes

$$
\begin{aligned}
Y(f) &= \frac{1}{T}\int_T \frac{1}{T}\int_T [h(s)\exp(-j2\pi f(s+\sigma)\,ds]x(\sigma)\,d\sigma\,dt \\
&= \frac{1}{T}\int_T \frac{1}{T}\int_T [h(s)\exp(-j2\pi fs)\,ds]x(\sigma)\exp(-j2\pi f\sigma)\,d\sigma\,dt \\
&= \frac{1}{T}\int_T H(f)x(\sigma)\exp(-j2\pi\, f\sigma)\,d\sigma \\
&= H(f)\frac{1}{T}\int_T x(\sigma)\exp(-j2\pi f\sigma)\,d\sigma \\
&= H(f)X(f) \qquad (3.8)
\end{aligned}
$$

Therefore the spectral image of the convolution of $x(t)$ with $h(t)$ is a complex number. Furthermore, $x(t)*h(t)$ and $H(f)\ X(f)$ are Fourier transform pairs. That is,

$$h(t)*x(t) \underset{\mathcal{F}^{-1}}{\overset{\mathcal{F}}{\rightleftarrows}} H(f)X(f) \qquad (3.9)$$

Under SPECTRUM IV control, the convolution of two signals can be accomplished. The data can be entered in the time or the frequency domain. The resultant convolution is presented to the user in the time domain. A convolution is mechanically produced by SPECTRUM IV as shown in Figure 3-4.

If one or more of the signals to be convolved is nonperiodic or corrupted by noise, ensemble averaging can be used to increase the statistical confidence of a convolution operation. In addition, as a service to the user of SPECTRUM IV, a WRAP-AROUND operation can be included in the convolution process. This option will provide the user with valid convolution data over a subset of the original time record length.

Execution of CONVOLVE

A convolution operation can be performed on two input records by using

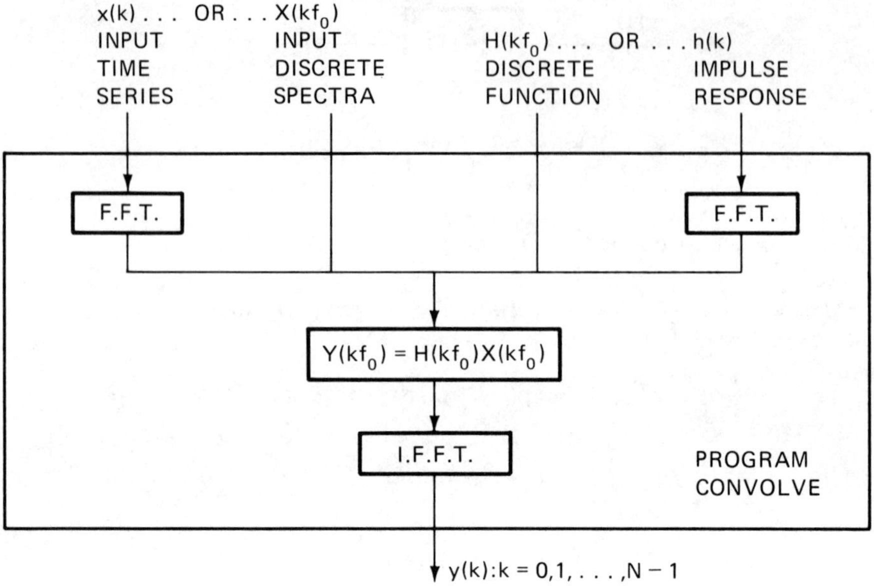

Figure 3-4. Program CONVOLVE.

the eight-letter mnemonic CONVOLVE. The structure of CONVOLVE requires the user to obey certain structural restrictions. The input records must reside in arrays B and C. As a convenience, a WRAP-AROUND option is available for any convolution operation. The result of a convolution operation is returned to array A. The output is in the time domain. Restrictions imposed on a CONVOLVE operation are:

1. The input records must reside in arrays B and C and be in the time (TIME) domain.
2. Arrays B and C must contain the same number of data points.
3. Sample frequencies associated with arrays B and C must be equal.
4. Since the convolved data is returned to array A, array A must be free of memory protection.
5. Neither array B nor array C can be the null array.

The structure of a CONVOLVE operation is shown in Table 3-1.

The output from a CONVOLVE call contains labels describing the nature of the operation in terms of sample points, frequency, and location of input-output data records. The output record resides in the time domain. If the input time-series records are of length N, the output record is of length N also, provided no WRAP-AROUND operation is performed. If a WRAP-AROUND operation is requested, the resulting output record is of

Table 3-1
Structure of a CONVOLVE Call

Column Number	*Description*	*Format or Contents*
Primary information card		
1-8	Calls CONVOLVE	CONVOLVE
15	First input array designator (B or C)	B or C
20	Second input array designator (C or B)	C or B
80	WRAP-AROUND option = 1 (default = 0)	1 or void

length $N/2$. These data values represent the first and fourth quadrant of the original convolution data record. After the execution of a CONVOLVE operation, the input arrays B and C will be returned to those locations in the frequency domain.

Example. The following example illustrates the use of program CONVOLVE. An input signal $x(t)$ is to be convolved with a system impulse response $h(t)$, where

$$x(t) = \delta(t) \qquad \text{an impulse}$$

$$h(t) = \exp(-4.0t) \qquad \text{an exponential}$$

The result of convolving these two signals is theoretically equal to $h(t)$. That is,

$$x(t)^*h(t) = h(t)$$

for $x(t)$ and $h(t)$ defined above.

The card control sequence associated with this experiment is found in Figure 3-5. The input process $x(t)$ and system impulse response $h(t)$ are synthesized by using USER LIB. The source coding of these two signals is found in Figure 3-6. Note that subroutine OWN is constructed so that the two user-supplied functions can be addressed directly through the indirect address parameter found on the USER LIB card. The impulse used was designed to have a maximum amplitude of 64. Although this was not a discrete unit impulse, it is an impulse. The user often will find it desirable to use a high-energy impulse to avoid magnitude scaling problems that result from small spectral values of the discrete unit impulse. The time-series representation of the input signal processes is found in Figure 3-7. The time-series characterization of the system impulse response is found in Figure 3-8 with the actual system output displayed in Figure 3-9. The output, as defined by the convolution process of an impulse response with an impulse, is the impulse response.

B. Transfer Function

One of the most useful modeling techniques used in linear systems analysis is the transfer function. A transfer function is defined in the frequency domain. It is a measure of a filter's capability to alter the magnitude and phase of an inputted pure sinusoid—that is, a pure sinusoid presented to a filter will appear at the output with a new magnitude and phase. The degree of change is measured by the transfer function. However, such information is desired for all possible input frequencies. You will recall from part B of Chapter 2 that an impulse has all possible frequencies. Therefore the transfer function and impulse response representation of a filter convey identical information.[b] The difference is that the impulse response resides in the two domain, whereas the transfer function belongs to the frequency domain.

Information about filter response times, bandpass and bandreject capabilities, and stability can be abstracted from the transfer function. Filters that pass only low frequencies and severely attenuate high frequencies are called low-pass filters. If an impulse were introduced to such a filter, the output would be dominated by low-frequency sinusoids. The inability of a low-frequency sinusoid to change its value rapidly suggests that such a device has a long response time. If a filter can pass high-frequency signals and attenuate low-frequency signals, it is said to be a high-pass filter. Using a similar argument, one would conclude that such a device has fast response times. Bandpass and bandreject filters selectively pass or attenuate signals that reside at prespecified frequency locations. Therefore a user often can predict what effect a filter would have on system performance based solely on an inspection of the transfer function.

Finally, it is often desirable to test the performance of a system by using simulation. To use simulation methods, a mathematical model of the system must be constructed. Mathematical models of a filter that exhibit prespecified transfer function behavior can be produced. Using modeling methods, a mathematical model can be abstracted from experimental data or a physical understanding of the filter. Once a satisfactory model of an equivalent transfer function has been obtained, the system can be tested with respect to any arbitrary input stimuli. SPECTRUM IV has a program called SYSTEM that will allow the user to synthesize a transfer function.

Theory

Let a linear system have impulse response $h(t)$ and an input $r(t)$. The

[b] A transfer function is defined under the hypothesis that all system initial conditions are zero.

```
CARD      COLUMN                                                                      8Ø
          123456789Ø12       .       .       .       .       .       .       .
-----------------------------------------------------------------------------------------
1         USER LIB      B                                             64       1.ØØ     1
2         THIS WILL CREATE A UNIT IMPULSE
3         PLOTTER       B                                             64
4         TIME                 1   64    THIS IS A TIME PLOT OF A UNIT IMPULSE FUNCTION
5         USER LIB      C                                             64       1.ØØ     2
6         AN EXPONENTIAL FUNCTION F(X)=EXP(-4T/N)
7         PLOTTER       C                                             64
8         TIME                 1   64    THIS IS A TIME PLOT OF AN EXPONENTIAL FUNCTION
9         CONVOLVE      B    C
1Ø        PLOTTER       A                                             64
11        TIME                 1   64    THE CONVOLUTION OF THE IMPULSE AND THE EXPONENTIAL
12        TERM
                 .       .       .       .       .       .       .       .
```

Figure 3-5. Card Control Sequence for Convolution Example.

```
FORTRAN IV G LEVEL  21                OWN                DATE = 75156          15/52/50                PAGE 0001

 0001                SUBROUTINE OWN
               C
               C   THE FOLLOWING FIVE STATEMENTS SHOULD BE INCLUDED IN ANY SUBROUTINE OWN
 0002                REAL*8 BAN
 0003                INTEGER DSO,E,F,TIME,FREQ,SPL
 0004                COMMON REST(6148),TEMR(1024),TEMC(1024),FRN(20),FCN(20),FRD(20),
                    1FCD(20),PN(21),PD(21),REST1(82),NPOINT,REST2(5),SPL,REST3(2)
 0005                COMMON /LETTER/ F,E,MAR(3),LAIS(60),TIME,FREQ,IBAN,BAN,LN,NN,NP
               C
               C
 0006                WRITE(LN,3) SPL
 0007              3 FORMAT(10X,'USER PROGRAM NUMBER ',I2,/)
 0008                IF(SPL .EQ. 2) GO TO 20
               C
               C
               C   USER PROGRAM 1 CREATES A TIME DATA SET FOR A UNIT IMPULSE
 0009             10 TEMR(1)= FLOAT(NPOINT)
 0010                GO TO 99
               C
               C
               C   USER PROGRAM 2 CREATES A TIME DATA SET FOR THE EXPONENTIAL FUNCTION
               C           EXP(-4T/NPOINT)
 0011             20 DO 1 I=1,NPOINT
 0012              1 TEMR(I)=EXP(-4.*FLOAT(I-1)/FLOAT(NPOINT))
               C
               C
 0013             99 CONTINUE
 0014                RETURN
 0015                RETURN
               $
***********01)  IEY002I LABEL*****************************************************************************************
 0016                END
```

Figure 3-6. Subroutine OWN (Convolution Example).

output—say, $s(t)$—is defined to be the convolution of $h(t)$ with $r(t)$. That is,

$$r(t) = h(t)*s(t) = \int_0^t h(t - \sigma)\, s(\sigma)\, d\sigma \tag{3.10}$$

The computational problems associated with convolution integral can be replaced with a product of Laplace transformed function. Let

$$S(s) = \mathcal{L}\,[s(t)]$$
$$H(s) = \mathcal{L}\,[h(t)]$$
$$R(s) = \mathcal{L}\,[r(t)]$$

From the convolution theorem of Laplace transforms,

$$R(s) = \mathcal{L}\,[h(t)*s(t)] = H(s)\, S(s) \tag{3.11}$$

The input-output relationship in the s domain is $H(s)$, where

$$H(s) = \frac{S(s)}{R(s)} \tag{3.12}$$

The steady state input-output relationship is called the system's transfer function, and it is denoted $H(f)$, where

$$H(f) = \frac{S(f)}{R(f)} \tag{3.13}$$

A transfer function can be realized experimentally. If the input record $r(t)$ and output record $s(t)$ are sampled and converted into the frequency domain with a DFT, the ratio of $R(f_i)$ into $S(f_i)$ at the discrete frequencies f_i will produce a discrete transfer function $R(f_i)$. That is,

$$H(f_i) = \frac{S(f_i)}{R(f_i)} = |\, H(f_i)\, | \angle \theta_{f_i} \tag{3.14}$$

Since $S(f_i)$ and $R(f_i)$ are complex numbers, $H(f_i)$ is complex also. Thus $H(f_i)$ can be represented as a gain and phase. At frequency f_i the filter will exhibit a gain equal to $|H(f_i)|$. The filter's phase shift at frequency f_i is given by $\theta_{f_i} = \tan^{-1}$ (Imaginary $\{H(f_i)\}$/Real $\{H(f_i)\}$). Usually this information is present graphically in gain-phase or Bode plot form. Therefore, if an input sinusoid has a magnitude S and a phase θ_{s_i} at frequency f_i, it will produce an output sinusoid of frequency f_i having a magnitude $|S|\,|H(f_i)|$ and a phase $\theta_{s_i} + \theta_{f_i}$.

The generation of a transfer function is accomplished through the ratioing of an input and output spectrum. In block diagram form, a computer-generated transfer function is accomplished as shown in Figure 3-10.

THIS IS A TIME PLOT OF A UNIT IMPULSE FUNCTION

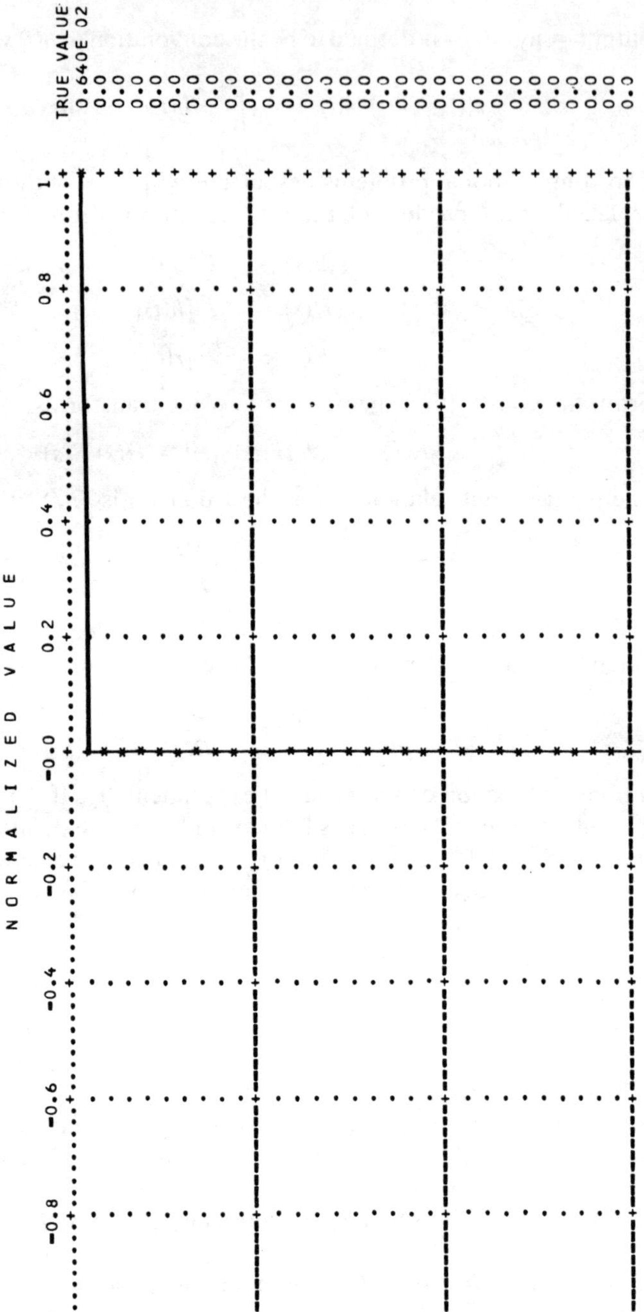

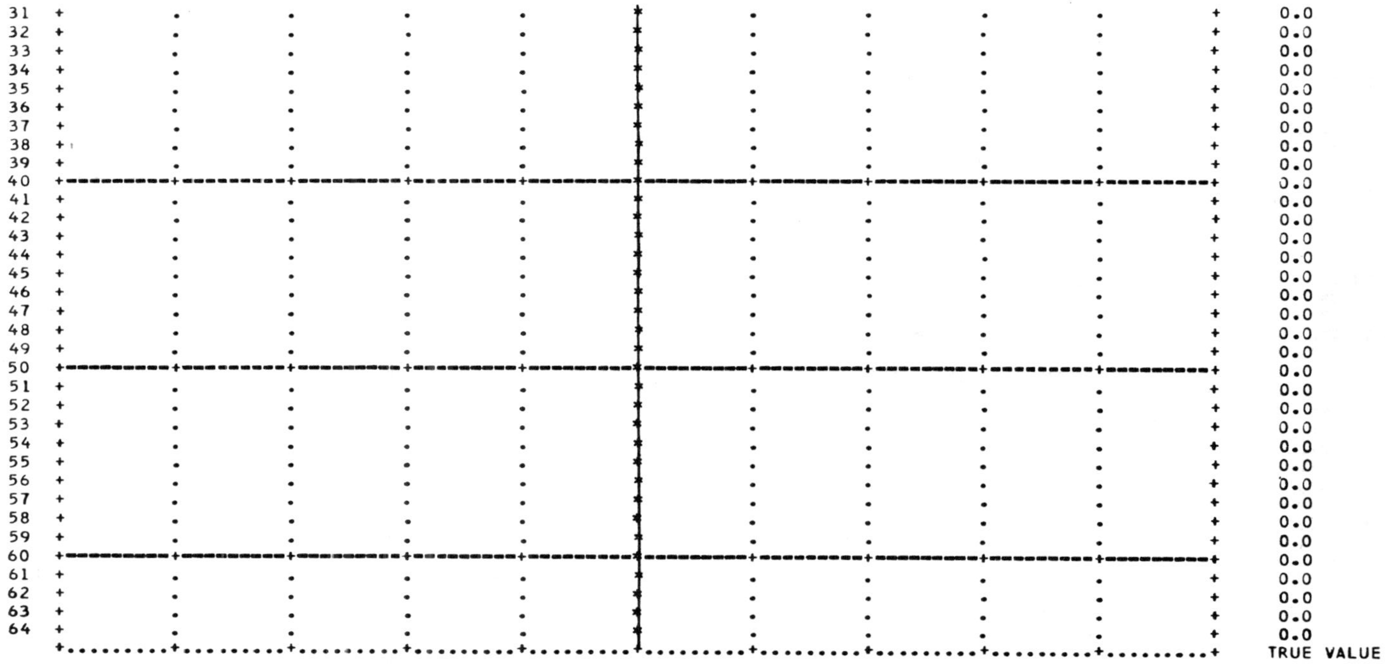

Figure 3-7. Input Time Series (Convolution Example).

THIS IS A TIME PLOT OF AN EXPONTIAL FUNCTION

N C R M A L I Z E D   V A L U E

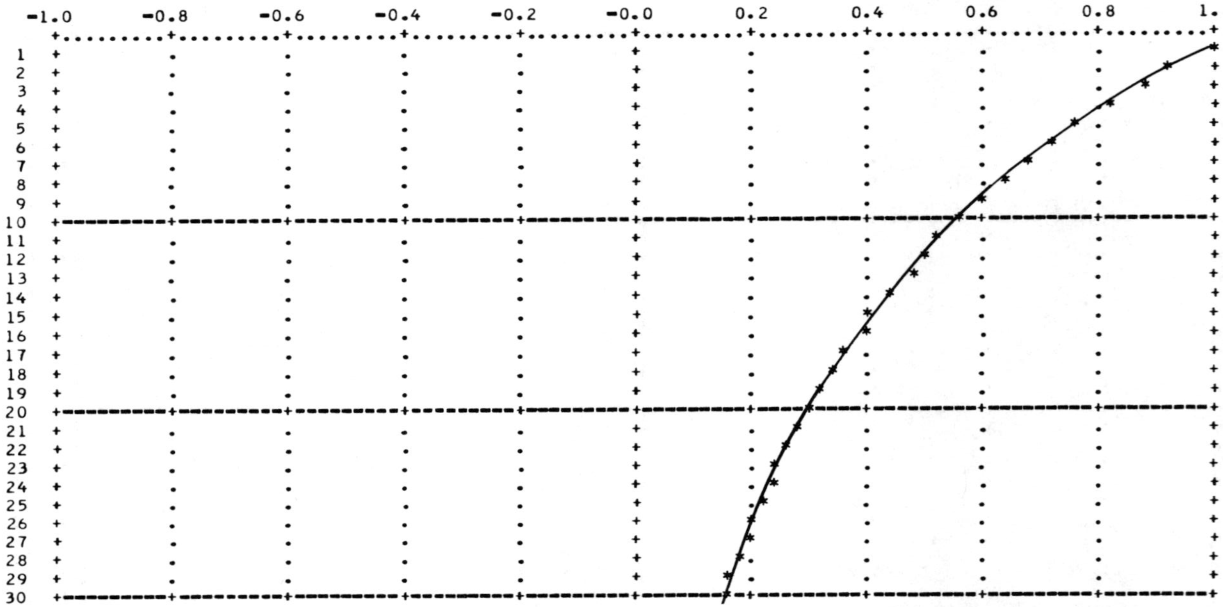

TRUE VALUE
0.100E 01
0.939E 00
0.882E 00
0.829E 00
0.779E 00
0.732E 00
0.687E 00
0.646E 00
0.607E 00
0.570E 00
0.535E 00
0.503E 00
0.472E 00
0.444E 00
0.417E 00
0.392E 00
0.368E 00
0.346E 00
0.325E 00
0.305E 00
0.287E 00
0.269E 00
0.253E 00
0.238E 00
0.223E 00
0.210E 00
0.197E 00
0.185E 00
0.174E 00
0.163E 00

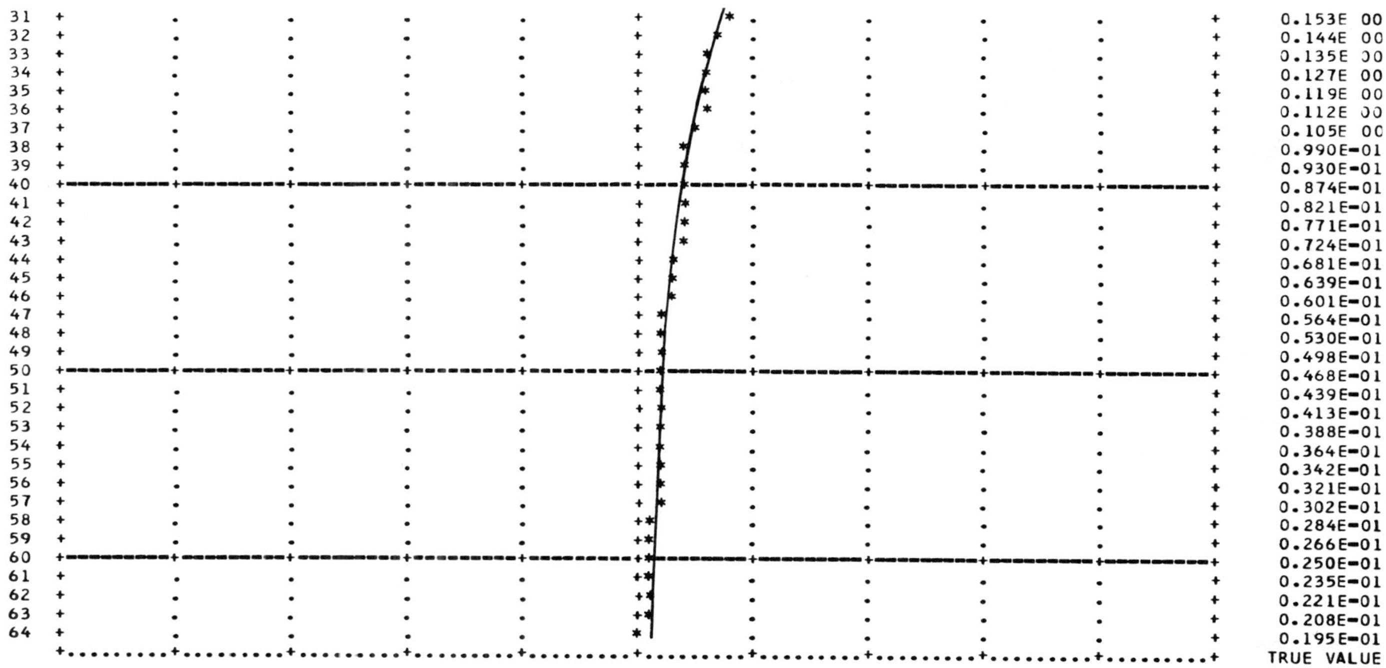

Figure 3-8. Impulse Response (Convolution Example).

THE CONVOLUTION OF THE IMPULSE AND THE EXPONENTIAL

NORMALIZED VALUE

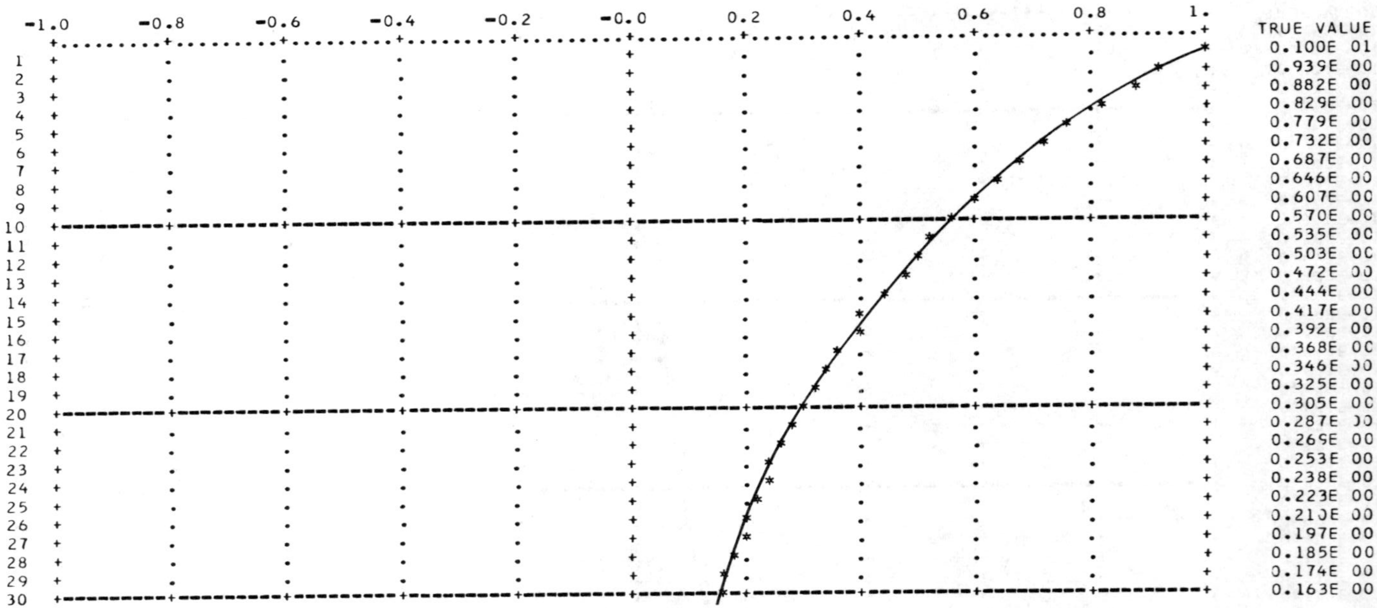

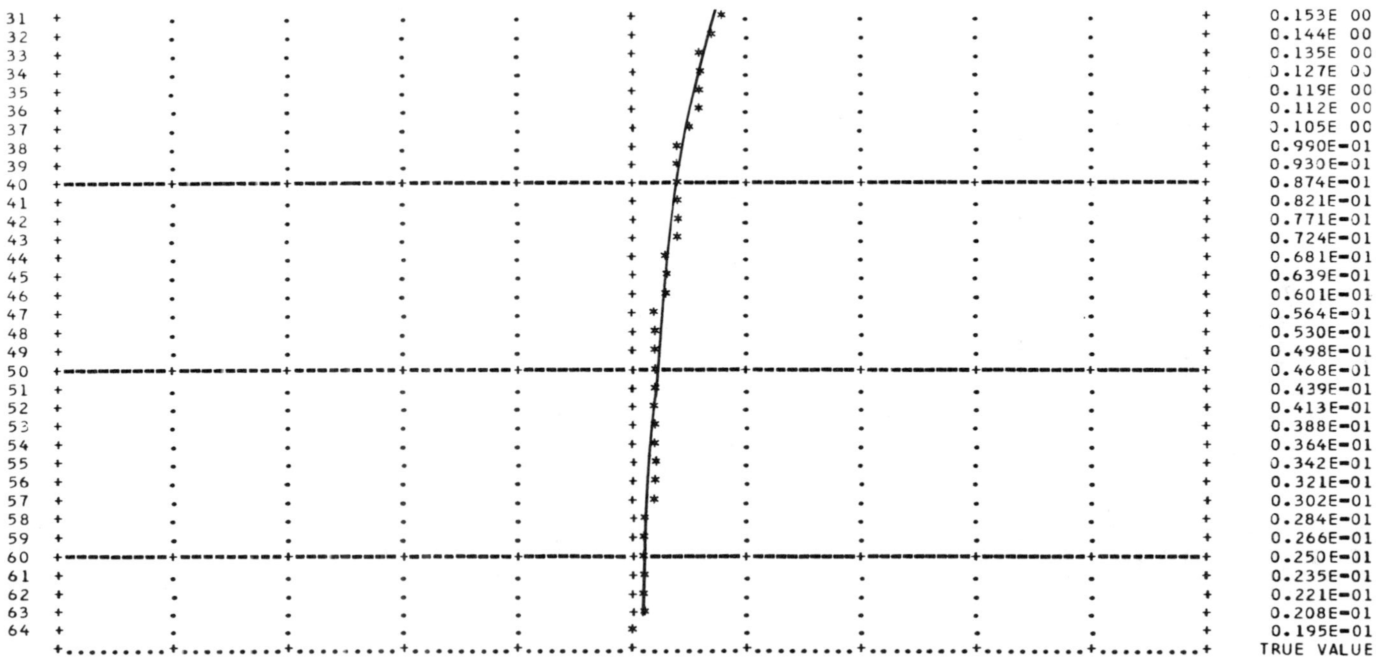

Figure 3-9. Output Time Series (Convolution Example).

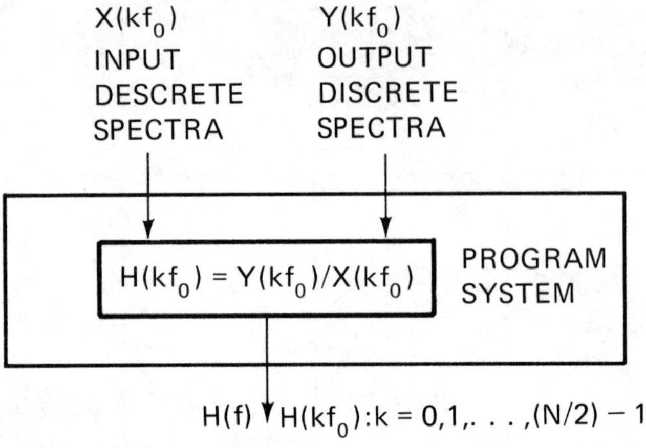

Figure 3-10. Program SYSTEM.

Execution of SYSTEM

A transfer function can be generated under SPECTRUM IV control using the six-letter mnemonic SYSTEM. The structure of SYSTEM requires that certain syntactic and format rules be obeyed. The resulting transfer function always resides in array A. Restrictions imposed on the use of SYSTEM are:

1. The input record must be entered into array C, and the data in array C must be in the frequency domain.
2. The output record must be entered into array B, and the data in array B must be in the frequency domain.
3. Since the transfer function is returned to array A, array A must be free of memory protection.
4. The number of data points in the input and output records must be the same.
5. The sampling frequencies associated with the input and output records must be the same.

The structure of program SYSTEM is shown in Table 3-2. Program SYSTEM computes the transfer function

$$H(f) = \frac{Y(f)}{X(f)}$$

in a direct manner unless a divide fault occurs (overflow). If a divide fault occurs, SYSTEM will branch to a subroutine that performs a linear in-

Table 3-2
Structure of a SYSTEM Call

Column Number	*Description*	*Format or Contents*
Preliminary information card		
1-6	Calls SYSTEM	SYSTEM

terpolation. If the interpolation is successful, the computation of $H(f)$ continues. A message is supplied automatically by SPECTRUM IV, attesting that a successful interpolation was accomplished. If the division fault cannot be resolved, an error message is produced automatically by SPECTRUM IV. The output stored in array A is identified automatically in terms of size and sampling frequency by the output phase of SYSTEM. In addition, the contents of array A are protected.

Example. We have noted that a transfer function is the Fourier transform of an impulse response. Therefore, if the input to a system is an impulse, the Fourier transform of the output represents the system transfer function. Suppose the output of a system, to a unit input stimulus is $x(t)$, where

$$x(t) = \frac{\exp(-4t)}{4}$$

Then the system transfer function is given by $X(f)$, where

$$X(f) = \frac{1}{4}\left(\frac{1}{s-4}\right)\Bigg|_{\underbrace{s = j2\pi f}} = \frac{1}{4}\left(\frac{1}{j2\pi f - 4}\right)$$

which is recognized to be a single-pole low-pass filter. To produce this result under SPECTRUM IV control, the following control structure is used:

A unit-strength 64-point input impulse is generated using program USER LIB. That is, an impulse denoted $\delta(k)$ is constructed to satisfy

$$\delta(k) = \left\{\begin{array}{l} 64 \text{ if } k = 0 \\ \\ 0 \text{ if } k = 1, 2, \ldots, 63 \end{array}\right\}$$

The strength of the impulse is given by its average value, which is unity. The impulse is to be generated in USER LIB.

The card control structure required to perform these operations can be found in Figure 3-11. The card control sequence associated with this problem indicates that an array switch occurs after the first and second FFT calls. This operation is used to load the contents of array A—which is

```
CARD          COLUMN                                                              8Ø
              123456789Ø12      .          .          .          .          .          .          .
--------------------------------------------------------------------------------------------------
1             USER LIB     A                                        64         1Ø.        1
2             INPUT IMPULSE
3             FFT
4             SWITCH       A    C
5             USER LIB     A                                        64         1Ø.        2
6             OUTPUT TIME SERIES
7             PLOTTER      A                                        64
8             TIME              1    64    OUTPUT TIME SERIES
9             FFT
1Ø            SWITCH       A    B
11            SYSTEM
12            PLOTTER      A
13            FREQ   MAG        1    32    TRANSFER FUNCTION
14            TERM
                    .          .          .          .          .          .          .          .
```

Figure 3-11. Card Control Sequence for System Transfer Function Experiment.

there as a result of an FFT operation—into the proper location for a future SYSTEM operation. In addition, the SWITCH operation will remove the memory protection given to array A by the FFT operation, thereby allowing the user to reuse array A. The synthesis of the input and output exponential, whose source is subroutine OWN, is documented in Figure 3-12. The output time series is displayed in Figure 3-13. Finally, the magnitude spectra associated with the simple single-pole filter can be found in Figure 3-14. The created transfer function is in good agreement with theory.

C. Cross-correlation

We have noted that the autocorrelation function is a measure of the average similarity that exists within a signal. Signal features such as periodicity and correlation times can be obtained through an autocorrelation operation. The frequency-domain version of autocorrelation was the power spectral density, which was a display of the power in a signal on a per-hertz basis. If two different signals are considered simultaneously, a similar operation can be performed. In the time domain the operation is called a cross-correlation. In the frequency domain the operation is called cross-power spectral density. Cross-correlation is the measure of the similarity between signals, say, $x(t)$ and $y(t + \tau)$. Here τ is called the delay parameter. That is, $y(t + \tau)$ is $y(t)$ delayed τ seconds of time. The cross-correlation function is defined in the time domain and is denoted $R_{xy}(\tau)$. If $x(t)$ and $y(t)$ are real signals, then $R_{xy}(\tau)$ is real for all τ. If $R_{xy}(\tau)$ is a large positive number, then on the average $x(t)$ and $y(t + \tau)$ are varying in harmony for that value of τ. If $R_{xy}(\tau)$ is near zero, then on the average $x(t)$ and $y(t + \tau)$ have very little in common for that value of τ. If $R_{xy}(\tau)$ is a large negative number, then on the average $x(t)$ and $y(t + \tau)$ are varying out of harmony for that value of τ. That is, $x(t)$ and $y(t + \tau)$ are inversely related.

Cross-correlation has great utility in the study of linear systems. For example, it has been successfully used on radar, biological, and societal problems. Specifically, in a radar application, range information is contained in the time delay between the transmission and reception of a pulse. Using the cross-correlation method, the delay time τ to maximum cross-correlation can be found. At this time the transmitted signal and its delayed received version are most similar. In a biological application, signals sharing a common source, such as the heart, can be analyzed through a cross-correlation. If signals are measured at two separate locations of the biological system, a cross-correlation of two of these signals will yield information about delays and distortions that may exist within the biological media. In a societal problem, scientists are often interested in deter-

```
FORTRAN IV G LEVEL  21                  OWN               DATE = 75156          17/14/29              PAGE 0001

0001              SUBROUTINE OWN
            C
            C   THE FOLLOWING FIVE STATEMENTS SHOULD BE INCLUDED IN ANY SUBROUTINE OWN
0002              REAL*8 BAN
0003              INTEGER DSO,E,F,TIME,FREQ,SPL
0004              COMMON REST(6148),TEMR(1024),TEMC(1024),FRN(20),FCN(20),FRD(20),
                 1FCD(20),PN(21),PD(21),REST1(82),NPOINT,REST2(5),SPL,REST3(2)
0005              COMMON /LETTER/ F,E,MAR(3),LAIS(60),TIME,FREQ,IBAN,BAN,LN,NN,NP
            C
            C
0006              WRITE(LN,3) SPL
0007            3 FORMAT(10X,'USER PROGRAM NUMBER ',I2,/)
0008              IF (SPL.EQ.2) GO TO 20
0009              TEMR(1)=64.
0010              GO TO 99
0011           20 DO 30 I=1,NPOINT
0012              DD3=I
0013           30 TEMR(I)=EXP(-DD3*4/NPOINT)
0014           99 CONTINUE
0015              RETURN
0016              END
```

Figure 3-12. Subroutine OWN (System Transfer Function Experiment).

mining the strength of interrelations that may exist within a social model. In general, a particular societal event will suffer propagation delays. In addition, the event will be modified in time because of other societal forces existing within the system. Cross-correlation methods can be used to investigate such behaviors.

Sometimes dissimilarity is desired—that is, the cross-correlation function $R_{xy}(\tau)$ is zero or near zero for all τ. Theories of communication and control require that random input signals be decomposable into a pure signal and noise process. It is also required that the noise and signal process be uncorrelated. If this hypothesis is true, then there are methods that can mimimize the effects of the noise. Cross-correlation methods can be used to test this hypothesis.

A convenient technique used to interpret cross-correlation information is the cross-correlation coefficient, a real number that is bounded between plus one and minus one and denoted $\rho_{xy}(\tau)$. It measures the relative similarity of $x(t)$ and $y(t + \tau)$. A value of $\rho_{xy}(\tau)$ equal to or near one, zero, or minus one implies that $x(t)$ and $y(t + \tau)$ are strongly (in a harmonious sense), weakly, or strongly (in an inverse sense) correlated. Program CROSS-C is included in SPECTRUM IV to perform cross-correlation operations.

Theory

The cross-correlation of some $x(t)$ with $y(t)$ is given by $R_{xy}(\tau)$, where

$$R_{xy}(\tau) = \frac{1}{T}\int_T x(t)y(t - \tau)\,dt \tag{3.15}$$

as $T \rightarrow \infty$. Therefore the cross-correlation of $x(t)$ with $y(t)$ is a measure of the time average value of $x(t)$ with $y(t)$ displaced τ seconds. If $R_{xy}(\tau)$ has large positive (negative) value, x and y are said to be positively (negatively) correlated at τ. Positive correlation implies that $x(t)$ and $y(t - \tau)$ are changing in harmony. Negative correlation implies that $x(t)$ and $y(t - \tau)$ are moving in opposite directions on the average. If $R_{xy}(\tau)$ equals zero, x and y are said to be uncorrelated.

However, computational savings can be obtained by accomplishing time-domain calculations in the frequency domain. Consider again, as $T \rightarrow \infty$,

$$R_{xy}(\tau) = \frac{1}{T}\int_T x(t)y(t - \tau)\,dt \tag{3.15}$$

Then $\mathscr{F}[R_{xy}(\tau)]$ is given by

OUTPUT TIME SERIES

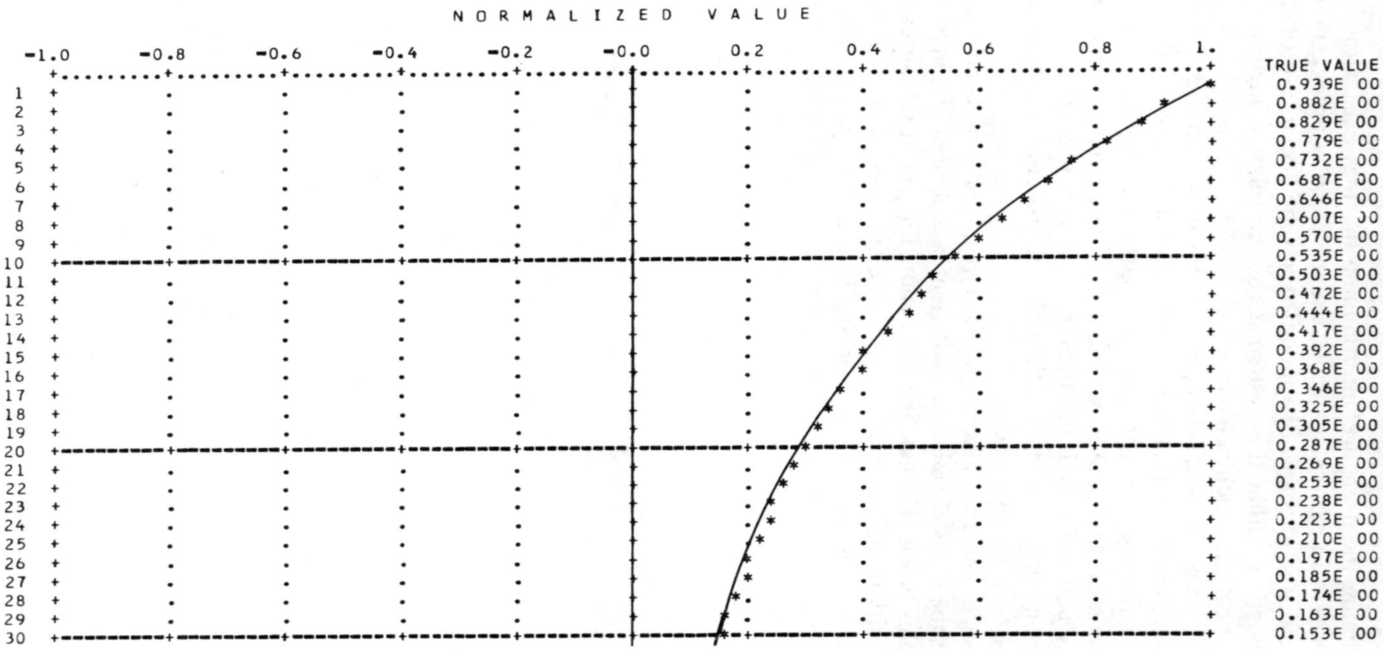

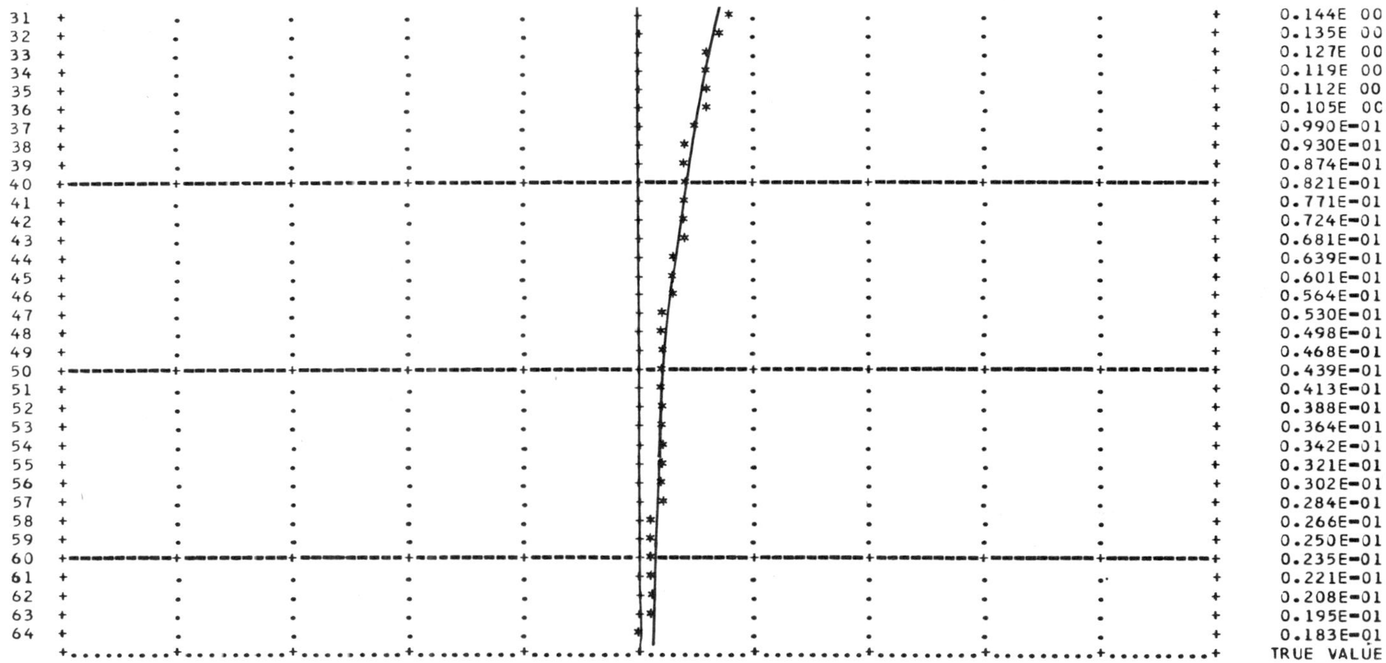

Figure 3-13. Output Time Series (System Transfer Function Experiment).

TRANSFER FUNCTION

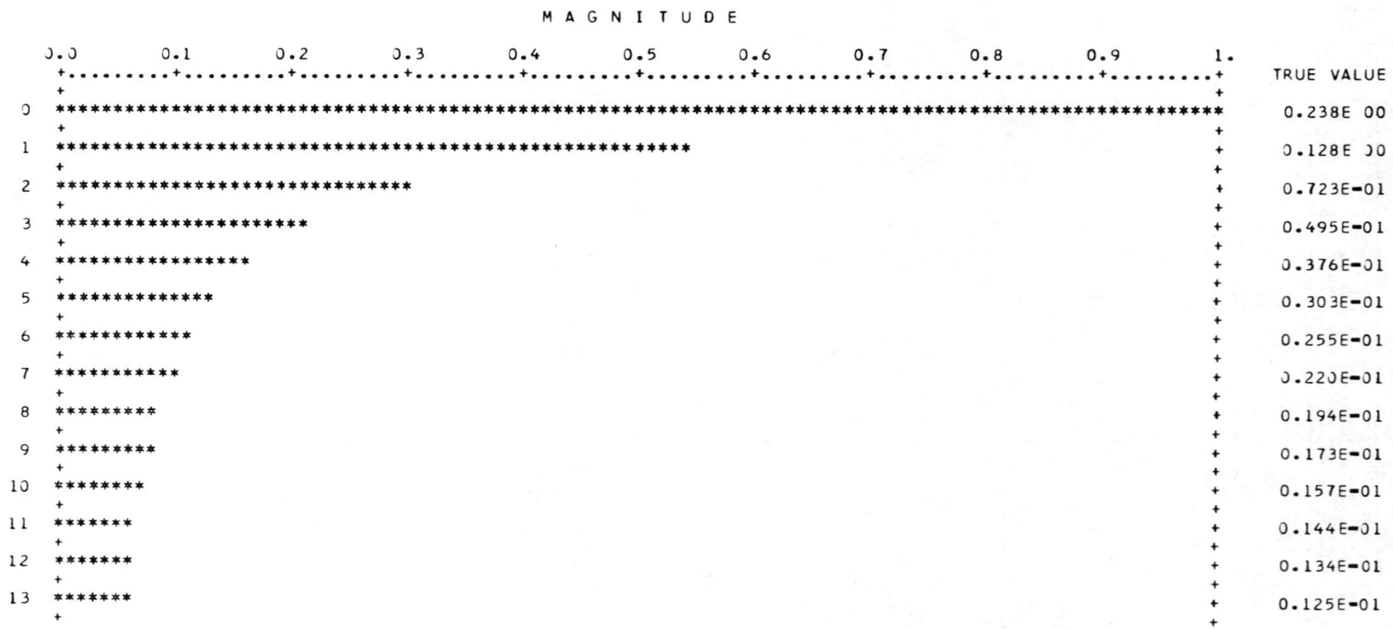

```
14  ******                                                     +   0.117E-01
     +                                                         +
15  ******                                                     +   0.111E-01
     +                                                         +
16  *****                                                      +   0.105E-01
     +                                                         +
17  *****                                                      +   0.100E-01
     +                                                         +
18  *****                                                      +   0.961E-02
     +                                                         +
19  *****                                                      +   0.925E-02
     +                                                         +
20  *****                                                      +   0.893E-02
     +                                                         +
21  *****                                                      +   0.866E-02
     +                                                         +
22  *****                                                      +   0.842E-02
     +                                                         +
23  *****                                                      +   0.822E-02
     +                                                         +
24  *****                                                      +   0.804E-02
     +                                                         +
25  *****                                                      +   0.789E-02
     +                                                         +
26  *****                                                      +   0.776E-02
     +                                                         +
27  *****                                                      +   0.766E-02
     +                                                         +
28  *****                                                      +   0.758E-02
     +                                                         +
29  *****                                                      +   0.751E-02
     +                                                         +
30  *****                                                      +   0.747E-02
     +                                                         +
31  *****                                                      +   0.744E-02
    +.........+.........+.........+.........+.........+.........+.........+.........+.........+.........+   TRUE VALUE
```

Figure 3-14. Low-pass, Single-pole Transfer Function (System Transfer Function Experiment).

$$\mathscr{F}[R_{xy}(\tau)] = \frac{1}{T}\int_T\left[\frac{1}{T}\int_T x(t)y(t-\tau)\,dt\right]e^{-j2\pi f\tau}\,d\tau\,dt$$

$$= \frac{1}{T}\int_T x(t)\left[\frac{1}{T}\int_T y(t-\tau)e^{-j2\pi f\tau}\,d\tau\right]dt \qquad (3.16)$$

Define a variable λ to be

$$\lambda = t - \tau$$

Then, defining $G_{xy}(f) = \mathscr{F}[R_{xy}(\tau)]$, one obtains

$$G_{xy}(f) = \frac{1}{T}\int_T x(t)\left[\frac{1}{T}\int_T y(\lambda)e^{-j2\pi f(t-\lambda)}\,d\lambda\right]dt$$

$$= \frac{1}{T}\int_T x(t)e^{-j2\pi ft}\left[\frac{1}{T}\int_T y(\lambda)e^{-j2\pi(-f)\lambda}\,d\lambda\right]dt$$

$$= \frac{1}{T}\int_T x(t)e^{-j2\pi ft}\,Y(-f)\,dt$$

$$= \left[\frac{1}{T}\int_T x(t)e^{-j2\pi ft}\,dt\right]Y(-f)$$

$$= X(f)Y(-f)$$

$$= \{Re[X(f)] + jIm[X(f)]\}\{Re[y(f) - jIm[Y(f)]\} \qquad (3.17)$$

The product $X(f)Y(-f)$ is a complex number called cross-power spectral density. Therefore cross correlation and cross-power spectral density are a Fourier transform pair, and the DFT of $x(t)$ and $y(t)$ can be used directly to construct the cross-correlation function. Since the DFT presumes periodic behavior over T and the time-series record of $x(t)$ and $y(t)$ represent only one experiment, the cross-correlation function is often generated from an ensemble average of cross-power spectra. Finally, cross-correlation is subject to the same WRAP-AROUND error that was found in the autocorrelation section. If the data records are aperiodic, it is suggested that a WRAP-AROUND error removal operation be undertaken. SPECTRUM IV will allow the user to compute both cross-correlation and spectral density measures. If $x(t)$ and $y(t)$ are real time series, then $R_{xy}(\tau)$ is also real.

A sometimes-used measure of cross-correlation is called the correlation coefficient. Denoted $\rho_{xy}(\tau)$, it is given by

$$\rho_{xy}(\tau) = R_{xy}(\tau)/\sqrt{R_{xx}(0)R_{yy}(0)} \qquad (3.18)$$

and is known to be bounded between plus and minus one. That is,

$$-1 \leq \rho_{xy}(\tau) \leq 1 \qquad (3.19)$$

You will recall that $R_{xx}(0)$ and $R_{yy}(0)$ are real positive numbers and that they represent the mean-squared behavior of the processes x and y. Therefore, under the hypothesis that $x(t)$ and $y(t)$ are real time series, $\rho_{xy}(\tau)$ is also real.

The cross-correlation coefficient can be produced under SPECTRUM IV control. The generation of this measure is accomplished through the sequenced applications of CROSS-C and AUTO-C operations. The task is performed as follows:

1. Perform a CROSS-C operation using option 0 on time-series records in arrays B and C. The result is returned to array A. In addition, the contents of array B and C are now in the frequency domain.
2. Perform an AUTO-C operation on the frequency-domain contents of array B. The resulting auto-correlated data are returned to B.
3. Repeat step 2 on the contents of array C.
4. Construct the cross-correlation coefficient using a CROSS-C operation with option 3. This option will use the data found in arrays A, B, and C in the manner specified by Equation (3.18).

A cross-correlation is accomplished under SPECTRUM IV control as shown in Figure 3-15.

Execution of CROSS-C

A cross-correlation or power spectral density operation can be accomplished by using the six-letter mnemonic CROSS-C. The records to be processed are required to reside in arrays B and C, and the processed data are returned to array A. Either cross-correlation or power spectral density is performed by using a select code. The options are:

Option 0: Perform a cross-correlation on the data in array B or C, and return to array A in the time domain.

Option 1: Perform a cross-correlation on the records in arrays B and C. Perform a WRAP-AROUND operation on the data. Return the cross-correlated data to array A in the time domain. Only the first and fourth quadrants of the computed data array are valid. These quadrants are supplied to the user in the first and second quadrants of array A.

Option 2: Perform a cross-power spectral density on the contents of arrays B and C. The results are returned to array A in the frequency domain.

Option 3: Compute the cross-correlation coefficient belonging to arrays B and C. This operation must be preceded by the series of operations outlined in the cross-correlation coefficient narra-

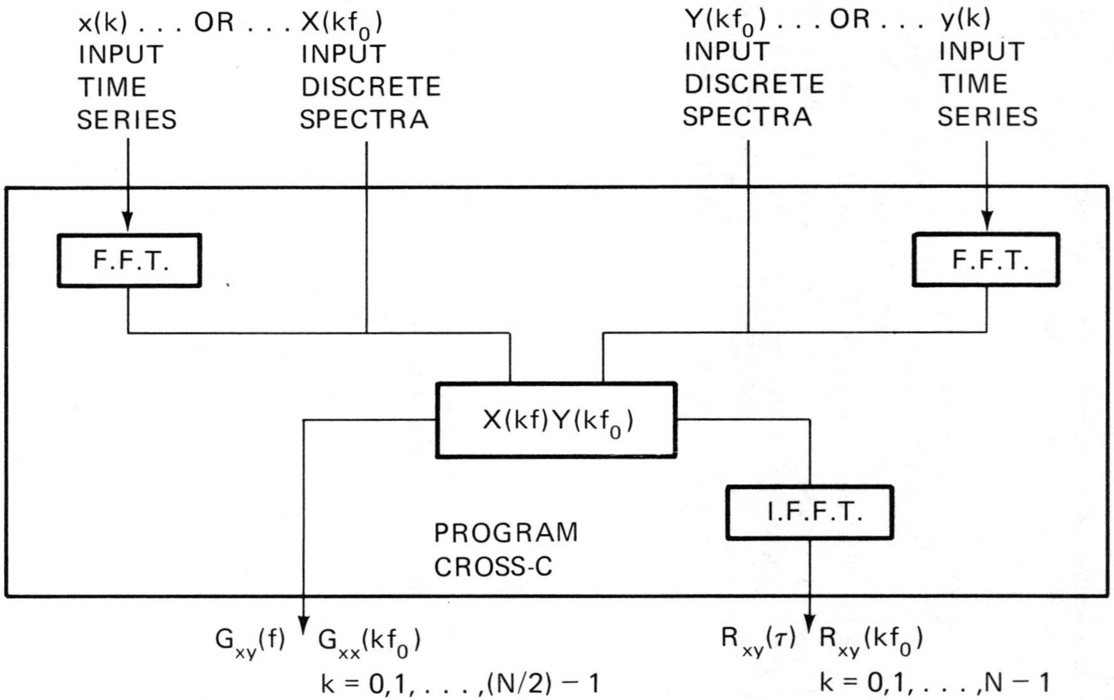

Figure 3-15. Program CROSS-C.

tive. The cross-correlation coefficient is returned to array A in the time domain.

Cross-correlation and power spectral density operations require that the input data be interpreted in the frequency domain. Therefore, if the data in array B or C is a time series, a DFT is performed on it. Upon completion of a CROSS-C operation, using any of the admissible options, the user will find the original input data in arrays B and C in the frequency domain.

Restrictions imposed on the use of CROSS-C are:

1. Arrays B and C must contain the same number of points.
2. The sampling frequencies associated with arrays B and C must be equal.
3. Since the data is returned to array A, array A must be free of memory protection.
4. Neither array B nor C can be the null array.

The control card requirements of CROSS-C are shown in Table 3-3.

Upon completion of a CROSS-C operation, SPECTRUM IV will supply to the user labels indicating array sizes, sampling frequencies, and select code information. Since CROSS-C uses an FFT operation, the data in array A are assigned memory protection.

Example. A sine wave is a cosine wave displaced by 90 degress ($\pi/2$ radians). Therefore the cross-correlation of a sine and cosine wave should reflect this deterministic relationship. Theoretically, if

$$x(t) = \sin(\omega_o t)$$

$$y(t) = \cos(\omega_o t)$$

then

$$R_{xy}(\tau) = \frac{1}{T}\int_T \sin(\omega_o t)\cos[\omega_o (t + \tau)]dt$$

$$= \frac{1}{2}\sin(\omega_o \tau).$$

Similarly, the cross-power spectral density function belonging to these two test signals becomes

$$\mathscr{F}[R_{xy}(\tau)] = \mathscr{F}\left[\frac{1}{2}\sin(\omega_o \tau)\right] = \frac{1}{4}\delta(\omega - \omega_o)$$

Both the correlation and cross-power spectral density can be produced under SPECTRUM IV control. The card sequence associated with this operation can be found in Figure 3-16. The card sequence requests that a

Table 3-3
Structure of a CROSS-C Call

Column Number	*Description*	*Format or Contents*
Primary information card		
1-7	Calls CROSS-C	CROSS-C
15	First input array (B or C)	B or C
20	Second input array (C or B)	C or B
80	Select code (option 0, 1, 2, or 3)	I1

sine and cosine wave be generated in the system library and plotted (see Figures 3-17 and 3-18). These signals, which were loaded into working arrays A and B, are then correlated using program CROSS-C. The result is plotted in the time domain (see Figure 3-19). The second phase of this experiment requires that the cross-power spectral density be derived. This can be accomplished several ways. The most direct approach would be to perform an FFT on the time-domain cross-correlation function found in array A. Another approach would be to regenerate the test signal and perform a CROSS-C operation using the power spectral density option. Still another approach would be to synthesize the original input from their spectral images found in arrays B and C. Consider this approach, recalling that FFT and IFFT operations are performed on array A data only. Therefore A must first be cleared of the previously computed cross-correlation function. Array B data are entered into array A where an IFFT is performed. Then the resulting time domain data are returned to B. The same operation is performed on the contents of array C. The two time-domain records located in arrays B and C are now operated on by CROSS-C using option 2. The resulting cross-power spectral density is then plotted (see Figure 3-20).

Example: Cross-correlation coefficient experiment. The cross-correlation coefficient will inform the user if basic similarities exist between two signal processes, independent of their individual signal strengths or amplitudes. In order to produce a cross-correlation measure under SPECTRUM IV control, the two signals under investigation must undergo preliminary signal manipulation. Suppose $x(t)$ and $y(t)$ are the signal processes to be analyzed. To create the cross-correlation coefficient given by

$$\rho_{xy}(\tau) = R_{xy}(\tau)/\sqrt{R_{xx}(0)R_{yy}(0)}$$

the following operations must be performed:

1. Produce R_{xy} using program CROSS-C

```
CARD       COLUMN                                                          8Ø
           123456789Ø12    .       .       .       .       .       .       .
-----------------------------------------------------------------------------
1          LIBRARY    B                                  64         64.ØØ
2          THIS IS A SINUSOID OF FREQUENCY 4.HZ     1  1.Ø  Ø.Ø    4.ØØ
3          LIBRARY    C                                  64         64.ØØ
4          THIS IS A COSINUSOID OF FREQUENCY 4. HZ  6  1.Ø  Ø.Ø    4.ØØ
5          PLOTTER    B                                  64
6          TIME            1   64   THIS IS A SINUSOID OF FREQUENCY 4 HZ
7          PLOTTER    C                                  64
8          TIME            1   64   THIS IS A COSINUSOID OF FREQUENCY 4.Ø HZ
9          CROSS-C    B    C                                                 Ø
1Ø         PLOTTER    A                                  64
11         TIME            1   64   THIS IS A CROSS-CORRELATION OF THE SINE AND COSINE
12         ZERO=OUT   A
13         SWITCH     A    B
14         IFFT
15         SWITCH     A    B
16         SWITCH     A    C
17         IFFT
18         SWITCH     A    C
19         CROSS-C    B    C                                                 2
2Ø         PLOTTER    A                                  32
21         FREQ   MAG      1   32   THE MAGNITUDE OF THE CROSS-POWER SPECTRAL DENSITY
22         TERM
                   .       .       .       .       .       .       .       .
```

Figure 3-16. Card Control Sequence for Sinusoidal Cross-correlation Experiment.

THIS IS A SINEUSOID OF FREQUENCY 4.0 HZ.

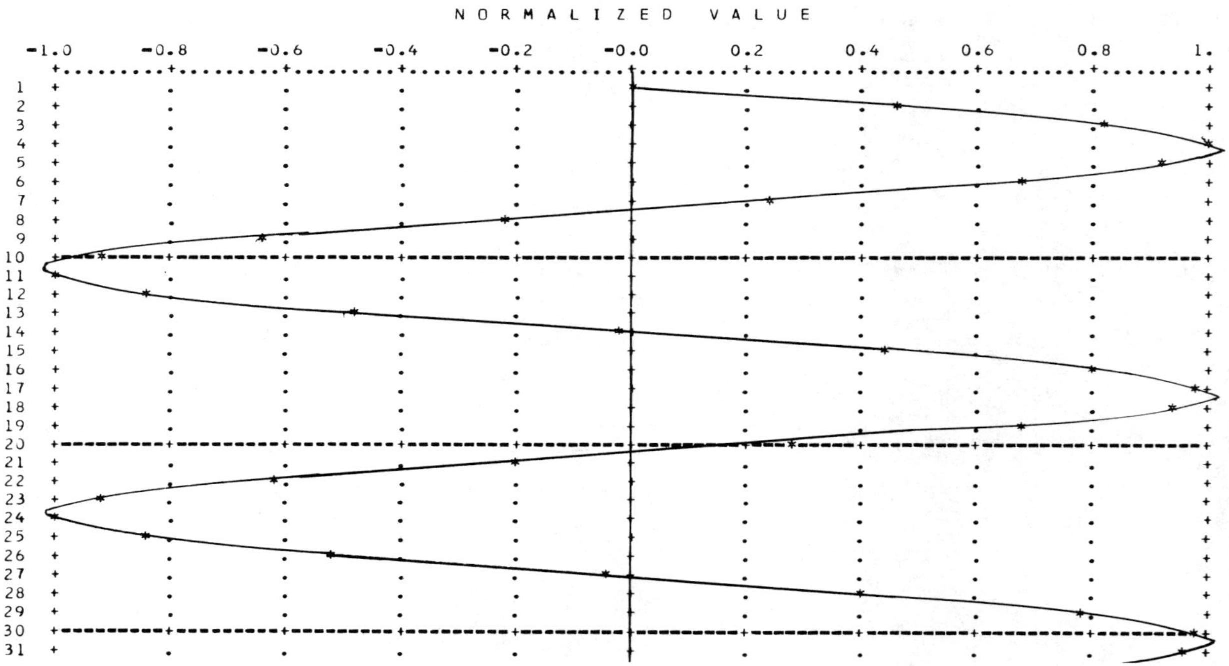

	TRUE VALUE
1	0.0
2	0.463E 00
3	0.820E 00
4	0.992E 00
5	0.938E 00
6	0.672E 00
7	0.252E 00
8	-0.224E 00
9	-0.649E 00
10	-0.928E 00
11	-0.995E 00
12	-0.837E 00
13	-0.489E 00
14	-0.295E-01
15	0.436E 00
16	0.803E 00
17	0.988E 00
18	0.948E 00
19	0.693E 00
20	0.281E 00
21	-0.195E 00
22	-0.627E 00
23	-0.916E 00
24	-0.998E 00
25	-0.853E 00
26	-0.514E 00
27	-0.589E-01
28	0.410E 00
29	0.785E 00
30	0.983E 00
31	0.957E 00

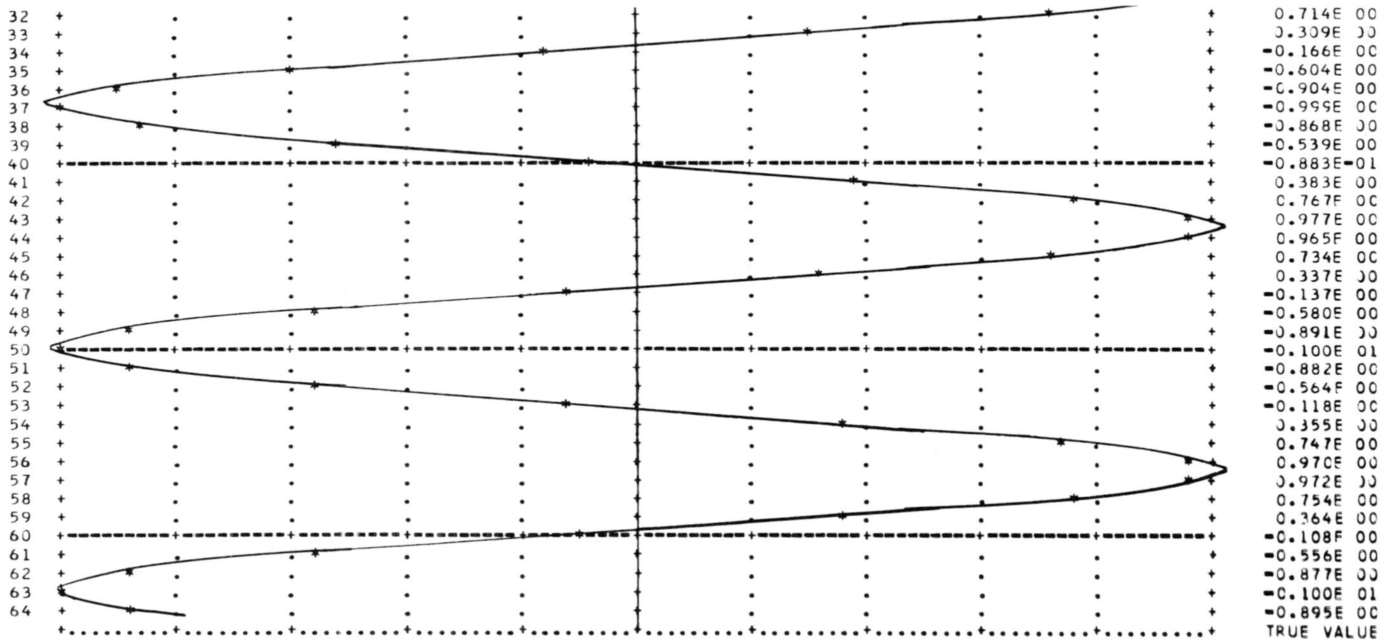

Figure 3-17. $x(t)$ Time Series (Sinusoidal Cross-correlation Experiment).

THIS IS A COSINEUSOID OF FREQUENCY 4.0 HZ.

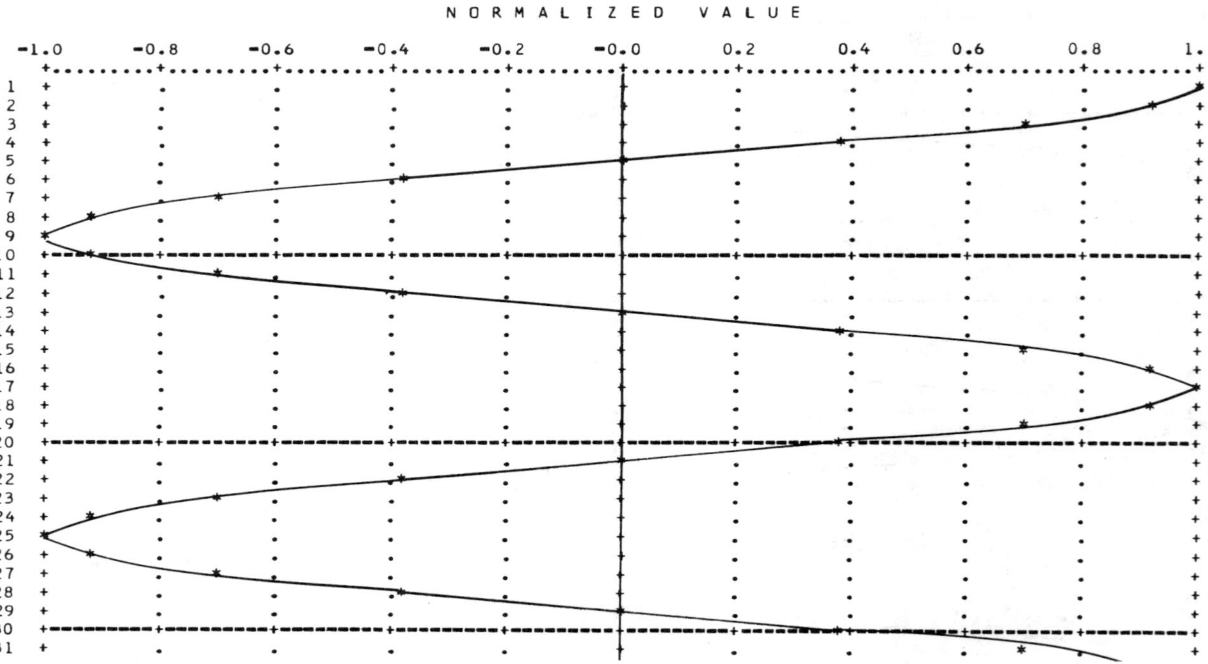

	TRUE VALUE
1	0.100E 01
2	0.924E 00
3	0.707E 00
4	0.383E 00
5	0.628E-06
6	-0.383E 00
7	-0.707E 00
8	-0.924E 00
9	-0.100E 01
10	-0.924E 00
11	-0.707E 00
12	-0.383E 00
13	-0.221E-05
14	0.383E 00
15	0.707E 00
16	0.924E 00
17	0.100E 01
18	0.924E 00
19	0.707E 00
20	0.383E 00
21	0.930E-06
22	-0.383E 00
23	-0.707E 00
24	-0.924E 00
25	-0.100E 01
26	-0.924E 00
27	-0.707E 00
28	-0.383E 00
29	-0.347E-05
30	0.383E 00
31	0.707E 00

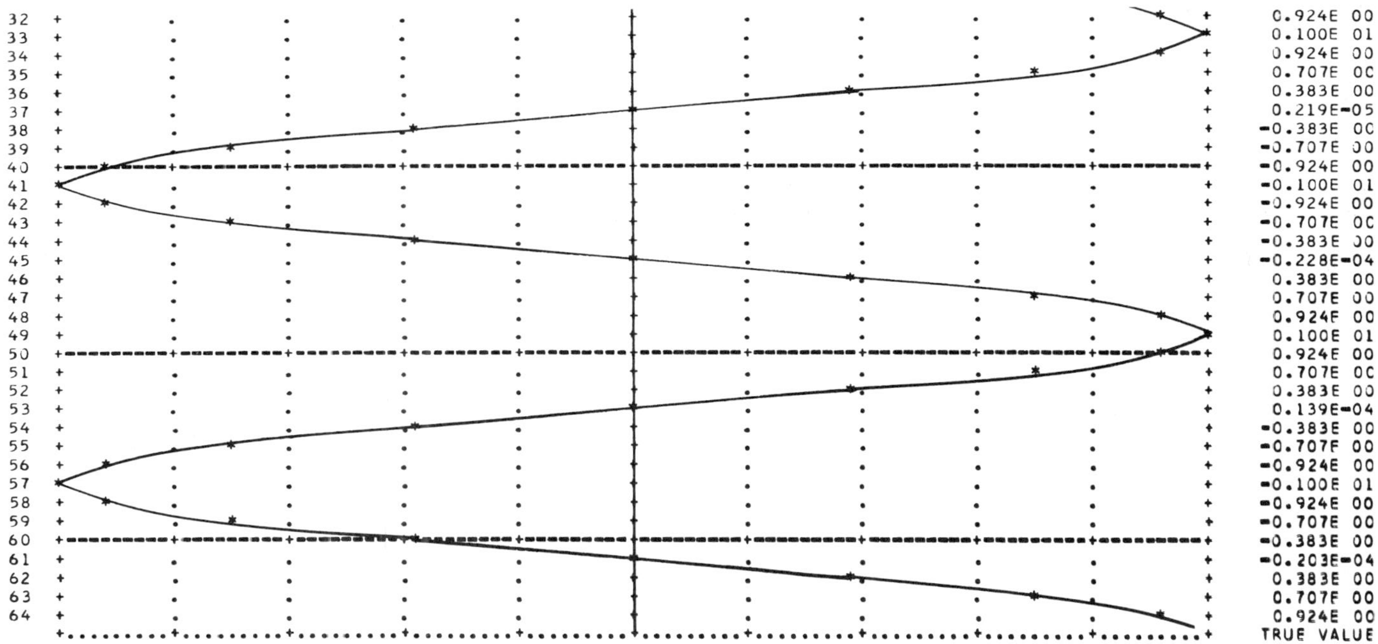

Figure 3-18. $y(t)$ Time Series (Sinusoidal Cross-correlation Experiment).

THIS IS A CROSS-CORRELATION OF THE SINE AND COSINE

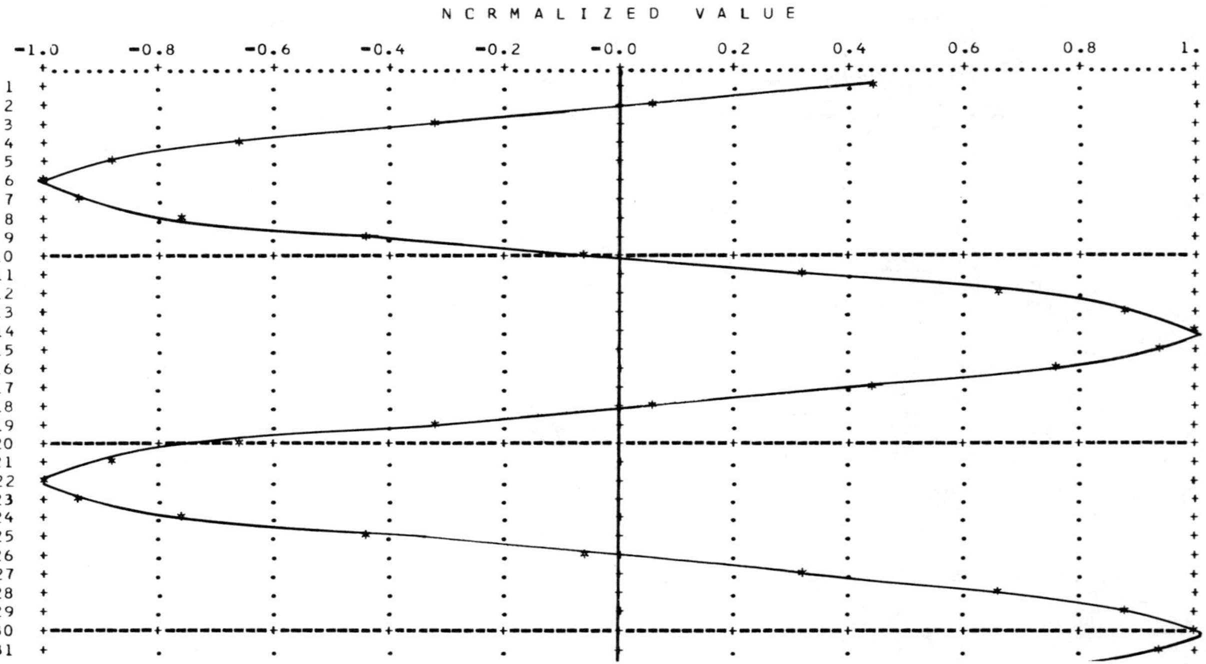

	TRUE VALUE
1	0.231E-01
2	0.332E-02
3	-0.169E-01
4	-0.346E-01
5	-0.470E-01
6	-0.523E-01
7	-0.496E-01
8	-0.393E-01
9	-0.231E-01
10	-0.332E-02
11	0.169E-01
12	0.346E-01
13	0.470E-01
14	0.523E-01
15	0.496E-01
16	0.393E-01
17	0.231E-01
18	0.332E-02
19	-0.169E-01
20	-0.346E-01
21	-0.470E-01
22	-0.523E-01
23	-0.496E-01
24	-0.393E-01
25	-0.231E-01
26	-0.332E-02
27	0.169E-01
28	0.346E-01
29	0.470E-01
30	0.523E-01
31	0.496E-01

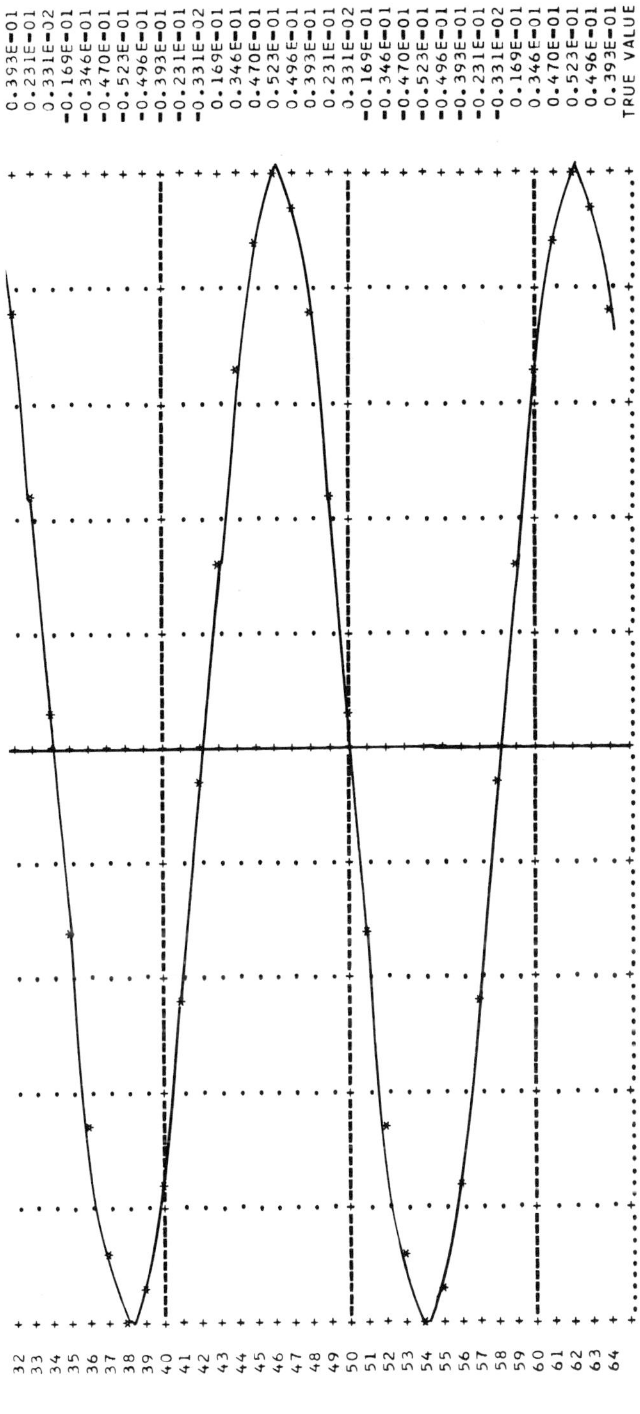

Figure 3-19. Cross-correlation (Sinusoidal Cross-correlation Experiment).

THE MAGNITUDE OF THE CROSS POWER SPECTRAL DENSITY

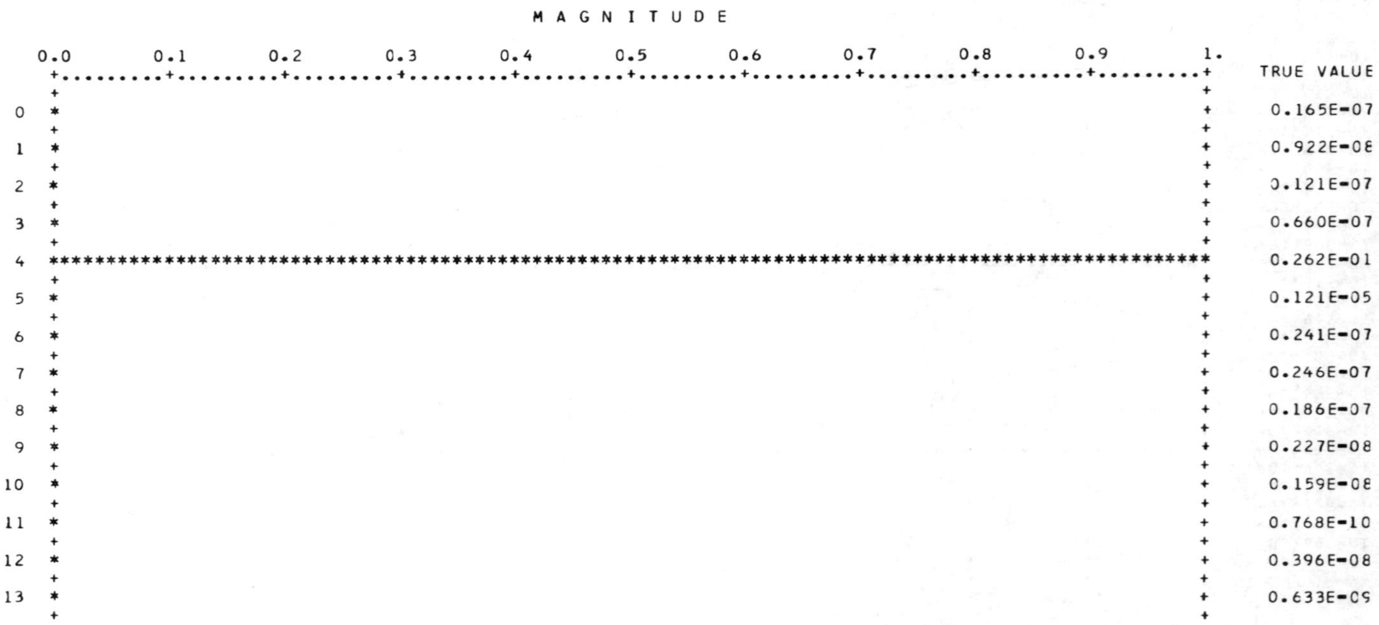

Figure 3-20. $G_{xy}(f)$ (Sinusoidal Cross-correlation Experiment).

2. Produce R_{xx} using program AUTO-C
3. Produce R_{yy} using program AUTO-C

These computations will be done using option 0 if no WRAP-AROUND protection is required; option 1 will be used otherwise. Once these preliminary calculations have been performed and the results stored in arrays A, B, and C, the cross-correlation coefficient can be synthesized. It is produced by calling program CROSS-C option 3.

To demonstrate this SPECTRUM IV capability, the following experiment is performed. Let $x(t)$ and $y(t)$ be defined as follows:

$$x(t) = \text{a pulse of duty cycle } 0.5$$

$$y(t) = x(t) + N(0.0,\ 1.0)$$

where $N(0.0,1.0)$ denotes normally distributed, zero mean, variance one noise.

The control card sequence associated with this experiment is found in Figure 3-21. It can be noted that the final CROSS-C call is with respect to option 3. The signal source $x(t)$ and $y(t)$ can be found in Figures 3-22 and 3-23 respectively. The result of preprocessing the data in the manner previously specified can be found in Figures 3-24, 25 and 26. Finally, the desired cross-correlation coefficient is found in Figure 3-27. Note that this coefficient indicates that the pulse and pulse plus noise have a similarity profile like that found when a pulse is correlated with itself. If $y(t)$ were completely devoid of noise, the resulting cross-correlation coefficient would have value 1 at $\tau = 0$, and value 0 at $\tau = 0.5$ seconds. However, the additive noise never allows $x(t)$ and $y(t)$ to become totally identical or dissimilar. Therefore the values of the cross-correlation never achieve a value of 1 or 0.

D. Coherence Function

It has been stated that a transfer function is indispensable to linear system theory. Implicit in the definition of a transfer function are certain assumptions. If a transfer function $H(f)$ is defined in terms of an input process $x(t)$ and output process $y(t)$ as follows:

$$H(f) = \frac{Y(f)}{X(f)}$$

the system is assumed: (1) to be linear; (2) to be free from any internal noise source; and (3) to have only one input signal source, namely, $x(t)$.[c] That is,

[c] A nonzero initial condition can be thought of as an extraneous input, that is, not included in $x(t)$.

```
CARD        COLUMN                                                                          8Ø
            123456789Ø12     .        .        .        .        .        .        .

1           LIBRARY       B                                                    4Ø       4Ø.ØØ
2           THIS IS A SQUARE PULSE                            2  2.Ø  Ø.Ø        .5ØØ
3           PLOTTER       B                                                    4Ø
4           TIME               1   4Ø   THIS IS THE PULSE AMP=2.Ø   DUTY CYCLE .5
5           LIBRARY       C                                                    4Ø       4Ø.ØØ
6           THIS IS A PULSE + N(Ø.Ø,1.Ø)                      9  2.Ø  Ø.Ø        .5Ø 1.ØØ
7           PLOTTER       C                                                    4Ø
8           TIME               1   4Ø   PULSE + GAUSSIAN NOISE N(Ø.Ø,1.Ø)
9           CROSS-C       B    C
1Ø          PLOTTER       A                                                    4Ø
11          TIME               1   4Ø   THIS IS THE CROSS-CORRELATION RESULTS
12          AUTO-C        B
13          PLOTTER       B                                                    4Ø
14          TIME               1   4Ø   THIS IS THE AUTO-CORRELATION OF THE PULSE
15          AUTO-C        C
16          PLOTTER       C                                                    4Ø
17          TIME               1   4Ø   THIS IS THE AUTO-CORRELATION OF PULSE + N(Ø.Ø,1.Ø)
18          CROSS-C       B    C                                                             3
19          PLOTTER       A                                                    4Ø
2Ø          TIME               1   4Ø   THIS IS THE CROSS-CORRELATION COEFFICIENT
21          TERM
                    .        .        .        .        .        .        .        .
```

Figure 3-21. Card Control Sequence for Cross-correlation Experiment.

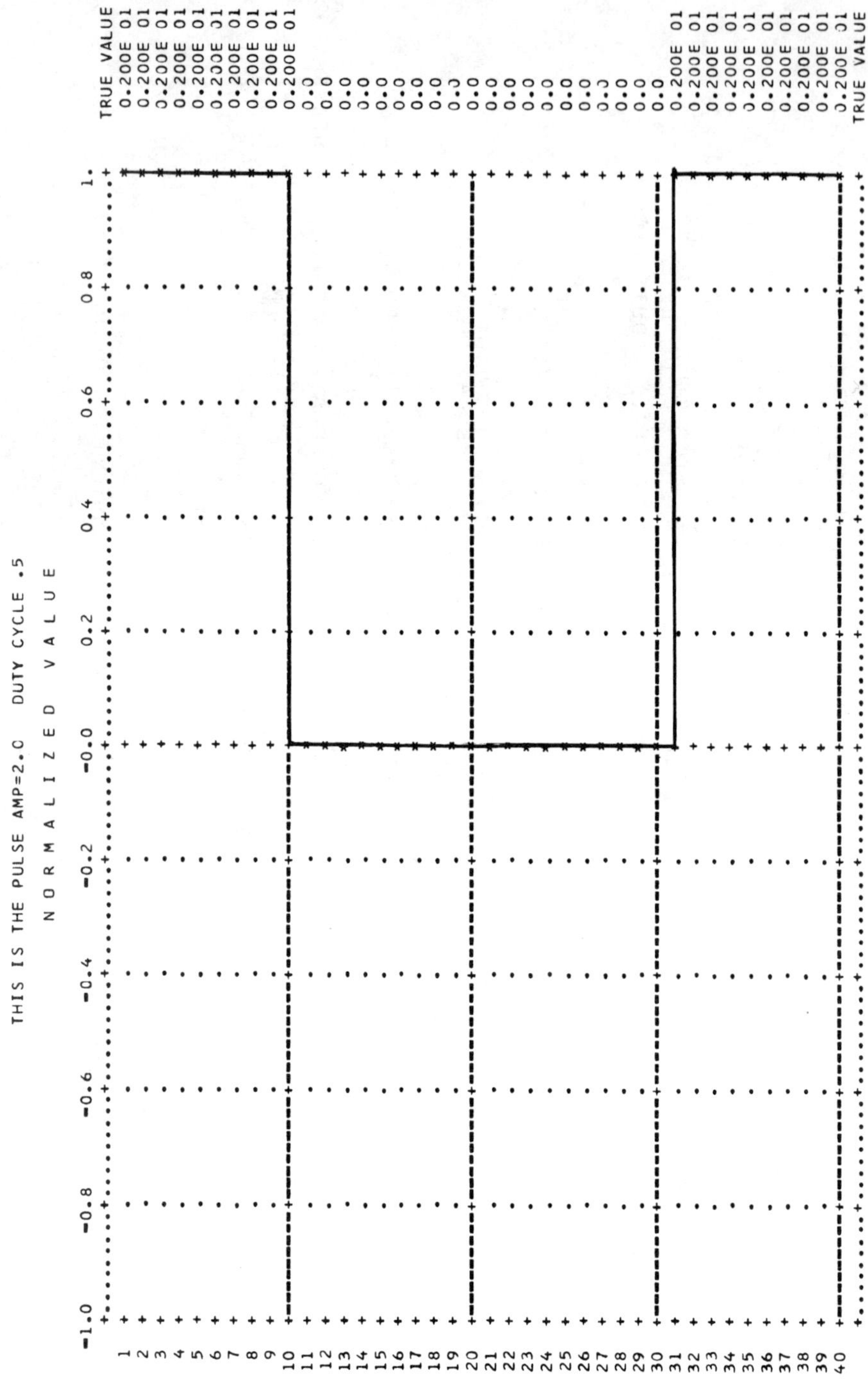

Figure 3-22. $x(t)$ Time Series (Cross-correlation Experiment).

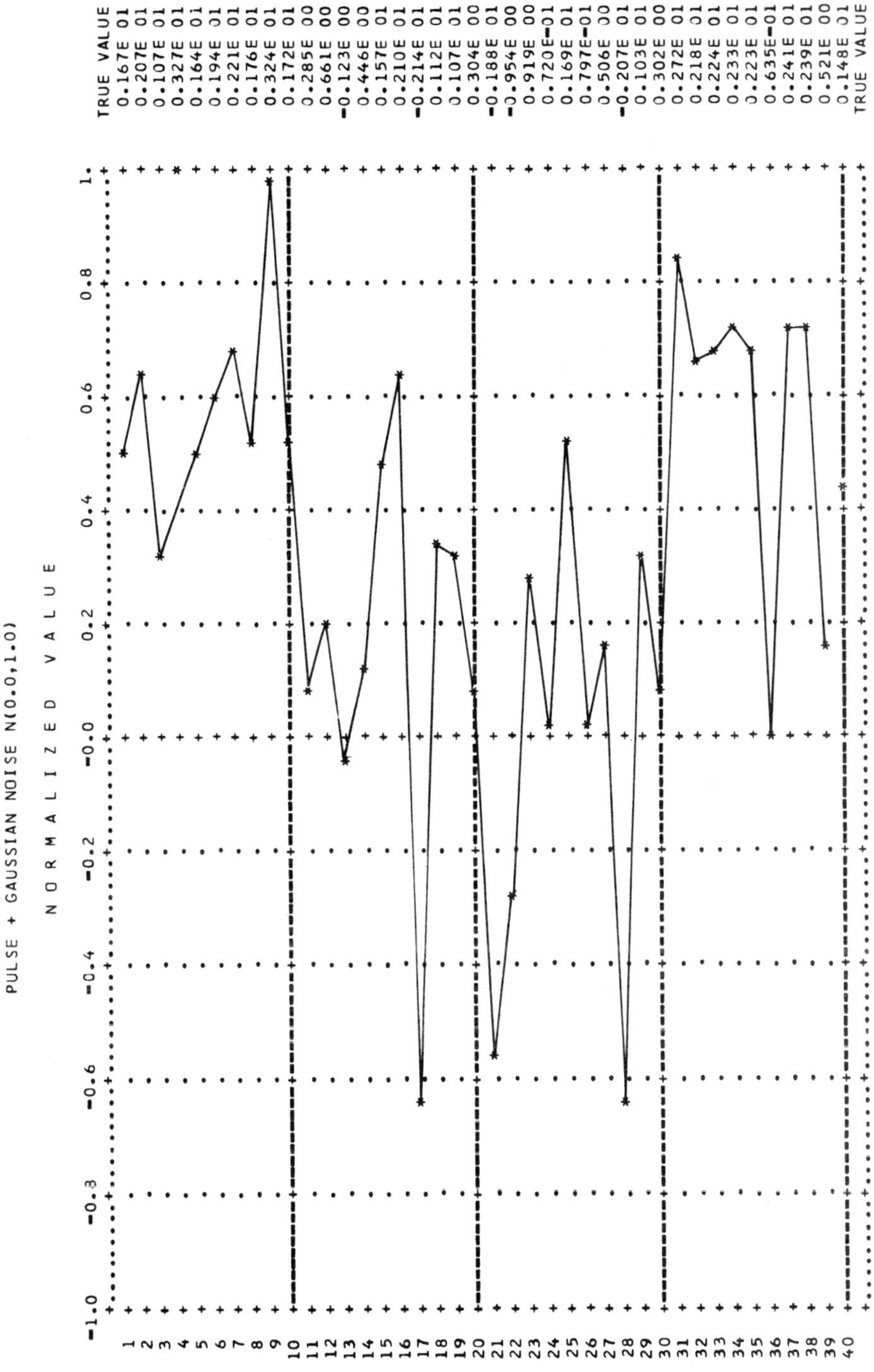

Figure 3-23. $y(t)$ Time Series (Cross-correlation Experiment).

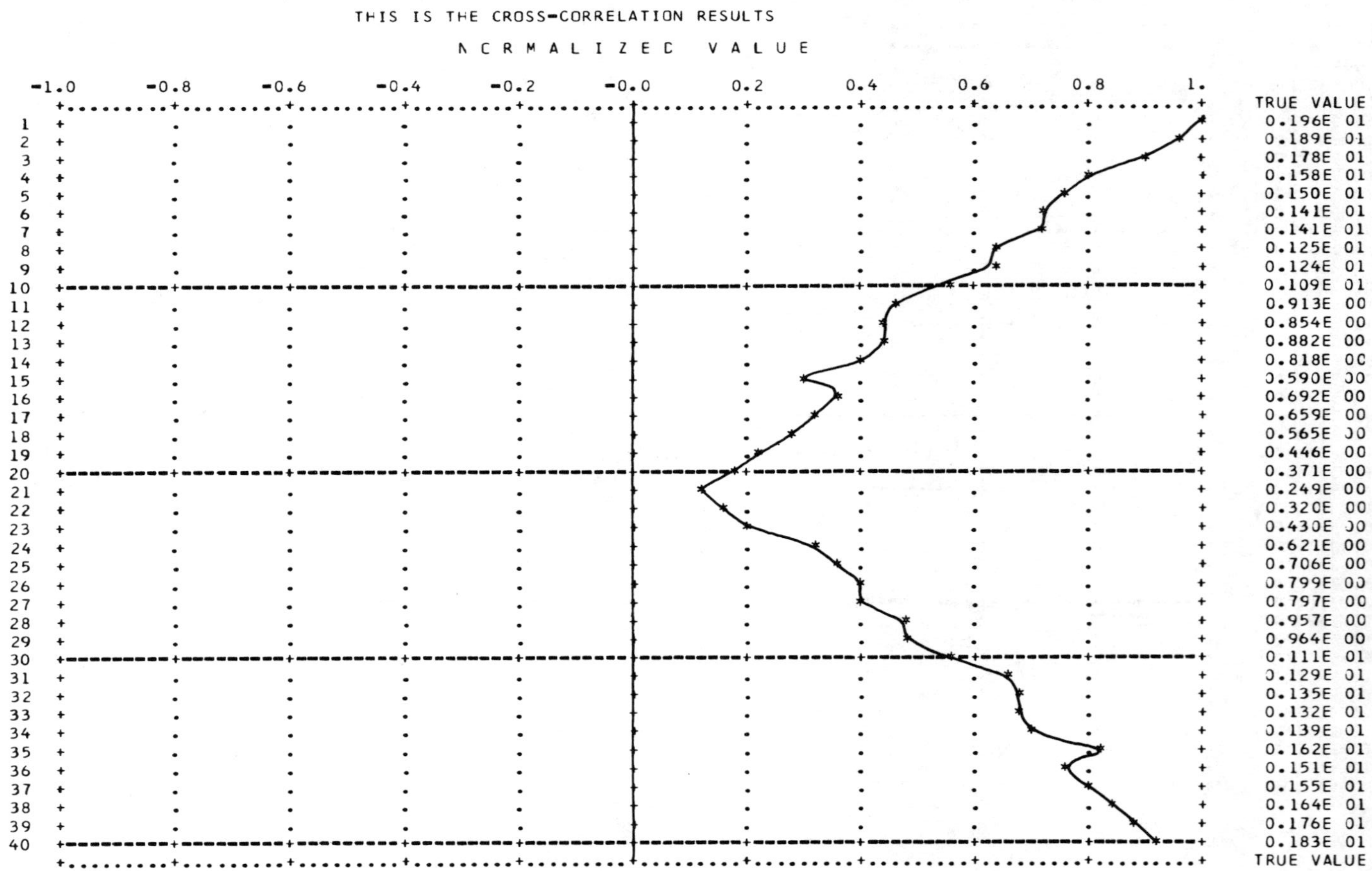

Figure 3-24. Cross-correlation.

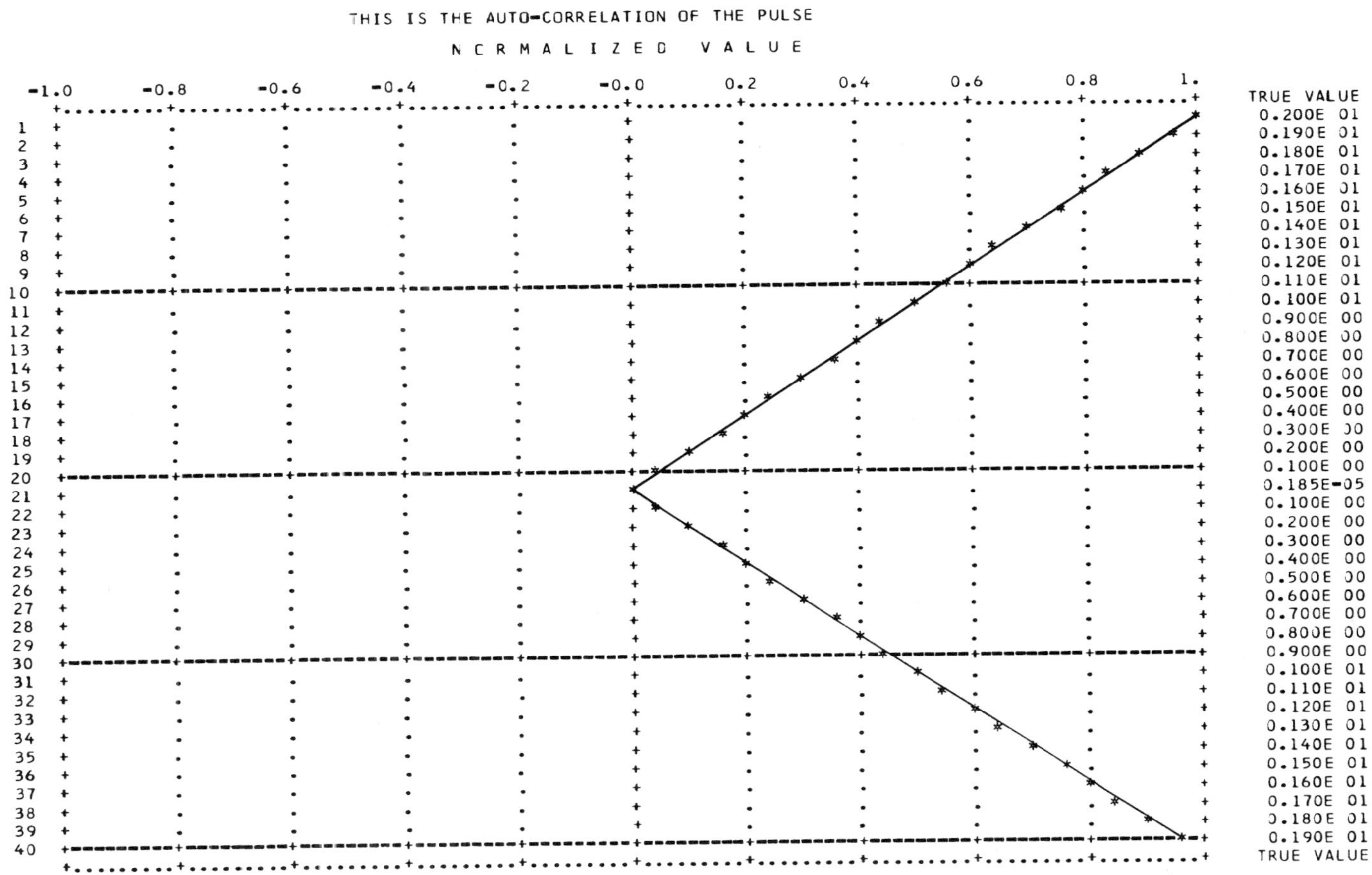

Figure 3-25. Autocorrelation of $x(t)$ (Cross-correlation Experiment).

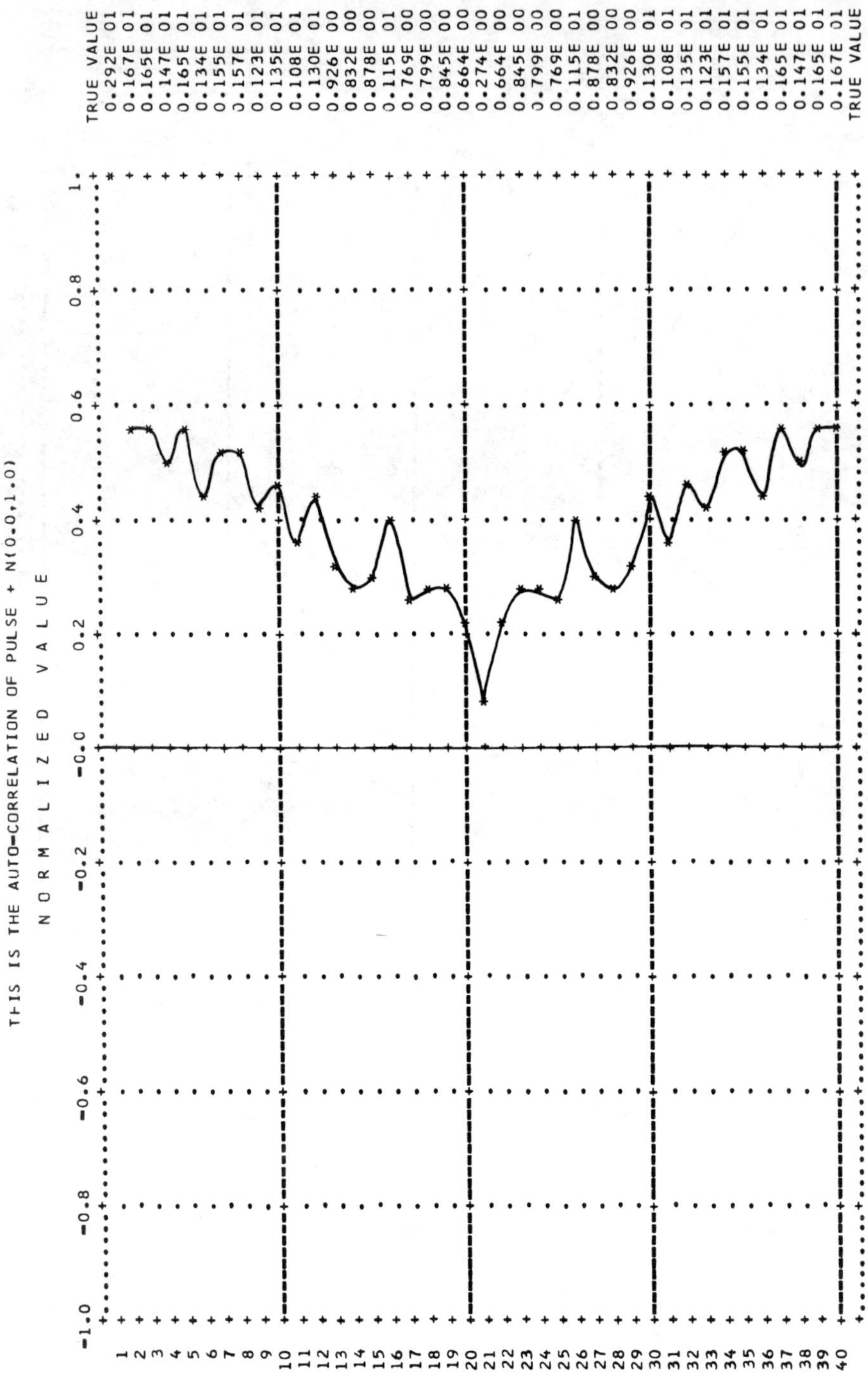

Figure 3-26. Autocorrelation of $y(t)$ (Cross-correlation Experiment).

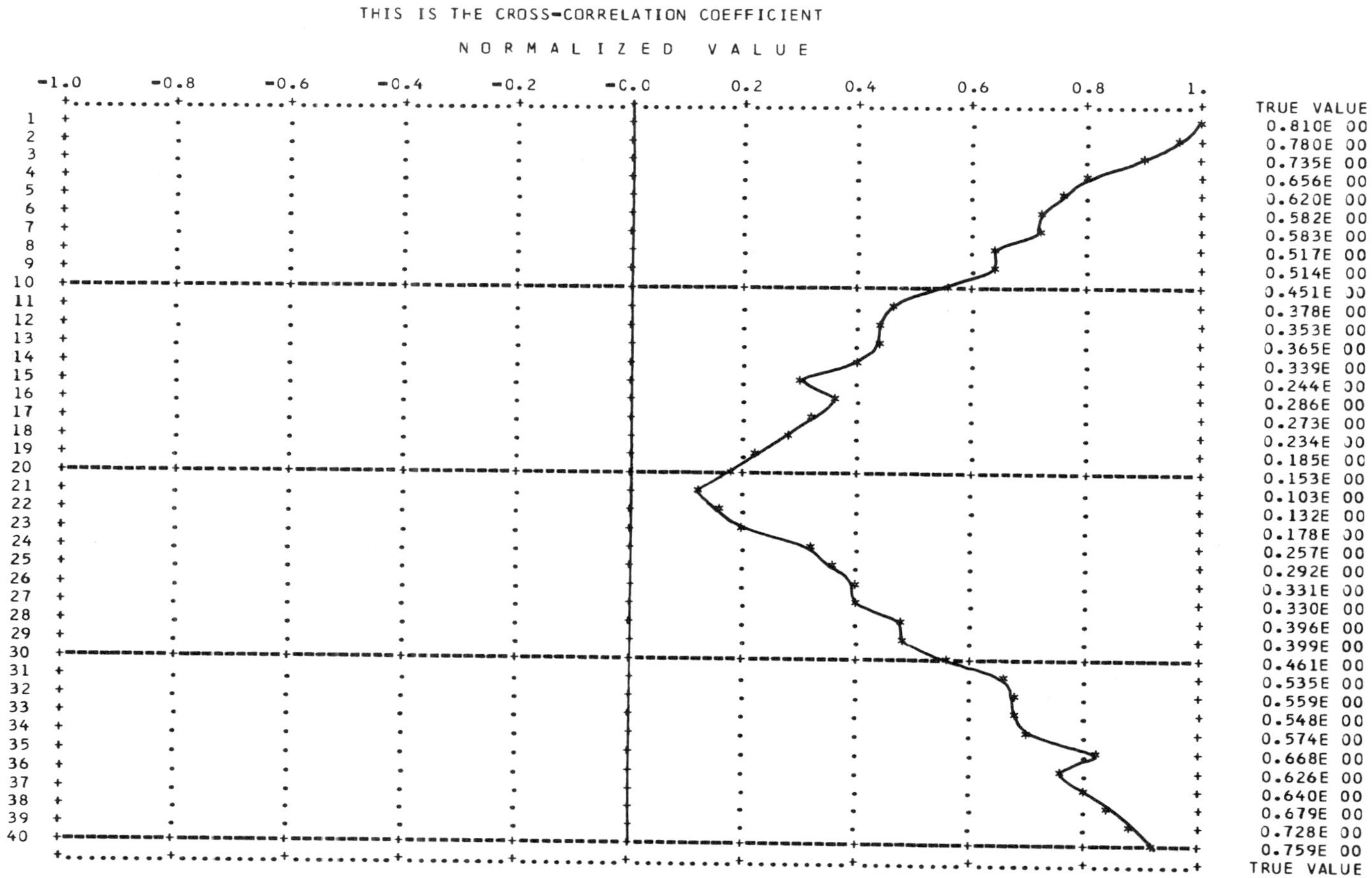

Figure 3-27. Cross-correlation Coefficient.

there are no extraneous system inputs. However, the system under consideration may not conform to this hypothesis. The possible deviations can be the result of nonlinearities, noise, or multiple signal sources (see Figure 3-28).

If the degree of nonlinearity, internal noise, or extraneous input activity is small, a linear model may be sufficiently accurate as an analysis tool. However, without a detailed theoretical or experimental analysis, the true nature of the system may not be completely understood. There is, however, a useful technique that will allow the user to test a system against hypothesis one through three. This test is called the coherence function.

The coherence function will test the validity of a transfer function representation of a system, which is sometimes referred to as a measure of linear causality. That is, it measures what portion of a system's output is due to a linear operation on its input. The coherence function will test a system only against hypotheses one through three. It will not tell the user the nature of any system distortion—that is, the coherence function cannot differentiate between nonlinearities, noise sources, or multiple inputs. Only the existence of such distortions can be detected through a coherence analysis.

The coherence function has a value between zero and one. A value of one indicates that the output is due to a linear operation on the input. A value of zero indicates that the output was not due to a linear operation solely on the input process $x(t)$. Values between one and zero are to be interpreted with respect to the limiting case previously stated. Program COHERNCE will allow a SPECTRUM IV user to perform a coherence operation on an input-output pair.

Theory

Consider Figure 3-29. Let the noise process $n(t)$ represent the effects of internal random noise, nonlinearities, and multiple inputs.

To measure the linear dependence of the output $z(t)$ on an input $x(t)$, one might look at their cross-correlation, or equivalently, investigate their cross-power spectral density. It was noted in the cross-correlation section that the cross-power spectral density of two signals, say, $z_1(t)$ and $z_2(t)$, whose transforms are $Z_1(f)$ and $Z_2(f)$, respectively, is given by $G_{z_1z_2}(f)$, where

$$\begin{aligned} G_{z_1z_2}(f) &= Z_1(f)\overset{*}{Z_2(f)} \\ &= [Re\{Z_1(f)\} + iI_m\{Z_1(f)\}]\,[Re\{Z_2(f)\} - iI_m\{Z_2(f)\}] \end{aligned} \tag{3.20}$$

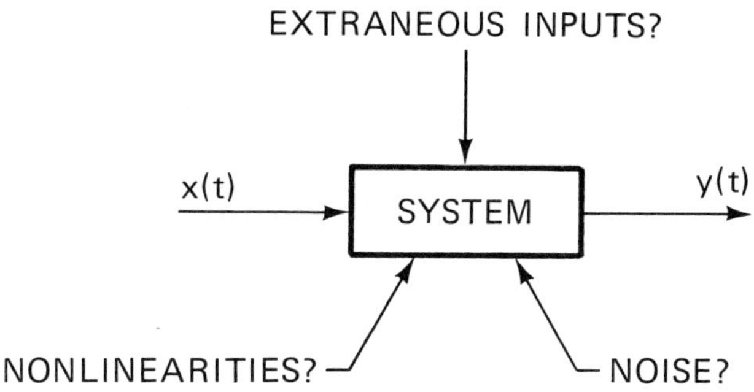

Figure 3-28. Generalized System.

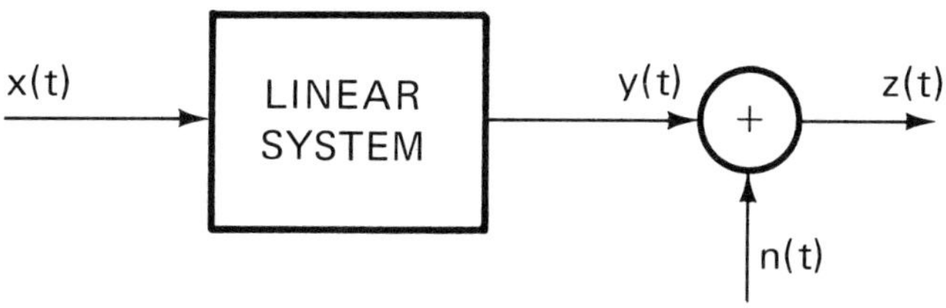

Figure 3-29. System Model.

Noting $z(t) = y(t) + n(t)$, which implies $Z(f) = Y(f) + N(f)$, the cross-power spectral density of output $z(t)$ to input $x(t)$ is

$$\begin{aligned} G_{zx}(f) &= [Y(f) + N(f)]X^*(f) \\ &= [Y(f)X^*(f) + N(f)X^*(f)] \\ &= G_{yx}(f) + G_{nx}(f) \end{aligned} \tag{3.21}$$

Since $G_{zx}(f)$ is the sum of a noise-free process $G_{yx}(f)$ and a noisy process $G_{nx}(f)$, it is impossible to measure what the relative strength of each is, looking only at $G_{zx}(f)$.

However, if this experiment was repeated a sufficient number of times, a trend might be identified. Let $\mathscr{E}$ denote the expectation operator such that the average value of an arbitrary random process, say q, is

$$\mathscr{E}(q) = \frac{1}{N}\sum_{i=1}^{N} q_i \tag{3.22}$$

The contributions of $x(t)$ to $z(t)$ can now be measured as follows:

Define $\delta^2(f)$ to be the coherence function, where

$$\delta^2(f) = \frac{\mathscr{E}[G_{yy}(f)]}{\mathscr{E}[G_{yy}(f)] + \mathscr{E}[G_{nn}(f)]} \tag{3.23}$$

Equation (3.23) defines a real number between 0 and 1. If δ^2 is near unity, the noise-free signal $y(t)$ dominates the noise process $n(t)$. If δ^2 has a value near zero, the contrapositive is true. However, from a physical standpoint, it is not reasonable to expect that the signal $y(t)$ is obtainable from direct measurements. Therefore the following formula for δ^2 is presented in terms of the directly measured input-output variables $x(t)$ and $z(t)$, respectively. Note

$$\begin{aligned}\delta^2(f) &= \frac{\mathscr{E}[G_{yy}(f)]}{\mathscr{E}[G_{yy}(f)] + \mathscr{E}[G_{nn}(f)]} \\ &= \frac{\mathscr{E}[G_{xx}(f)][G_{yy}(f)]}{\mathscr{E}[G_{xx}(f)]\{\mathscr{E}[G_{yy}(f)] + \mathscr{E}[G_{nn}(f)]\}}\end{aligned} \tag{3.24}$$

It is reasonable to consider the noise process $n(t)$ to be uncorrelated with either noise-free process $x(t)$ or $y(t)$. That is, if a sufficient number of individual experiments are performed, on the average,

$$\mathscr{E}[R_{nx}(\tau)] \to 0 \tag{3.25}$$

and

$$\mathscr{E}[R_{ny}(\tau)] \to 0 \tag{3.26}$$

then

$$\mathscr{E}[G_{nx}(f)] \to 0 \tag{3.27}$$

and

$$\mathscr{E}[G_{ny}(f)] \to 0 \tag{3.28}$$

Therefore, from $z(t) = y(t) + n(t)$, a direct computation yields

$$\begin{aligned}\mathscr{E}[G_{zz}(f)] &= \mathscr{E}\{[Y(f) + N(f)][Y(f) + N(f)]^*\} \\ &= \mathscr{E}[G_{yy}(f)] + \mathscr{E}[G_{nn}(f)] + \mathscr{E}[G_{ny}(f)] + \mathscr{E}[G_{yn}(f)] \\ &= \mathscr{E}[G_{yy}(f)] + \mathscr{E}[G_{nn}(f)]\end{aligned} \tag{3.29}$$

Therefore Equation (3.24) can be written as

$$\delta^2(f) = \frac{\mathscr{E}[G_{xx}(f)]\,\mathscr{E}[G_{yy}(f)]}{\mathscr{E}[G_{xx}(f)]\,\mathscr{E}[G_{zz}(f)]} \tag{3.30}$$

Finally, note that the numerator of (3.30) can be rewritten as

$$\mathscr{E}[G_{xx}(f)]\,\mathscr{E}[G_{yy}(f)] = \mathscr{E}[X(f)X(f)^*]\,\mathscr{E}[Y(f)Y(f)]^*$$

$$= \mathscr{E}[X(f)Y^*(f)]\,\mathscr{E}[Y(f)X^*(f)]$$
$$= \mathscr{E}[G_{yx}(f)]\,\mathscr{E}[G_{xy}{}^*(f)]$$
$$= |[G_{yx}(f)]|^2 \qquad (3.31)$$

But from Equation (3.21),

$$\mathscr{E}[G_{zx}(f)] = \mathscr{E}[G_{yx}(f)] + \mathscr{E}[G_{nx}(f)]$$
$$= \mathscr{E}[G_{yx}(f)] \qquad (3.32)$$

Therefore, combining (3.30),(3.31), and (3.32) one obtains δ^2 in terms of $x(t)$ and $z(t)$ only, namely,[d]

$$\delta^2 = \frac{|\mathscr{E}[G_{zx}(f)]|^2}{\mathscr{E}[G_{zz}(f)]\,\mathscr{E}[G_{xx}(f)]} \qquad (3.33)$$

It can be noted that δ^2 of Equation (3.33) is defined in terms of measurable input-output quantities, namely, $x(t)$ and $z(t)$. If the system is a noise-free, single-input linear system, then from Equation (3.29),

$$\mathscr{E}[G_{zz}(f)] = G_{yy}(f) \qquad (3.34)$$

and from Equation (3.32),

$$\mathscr{E}[G_{zx}(f)] = G_{yx}(f)$$

Therefore

$$\delta^2(f) = \frac{|G_{yx}(f)|^2}{G_{yy}(f)G_{xx}(f)} = 1$$

for all frequency *independent of the system transfer function*. δ^2 is computed independent of any transfer function knowledge or model. This is important to the experimental scientist. If there is a noise contribution in $z(t)$, at frequency f, then $\delta^2(f) < 1$. Some frequencies may exhibit a high degree of causality, whereas other frequencies have a low measure of causality. Program COHERNCE will allow a SPECTRUM IV user to perform a coherence operation. The coherence function is produced as shown in Figure 3-30.

Execution of COHERNCE

A coherence operation can be performed by using the eight-letter mnemonic COHERNCE. COHERNCE will operate on cross-spectral

[d] Ensemble averaging is accomplished under SPECTRUM IV control through the application of FREQ-AVG.

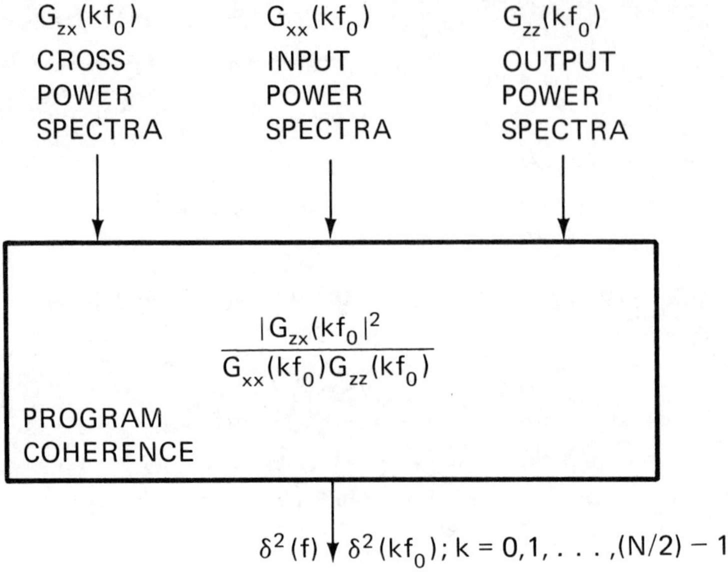

Figure 3-30. Program COHERNCE.

density data (entered into array A) and PSD representations of the measurable input and output time-series processes (entered into array B and C). The working arrays A, B, and C are in use simultaneously during a coherence operation. It is desired that these arrays be nonvolatile, that is, that they not be destroyed. Therefore a storage array does not exist into which $\delta^2(f)$ can be inserted. Under SPECTRUM IV control the resulting coherence function is listed in tabular form as it is computed and simultaneously stored in a temporary location register. Because there is potentially a divide fault in the calculation of δ^2, the interpolation method discussed in the transfer function section of this chapter is incorporated in the COHERNCE program. Restrictions imposed on a COHERNCE operation are:

1. All arrays must be in the frequency domain.
2. All sampling frequencies must be equal.
3. The record length of all arrays must be equal.
4. The information must conform to the following array rule. Array

$$A \Rightarrow \mathscr{E}G_{zx}(f)$$

$$B \Rightarrow \mathscr{E}G_{xx}(f) \text{ or } G_{zz}(f)$$

$$C \Rightarrow \mathscr{E}G_{zz}(f) \text{ or } G_{xx}(f)$$

5. Array B or C cannot be the null array.

The control card sequence required of a COHERNCE operation is shown in Table 3-4. SPECTRUM IV automatically outputs labels defining sampling and record size values. A coherence call automatically outputs, in tabular form, the coherence values for all positive harmonics of the input sampling rate as well as storing the coherence data record in a temporary storage location. If desired or applicable, program DISK OUT can be used to store this temporary array on disk. The data that would now be on disk can be used for further SPECTRUM IV analysis or display. If a divide fault is encountered, COHERNCE will attempt to remove it through a linear interpolation. SPECTRUM IV will produce a message indicating whether the operation succeeded or failed.

The example problem in this section makes use of multiple nesting of many SPECTRUM IV operations. Found in this example are disk input operations and optional display calls. These operations are documented in the discussions of input requirements and output requirements in Chapter 1 and of disk information in Chapter 5. It is strongly suggested that the user duplicate the following example before attempting to create a COHERNCE analysis over an arbitary signal set.

Example. There are two methods of performing a coherence analysis under SPECTRUM IV control. They differ only in how the input-output signal processes are treated. In one approach, the input-output time series are destroyed after use (volatile input-output space) whereas the other technique stores the input-output space for possible future use (nonvolatile input-output space). The two methods are presented in block diagram form and in Figures 3-31a and b.

Suppose m input-output experiments are performed and their time series recorded. Then:

1. Volatile input-output space approach (see Figure 3-31a)
   A. Over m experiments
      Step 1. Enter input-output time series
      Step 2. Compute cross-power spectral density
      Step 3. Compute input-output power spectral densities
      Step 4. Store frequency-domain results of steps 2 and 3

Table 3-4
Structure of a COHERNCE Call

Column Number	*Description*	*Format or Contents*
Primary information card		
1-8	Calls COHERNCE	COHERNCE

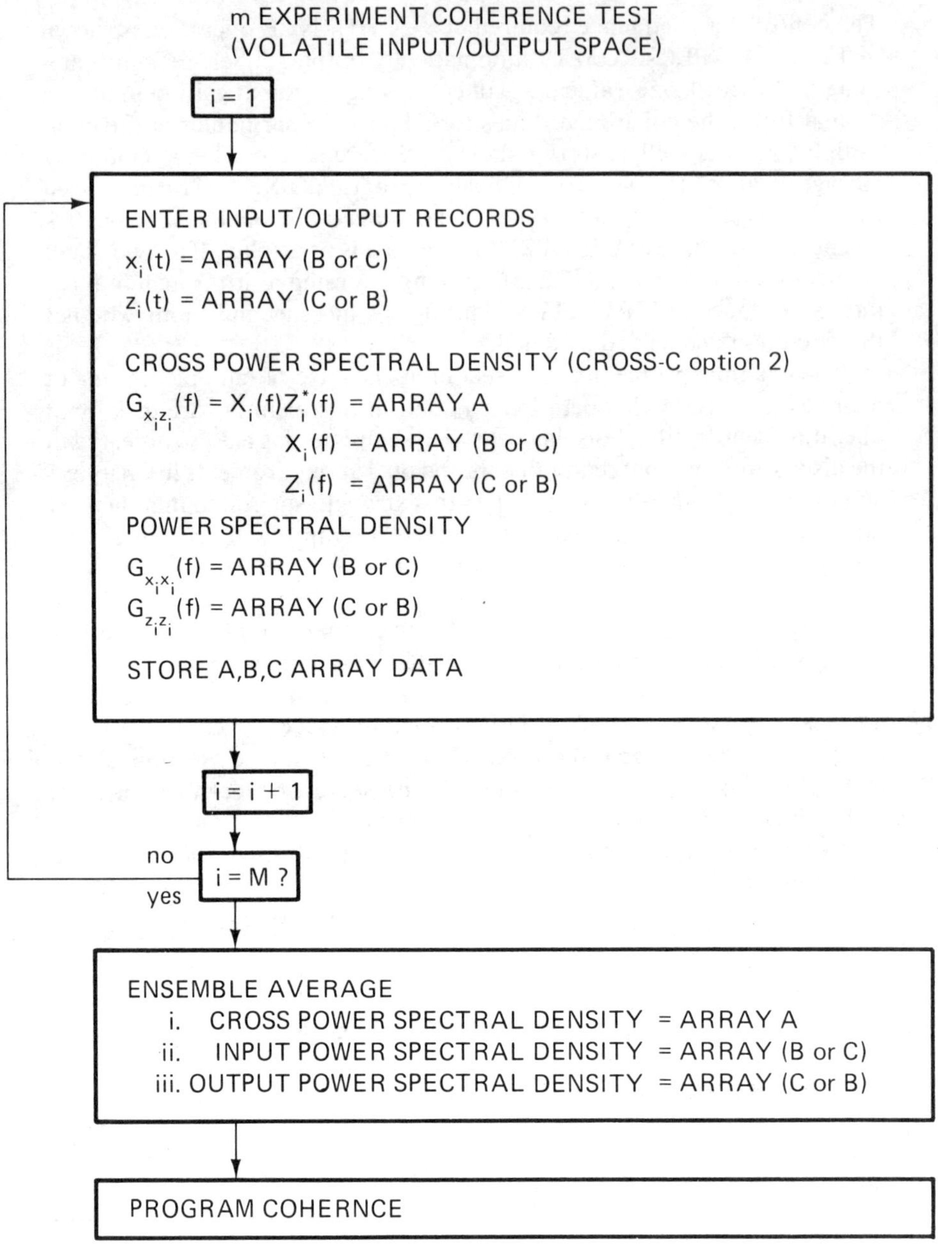

Figure 3-31. *m* Experiment Coherence Test: (a) Volatile Input-Output Space; (b) Nonvolatile Input-Output Space.

m EXPERIMENT COHERENCE TEST
(NON-VOLATILE INPUT/OUTPUT SPACE)

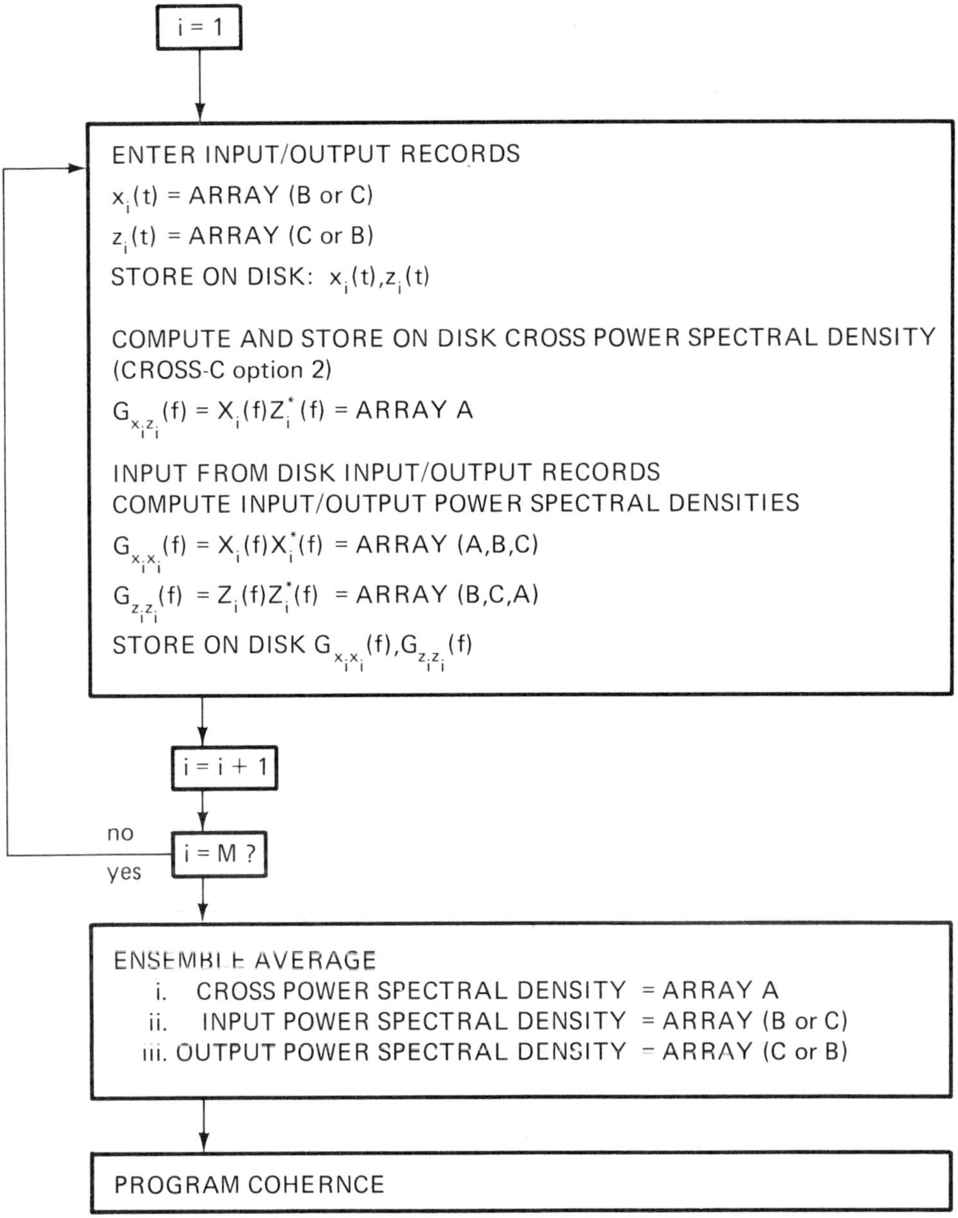

B. Ensemble average m frequency-domain data records

C. Perform coherence analysis

2. Nonvolatile input-ouput space approach (see Figure 3-31b)

A. Over m experiments

Step 1. Enter and store input-output time series
Step 2. Compute cross-power spectral density
Step 3. Re-enter input-output time series; compute input-output power spectral densities
Step 4. Store frequency-domain results

B. Ensemble average m frequency-domain data records

C. Perform coherence analysis

Recall that a coherence test requires that input-output cross-ensemble-averaged power spectral densities be presented to program COHERNCE. Ensemble averaging, in the frequency domain, is accomplished through a FREQ-AVG operation. (This SPECTRUM IV function is documented in Chapter 5.) Finally, the user should remain aware that the result of a COHERNCE call is found in a temporary array. Upon successfully completion of a COHERNCE operation, the contents of the temporary array is presented to the user in tabular form. If the user wishes to preserve this data for future use of display, it must be stored through a DISK OUT operation (see pp. 308-309 in Chapter 5.) There is an optional parameter policy that will allow the temporary data array to be preserved on disk.

The following numerical example is presented to demonstrate a Nonvolatile coherence analysis. Consider the following single-pole system whose transfer function is given by $H(s)$, where

$$H(s) = \frac{1}{(s + 3)}$$

If the system input, say, $x(t)$, is an impulse function, then the system output, in the absence of any noise corruption, will be $y(t)$, where

$$y(t) = \exp(-3t)$$

Suppose that noise is added to the output process in the form of $n(t)$. Then the actual system output would be some $z(t)$, where

$$z(t) = y(t) + n(t)$$

In the presence of additive output noise, it is reasonable to assume that at some frequencies of the output spectra there would be energy components that are not entirely a result of linear operations on the input process. Therefore it should be expected that a coherence analysis of this experiment should have nonunity values.

To test this hypothesis, consider the additive noise to be normally distributed, mean value zero, variance 0.1. (A flow chart of the experiment can be found in Figure 3-32.) The disk data record identification numbers are included in this diagram. The card control sequence required of this experiment can be found in Figure 3-33. Several points of interest are the use of an optional parameter to add the LIBRARY noise process number 10 to a USER LIB call through an augmentation process and the use of DISK IN and DISK OUT calls. The noise process used in this example was normally distributed, mean 0, variance 0.1. The user should note that the use of an optional disk control parameter, which will allow the user to store the temporary data array as a disk file. The noise-free input-output processes can be found in source form in Figure 3-34. Here the input impulse and output exponential appear as indirect address programs 50 and 1, respectively. The input and noise-corrupted output sample time series can be found in Figures 3-35 and 3-36.

In all, four individual experiments are performed in the manner specified by the nonvolatile approach to coherence analysis (see Figures 3-35 through 3-40). Note the disk file sequential numbering system associated with the DISK OUT operations. A coherence analysis over a single experiment (namely, the fourth experiment) is documented in Figure 3-41 and displayed in Figure 3-47. Using a FREQ-AVG call, the ensemble averages of the input-output/cross-power spectra are found in Figures 3-42 through 3-44. The coherence analysis performed on the ensemble-averaged data set is found in Figure 3-45 and displayed in Figure 3-49. The simple experiment coherence test is noted to have a value of unity everywhere. Based on a single experiment, the input and output spectra will be unique. Therefore transfer function (equivalently the impulse response), defined by the ratio of these spectra, is also unique. The single-record coherence test must assume that the measured output was entirely the result of the inputs being processed by this unique impluse-response function. However, over an ensemble-averaged data set, this is not true (see Figure 3-49). Here it can be noted that at low frequencies the output is primarily the result of a linear operation on the input. Recall that the uncorrupted system output $y(t)$ is rich in low frequencies. Therefore at low frequencies the output is dominated by pure signal power rather than noise power. At high frequencies, the opposite is true. If more than four experiments were performed, a smoother exponential decay of the coherence measure would become more apparent. Obviously, the quality of the coherence analysis is directly proportional to the number of experiments performed. Finally, the disk directory for the problem considered is found in Figure 3-50. A disk directory call can be exercised anytime after the disk system has been initialized (INITIAL).

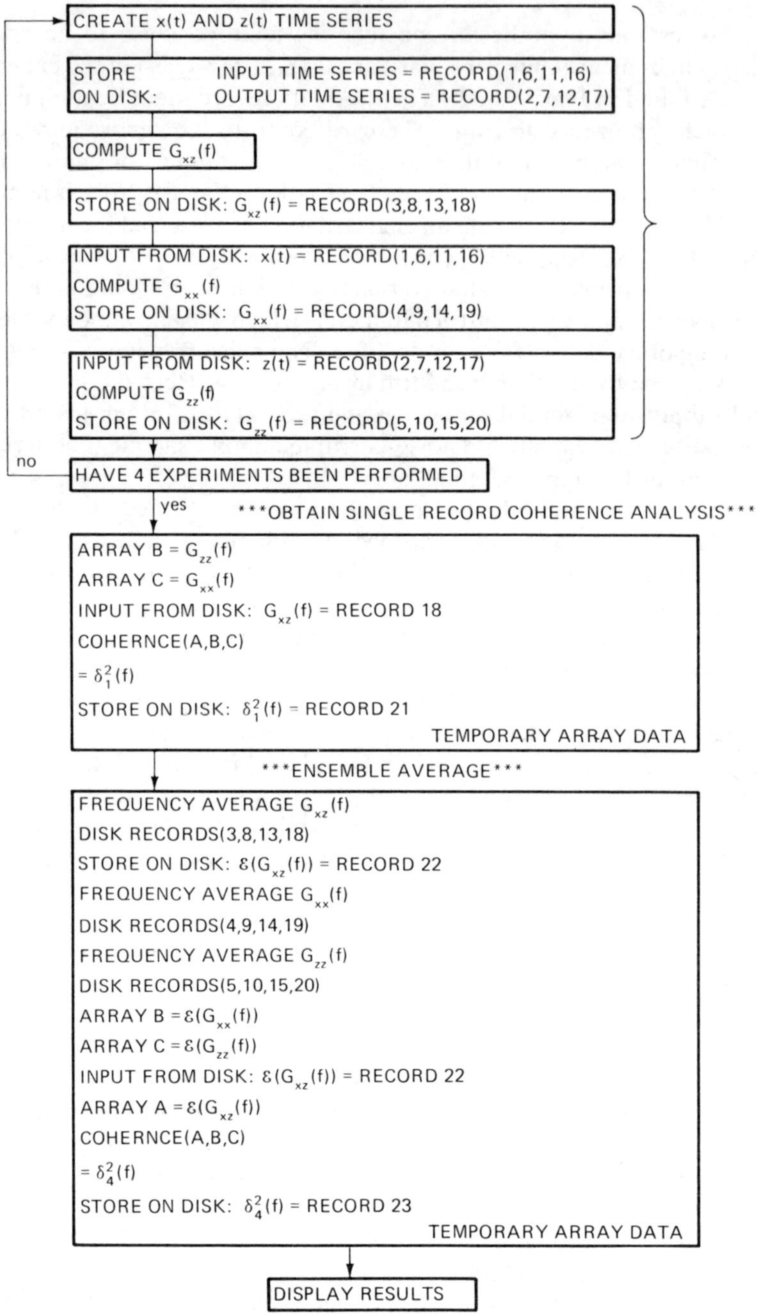

Figure 3-32. Flow Chart of Coherence Example.

```
CARD       COLUMN                                                                              8Ø
           123456789Ø12       .         .         .         .         .         .         .

1          STATUS
2          USER LIB      C                                           48      48.             1
3          THIS IS THE INPUT SIGNAL
4          PLOTTER       C                                           48
5          TIME               1   48    THIS IS THE INPUT SIGNAL
6          USER LIB      B                                           48      48.             2
7          THIS IS A PULSE OF DUTY CYCLE .5          1Ø                      .1
8          PLOTTER       B                                           48
9          TIME               1   48    THIS IS A PULSE OF DUTY CYCLE .5
1Ø         INITIAL
11         DISK OUT      C         TIME                              48      48.
12         THIS IS THE INPUT SIGNAL
13         DISK OUT      B         TIME                              48      48.
14         THIS IS THE OUTPUT SIGNAL PLUS NOISE
15         CROSS-C       B    C                                                              2
16         DISK OUT      A         TIME                              48      48.
17         THIS IS THE CROSS POWER SPECTRAL DENSITY FROM RECORD 1
18         CLEAR-AL
19         DISK IN       C         TIME                              48      48.             1
2Ø         DISK IN       B         TIME                              48      48.             2
21         PSD           C
22         PSD           B
23         DISK OUT      C         TIME                              48      48.
24         THIS IS THE INPUT POWER SPECRAL DENSITY  1
25         DISK OUT      B         TIME                              48      48.
26         THIS IS THE OUTPUT POWER SPECRAL DENSITY   1
27         CLEAR-AL
28         USER LIB      C                                           48      48.
29         THIS IS THE INPUT SIGNAL
```

Figure 3-33. Card Control Sequence for Coherence Example.

```
30     DISK OUT     C           TIME                          48      48.
31     THIS IS THE INPUT SIGNAL
32     USER LIB     B                                         48      48.
33     THIS IS A PULSE OF DUTY CYCLE  .5         1Ø                   .1
34     DISK OUT     B           TIME                          48      48.
33     THIS IS THE OUTPUT SIGNAL + NOISE
34     CROSS-C      B    C                                                     2
35     DISK OUT     A           FREQ                          48      48.
36     THIS IS THE CROSS POWER SPECRAL DENSITY FROM RECORD 2
37     CLEAR-AL
38     DISK IN      C           TIME                          48      48.      6
39     DISK IN      B           TIME                          48      48.      7
4Ø     PSD          C
41     PSD          B
42     DISK OUT     C           FREQ                          48      48.
43     THIS IS THE INPUT POWER SPECTRAL DENSITY  2
44     DISK OUT     B           FREQ                          48      48.
45     THIS IS THE OUTPUT POWER SPECTRAL DENSITY   2
46     CLEAR-AL

       (CONTINUE)

85     THIS IS THE OUTPUT POWER SPECTRAL DENSITY   4
86     DISK IN      A           FREQ                          48      48.     18
87     COHERNCE
88     DISK OUT     A           FREQ                          48      48.      1
89     THIS IS THE COHERENCE FUNCTION FOR A SINGLE RECORD

              (NOTE THE ABOVE COHERENCE ANALYSIS WAS PERFORMED OF
               THE FOURTH EXPERIMENTAL RECORD ONLY)
```

```
90        CLEAR-AL
91        FREQ-AVG                                                       2
92            4   48       48.
93          1  B
94        DISK IN      B          FREQ                    48      48.    3
95          1  B
96        DISK IN      B          FREQ                    48      48.    8
97          1  B
98        DISK IN      B          FREQ                    48      48.   13
99          1  B
100       DISK IN      B          FREQ                    48      48.   18
101       DISK OUT     A          FREQ                    48      48.
102       THIS IS ENSEMBLE AVERAGE OF CROSS POWER SPECTRAL DENSITIES
103       CLEAR-AL
104       FREQ-AVG                                                       2
105           4   48       48.
106         1  C
107       DISK IN      C          FREQ                    48      48.    4

113       DISK IN      C          FREQ                    48      48.   19
114       SWITCH       A    C
115       FREQ-AVG                                                       2
116           4   48       48.
117         1  B
118       DISK IN      B          FREQ                    48      48.    5

                   ( CONTINUE )
```

Figure 3-33. (cont.)

```
124        DISK IN      B            FREQ                               48       48.        2Ø
125        SWITCH       A    C
126        DISK IN      A            FREQ                               48       48.        22
126        COHERNCE
127        DISK OUT     A            FREQ                               48       48.
128        COHERENCE FUNCTION OBTAINED FROM ENSEMBLE AVERAGE

                        ( CONTINUE )

129        CLEAR-AL
13Ø        DISK IN      B            FREQ                               48       48.        21
131        DISK IN      A            FREQ                               48       48.        23
132        PLOTTER      B                                               24
133        FREQ   MAG        1   24    THIS IS A SINGLE RECORD COHERENCE FUNCTION
134        PLOTTER      A                                               24
135        FREQ   MAG        1   24    THIS IS AN ENSEMBLE AVERAGED COHERENCE
136        DIRECTRY
137        TERM
                 .         .         .         .         .         .         .         .
```

Figure 3-33. (cont.)

```
FORTRAN IV G LEVEL  21              OWN              DATE = 75190          14/18/44                 PAGE 0001

0001                SUBROUTINE OWN
              C
              C  THE FOLLOWING FIVE STATEMENTS SHOULD BE INCLUDED IN ANY SUBROUTINE OWN
0002                REAL*8 BAN
0003                INTEGER DSO,E,F,TIME,FREQ,SPL
0004                COMMON REST(6148),TEMR(1024),TEMC(1024),FRN(20),FCN(20),FRD(20),
                   1FCD(20),PN(21),PD(21),REST1(82),NPOINT,REST2(5),SPL,REST3(2)
0005                COMMON /LETTER/ F,E,MAR(3),LAIS(60),TIME,FREQ,IBAN,BAN,LN,NN,NP
              C
              C
0006                WRITE(LN,3) SPL
0007              3 FORMAT(10X,'USER PROGRAM NUMBER ',I2,/)
0008                GO TO (50,1),SPL
0009              1 DO 10 I = 1,NPOINT
0010             10 TEMR(I)=EXP(-3.*I/NPOINT)
0011                GO TO 99
0012             50 TEMR(1)=1
0013             99 RETURN
0014                END
```

Figure 3-34. Subroutine OWN (Coherence Example).

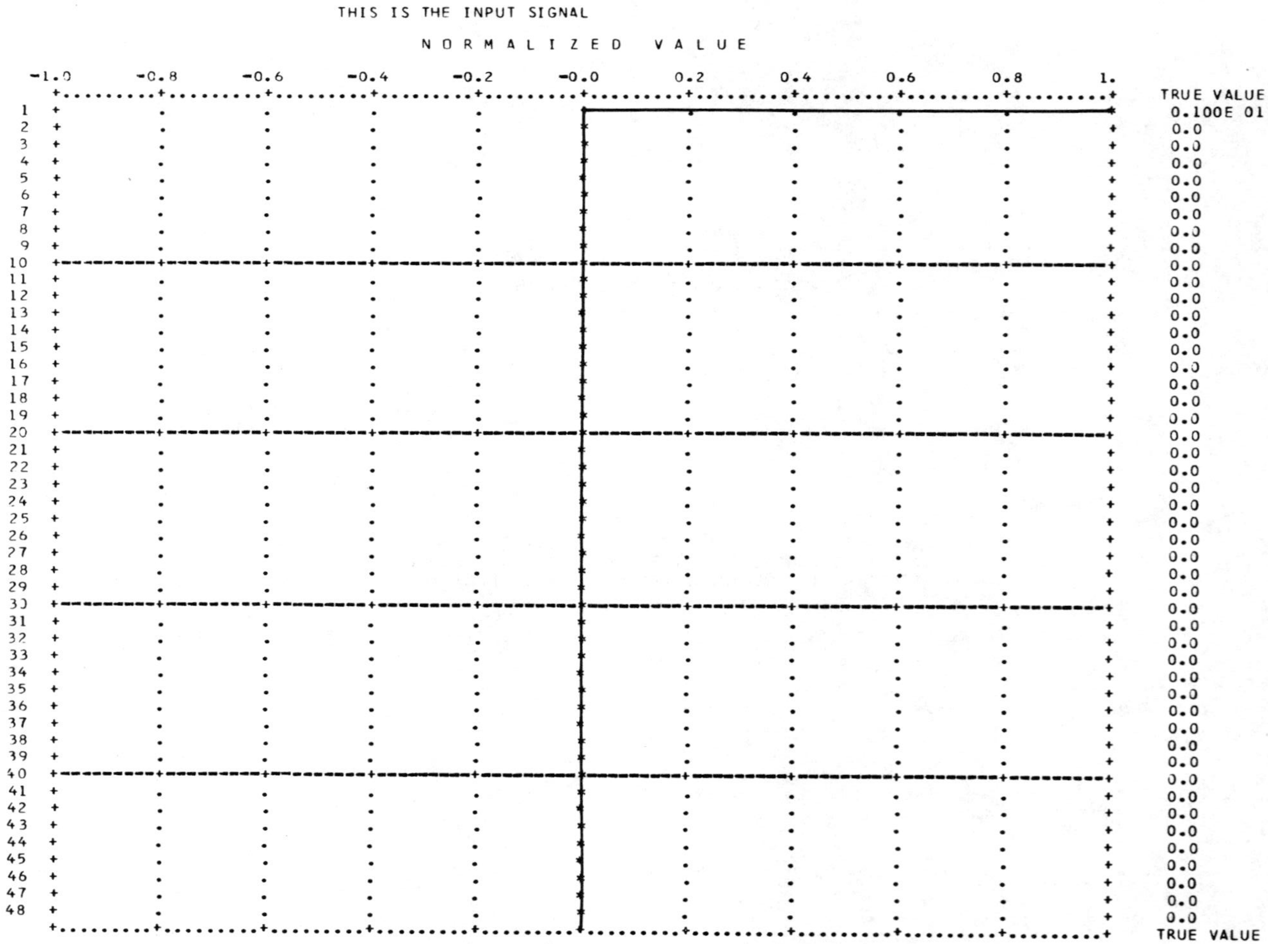

Figure 3-35. Input Time Series (Coherence Example).

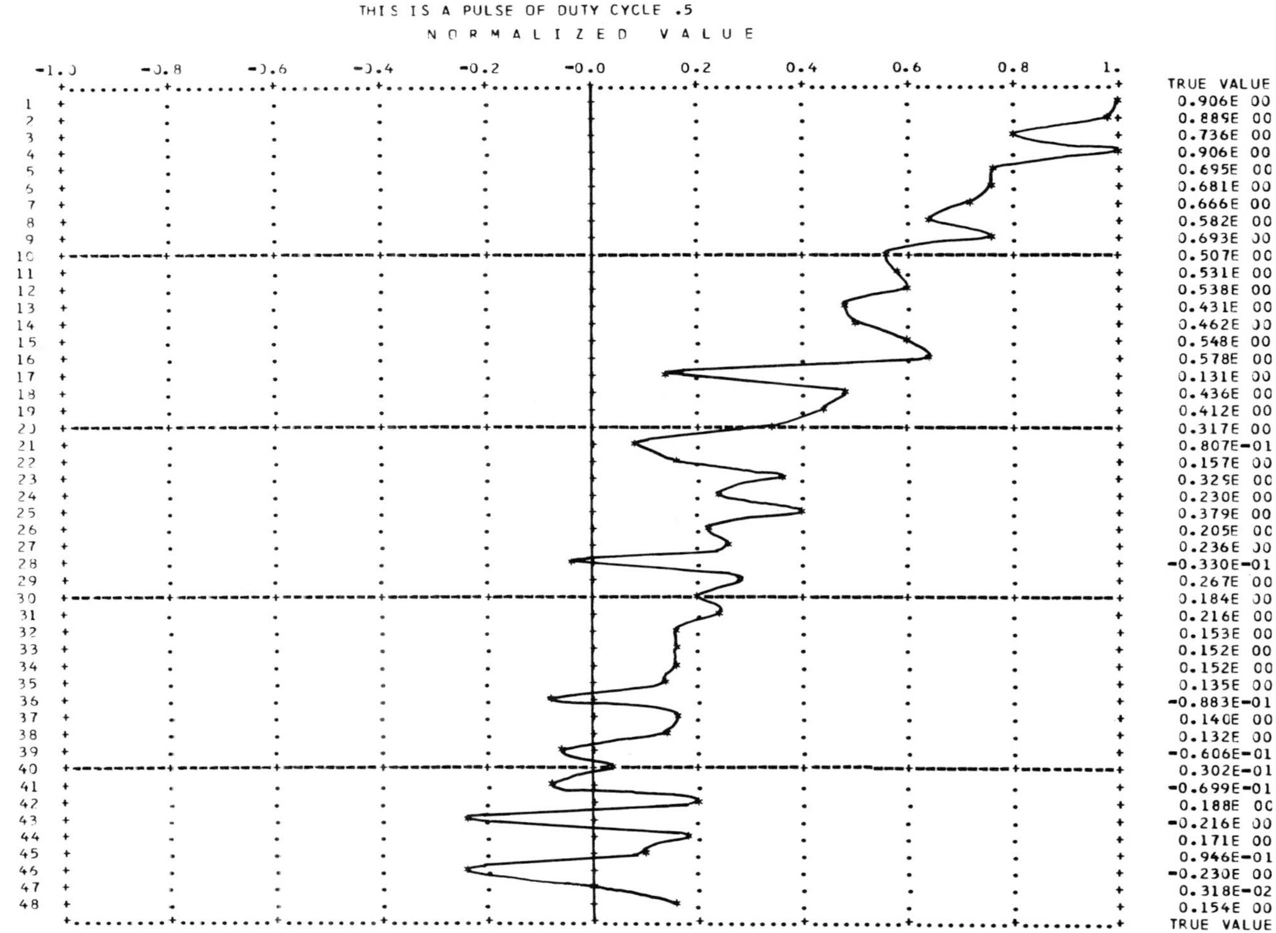

Figure 3-36. Sample Output Time Series (Coherence Example).

```
DISK STORAGE INITIALIZATION FUNCTIONAL TASK

              USER REQUIREMENTS

(1) A RECORD MUST BE WRITTEN BEFORE IT IS READ FROM DISK

(2) INFORMATION ABOUT ALL RECORDS STORED ON DISK IS OBTAINED BY THE DIRECTORY SUBROUTINE

(3) NUMBER OF POINTS, DOMAIN, AND SAMPLING FREQUENCY MUST BE KNOWN TO GET A RECORD OFF OF DISK

(4) RECORD MUST BE IDENTIFIED BY ITS RECORD NUMBER TO BE READ OFF DISK

(5)  RECORD NUMBER IS ASSIGNED TO DATA WHEN IT IS OUTPUTED TO THE DISK

DISK CONTAINING DATA SET NUMBER 4 FOR USE IN STORAGE OF SIGNAL ANALYSIS DATA HAS BEEN INITIALIZED AND IS READY FOR USE
```

```
DISK OUTPUT FUNCTIONAL TASK

INFORMATION COMES FROM ARRAY C

NUMBER OF DATA POINTS   48

SAMPLING FREQUENCY OF THE DATA        48.0

INFORMATION IS IN THE TIME DOMAIN

IDENTIFICATION  THIS IS THE INPUT SIGNAL

RECORD NUMBER ASSIGNED TO THIS DATA    1
```

```
DISK OUTPUT FUNCTIONAL TASK

INFORMATION COMES FROM ARRAY B

NUMBER OF DATA POINTS   48

SAMPLING FREQUENCY OF THE DATA        48.0

INFORMATION IS IN THE TIME DOMAIN

IDENTIFICATION  THIS IS THE OUTPUT SIGNAL + NOISE

RECORD NUMBER ASSIGNED TO THIS DATA    2
```

```
CROSS CORRELATION FUNCTIONAL TASK

NUMBER OF SAMPLE POINTS IS    48

SAMPLING FREQUENCY OF THIS SYSTEM IS        48.0

DATA IS STORED IN THE FREQ DOMAIN

DATA IS STORED IN THE A ARRAY

INPUT AND OUTPUT SIGNALS ARE IN ARRAYS B AND C IN THE FREQUENCY DOMAIN


DISK OUTPUT FUNCTIONAL TASK

INFORMATION COMES FROM ARRAY A

NUMBER OF DATA POINTS   48

SAMPLING FREQUENCY OF THE DATA        48.0

INFORMATION IS IN THE FREQ DOMAIN

IDENTIFICATION  THIS IS THE CROSS POWER SPECTRAL DENSITY FROM RECORD  1

RECORD NUMBER ASSIGNED TO THIS DATA     3
```

Figure 3-37. Complete First-pass Analysis (Coherence Example).

```
DISK INPUT FUNCTIONAL TASK

INFORMATION PUT INTO ARRAY C

NUMBER OF INFORMATION POINTS        48

DOMAIN OF INFORMATION          TIME

SAMPLING FREQUENCY OF DATA        48.0

INFORMATION FROM DISK RECORD     1


POWER SPECTRAL DENSITY FUNCTIONAL TASK

RESULTS STORED IN ARRAY  C

NUMBER OF SAMPLE POINTS IS    48

DATA WAS SAMPLED AT THE RATE OF        48.0 HZ

DATA STORED IN THE FREQUENCY DOMAIN
```

```
DISK INPUT FUNCTIONAL TASK

INFORMATION PUT INTO ARRAY B

NUMBER OF INFORMATION POINTS        48

DOMAIN OF INFORMATION          TIME

SAMPLING FREQUENCY OF DATA        48.0

INFORMATION FROM DISK RECORD     2


POWER SPECTRAL DENSITY FUNCTIONAL TASK

RESULTS STORED IN ARRAY  B

NUMBER OF SAMPLE POINTS IS    48

DATA WAS SAMPLED AT THE RATE OF        48.0 HZ

DATA STORED IN THE FREQUENCY DOMAIN
```

```
DISK OUTPUT FUNCTIONAL TASK

INFORMATION COMES FROM ARRAY C

NUMBER OF DATA POINTS   48

SAMPLING FREQUENCY OF THE DATA        48.0

INFORMATION IS IN THE FREQ DOMAIN

IDENTIFICATION  THIS IS THE INPUT POWER SPECTRAL DENSITY  1

RECORD NUMBER ASSIGNED TO THIS DATA    4


DISK OUTPUT FUNCTIONAL TASK

INFORMATION COMES FROM ARRAY B

NUMBER OF DATA POINTS   48

SAMPLING FREQUENCY OF THE DATA        48.0

INFORMATION IS IN THE FREQ DOMAIN

IDENTIFICATION  THIS IS THE OUTPUT POWER SPECTRAL DENSITY   1

RECORD NUMBER ASSIGNED TO THIS DATA    5
```

Figure 3-37. (cont.)

```
LIBRARY INPUT FUNCTIONS FUNCTIONAL TASK

USER PROGRAM NUMBER  1
INFORMATION PUT INTO ARRAY C

NUMBER OF SAMPLE POINTS IS   48

SAMPLING FREQUENCY OF DATA IS        48.0

INPUT IDENTIFICATION  THIS IS THE INPUT SIGNAL
```

```
DISK OUTPUT FUNCTIONAL TASK

INFORMATION COMES FRCM ARRAY C

NUMBER OF DATA POINTS   48

SAMPLING FREQUENCY OF THE DATA        48.0

INFORMATION IS IN THE TIME DOMAIN

IDENTIFICATION  THIS IS THE INPUT SIGNAL

RECORD NUMBER ASSIGNED TO THIS DATA    6
```

```
LIBRARY INPUT FUNCTIONS FUNCTIONAL TASK

USER PROGRAM NUMBER  2
INFORMATION PUT INTO ARRAY B

NUMBER OF SAMPLE POINTS IS   48

SAMPLING FREQUENCY OF DATA IS        48.0

ADDITIVE GAUSSIAN NOISE OF MEAN   0.0 VARIANCE      0.100  HAS BEEN SYNTHESIZED BY THE LIBRARY
INPUT IDENTIFICATION  THIS IS A PULSE CF DUTY CYCLE .5
```

```
DISK OUTPUT FUNCTIONAL TASK

INFORMATION COMES FROM ARRAY B

NUMBER OF DATA POINTS   48

SAMPLING FREQUENCY OF THE DATA        48.0

INFORMATION IS IN THE TIME DOMAIN

IDENTIFICATION  THIS IS THE OUTPUT SIGNAL + NOISE

RECORD NUMBER ASSIGNED TO THIS DATA    7


CROSS CORRELATION FUNCTIONAL TASK

NUMBER OF SAMPLE POINTS IS   48

SAMPLING FREQUENCY OF THIS SYSTEM IS        48.0

DATA IS STORED IN THE FREQ DOMAIN

DATA IS STORED IN THE A ARRAY

INPUT AND OUTPUT SIGNALS ARE IN ARRAYS B AND C IN THE FREQUENCY DOMAIN
```

Figure 3-38. Complete Second-pass Analysis (Coherence Example).

```
DISK OUTPUT FUNCTIONAL TASK

INFORMATION COMES FROM ARRAY A

NUMBER OF DATA POINTS   48

SAMPLING FREQUENCY OF THE DATA        48.0

INFORMATION IS IN THE FREQ DOMAIN

IDENTIFICATION  THIS IS THE CROSS POWER SPECTRAL DENSITY FROM RECORD   2

RECORD NUMBER ASSIGNED TO THIS DATA    8


DISK INPUT FUNCTIONAL TASK

INFORMATION PUT INTO ARRAY C

NUMBER OF INFORMATION POINTS       48

DOMAIN OF INFORMATION         TIME

SAMPLING FREQUENCY OF DATA         48.0

INFORMATION FROM DISK RECORD    6


DISK INPUT FUNCTIONAL TASK

INFORMATION PUT INTO ARRAY B

NUMBER OF INFORMATION POINTS       48

DOMAIN OF INFORMATION         TIME

SAMPLING FREQUENCY OF DATA         48.0

INFORMATION FROM DISK RECORD    7
```

```
POWER SPECTRAL DENSITY FUNCTIONAL TASK

RESULTS STORED IN ARRAY  C

NUMBER OF SAMPLE POINTS IS   48

DATA WAS SAMPLED AT THE RATE OF        48.0 HZ

DATA STORED IN THE FREQUENCY DOMAIN


DISK OUTPUT FUNCTIONAL TASK

INFORMATION COMES FROM ARRAY C

NUMBER OF DATA POINTS   43

SAMPLING FREQUENCY OF THE DATA        48.0

INFORMATION IS IN THE FREQ DOMAIN

IDENTIFICATION  THIS IS THE INPUT POWER SPECTRAL DENSITY  2

RECORD NUMBER ASSIGNED TO THIS DATA    9
```

```
POWER SPECTRAL DENSITY FUNCTIONAL TASK

RESULTS STORED IN ARRAY  B

NUMBER OF SAMPLE POINTS IS   48

DATA WAS SAMPLED AT THE RATE OF        48.0 HZ

DATA STORED IN THE FREQUENCY DOMAIN


DISK OUTPUT FUNCTIONAL TASK

INFORMATION COMES FROM ARRAY B

NUMBER OF DATA POINTS   48

SAMPLING FREQUENCY OF THE DATA        48.0

INFORMATION IS IN THE FREQ DOMAIN

IDENTIFICATION  THIS IS THE OUTPUT POWER SPECTRAL DENSITY   2

RECORD NUMBER ASSIGNED TO THIS DATA    10
```

Figure 3-38. (cont.)

```
LIBRARY INPUT FUNCTIONS FUNCTIONAL TASK

USER PROGRAM NUMBER  1
INFORMATION PUT INTO ARRAY C

NUMBER OF SAMPLE POINTS IS   48

SAMPLING FREQUENCY OF DATA IS       48.0

INPUT IDENTIFICATION  THIS IS THE INPUT SIGNAL


LIBRARY INPUT FUNCTIONS FUNCTIONAL TASK

USER PROGRAM NUMBER  2
INFORMATION PUT INTO ARRAY B

NUMBER OF SAMPLE POINTS IS   48

SAMPLING FREQUENCY OF DATA IS       48.0

ADDITIVE GAUSSIAN NOISE OF MEAN   0.0 VARIANCE      0.100  HAS BEEN SYNTHESIZED BY THE LIBRARY
INPUT IDENTIFICATION  THIS IS A PULSE OF DUTY CYCLE .5
```

```
DISK OUTPUT FUNCTIONAL TASK

INFORMATION COMES FROM ARRAY C

NUMBER OF DATA POINTS    48

SAMPLING FREQUENCY OF THE DATA         48.0

INFORMATION IS IN THE TIME DOMAIN

IDENTIFICATION   THIS IS THE INPUT SIGNAL

RECORD NUMBER ASSIGNED TO THIS DATA    11
```

```
DISK OUTPUT FUNCTIONAL TASK

INFORMATION COMES FROM ARRAY B

NUMBER OF DATA POINTS    48

SAMPLING FREQUENCY OF THE DATA         48.0

INFORMATION IS IN THE TIME DOMAIN

IDENTIFICATION   THIS IS THE OUTPUT SIGNAL + NOISE

RECORD NUMBER ASSIGNED TO THIS DATA    12
```

```
CROSS CORRELATION FUNCTIONAL TASK

NUMBER OF SAMPLE POINTS IS    48

SAMPLING FREQUENCY OF THIS SYSTEM IS         48.0

DATA IS STORED IN THE FREQ DOMAIN

DATA IS STORED IN THE A ARRAY

INPUT AND OUTPUT SIGNALS ARE IN ARRAYS B AND C IN THE FREQUENCY DOMAIN
```

Figure 3-39. Complete Third-pass Analysis (Coherence Example).

```
DISK OUTPUT FUNCTIONAL TASK

INFORMATION COMES FRCM ARRAY A

NUMBER OF DATA POINTS   48

SAMPLING FREQUENCY OF THE DATA        48.0

INFORMATION IS IN THE FREQ DOMAIN

IDENTIFICATION  THIS IS THE CROSS POWER SPECTRAL DENSITY FROM RECORD    3

RECORD NUMBER ASSIGNED TO THIS DATA    13
```

```
DISK INPUT FUNCTIONAL TASK

INFORMATION PUT INTO ARRAY C

NUMBER OF INFORMATION POINTS        48

DOMAIN OF INFORMATION          TIME

SAMPLING FREQUENCY OF DATA         48.0

INFORMATION FROM DISK RECORD   11
```

```
DISK INPUT FUNCTIONAL TASK

INFORMATION PUT INTO ARRAY B

NUMBER OF INFORMATION POINTS        48

DOMAIN OF INFORMATION          TIME

SAMPLING FREQUENCY OF DATA         48.0

INFORMATION FROM DISK RECORD   12
```

```
POWER SPECTRAL DENSITY FUNCTIONAL TASK

RESULTS STORED IN ARRAY  C

NUMBER OF SAMPLE POINTS IS   48

DATA WAS SAMPLED AT THE RATE OF        48.0 HZ

DATA STORED IN THE FREQUENCY DOMAIN
```

```
POWER SPECTRAL DENSITY FUNCTIONAL TASK

RESULTS STORED IN ARRAY  B

NUMBER OF SAMPLE POINTS IS   48

DATA WAS SAMPLED AT THE RATE OF        48.0 HZ

DATA STORED IN THE FREQUENCY DOMAIN


DISK OUTPUT FUNCTIONAL TASK

INFORMATION COMES FROM ARRAY B

NUMBER OF DATA POINTS   48

SAMPLING FREQUENCY OF THE DATA        48.0

INFORMATION IS IN THE FREQ DOMAIN

IDENTIFICATION  THIS IS THE OUTPUT POWER SPECTRAL DENSITY  3

RECORD NUMBER ASSIGNED TO THIS DATA   15
```

```
DISK OUTPUT FUNCTIONAL TASK

INFORMATION COMES FROM ARRAY C

NUMBER OF DATA POINTS   48

SAMPLING FREQUENCY OF THE DATA        48.0

INFORMATION IS IN THE FREQ DOMAIN

IDENTIFICATION  THIS IS THE INPUT POWER SPECTRAL DENSITY 3

RECORD NUMBER ASSIGNED TO THIS DATA   14
```

Figure 3-39. (cont.)

```
LIBRARY INPUT FUNCTIONS FUNCTIONAL TASK

USER PROGRAM NUMBER  1

INFORMATION PUT INTO ARRAY C

NUMBER OF SAMPLE POINTS IS   48

SAMPLING FREQUENCY OF DATA IS        48.0

INPUT IDENTIFICATION  THIS IS THE INPUT SIGNAL



LIBRARY INPUT FUNCTIONS FUNCTIONAL TASK

USER PROGRAM NUMBER  2

INFORMATION PUT INTO ARRAY B

NUMBER OF SAMPLE POINTS IS   48

SAMPLING FREQUENCY OF DATA IS        48.0

ADDITIVE GAUSSIAN NOISE OF MEAN   0.0 VARIANCE      0.100  HAS BEEN SYNTHESIZED BY THE LIBRARY

INPUT IDENTIFICATION  THIS IS A PULSE CF DUTY CYCLE .5
```

```
DISK OUTPUT FUNCTIONAL TASK

INFORMATION COMES FROM ARRAY C

NUMBER OF DATA POINTS   48

SAMPLING FREQUENCY OF THE DATA        48.0

INFORMATION IS IN THE TIME DOMAIN

IDENTIFICATION  THIS IS THE INPUT SIGNAL

RECORD NUMBER ASSIGNED TO THIS DATA   16

CROSS CORRELATION FUNCTIONAL TASK

NUMBER OF SAMPLE POINTS IS   48

SAMPLING FREQUENCY OF THIS SYSTEM IS        48.0

DATA IS STORED IN THE FREQ DOMAIN

DATA IS STORED IN THE A ARRAY

INPUT AND OUTPUT SIGNALS ARE IN ARRAYS B AND C IN THE FREQUENCY DOMAIN
```

```
DISK OUTPUT FUNCTIONAL TASK

INFORMATION COMES FROM ARRAY B

NUMBER OF DATA POINTS   48

SAMPLING FREQUENCY OF THE DATA        48.0

INFORMATION IS IN THE TIME DOMAIN

IDENTIFICATION  THIS IS THE OUTPUT SIGNAL + NOISE

RECORD NUMBER ASSIGNED TO THIS DATA   17
```

Figure 3-40. Complete Fourth-pass Analysis (Coherence Example).

```
DISK OUTPUT FUNCTIONAL TASK

INFORMATION COMES FROM ARRAY A

NUMBER OF DATA POINTS   48

SAMPLING FREQUENCY OF THE DATA        48.0

INFORMATION IS IN THE FREQ DOMAIN

IDENTIFICATION  THIS IS THE CROSS POWER SPECTRAL DENSITY FROM RECORD    4

RECORD NUMBER ASSIGNED TO THIS DATA   18
```

```
DISK INPUT FUNCTIONAL TASK

INFORMATION PUT INTO ARRAY C

NUMBER OF INFORMATICN POINTS        48

DOMAIN OF INFORMATION          TIME

SAMPLING FREQUENCY OF DATA         48.0

INFORMATION FROM DISK RECORD   16
```

```
DISK INPUT FUNCTIONAL TASK

INFORMATION PUT INTO ARRAY B

NUMBER OF INFORMATICN POINTS        48

DOMAIN OF INFORMATION          TIME

SAMPLING FREQUENCY OF DATA         48.0

INFORMATION FROM DISK RECORD   17
```

```
POWER SPECTRAL DENSITY FUNCTIONAL TASK

RESULTS STORED IN ARRAY  C

NUMBER OF SAMPLE POINTS IS   48

DATA WAS SAMPLED AT THE RATE OF        48.0 HZ

DATA STORED IN THE FREQUENCY DOMAIN
```

```
DISK OUTPUT FUNCTIONAL TASK

INFORMATION COMES FRCM ARRAY C

NUMBER OF DATA POINTS   48

SAMPLING FREQUENCY OF THE DATA        48.0

INFORMATION IS IN THE FREQ DOMAIN

IDENTIFICATION  THIS IS THE INPUT POWER SPECTRAL DENSITY  4

RECORD NUMBER ASSIGNED TO THIS DATA   19
```

```
POWER SPECTRAL DENSITY FUNCTIONAL TASK

RESULTS STORED IN ARRAY  B

NUMBER OF SAMPLE POINTS IS   48

DATA WAS SAMPLED AT THE RATE OF        48.0 HZ

DATA STORED IN THE FREQUENCY DOMAIN
```

```
DISK OUTPUT FUNCTIONAL TASK

INFORMATION COMES FRCM ARRAY B

NUMBER OF DATA POINTS   48

SAMPLING FREQUENCY OF THE DATA        48.0

INFORMATION IS IN THE FREQ DOMAIN

IDENTIFICATION  THIS IS THE OUTPUT POWER SPECTRAL DENSITY   4

RECORD NUMBER ASSIGNED TO THIS DATA   20
```

Figure 3-40 (Continued)

```
DISK INPUT FUNCTIONAL TASK

INFORMATION PUT INTO ARRAY A

NUMBER OF INFORMATION POINTS        48

DOMAIN OF INFORMATION        FREQ

SAMPLING FREQUENCY OF DATA        48.0

INFORMATION FROM DISK RECORD   18

COHERENCE FUNCTION FUNCTIONAL TASK

CROSS-CORRELATION SHCULD BE STORED IN ARRAY A

INPUT-OUTPUT SIGNALS SHOULD BE STORED IN ARRAYS B AND C

ALL INFORMATION SHOULD BE IN THE FREQUENCY DOMAIN

NUMBER OF DATA POINTS IN THIS SYSTEM IS   48

DATA WAS SAMPLED AT THE RATE OF        48.0 HZ

THE  VALUE  OF THE COHERENCE FUNCTION AT EACH HARMONIC IS LISTED BELOW

ANY COHERENCE VALUES OUTSIDE THE RANGE  0<X<1  INDICATE NONLINEARITIES IN THE SYSTEM

        HARMONIC                          VALUE OF COHERENCE FUNCTION


           0                                  0.10000E 01
           1                                  0.10000E 01
           2                                  0.10000E 01
```

```
   3          0.10000E 01
   4          0.10000E 01
   5          0.10000E 01
   6          0.10000E 01
   7          0.10000E 01
   8          0.10000E 01
   9          0.10000E 01
  10          0.10000E 01
  11          0.10000E 01
  12          0.10000E 01
  13          0.10000E 01
  14          0.10000E 01
  15          0.10000E 01
  16          0.10000E 01
  17          0.10000E 01
  18          0.10000E 01
  19          0.10000E 01
  20          0.10000E 01
  21          0.10000E 01
  22          0.10000E 01
  23          0.10000E 01

DISK OUTPUT FUNCTIONAL TASK

INFORMATION COMES FROM TEMPORARY ARRAYS

HEADER INFORMATION COMES FROM ARRAY A

NUMBER OF DATA POINTS   48

SAMPLING FREQUENCY OF THE DATA       48.0

INFORMATION IS IN THE FREQ DOMAIN

IDENTIFICATION   THIS IS THE COHERENCE FUNCTION FOR A SINGLE RECORD

RECORD NUMBER ASSIGNED TO THIS DATA  21
```

Figure 3-41. Single-experiment Coherence Test (Coherence Example).

```
FREQUENCY ENSEMBLE AVERAGING FUNCTIONAL TASK

NUMBER OF DATA SETS TO BE AVERAGED   4

NUMBER OF DATA POINTS IN EACH SIGNAL   48

SAMPLING RATE OF THE DATA IS        48.0 HZ


*****DATA SET   1  NUMBER  OF INTERMEDIATE OPERATIONS IS  1  RESULTS WILL COME FROM ARRAY B TO BE AVERAGED*****

     FREQ DOMAIN INFORMATION CONSISTING OF   48 POINTS WAS READ FROM DISK RECORD    3 INTO ARRAY B

*****DATA SET   2  NUMBER  OF INTERMEDIATE OPERATIONS IS  1  RESULTS WILL COME FROM ARRAY B TO BE AVERAGED*****

     FREQ DOMAIN INFORMATION CONSISTING OF   48 POINTS WAS READ FROM DISK RECORD    8 INTO ARRAY B

*****DATA SET   3  NUMBER  OF INTERMEDIATE OPERATIONS IS  1  RESULTS WILL COME FROM ARRAY B TO BE AVERAGED*****

     FREQ DOMAIN INFORMATICN CONSISTING OF   48 POINTS WAS READ FROM DISK RECORD   13 INTO ARRAY B
```

```
*****DATA SET   4  NUMBER  OF INTERMEDIATE OPERATIONS IS  1  RESULTS WILL COME FROM ARRAY B TO BE AVERAGED*****

     FREQ DOMAIN INFORMATION CONSISTING OF    48 POINTS WAS READ FROM DISK RECORD   18 INTO ARRAY B

                 **********ALL ENSEMBLE AVERAGING COMPLETED  ***  RESULTS STORED IN ARRAY A**********


     DISK OUTPUT FUNCTIONAL TASK

     INFORMATION COMES FROM ARRAY A

     NUMBER OF DATA POINTS   48

     SAMPLING FREQUENCY OF THE DATA        48.0

     INFORMATION IS IN THE FREQ DOMAIN

     IDENTIFICATION  THIS IS ENSEMBLE AVERAGE OF CROSS POWER SPECTRAL DENSITIES

     RECORD NUMBER ASSIGNED TO THIS DATA   22
```

Figure 3-42. Ensemble-averaged Cross-power Spectra Data (Coherence Example).

```
FREQUENCY ENSEMBLE AVERAGING FUNCTIONAL TASK

NUMBER OF DATA SETS TO BE AVERAGED   4

NUMBER OF DATA POINTS IN EACH SIGNAL   48

SAMPLING RATE OF THE DATA IS       48.0 HZ


*****DATA SET   1  NUMBER  OF INTERMEDIATE OPERATIONS IS  1  RESULTS WILL COME FROM ARRAY C TO BE AVERAGED*****

     FREQ DOMAIN INFORMATION CONSISTING OF   48 POINTS WAS READ FROM DISK RECORD    4 INTO ARRAY C

*****DATA SET   2  NUMBER  OF INTERMEDIATE OPERATIONS IS  1  RESULTS WILL COME FROM ARRAY C TO BE AVERAGED*****

     FREQ DOMAIN INFORMATION CONSISTING OF   48 POINTS WAS READ FROM DISK RECORD    9 INTO ARRAY C

*****DATA SET   3  NUMBER  OF INTERMEDIATE OPERATIONS IS  1  RESULTS WILL COME FROM ARRAY C TO BE AVERAGED*****

     FREQ DOMAIN INFORMATION CONSISTING OF   48 POINTS WAS READ FROM DISK RECORD   14 INTO ARRAY C
```

```
*****DATA SET    4  NUMBER  OF INTERMEDIATE OPERATIONS IS  1  RESULTS WILL COME FROM ARRAY C TO BE AVERAGED*****

     FREQ DOMAIN INFORMATICN CONSISTING OF    48 POINTS WAS READ FROM DISK RECORD    19 INTO ARRAY C


            **********ALL ENSEMBLE AVERAGING COMPLETED  ***  RESULTS STORED IN ARRAY A**********



     RESULTS OF THE ARRAY SWITCHING FUNCTIONAL TASK

     ARRAYS                                A    AND    C

     NUMBER OF SAMPLE POINTS               0          48

     SAMPLING FREQUENCIES                0.0        48.0

     DOMAIN                             NONE        FREQ
```

Figure 3-43. Ensemble-averaged Input Power Spectra Data (Coherence Example).

```
     FREQUENCY ENSEMBLE AVERAGING FUNCTIONAL TASK

     NUMBER OF DATA SETS TO BE AVERAGED   4

     NUMBER OF DATA POINTS IN EACH SIGNAL   48

     SAMPLING RATE OF THE DATA IS       48.0 HZ


*****DATA SET   1  NUMBER  OF INTERMEDIATE OPERATIONS IS  1  RESULTS WILL COME FROM ARRAY B TO BE AVERAGED*****

     FREQ DOMAIN INFORMATION CONSISTING OF   48 POINTS WAS READ FROM DISK RECORD    5 INTO ARRAY B


*****DATA SET   2  NUMBER  OF INTERMEDIATE OPERATIONS IS  1  RESULTS WILL COME FROM ARRAY B TO BE AVERAGED*****

     FREQ DOMAIN INFORMATION CONSISTING OF   48 POINTS WAS READ FROM DISK RECORD   10 INTO ARRAY B


*****DATA SET   3  NUMBER  OF INTERMEDIATE OPERATIONS IS  1  RESULTS WILL COME FROM ARRAY B TO BE AVERAGED*****

     FREQ DOMAIN INFORMATION CONSISTING OF   48 POINTS WAS READ FROM DISK RECORD   15 INTO ARRAY B
```

```
*****DATA SET   4  NUMBER  OF INTERMEDIATE OPERATIONS IS  1  RESULTS WILL COME FROM ARRAY B TO BE AVERAGED*****

FREQ DOMAIN INFORMATION CONSISTING OF   48 POINTS WAS READ FROM DISK RECORD   20 INTO ARRAY B

          **********ALL ENSEMBLE AVERAGING COMPLETED  ***  RESULTS STORED IN ARRAY A**********

RESULTS OF THE ARRAY SWITCHING FUNCTIONAL TASK            DISK INPUT FUNCTIONAL TASK

ARRAYS                               A    AND    B        INFORMATION PUT INTO ARRAY A

NUMBER OF SAMPLE POINTS              0           48       NUMBER OF INFORMATION POINTS        48

SAMPLING FREQUENCIES               0.0         48.0       DOMAIN OF INFORMATION         FREQ

DOMAIN                            NONE         FREQ       SAMPLING FREQUENCY OF DATA        48.0

                                                          INFORMATION FROM DISK RECORD   22
```

Figure 3-44. Ensemble-averaged Output Power Spectra Data (Coherence Example).

COHERENCE FUNCTION FUNCTIONAL TASK

CROSS-CORRELATION SHOULD BE STOREC IN ARRAY A

INPUT-OUTPUT SIGNALS SHOULD BE STORED IN ARRAYS B AND C

ALL INFORMATION SHOULC BE IN THE FREQUENCY DOMAIN

NUMBER OF DATA POINTS IN THIS SYSTEM IS 48

DATA WAS SAMPLED AT THE RATE OF 48.0 HZ

THE VALUE OF THE COHERENCE FUNCTION AT EACH HARMONIC IS LISTED BELOW

ANY COHERENCE VALUES OUTSIDE THE RANGE 0<X<1 INDICATE NONLINEARITIES IN THE SYSTEM

HARMONIC	VALUE OF COHERENCE FUNCTION
0	0.99842E 00
1	0.99017E 00
2	0.95315E 00
3	0.94004E 00
4	0.94778E 00
5	0.89390E 00
6	0.95598E 00
7	0.62965E 00
8	0.94963E 00
9	0.39331E 00
10	0.57976E 00
11	0.95120E 00
12	0.59961E 00
13	0.81448E 00

```
14                                   0.79731E 00
15                                   0.15122E 00
16                                   0.57047E 00
17                                   0.40370E 00
18                                   0.29351E 00
19                                   0.88288E-01
20                                   0.81448E 00
21                                   0.66583E 00
22                                   0.44802E 00
23                                   0.20820E 00

DISK OUTPUT FUNCTIONAL TASK

INFORMATION COMES FROM TEMPORARY ARRAYS

HEADER INFORMATION COMES FROM ARRAY A

NUMBER OF DATA POINTS    48

SAMPLING FREQUENCY OF THE DATA        48.0

INFORMATION IS IN THE FREQ DOMAIN

IDENTIFICATION  COHERENCE FUNCTION OBTAINED FROM ENSEMBLE AVERAGE

RECORD NUMBER ASSIGNED TO THIS DATA
```

Figure 3-45. Ensemble Coherence Test (Coherence Example).

```
DISK INPUT FUNCTIONAL TASK

INFORMATION PUT INTO ARRAY B

NUMBER OF INFORMATION POINTS        48

DOMAIN OF INFORMATION         FREQ

SAMPLING FREQUENCY OF DATA          48.0

INFORMATION FROM DISK RECORD   21


LINE PLOTTER FUNCTIONAL TASK

INFORMATION TO BE PLOTTED CAME FROM ARRAY B

NUMBER OF DATA POINTS IN THE ARRAY IS   48

SAMPLING FREQUENCY OF THE DATA IS       48.0

DATA IS IN THE FREQ DOMAIN

FREQUENCY RESOLUTION IS       1.000 HZ
```

```
DISK INPUT FUNCTIONAL TASK

INFORMATION PUT INTC ARRAY A

NUMBER OF INFORMATICN POINTS        48

DOMAIN OF INFORMATION         FREQ

SAMPLING FREQUENCY OF DATA          48.0

INFORMATION FROM DISK RECORD   23
```

Figure 3-46. Store Temporary Data (Coherence Example).

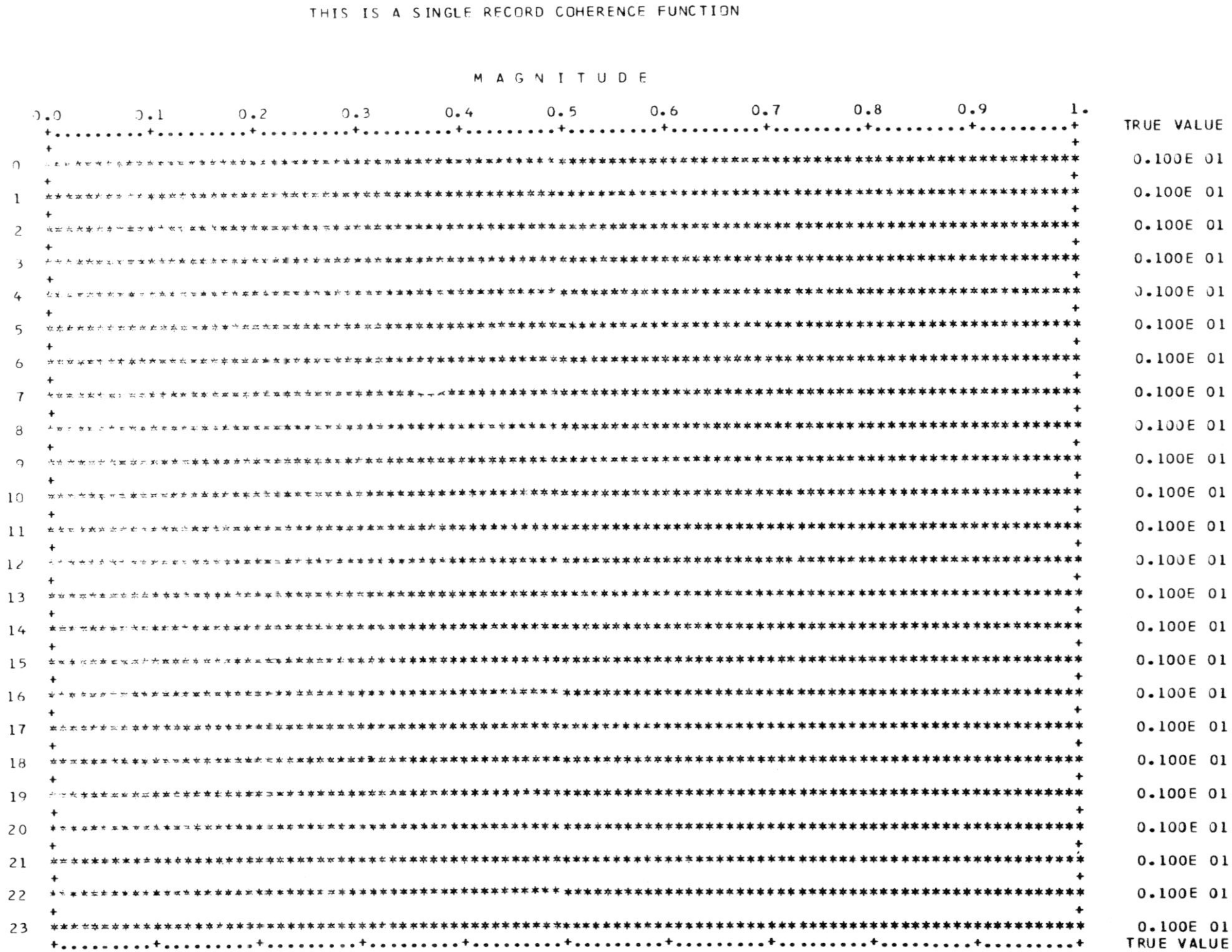

Figure 3-47. Single-record Coherence Test (Coherence Example).

```
LINE PLOTTER FUNCTIONAL TASK

INFORMATION TO BE PLOTTED CAME FROM ARRAY A

NUMBER OF DATA POINTS IN THE ARRAY IS    48

SAMPLING FREQUENCY OF THE DATA IS        48.0

DATA IS IN THE FREQ DOMAIN

FREQUENCY RESOLUTION IS       1.000 HZ
```

Figure 3-48. Request Pilot (Coherence Example).

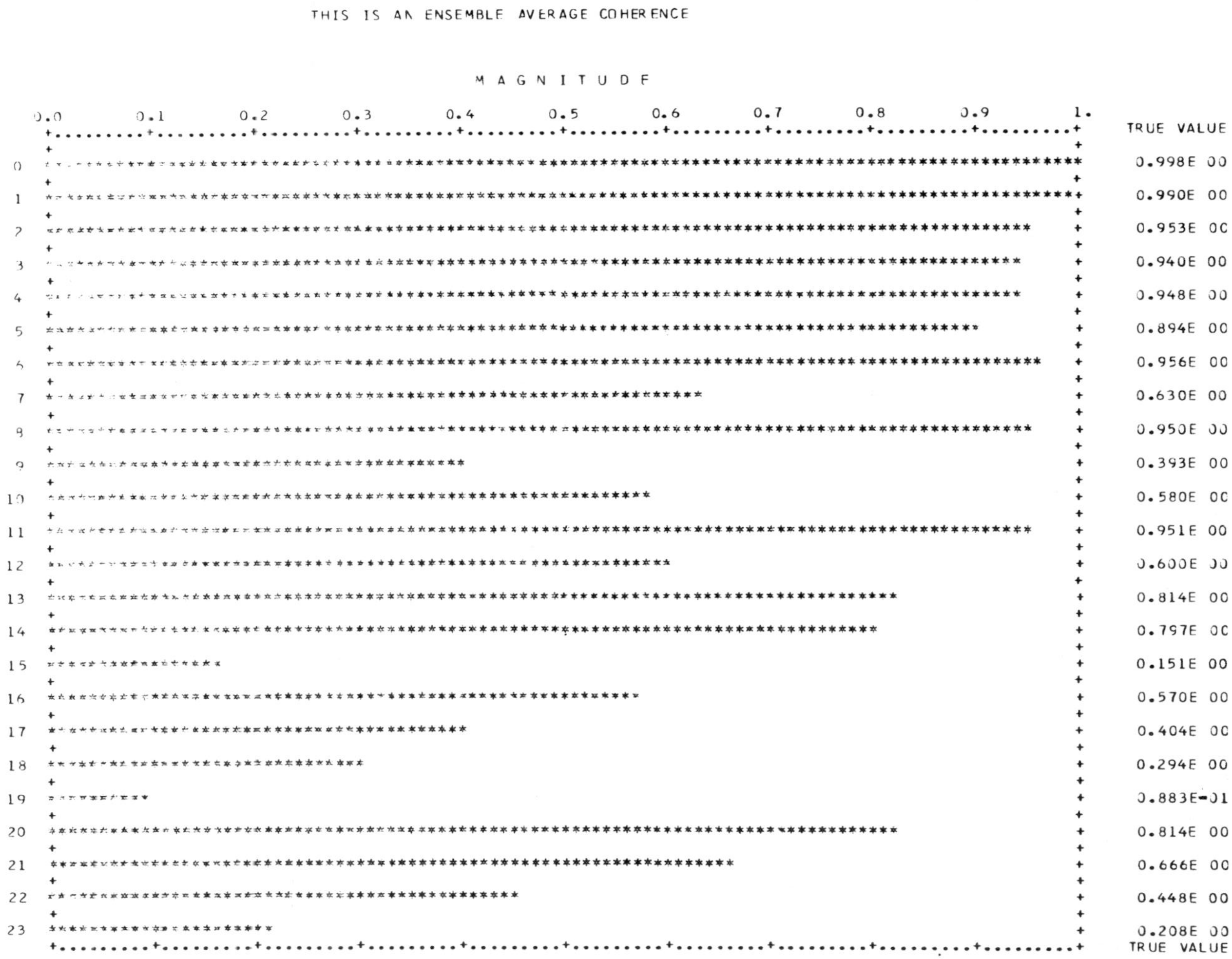

Figure 3-49. Ensemble Average Test (Coherence Example).

THE FOLLOWING, ARE THE 23 SIGNAL RECORDS ON DISK FILE 4

DOMAIN	SAMPLES	SAMPLING FREQUENCY	IDENTIFICATION OF DATA	RECORD NUMBER
TIME	48	48.0	THIS IS THE INPUT SIGNAL	1
TIME	48	48.0	THIS IS THE OUTPUT SIGNAL + NOISE	2
FREQ	48	48.0	THIS IS THE CROSS POWER SPECTRAL DENSITY FROM RECORD 1	3
FREQ	48	48.0	THIS IS THE INPUT POWER SPECTRAL DENSITY 1	4
FREQ	48	48.0	THIS IS THE OUTPUT POWER SPECTRAL DENSITY 1	5
TIME	48	48.0	THIS IS THE INPUT SIGNAL	6
TIME	48	48.0	THIS IS THE OUTPUT SIGNAL + NOISE	7
FREQ	48	48.0	THIS IS THE CROSS POWER SPECTRAL DENSITY FROM RECORD 2	8
FREQ	48	48.0	THIS IS THE INPUT POWER SPECTRAL DENSITY 2	9
FREQ	48	48.0	THIS IS THE OUTPUT POWER SPECTRAL DENSITY 2	10
TIME	48	48.0	THIS IS THE INPUT SIGNAL	11

```
TIME   48   48.0   THIS IS THE OUTPUT SIGNAL + NCISE                                   12
FREQ   48   48.0   THIS IS THE CRCSS POWER SPECTRAL DENSITY FROM RECORD    3           13
FREQ   48   48.0   THIS IS THE INPUT POWER SPECTRAL DENSITY 3                          14
FREQ   48   48.0   THIS IS THE CUTPUT POWER SPECTRAL DENSITY  3                        15
TIME   48   48.0   THIS IS THE INPUT SIGNAL                                            16
TIME   48   48.0   THIS IS THE OUTPUT SIGNAL + NOISE                                   17
FREQ   48   48.0   THIS IS THE CROSS POWER SPECTRAL DENSITY FROM RECORD    4           18
FREQ   48   48.0   THIS IS THE INPUT POWER SPECTRAL DENSITY  4                         19
FREQ   48   48.0   THIS IS THE OUTPUT POWER SPECTRAL DENSITY   4                       20
FREQ   48   48.0    THIS IS THE COHERENCE FUNCTICN FOR A SINGLE RECORD                 21
FREQ   48   48.0   THIS IS ENSEMBLE AVERAGE OF CRCSS POWER SPECTRAL DENSITIES          22
FREQ   48   48.0   COHERENCE FUNCTICN OBTAINED FROM ENSEMBLE AVERAGE                   23
```

Figure 3-50. Directory (Coherence Example).

4 Filters

Filters are used to modify the time- or frequency-domain behavior of a signal. The ability to perform such an operation is critical to the study of linear systems. A filter can be constructed that will accelerate, delay, or retard the dynamics of a time-domain process. Similarly, a filter can be constructed that will pass only low, high, or a range of input frequencies. In addition, a filter can be constructed that will introduce a prespecified phase shift to a processed signal. The objectives of filtering are embodied in a design criterion, which is a statement, authored by the user, that specifies the filter criterion of success. This criterion may be heuristic—such as the removal of frequencies above a prespecified value—or mathematical—such as the optimization of a system's signal-to-noise ratio.

Often heuristic filter criteria are found in linear signal analysis. For example, a biological scientist may require a filter that will pass only alpha brain waves, thereby removing ambiguous signal sources. The socioeconomic scientist may be interested in inserting into a model a filter that would have averaging capabilities. A societal engineer may be interested in introducing a data propagation delay in a societal model. A control engineer might want to design a stabilization filter that would pass only low frequencies. An instrumentation engineer may want the filter to block all multiples of 60 Hz that may be present in a measurement system.

Mathematical design criteria generally fall into one of two classes—the maximization of signal-to-noise ratios or the minimization of estimation errors. The maximizing of signal-to-noise ratio is applicable to problems where the signal is known, but appears in the presence of noise. For example, a radar return detection problem would fall into this class. Here a filter would be used to improve the signal-to-noise measure found in the radar signal-plus-noise return. The processed data would provide the signal analysis portion of the radar system with a significantly improved data base. In other applications, an estimation of the actual value of a noise-corrupted signal is desired. Here the difference between the true signal and its estimated value is to be the estimation error. Provided certain information about the noise process is known, filters that will minimize the estimation error can be designed. These filters can be used, for example, to improve the performance of a speech-recognition or communication system.

SPECTRUM IV provides the user with a collection of filtering strategies that cover both the heuristic and mathematical approaches to filter design and analysis. In all cases the filter philosophy has been merged with time-series and digital spectral analysis techniques. Therefore, to use SPECTRUM IV, only a parameter set that characterizes the desired filter function need be supplied. SPECTRUM IV will perform the required filter operation and return to the user the results of that analysis.

In particular, SPECTRUM IV contains the following filter options:

1. Transfer function synthesis (TRANSFER)
2. Ideal digital filter (D-FILTER)
3. Digital recursive filter (DISCRETE)
4. Matched filter (MATCH)
5. Wiener filter (WIENER)
6. Hanning filter (HANNING)

The purpose of the first three filter functions is that they are consistent with the heuristic approach to filtering. These digital filters can perform low-pass, high-pass, or bandpass operations. The next two digital filters satisfy prespecified mathematical design criteria. The HANNING filter function is a special purpose device; it serves to introduce periodicity in aperiodic data records.

A. Transfer Function Synthesis

From an analysis viewpoint, the concept of a transfer function was developed in Chapter 3, Section B. At that time it was shown that a transfer function was a powerful analysis tool that represented the system capability to modify the frequency-domain representation of an input process. Using time-series and spectral analysis methods, it was shown that a transfer function could be directly computed from obscured input-output behavior. However, there are many situations where synthesis, rather than analysis, is required.

Analog filter synthesis is a well-developed science. A filter may be as simple as a one-pole device or as complex as a multipole device. Some commonly used multiple-pole philosophies are those of Butterworth and Chebyshev. These filters can be configured as a low-pass, high-pass, or bandpass. Such devices have many applications. For example, they can be used to remove high-frequency electronic noise or low-frequency mechanical noise from a signal process. A bandpass filter can be used to process a select band of frequencies from a seismic signal for geological analysis purposes. In a communications application, a band of frequencies may be occupied by many signal channels, each separated from its neighbor in frequency. A highly selective filter (called a resonator) that will pass but one signal channel can be designed. Such a filter would allow a prespecified information channel to be interrogated at the exclusion of all others. A filter that will pass all but a narrow band of frequencies is called a notch filter. Such a filter can be used to remove a periodic noise source, such as 60-Hz noise.

If a filter is used to augment an existing filter, it is called a compensator. A compensator can be used to accelerate or retard system performance. In addition, it can be used to stabilize linear systems through selective phase manipulation. A transfer function can be synthesized under SPECTRUM IV control through program TRANSFER.

Theory

In general, a transfer function can be represented as the ratio of two polynomials. The polynomials can be written in either factored or unfactored form. That is, if *H(s)* is a transfer function, then it will appear in unfactored form as

$$H(s) = K_1 \sum_{i=1}^{N} \alpha_i s^{i-1} \Big/ \sum_{i=1}^{D} \beta_i s^{i-1} \tag{4.1}$$

or in factored form as

$$H(s) = K_2 \prod_{i=1}^{N} (s + \gamma_i) \Big/ \prod_{i=1}^{D} (s + \lambda_i) \tag{4.2}$$

where γ_i and λ_i are historically called the system zero and poles, respectively. The steady-state performance of these filters is denoted $H(f)$, where

$$H(f) = H(s)\big|_{s=j2\pi f} \tag{4.3}$$

The steady-state unfactored and factored forms thus become

$$H(f) = K_1 \sum_{i=1}^{N} \alpha_i (j2\pi f)^{i-1} \Big/ \sum_{i=1}^{D} \beta_i (j2\pi f)^{i-1} \tag{4.4}$$

$$H(f) = K_2 \prod_{i=1}^{N} (j2\pi f + \gamma_1) \Big/ \prod_{i=1}^{D} (j2\pi f + \lambda_i) \tag{4.5}$$

respectively. Program TRANSFER is used to generate a spectral representation of a filter given its mathematical characterization of $H(s)$. The source of this information can reside in OWN or on data cards. During execution, $H(s)$ is interpreted as $H(kf_o)$, where $f_0 = 1/T_s$, T_s is the sampling rate, and $k = 0, 1, \ldots, N - 1$.

A transfer operation is performed under SPECTRUM IV control as shown in Figure 4-1.

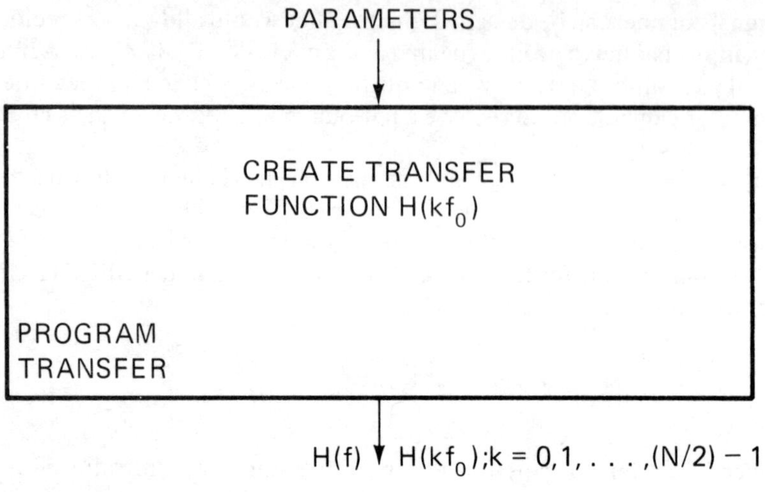

Figure 4-1. Program Transfer.

Execution of Transfer

To define a transfer function properly, the user must provide the program with all filter-defining parameters. This information includes the filter coefficients. SPECTRUM IV allows the user to accomplish this task in the following ways:

1. Read polynomial coefficients from cards.
2. Read complex coefficients from cards.
3. Read either polynomial or complex coefficients from user-supplied subprogram OWN.

Program TRANSFER will recognize the following five different kinds of data cards:

1. Primary information card, which is the first card to appear in a TRANSFER operation and is used to call program TRANSFER. See Table 4-1.
2. Secondary information card, which supplies the following information (See Table 4-2):
   a. Are the coefficients in polynomial or factored form?
   b. If their source is cards, are the data found in E or F format?
   c. What is the value of gain K_1 or K_2?
3. Origin-of-data card, which supplies the following information (see Table 4-3):
   a. Do the program parameters come from cards or a user-supplied subroutine?

Table 4-1
Primary Information Card for a TRANSFER Call

Column Number	*Description*	*Format or Contents*
Primary information card		
1-8	Calls TRANSFER	TRANSFER
15	Array to hold transfer function (A, B, or C)	A1
57-60	Number of positive harmonics to be generated	I4
61-72	Sampling frequency	F12.2
80	First user program (if applicable)	I1

Table 4-2
Secondary Information Card for a TRANSFER Call

Column Number	*Description*	*Format or Contents*
Secondary information card		
1-8	Type of data FACTORS denote complex roots of a factored polynomial POLY-JW denotes polynomial coefficients	FACTORS or POLY-JW
10	Format used (E or F)	A1
11-20	Gain K_1 or K_2	E10.3

Table 4-3
Origin-of-data Card for a TRANSFER Call

Column Number	*Description*	*Format or Contents*
Origin-of-data Card		
1-8	Data source CARDS = cards USER = user subroutine	CARDS or USER
10	Numerator = N or Denominator = D	N or D
14-15	Order of the resultant polynomial ($0 \leq$ NORDER ≤ 20)	I2

b. Do the current data being entered into program TRANSFER represent numerator of denominator coefficients?

c. What is the order of the derived numerator or denominator?

4. Data cards, which contain either the complex factor or polynominal filter coefficients. Their use is constrained as follows:

   a. A maximum of 7 polynomial coefficients per card.

   b. A maximum of 3 complex coefficients per card.

   c. A maximum of 20 complex or 21 polynomial coefficients per filter.

   d. The data must appear in either E10.3 or F10.3 format.

   Data-card utilization for a TRANSFER operation is similiar to that found in the discussion of READ IN in Chapter 1. READ IN. The reader is directed to seek detailed information about data-card input operations in that section. Briefly, the card structure appears as shown in Figure 4-2.

5. End-of-file card, which is required only when entering coefficient data from cards. It is used as follows (see also Figure 4-3):

   a. Use the six-letter mnemonic NNNNNN to terminate a numerator read-in operation.

   b. Use the six-letter mnemonic DDDDDD to terminate a denominator read-in operation.

Restrictions imposed on the use of program TRANSFER are:

1. The order of the defined polynomial must be bounded as follows:

$$0 \leq N \leq 20$$

2. When calling a user-supplied subroutine for the first time, the user must notify the program where to find the second data source. This is accomplished by using the parameter SPL

   SPL = nn:nn is the indirect address of the subprogram of subroutine OWN to be called.

3. Both the filter numerator and denominator must be defined.

4. A 0th order polynomial is to be interpreted to be a constant.

The use of program TRANSFER can be accomplished through the interaction of many combinations of control cards. Several non-numerical example problems will be offered to assist the user in resolving any ambiguity associated with the formal use of program TRANSFER.

Consider the problem of synthesizing the polynomial transfer function

$$H(s) = 5.0\frac{A + Bs + Cs^2 + Ds^3 + Es^4 + Fs^5}{A_1 + B_1s + C_1s^2}$$

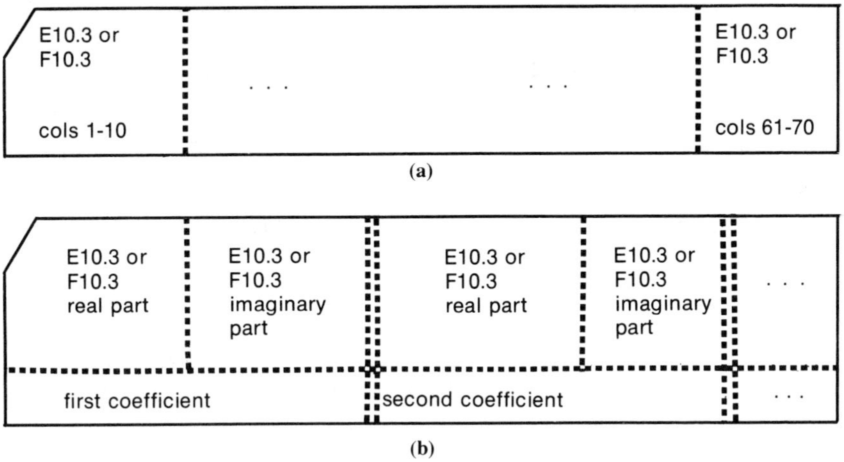

Figure 4-2. Polynomial Coefficient Card (a) and Complex Coefficient (b).

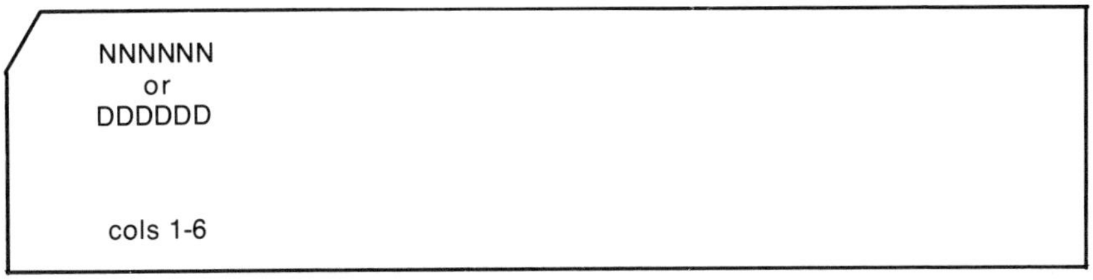

Figure 4-3. End-of-file Card.

With respect to the programming variables found in subroutine OWN, the following is true:

PN(1) = A	PD(1) = A_1
PN(2) = B	PD(2) = B_1
PN(3) = C	PD(3) = C_1
PN(4) = D	
PN(5) = E	
PN(6) = F	

The first example will treat the problem of entering polynomial filter coefficients into program TRANSFER from a user-supplied subroutine. The card control sequence required of such a task is shown in Figure 4-4, and subprogram OWN would contain the elements shown in Figure 4-5.

A transfer function will be synthesized through the following sequence of events:

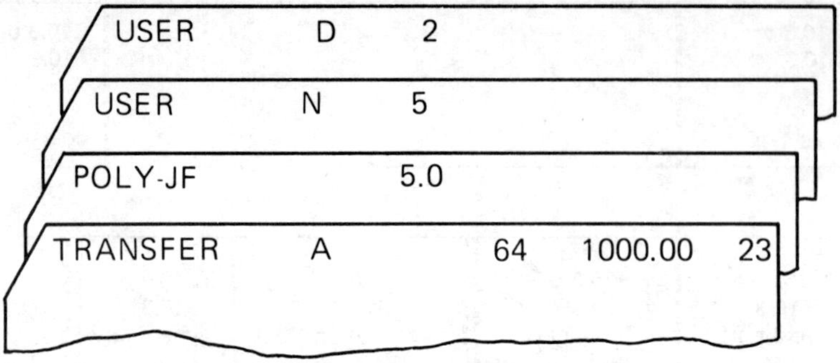

Figure 4-4. Numerator and Denominator Polynomial Synthesis.

```
 5 6 7
          OWN
          . . .
          . . .
          IF (SPLEQ.23) GO TO 23
          IF (SPLEQ.3) GO TO 3
          . . .
          . . .
23        create numerator coefficients
          . . . A,B,C,D,E,F . . .
          . . .                      SAMPLE PROBLEM
          SPL=3
          GO TO 99
          . . .
3         create denominator coefficients
          . . . A1,B1,C1 . . .
          . . .
          GO TO 99
          . . .
99        RETURN
```

Figure 4-5. Subroutine OWN.

1. A 64-point representation of a transfer function is requested for a sampling frequency of 1000 Hz. The first set of polynominal coefficients is declared to be resident at indirect address 23 of user-supplied subprogram OWN.

2. The filter to be synthesized is defined in terms of numerator and denominator polynomials having a maximal order of five (5).
3. Numerator coefficients are read from the user-supplied subroutine. The entry point has been given the prespecified value of 23. Before leaving this calculation, the next entry point is established. The indirect address for a re-entry into subprogram OWN is defined to be SPL = 3.
4. The remaining two-denominator coefficients are presented to program TRANSFER. They are found by entering subprogram OWN at indirect address 3.

Consider now the problem of synthesizing a filter of the form:

$$H(s) = 100 \frac{1.0}{(\mathrm{s} + \mathbf{A}_1 + \mathrm{j}\mathbf{B}_1)(\mathrm{s} + \mathbf{A}_2 + \mathrm{j}\mathbf{B}_2)}$$

through the use of a user-supplied subprogram. With respect to the programming variables found in routine OWN, the following is true:

$$\begin{aligned} \mathrm{FRD}(1) &= \mathbf{A}_1 \\ \mathrm{FRD}(2) &= \mathbf{A}_2 \\ \mathrm{FCD}(1) &= \mathbf{B}_1 \\ \mathrm{FCD}(2) &= \mathbf{B}_2 \end{aligned}$$

The card control sequence required by this task is shown in Figure 4-6. The operative sequence is similar to the previously discussed problem. Here the real and complex terms of a factored form filter are read into the program. The handling of indirect address is the same. Since the filter numerator is 0th order, the programming variable PN found in subprogram OWN is assigned the value PN(1)=1. During program execution, the factored denominator terms are multiplied together to produce a polynomial. Under SPECTRUM IV control the filter function is analyzed for 80 positive harmonics, defined in terms of a 105-Hz sample rate, and then stored in array B.

The problem of constructing a filter characterized by a fourteenth-order denominator and a third-order numerator from a card based data source would be accomplished as shown in Figure 4-7. In this example,

1. Four numerator polynomial coefficients are read from cards. This defines the third-order numerator.
2. Fifteen polynomial denominator coefficients are read from cards. This defines the fourteenth-order denominator.
3. All read operations are done in F format.
4. The value of K_1 is specified to be 10.0.
5. The transfer function is created over 50 positive harmonics using a sample frequency of 100 Hz.

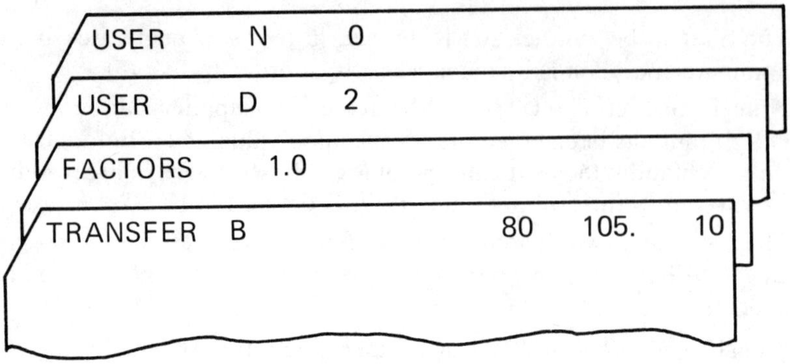

Figure 4-6. Numerator and Denominator Factor Synthesis.

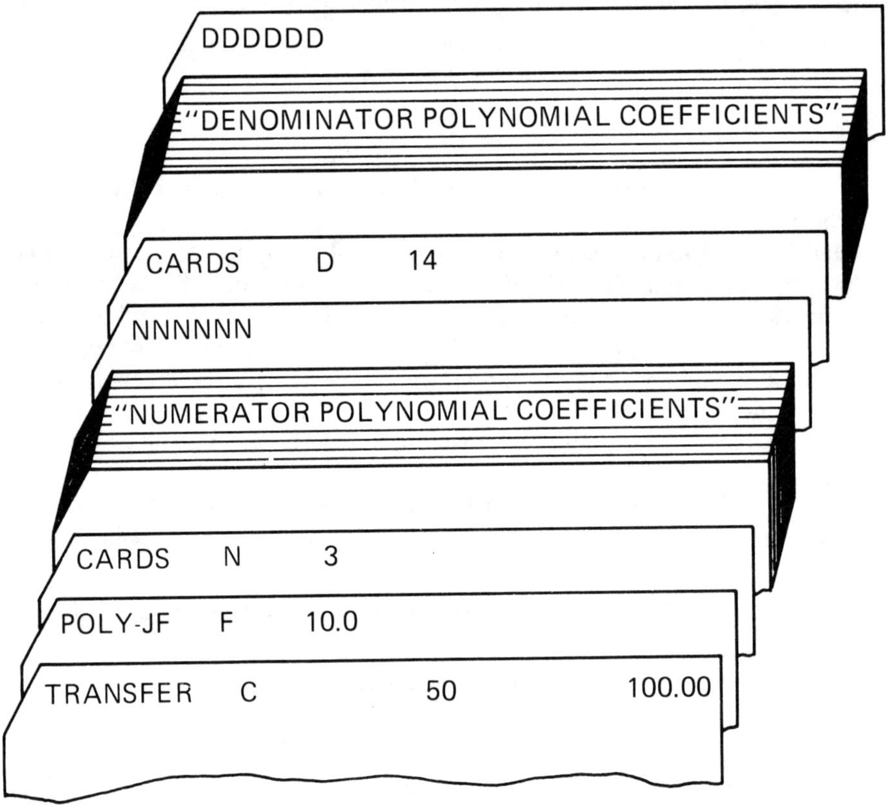

Figure 4-7. Filter Synthesis from Card Data.

6. The resultant filter is stored in array C.

As a final example, consider the problem of constructing a transfer function defined in terms of a fifteenth-order denominator and a third-order numerator. Furthermore, let the filter coefficients be derived from user-supplied subroutine and card-based data sets. See Figure 4-8, where:

1. Fifteen denominator complex factors are read from cards to construct the fifteenth-order denominator.
2. Three complex numerator coefficients are read from subroutine OWN at indirect address 5. The coefficients define a third-order numerator.
3. The data are read in E format.
4. The filter gain is set equal to 20.0
5. The transfer function is defined over 25 positive harmonics defined in terms of a 200-Hz sample rate.
6. The filter is stored in array A.

Example. Consider the following second-order transfer function denoted $H(s)$:

$$H(s) = 10.0 \frac{1.0}{s^2 + 10s + 125} = 10.0 \frac{1.0}{(s + 5 + j10)(s + 5 - j10)}$$

The filter's poles are located at

$$s = 0.5 \pm j10$$

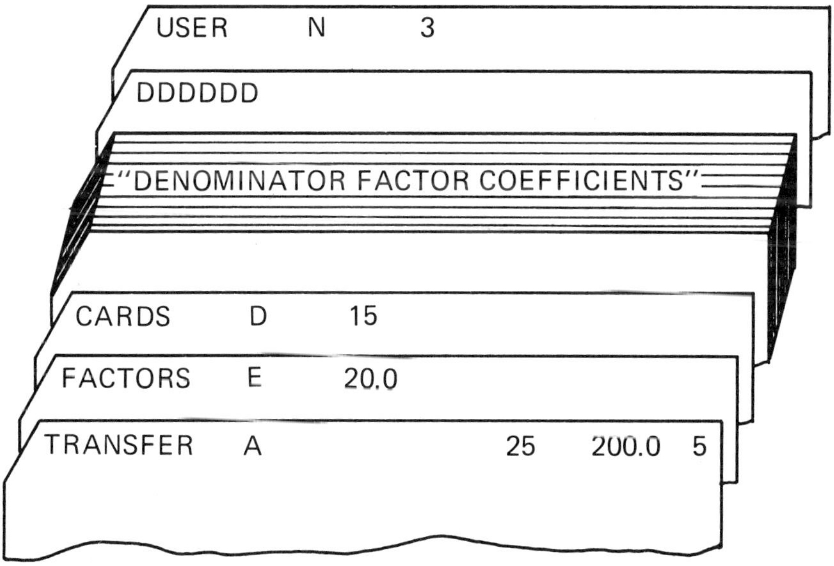

Figure 4-8. Filter Synthesis from User Supplied Data.

The analysis of such a filter was performed using three of the TRANSFER program input options:

1. Define $H(s)$ in terms of numerator and denominator polynomial coefficients that are resident on cards.
2. Define $H(s)$ in terms of numerator and denominator complex factors that are resident on cards.
3. Define $H(s)$ in terms of numerator and denominator complex factors that are generated in subprogram OWN.

The result of such an experiment can be found in Figures 4-9 through 4-14. The card control sequence required by this problem is found in Figure 4-9. Note the insertion of a STATUS card at the beginning and end of the program control deck.[a] (See section D of Chapter 5 for a detailed discussion of this SPECTRUM IV option.) The execution of a STATUS card will cause a memory "dump" of the contents of system control parameters and storage arrays. The remainder of the cards provide the program with the primary and secondary information required to produce the requested transfer function. Where applicable, data are supplied.

Subroutine OWN can be found in Figure 4-10. Note that the generation of the complex denominator roots is accomplished in accordance with the previously established rules of a USER LIB operation.

The magnitude spectra associated with the first 25 positive harmonics of all three experiments can be found in Figures 4-11, 4-12, and 4-13. The profile of the underdamped second-order transfer function is invariant to the method used to input data. The d-c gain of the filter is found to be 10/125 = 0.800E-2. The maximal filter gain is found at 9.0 Hz with a value of 0.9988E-2.

Finally, the example problem is completed with a memory dump through the application of a STATUS operation. The reader will note that the dump operation supplies control parameter as well as storage array data. This information can be an invaluable debugging aid.

B. Ideal Digital Filters

Purpose

It is often desirable to alter the gain and phase frequency-domain profile of some signals under analysis. These changes can range from the radical to the subtle. If, for example, one is interested in detecting the presence of a select number of frequencies in a complex signal, one would take the FFT of that signal and then radically alter it by setting all magnitude and phase

[a] See the discussion of STATUS on pp.311-312 in Chapter 6.

```
CARD    COLUMN                                                                        8ø
        123456789ø12      .         .         .         .         .         .         .
----------------------------------------------------------------------------------------
1       STATUS
2       TRANSFER      A                                  F        5ø      5ø.ø
3       POLY-UF  F      1.E1
4       CARDS    D    2
5          125.       1ø.         1.
6       DDDD
7       CARDS    N    ø
8            1.
9       NNNN
1ø      PLOTTER       A                                           25
11      FREQ   MAG         1   25    POLYNOMIAL FORM SYNTHESIS
12      ZERO-OUT      A
13      TRANSFER      A                                  F        5ø      5ø.
14      FACTORS  F      1.E1
15      CARDS    N    ø
16      NNNN
17      CARDS    D    2
18          -5.       1ø.       -5.      -1ø.
19      DDDD
2ø      PLOTTER       A                                           25
21      FREQ   MAG         1   25    FACTORED FORM SYNTHESIS
22      ZERO-OUT      A                                  F        5ø      5ø.         3
23      TRANSFER      A
24      FACTORS  F      1.E1
25      USER     N    ø
25      USER     D    2
26      PLOTTER       A                                           25
27      FREQ   MAG         1   25    POLYNOMIAL FORM USER LIBRARY
28      STATJS
29      TERM
                  .         .         .         .         .         .         .         .
```

Figure 4-9. Card Control Sequence for Transfer Function Experiment.

```
FORTRAN IV G LEVEL  21                  OWN                 DATE = 75156          16/12/01                 PAGE 0001

                SUBROUTINE OWN
          C
          C  THE FOLLOWING FIVE STATEMENTS SHOULD BE INCLUDED IN ANY SUBROUTINE OWN
                REAL*8 BAN
                INTEGER DSO,E,F,TIME,FREQ,SPL
                COMMON REST(6148),TEMR(1024),TEMC(1024),FRN(20),FCN(20),FRD(20),
               1FCD(20),PN(21),PD(21),REST1(82),NPOINT,REST2(5),SPL,REST3(2)
                COMMON /LETTER/ F,E,MAR(3),LAIS(60),TIME,FREQ,IBAN,BAN,LN,NN,NP
          C
          C
                WRITE(LN,3) SPL
              3 FORMAT(10X,'USER PROGRAM NUMBER ',I2,/)
                IF(SPL.EQ.3) GO TO 7
                GO TO 99
              7 FRD(1) =-5.0
                FRD(2) =-5.0
                FCD(1) = 10.
                FCD(2) =-10.
             99 CONTINUE
                RETURN
                END
```

Figure 4-10. Subroutine OWN (Transfer Function Experiment).

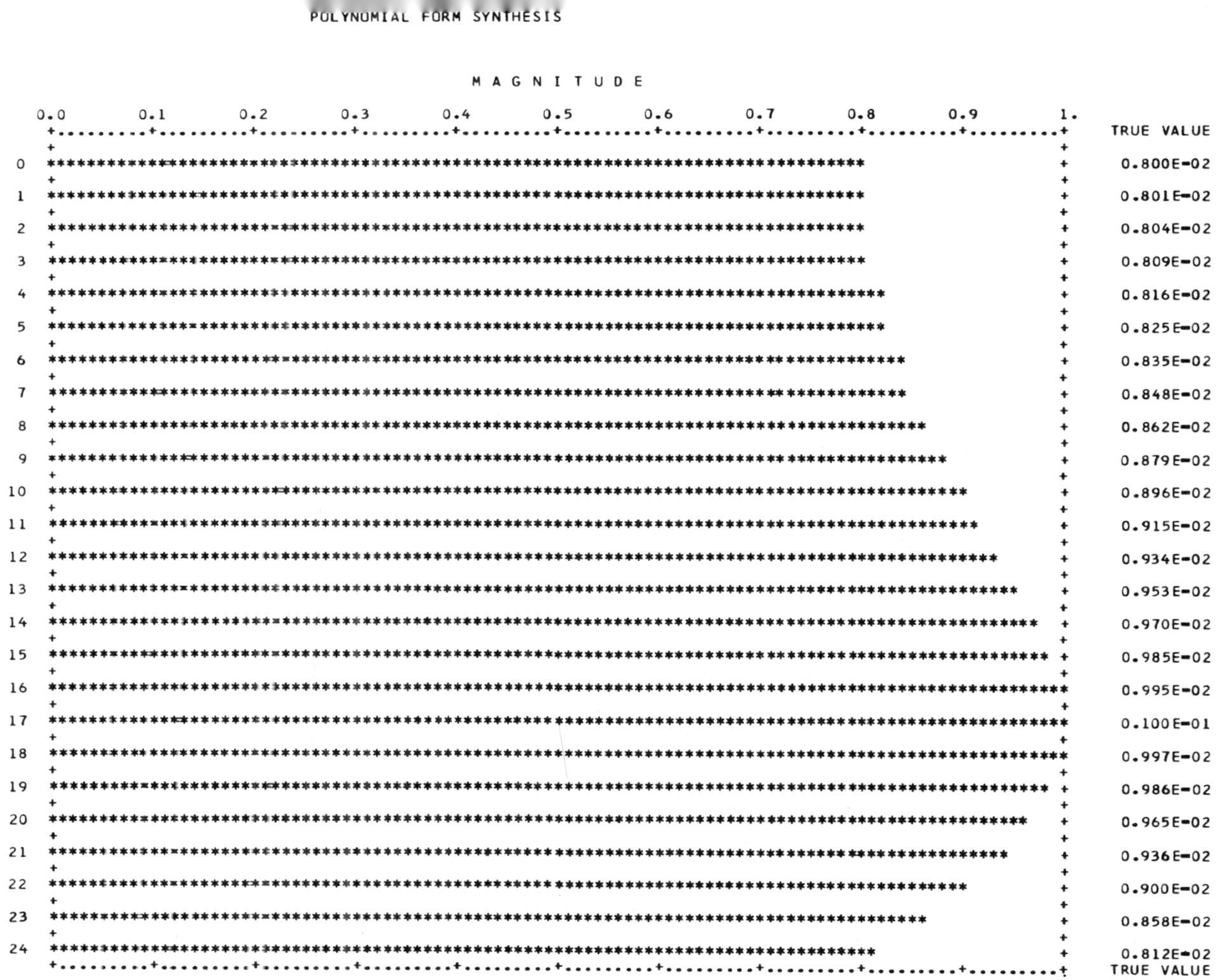

Figure 4-11. Magnitude Spectra of $H(s)$: POLY-JF (Transfer Function Experiment).

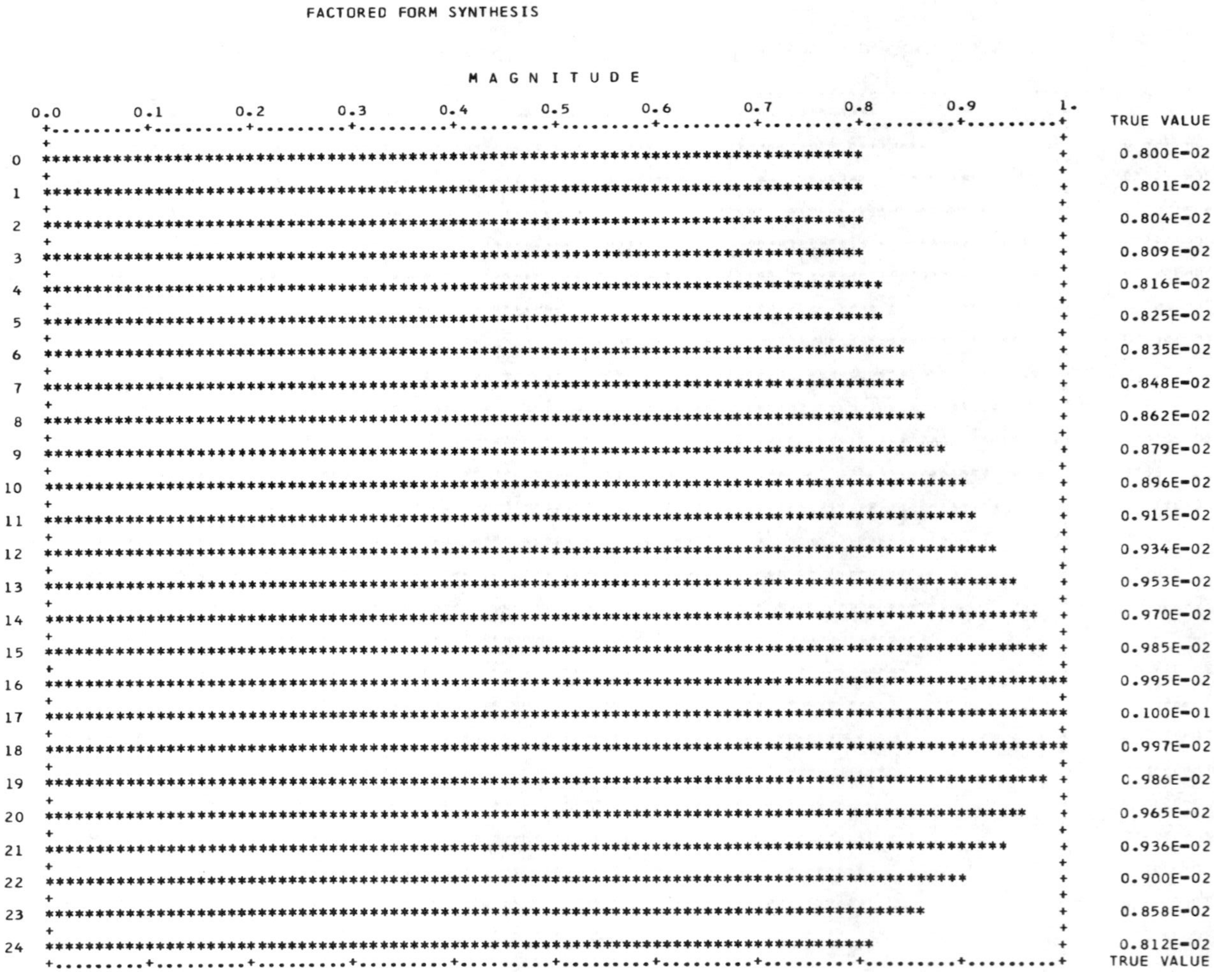

Figure 4-12. Magnitude Spectra of $H(s)$: FACTORS (Transfer Function Experiment).

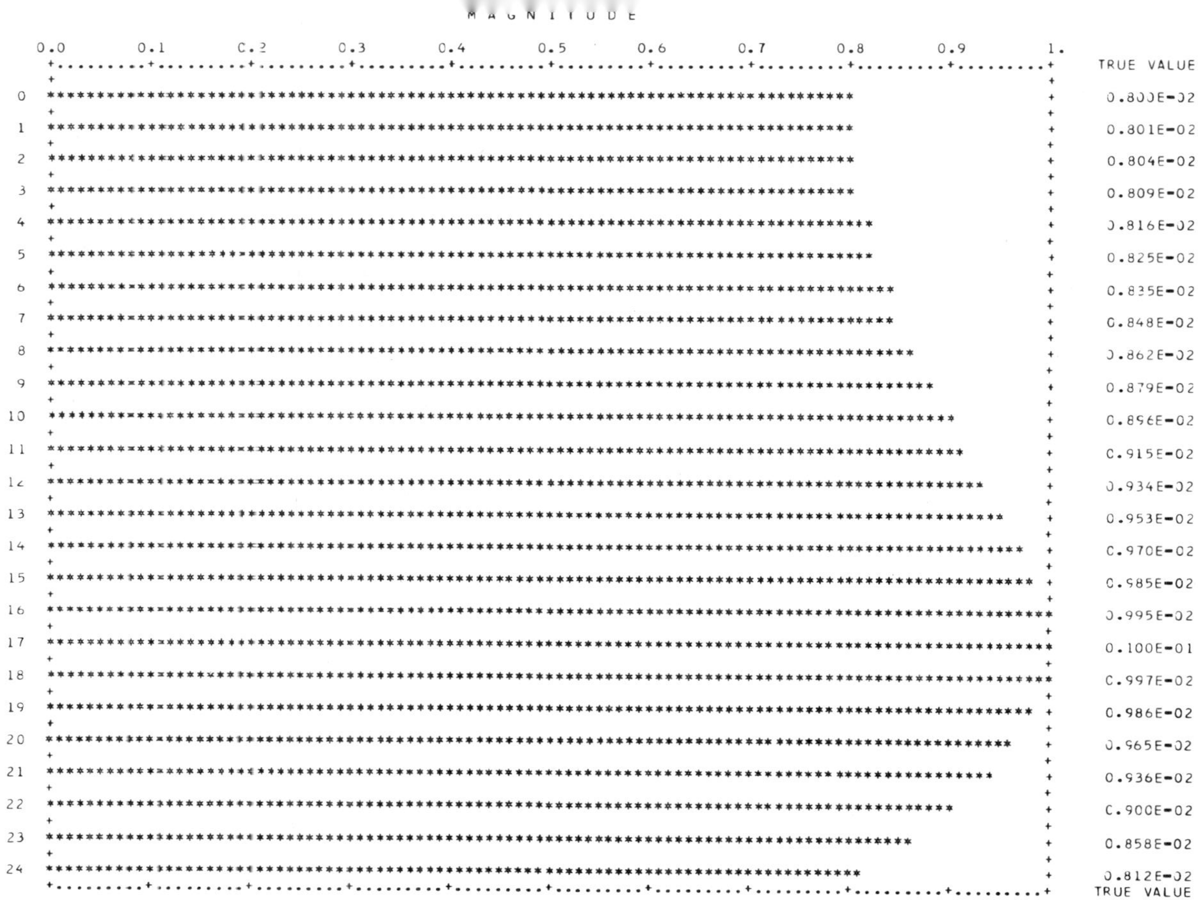

Figure 4-13. Magnitude Spectra of $H(s)$: OWN (Transfer Function Experiment).

ARRAY	A	B	C	ARRAY
NUMBER OF POINTS	99	0	0	NUMBER OF POINTS
DOMAIN	FREQ	NONE	NONE	DOMAIN
SAMPLE FREQUENCY	50.0	0.0	0.0	SAMPLE FREQUENCY

CONTROL PARAMETER	1	2	3	4	5	6	7	8	9	10
STATUS	1	0	0	0	0	0	0	0	0	0
CONTROL PARAMETER	11	12	13	14	15	16	17	18	19	20
STATUS	0	0	0	0	0	0	0	0	0	1

THESE ARE THE PRESENT CONTENTS OF ALL WORKING ARRAYS FOR 99 POINTS

ARRAY A		ARRAY B		ARRAY C		TEMPORARY ARRAY		
REAL	COMPLEX	REAL	COMPLEX	REAL	COMPLEX	REAL	COMPLEX	POINT
0.800E-02	0.0	0.0	0.0	0.0	0.0	0.800E-02	0.0	1
0.800E-02	-0.324E-03	0.0	0.0	0.0	0.0	0.801E-02	0.0	2
0.801E-02	-0.653E-03	0.0	0.0	0.0	0.0	0.804E-02	0.0	3
0.803E-02	-0.991E-03	0.0	0.0	0.0	0.0	0.809E-02	0.0	4
0.805E-02	-0.134E-02	0.0	0.0	0.0	0.0	0.816E-02	0.0	5
0.806E-02	-0.172E-02	0.0	0.0	0.0	0.0	0.825E-02	0.0	6
0.808E-02	-0.211E-02	0.0	0.0	0.0	0.0	0.835E-02	0.0	7
0.809E-02	-0.254E-02	0.0	0.0	0.0	0.0	0.848E-02	0.0	8
0.808E-02	-0.301E-02	0.0	0.0	0.0	0.0	0.862E-02	0.0	9
0.806E-02	-0.351E-02	0.0	0.0	0.0	0.0	0.879E-02	0.0	10
0.799E-02	-0.406E-02	0.0	0.0	0.0	0.0	0.896E-02	0.0	11
0.788E-02	-0.465E-02	0.0	0.0	0.0	0.0	0.915E-02	0.0	12
0.770E-02	-0.529E-02	0.0	0.0	0.0	0.0	0.934E-02	0.0	13

```
 0.743E-02 -0.596E-02   0.0   0.0   0.0   0.0   0.953E-02  0.0   14
 0.706E-02 -0.665E-02   0.0   0.0   0.0   0.0   0.970E-02  0.0   15
 0.656E-02 -0.735E-02   0.0   0.0   0.0   0.0   0.985E-02  0.0   16
 0.591E-02 -0.801E-02   0.0   0.0   0.0   0.0   0.995E-02  0.0   17
 0.513E-02 -0.858E-02   0.0   0.0   0.0   0.0   0.100E-01  0.0   18
 0.421E-02 -0.904E-02   0.0   0.0   0.0   0.0   0.997E-02  0.0   19
 0.320E-02 -0.932E-02   0.0   0.0   0.0   0.0   0.986E-02  0.0   20
 0.214E-02 -0.941E-02   0.0   0.0   0.0   0.0   0.965E-02  0.0   21
 0.110E-02 -0.930E-02   0.0   0.0   0.0   0.0   0.936E-02  0.0   22
 0.125E-03 -0.900E-02   0.0   0.0   0.0   0.0   0.900E-02  0.0   23
-0.731E-03 -0.855E-02   0.0   0.0   0.0   0.0   0.858E-02  0.0   24
-0.144E-02 -0.799E-02   0.0   0.0   0.0   0.0   0.812E-02  0.0   25
-0.201E-02 -0.737E-02   0.0   0.0   0.0   0.0   0.0        0.0   26
-0.243E-02 -0.674E-02   0.0   0.0   0.0   0.0   0.0        0.0   27
-0.273E-02 -0.611E-02   0.0   0.0   0.0   0.0   0.0        0.0   28
-0.293E-02 -0.552E-02   0.0   0.0   0.0   0.0   0.0        0.0   29
-0.304E-02 -0.497E-02   0.0   0.0   0.0   0.0   0.0        0.0   30
-0.309E-02 -0.447E-02   0.0   0.0   0.0   0.0   0.0        0.0   31
-0.308E-02 -0.402E-02   0.0   0.0   0.0   0.0   0.0        0.0   32
-0.305E-02 -0.362E-02   0.0   0.0   0.0   0.0   0.0        0.0   33
-0.299E-02 -0.326E-02   0.0   0.0   0.0   0.0   0.0        0.0   34
-0.291E-02 -0.294E-02   0.0   0.0   0.0   0.0   0.0        0.0   35
-0.282E-02 -0.266E-02   0.0   0.0   0.0   0.0   0.0        0.0   36
-0.273E-02 -0.241E-02   0.0   0.0   0.0   0.0   0.0        0.0   37
-0.263E-02 -0.219E-02   0.0   0.0   0.0   0.0   0.0        0.0   38
-0.253E-02 -0.200E-02   0.0   0.0   0.0   0.0   0.0        0.0   39
-0.244E-02 -0.182E-02   0.0   0.0   0.0   0.0   0.0        0.0   40
-0.234E-02 -0.167E-02   0.0   0.0   0.0   0.0   0.0        0.0   41
-0.225E-02 -0.153E-02   0.0   0.0   0.0   0.0   0.0        0.0   42
-0.216E-02 -0.141E-02   0.0   0.0   0.0   0.0   0.0        0.0   43
-0.207E-02 -0.130E-02   0.0   0.0   0.0   0.0   0.0        0.0   44
-0.199E-02 -0.120E-02   0.0   0.0   0.0   0.0   0.0        0.0   45
-0.191E-02 -0.111E-02   0.0   0.0   0.0   0.0   0.0        0.0   46
-0.184E-02 -0.103E-02   0.0   0.0   0.0   0.0   0.0        0.0   47
-0.176E-02 -0.955E-03   0.0   0.0   0.0   0.0   0.0        0.0   48
-0.170E-02 -0.888E-03   0.0   0.0   0.0   0.0   0.0        0.0   49
-0.163E-02 -0.828E-03   0.0   0.0   0.0   0.0   0.0        0.0   50
-0.163E-02  0.828E-03   0.0   0.0   0.0   0.0   0.0        0.0   51
-0.170E-02  0.888E-03   0.0   0.0   0.0   0.0   0.0        0.0   52
-0.176E-02  0.955E-03   0.0   0.0   0.0   0.0   0.0        0.0   53
-0.184E-02  0.103E-02   0.0   0.0   0.0   0.0   0.0        0.0   54
-0.191E-02  0.111E-02   0.0   0.0   0.0   0.0   0.0        0.0   55
-0.199E-02  0.120E-02   0.0   0.0   0.0   0.0   0.0        0.0   56
-0.207E-02  0.130E-02   0.0   0.0   0.0   0.0   0.0        0.0   57
-0.216E-02  0.141E-02   0.0   0.0   0.0   0.0   0.0        0.0   58
-0.225E-02  0.153E-02   0.0   0.0   0.0   0.0   0.0        0.0   59
-0.234E-02  0.167E-02   0.0   0.0   0.0   0.0   0.0        0.0   60
```

Figure 4-14. Status Dump (Transfer Function Experiment).

-0.244E-02	0.182E-02	0.0	0.0	0.0	0.0	0.0	0.0	61
-0.253E-02	0.200E-02	0.0	0.0	0.0	0.0	0.0	0.0	62
-0.263E-02	0.219E-02	0.0	0.0	0.0	0.0	0.0	0.0	63
-0.273E-02	0.241E-02	0.0	0.0	0.0	0.0	0.0	0.0	64
-0.282E-02	0.266E-02	0.0	0.0	0.0	0.0	0.0	0.0	65
-0.291E-02	0.294E-02	0.0	0.0	0.0	0.0	0.0	0.0	66
-0.299E-02	0.326E-02	0.0	0.0	0.0	0.0	0.0	0.0	67
-0.305E-02	0.362E-02	0.0	0.0	0.0	0.0	0.0	0.0	68
-0.308E-02	0.402E-02	0.0	0.0	0.0	0.0	0.0	0.0	69
-0.309E-02	0.447E-02	0.0	0.0	0.0	0.0	0.0	0.0	70
-0.304E-02	0.497E-02	0.0	0.0	0.0	0.0	0.0	0.0	71
-0.293E-02	0.552E-02	0.0	0.0	0.0	0.0	0.0	0.0	72
-0.273E-02	0.611E-02	0.0	0.0	0.0	0.0	0.0	0.0	73
-0.243E-02	0.674E-02	0.0	0.0	0.0	0.0	0.0	0.0	74
-0.201E-02	0.737E-02	0.0	0.0	0.0	0.0	0.0	0.0	75
-0.144E-02	0.799E-02	0.0	0.0	0.0	0.0	0.0	0.0	76
-0.731E-03	0.855E-02	0.0	0.0	0.0	0.0	0.0	0.0	77
0.125E-03	0.900E-02	0.0	0.0	0.0	0.0	0.0	0.0	78
0.110E-02	0.930E-02	0.0	0.0	0.0	0.0	0.0	0.0	79
0.214E-02	0.941E-02	0.0	0.0	0.0	0.0	0.0	0.0	80
0.320E-02	0.932E-02	0.0	0.0	0.0	0.0	0.0	0.0	81
0.421E-02	0.904E-02	0.0	0.0	0.0	0.0	0.0	0.0	82
0.513E-02	0.858E-02	0.0	0.0	0.0	0.0	0.0	0.0	83
0.591E-02	0.801E-02	0.0	0.0	0.0	0.0	0.0	0.0	84
0.656E-02	0.735E-02	0.0	0.0	0.0	0.0	0.0	0.0	85
0.706E-02	0.665E-02	0.0	0.0	0.0	0.0	0.0	0.0	86
0.743E-02	0.596E-02	0.0	0.0	0.0	0.0	0.0	0.0	87
0.770E-02	0.529E-02	0.0	0.0	0.0	0.0	0.0	0.0	88
0.788E-02	0.465E-02	0.0	0.0	0.0	0.0	0.0	0.0	89
0.799E-02	0.406E-02	0.0	0.0	0.0	0.0	0.0	0.0	90
0.806E-02	0.351E-02	0.0	0.0	0.0	0.0	0.0	0.0	91
0.808E-02	0.301E-02	0.0	0.0	0.0	0.0	0.0	0.0	92
0.809E-02	0.254E-02	0.0	0.0	0.0	0.0	0.0	0.0	93
0.808E-02	0.211E-02	0.0	0.0	0.0	0.0	0.0	0.0	94
0.806E-02	0.172E-02	0.0	0.0	0.0	0.0	0.0	0.0	95
0.805E-02	0.134E-02	0.0	0.0	0.0	0.0	0.0	0.0	96
0.803E-02	0.991E-03	0.0	0.0	0.0	0.0	0.0	0.0	97
0.801E-02	0.653E-03	0.0	0.0	0.0	0.0	0.0	0.0	98
0.800E-02	0.324E-03	0.0	0.0	0.0	0.0	0.0	0.0	99

Figure 4-14 (Continued)

components of all frequencies—execpt those to be detected—equal to zero. If certain frequencies in a spectra are undesired, they can be removed similarly. For example, suppose a signal has an unwanted frequency component at 60 Hz (see Figure 4-15). It is a simple task to construct an ideal digital filter, say, $H(f)$, that passes all but 60 Hz with unity gain.

A subtle change may be to uniformly change all phase components of a transformed signal. This might be accomplished for stability considerations. Program D-FILTER will allow SPECTRUM IV user to perform ideal filter operations.

Theory

An ideal filter is characterized by a linear phase shift as a function of frequency with unity gain over a given frequency range, zero gain elsewhere. Mathematically, if $H(f)$ is an ideal filter, then

$$H(f) = |H(f)| \angle \theta$$

where

$$|H(f)| = \begin{Bmatrix} 1 \text{ if } f_{\text{LOWER}} \leq f \leq f_{\text{UPPER}} \\ 0 \text{ otherwise} \end{Bmatrix}$$

and the phase angle θ is a linear function of frequency given by

$$\theta = \alpha f$$

graphically, $H(f)$ appears as shown in Figure 4-16.

The ideal filter considered in SPECTRUM IV admits only piecewise constant magnitude changes. The phase shift associated with the ideal filter considered by SPECTRUM IV is assumed to be zero.

Ideal filters are considered to be of one of the following four categories:

1. Low-pass

$$H(f) = \begin{Bmatrix} 1 \text{ if } 0 \leq f \leq f_{\text{UPPER}} \\ 0 \text{ otherwise} \end{Bmatrix}$$

2. High-pass

$$H(f) = \begin{Bmatrix} 1 \text{ if } f_{\text{LOWER}} \leq f \leq \infty \\ 0 \text{ otherwise} \end{Bmatrix}$$

3. Bandpass

$$H(f) = \begin{Bmatrix} 1 \text{ if } f_{\text{LOWER}} \leq f \leq f_{\text{UPPER}} \\ 0 \text{ otherwise} \end{Bmatrix}$$

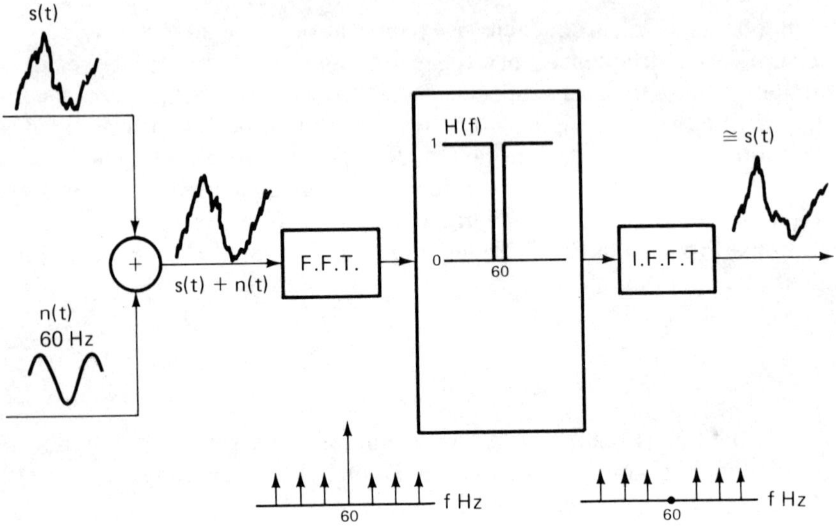

Figure 4-15. Ideal Digital Filtering.

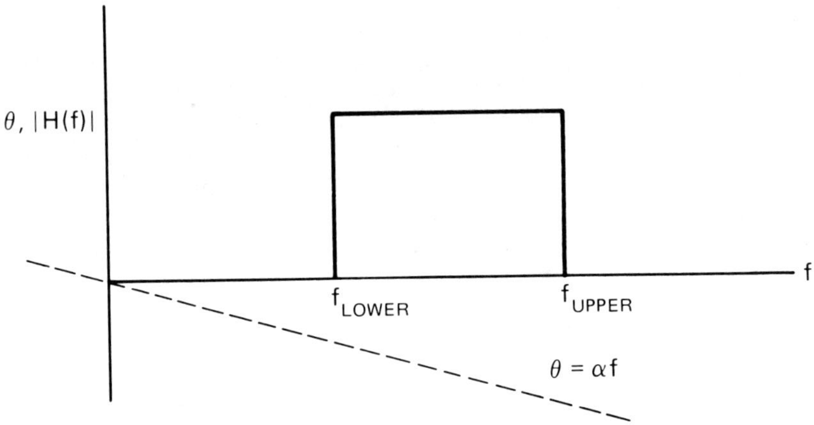

Figure 4-16. Ideal Filter.

4. Notch

$$H(f) = \begin{Bmatrix} 0 \text{ if } f = f_o \\ 1 \text{ otherwise} \end{Bmatrix}$$

Program D-FILTER of SPECTRUM IV will allow the user to perform any of the foregoing filter options. The filter options are selected by using an option code.

SPECTRUM IV performs an ideal filter operation in a direct manner. In block diagram, it appears as shown in Figure 4-17.

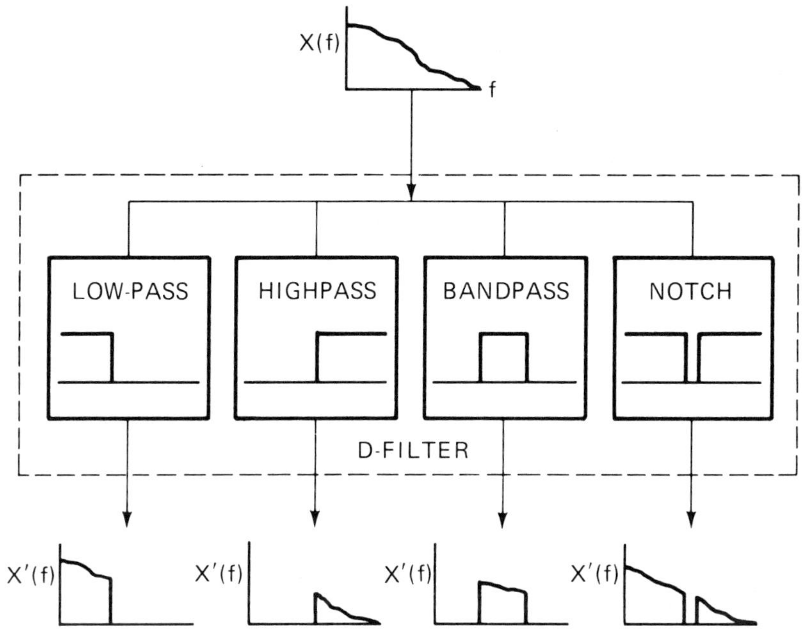

Figure 4-17. Program D-FILTER.

Execution of D-FILTER

An ideal filter operation is accomplished by using the eight-letter mnemonic D-FILTER. The filter operation is applied to the frequency domain record in a specific array. The desired filter category is assigned by using a code. The ideal filtered data are returned to the array they originated from. The control structure of D-FILTER is as follows:

1. Low-pass: D-FILTER will set to zero all frequency components greater than f_{UPPER}.
2. High-pass: D-FILTER will set to zero all frequency components less than f_{LOWER}.

3. Bandpass: D-FILTER will set to zero all frequencies outside the interval f_{LOWER} to f_{UPPER}.
4. Notch: D-FILTER will set to zero the harmonic nearest to f_o.

The control card required for a D-FILTER operation is shown in Table 4-4.

SPECTRUM IV will automatically output, upon the completion of a D-FILTER operation, information about the sample frequency and number of sample points used. In addition, cut-off or notch frequencies are echo-printed. The filter data record can be formed in the originally designated array and domain.

Example. Ideal filters can be used to exercise precise control over the spectral representation of a signal process. To exemplify this, two experiments are performed:

1. An ideal low-pass filter: A pulse of duty cycle 0.25 is created. The spectral representation of such a pulse train is rich in harmonic content. An ideal low-pass filter is used to annihilate the high-frequency components of that signal process. The low-pass time-series representation of the original pulse train is then displayed and analyzed.
2. Noise removal: A scientist often will find that electronically produced data can become contaminated with 60-Hz line frequency noise. An ideal digital notch filter can be used to remove the effects of such a noise process. To demonstrate, a 10-Hz signal process is corrupted with 60-Hz additive noise. The 60-Hz component is removed by a notch filter and the results analyzed.

The results of this experimentation can be found in Figures 4-18 through 4-27. Figure 4-18 contains the card control sequence associated with the experiment. A USER LIB operation is needed to support the experiment. This operation assigns the task of generating the 10- and 60-Hz signals of the second experiment to subroutine OWN.

The signal tested in the first experiment has harmonics at integer multiples of 9.615 Hz. Therefore a 100-Hz low-pass filter would allow only the first 10 positive harmonics to appear at the output (that is, harmonic 0 through 9). The result of the low-pass experiment is interpreted in Figures 4-20 through 4-23. Comparing the time series found in Figures 4-20 and 4-23, the effects of a low-pass filter became evident. Note that although the general shape of the original pulse train is preserved, the edge character is destroyed. It is well known that edges, which represent a rapid change in algebraic value, are characterized by high-frequency components. That is, high-frequency harmonics are required to support rapid changes in a signal profile. You may recall that an impulse signal process which has severe edge behavior, is characterized by an abundance of high-frequency components.

Table 4-4
Structure of a D-FILTER Call

Column Number	*Description*	*Format or Contents*
Primary information card		
1-8	Calls D-FILTER	D-FILTER
15	Array to filtered (A, B, or C)	A1
Secondary information card		
1-15	f_{LOWER}	F15.2
16-30	f_{UPPER}	F15.2
31-45	f_0	F15.2
49-56	Filter mnemonic designator LOW PASS or HIGH PASS or BANDPASS or NOTCH bbb	A8

The analysis of the second experiment is accomplished in a straightforward manner. The composite signal spectra, found in Figure 4-25, is composed of two distinct spectral lines located at 10 Hz and 60 Hz. The notch filter zeroes the 60-Hz line. The remaining 10-Hz line is then displayed in the frequency and time domain.

C. Recursive Digital Filter

Digital filters are classified as either recursive or nonrecursive. Recursive filters have feedback. Here, in a prespecified manner, part of the output is feedback to the input. A filter using throughput, at the exclusion of feedback, is classified as nonrecursive. Besides differing in structure, they differ in impulse response. Because a nonrecursive filter has no feedback, its impulse response must be of finite time duration. However, a recursive filter can use its feedback structure to continually resupply signal energy to the input. Therefore recursive digital filter often is called an infinite-impulse time-duration filter. To perform a given filter function, a recursive filter is generally more efficient than its nonrecursive counterpart. That is, generally a recursive filter will require fewer multiplications and additions than a nonrecursive mechanization.

Recursive digital filters have been successfully applied to a wide class of filtering problems. These filters can operate over a wide range of frequencies in a low-pass, high-pass, or bandpass configuration. The design philosophies associated with these filters either take advantage of the

```
CARD       COLUMN                                                                          8Ø
           123456789Ø12         .        .        .        .        .        .        .
-------------------------------------------------------------------------------------------
1          LIBRARY      A                                                  52      5ØØ.
2          PULSE TRAIN                                     2  1.Ø  Ø.Ø       .5ØØ
3          PLOTTER      A                                                  52
4          TIME                 1   52    PULSE TRAIN
5          FFT          A
6          PLOTTER      A                                                  26
7          FREQ   MAG           1   26    BEFORE FILTERING
8          D-FILTER     A
9                   1ØØ.                                       LOW-PASS
1Ø         PLOTTER      A                                                  26
11         FREQ   MAG           1   26    AFTER FILTERING
12         IFFT
13         PLOTTER      A                                                  52
14         TIME                 1   52    LOW-PASSED PULSE TRAIN
15         USER LIB     A                                                  6Ø      6ØØ.      1
16         SINE WAVE OF 1Ø HZ WITH 6Ø HZ NOISE
17         PLOTTER      A                                                  6Ø
18         TIME                 1   6Ø    PRF = 1Ø HZ PLUS 6Ø HZ NOISE
19         FFT          A
2Ø         PLOTTER      A                                                  3Ø
21         FREQ   MAG           1   3Ø    BEFORE FILTERING
22         D-FILTER     A
23                                                    6Ø.     NOTCH
24         PLOTTER      A
25         FREQ   MAG           1   3Ø    AFTER FILTERING
26         IFFT
27         PLOTTER      A                                                  6Ø
28         TIME                 1   6Ø    FILTER SIGNAL
29         TERM
                    .        .        .        .        .        .        .        .
```

Figure 4-18. Card Control Sequence for Ideal Filter Experiment.

```
FORTRAN IV G LEVEL  21                  OWN                 DATE = 75184          11/20/51                  PAGE 0001

0001                  SUBROUTINE OWN
                C
                C   THE FOLLOWING FIVE STATEMENTS SHOULD BE INCLUDED IN ANY SUBROUTINE OWN
0002                  REAL*8 BAN
0003                  INTEGER DSO,E,F,TIME,FREQ,SPL
0004                  COMMON REST(6148),TEMR(1024),TEMC(1024),FRN(20),FCN(20),FRD(20),
                     1FCD(20),PN(21),PD(21),REST1(82),NPOINT,REST2(5),SPL,REST3(2)
0005                  COMMON /LETTER/ F,E,MAR(3),LAIS(60),TIME,FREQ,IBAN,BAN,LN,NN,NP
                C
                C
0006                  WRITE(LN,3) SPL
0007                3 FORMAT(10X,'USER PROGRAM NUMBER ',I2,/)
0008                  PI2 = 8.0*ATAN(1.0)
0009                  DO 20 J=1,NPOINT
0010                  TEMR(J) = SIN((J-1)*PI2*10./600.) + SIN((J-1)*PI2*60./600.)
0011             20 CONTINUE
0012                  RETURN
0013                  END
```

Figure 4-19. Subroutine OWN (Ideal Filter Experiment).

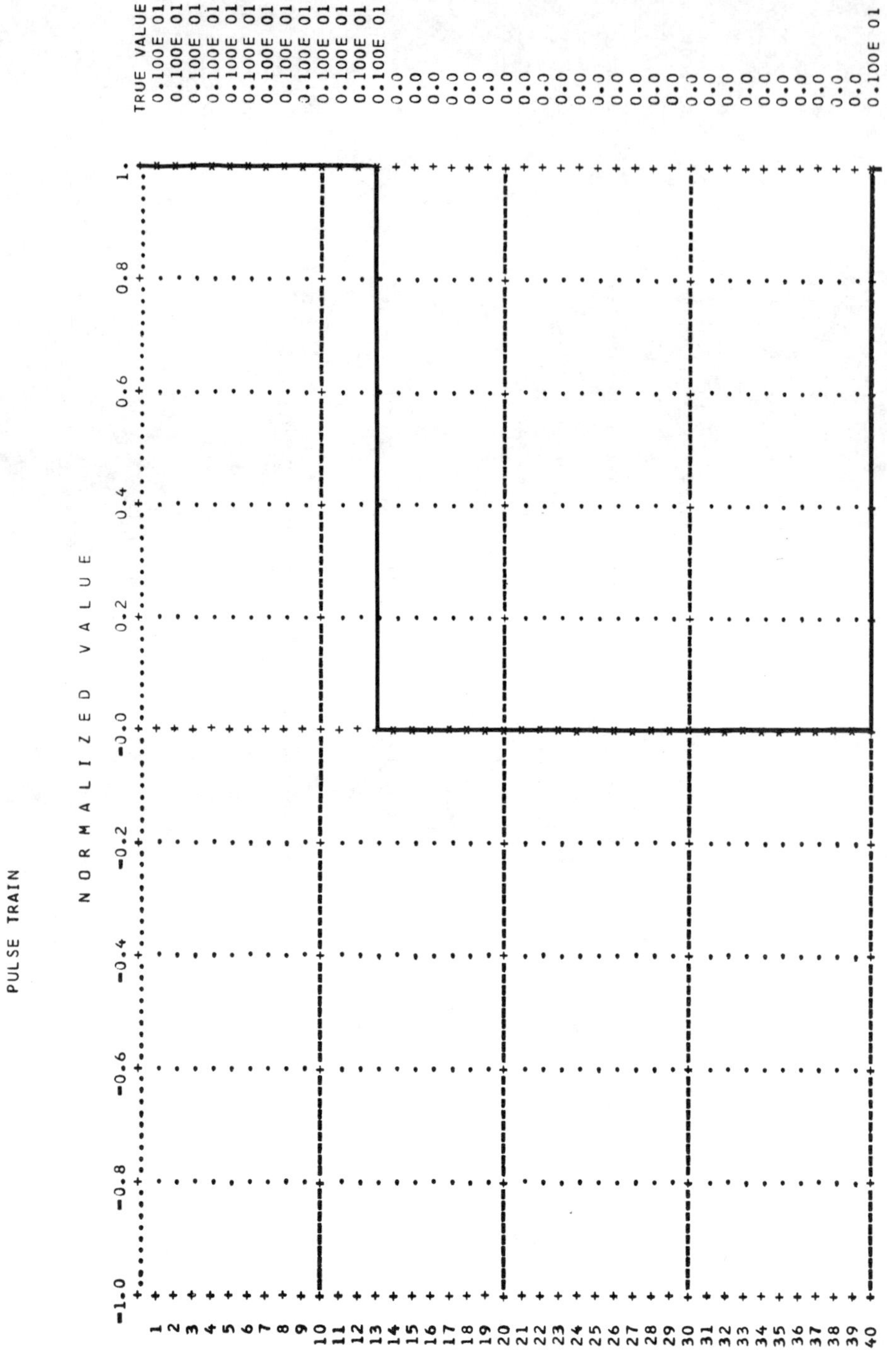
PULSE TRAIN
NORMALIZED VALUE
-1.0
-0.8
-0.6
-0.4
-0.2
-0.0
0.2
0.4
0.6
0.8
1.
TRUE VALUE

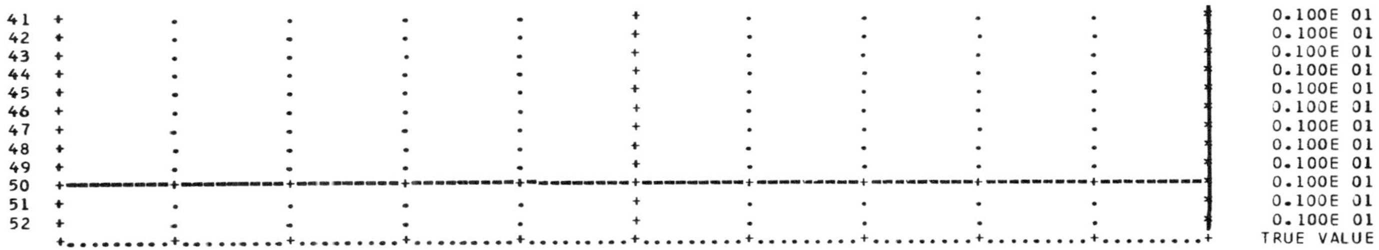


```
FAST FOURIER TRANSFORM FUNCTIONAL TASK

FFT HAS BEEN PERFORMED ON THE CONTENTS OF ARRAY A

THE INFORMATION IS NOW IN THE FREQUENCY DOMAIN

NUMBER OF POSITIVE AND NEGATIVE HARMONICS IS   52

SAMPLING FREQUENCY OF THE DATA IS       500.0

FREQUENCY RESOLUTION OR FUNDAMENTAL FREQUENCY IS         9.6 HZ
```

```
LINE PLOTTER FUNCTIONAL TASK

INFORMATION TO BE PLOTTED CAME FROM ARRAY A

NUMBER OF DATA POINTS IN THE ARRAY IS    52

SAMPLING FREQUENCY OF THE DATA IS       500.0

DATA IS IN THE FREQ DOMAIN

FREQUENCY RESOLUTION IS      9.615 HZ
```

Figure 4-20. Pulse Train (Ideal Filter Experiment).

BEFORE FILTERING

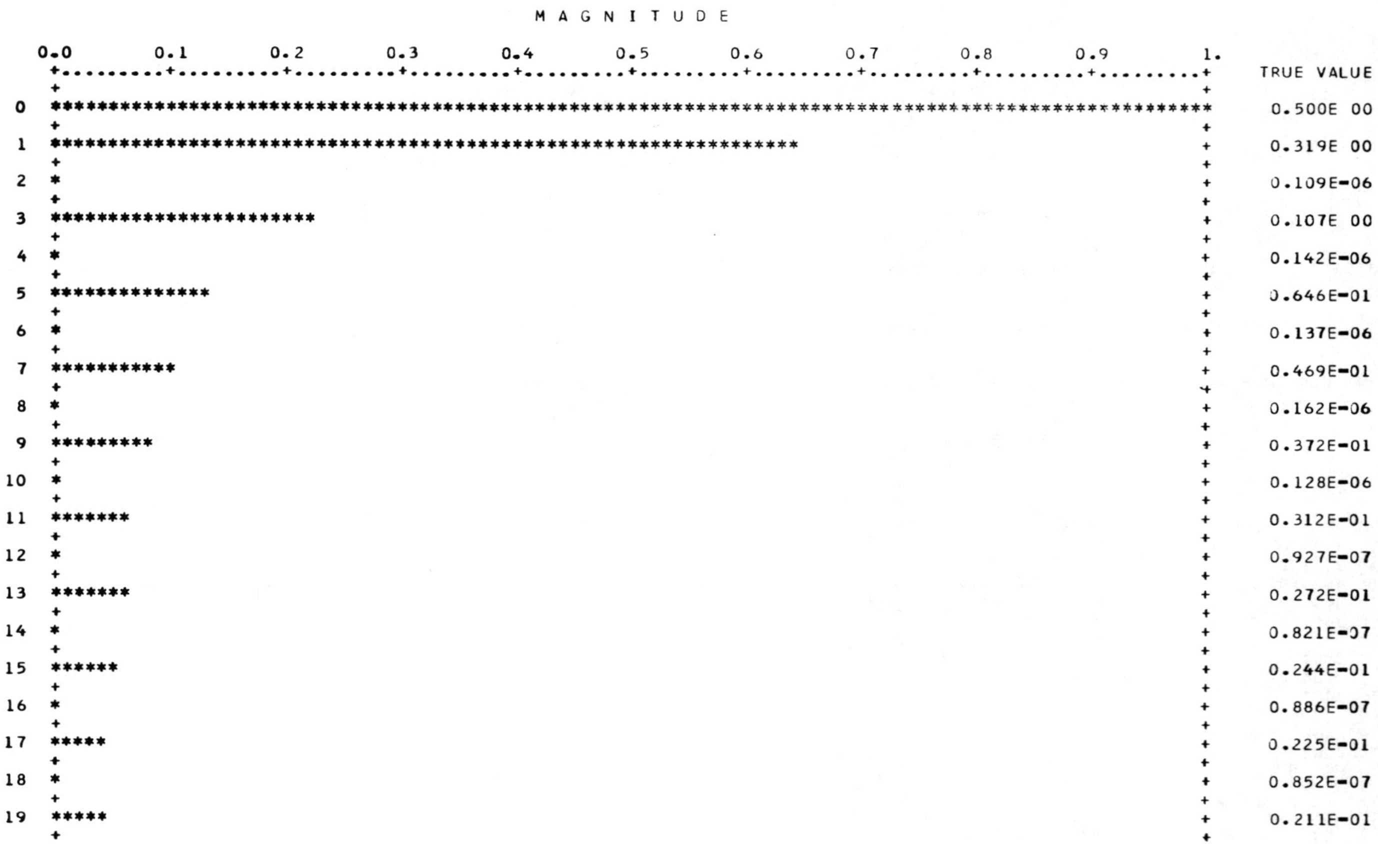

```
20  *                                                                                                   +     0.520E-07
    +                                                                                                   +
21  *****                                                                                               +     0.201E-01
    +                                                                                                   +
22  *                                                                                                   +     0.351E-07
    +                                                                                                   +
23  *****                                                                                               +     0.196E-01
    +                                                                                                   +
24  *                                                                                                   +     0.133E-07
    +                                                                                                   +
25  *****                                                                                               +     0.193E-01
    +.........+.........+.........+.........+.........+.........+.........+.........+.........+.........+    TRUE VALUE


DIGITAL FILTERING FUNCTIONAL TASK                                   LINE PLOTTER FUNCTIONAL TASK

DIGITAL FILTERING RESULTS STORED IN ARRAY A                         INFORMATION TO BE PLOTTED CAME FROM ARRAY A

NUMBER OF SAMPLE POINTS IS  52                                      NUMBER OF DATA POINTS IN THE ARRAY IS   52

DATA WAS SAMPLED AT THE RATE OF       500.0 HZ                      SAMPLING FREQUENCY OF THE DATA IS      500.0

INFORMATION STORED IN THE FREQ DOMAIN                               DATA IS IN THE FREQ DOMAIN

LOW-PASS DIGITAL FILTER      CUT-OFF FREQUENCY       100.0 HZ       FREQUENCY RESOLUTION IS      9.615 HZ
```

Figure 4-21. Spectra of PULSE (Ideal Filter Experiment).

AFTER FILTERING

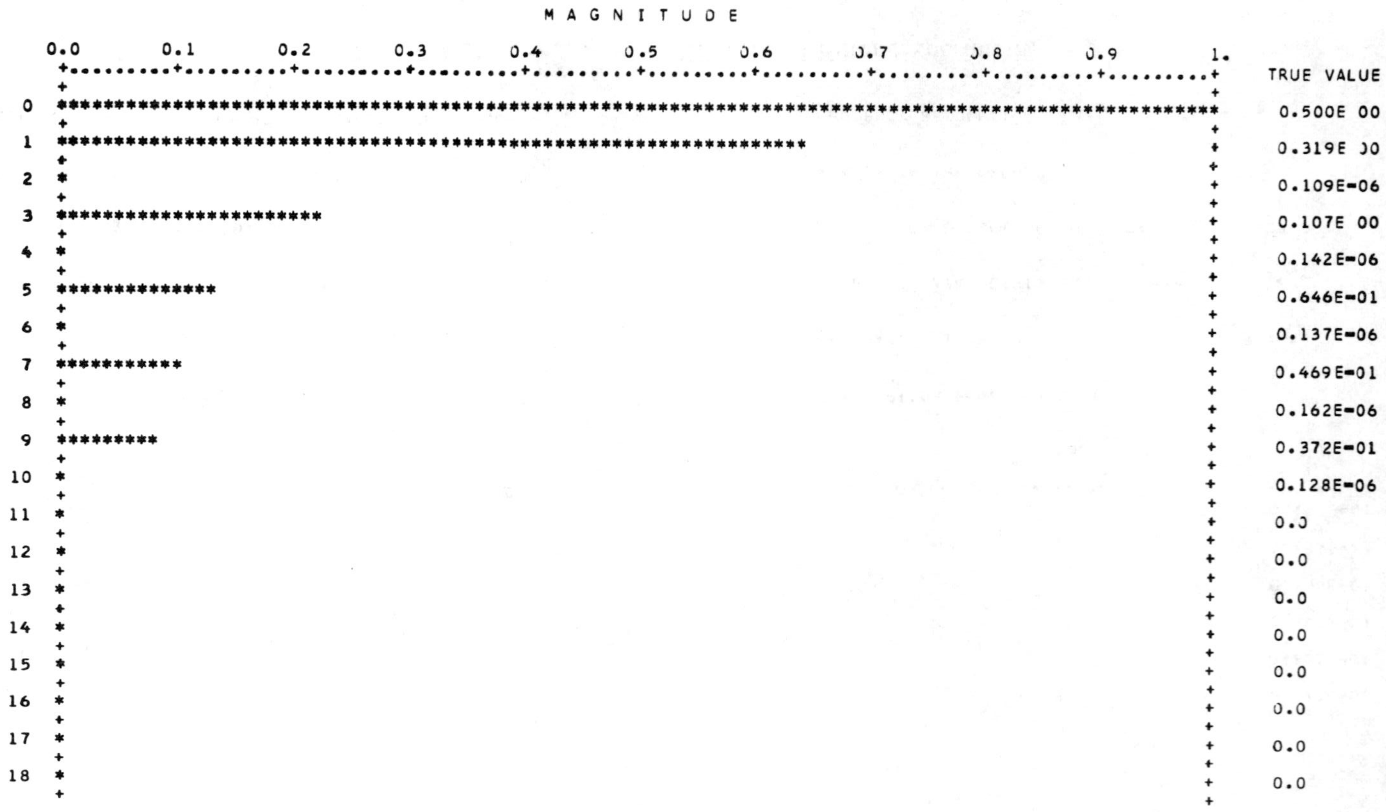

```
19  *                                                                                                  +      0.0
    +                                                                                                  +
20  *                                                                                                  +      0.0
    +                                                                                                  +
21  *                                                                                                  +      0.0
    +                                                                                                  +
22  *                                                                                                  +      0.0
    +                                                                                                  +
23  *                                                                                                  +      0.0
    +                                                                                                  +
24  *                                                                                                  +      0.0
    +                                                                                                  +
25  *                                                                                                  +      0.0
    +.........+.........+.........+.........+.........+.........+.........+.........+.........+.........+    TRUE VALUE

INVERSE FAST FOURIER TRANSFORM FUNCTIONAL TASK                    LINE PLOTTER FUNCTIONAL TASK

INVERSE FFT HAS BEEN PERFORMED ON THE CONTENTS OF ARRAY A        INFORMATION TO BE PLOTTED CAME FROM ARRAY A

THE INFORMATION IS NOW IN THE TIME DOMAIN                         NUMBER OF DATA POINTS IN THE ARRAY IS   52

NUMBER OF TIME DOMAIN POINTS IS   52                              SAMPLING FREQUENCY OF THE DATA IS      500.0

SAMPLING FREQUENCY OF THE DATA IS      500.0                      DATA IS IN THE TIME DOMAIN

                                                                  TIME INTERVAL BETWEEN SAMPLE POINTS IS   0.00200 SECONDS
```

Figure 4-22. Low-passed Spectra (Ideal Filter Experiment).

LOW PASSED PULSE TRAIN

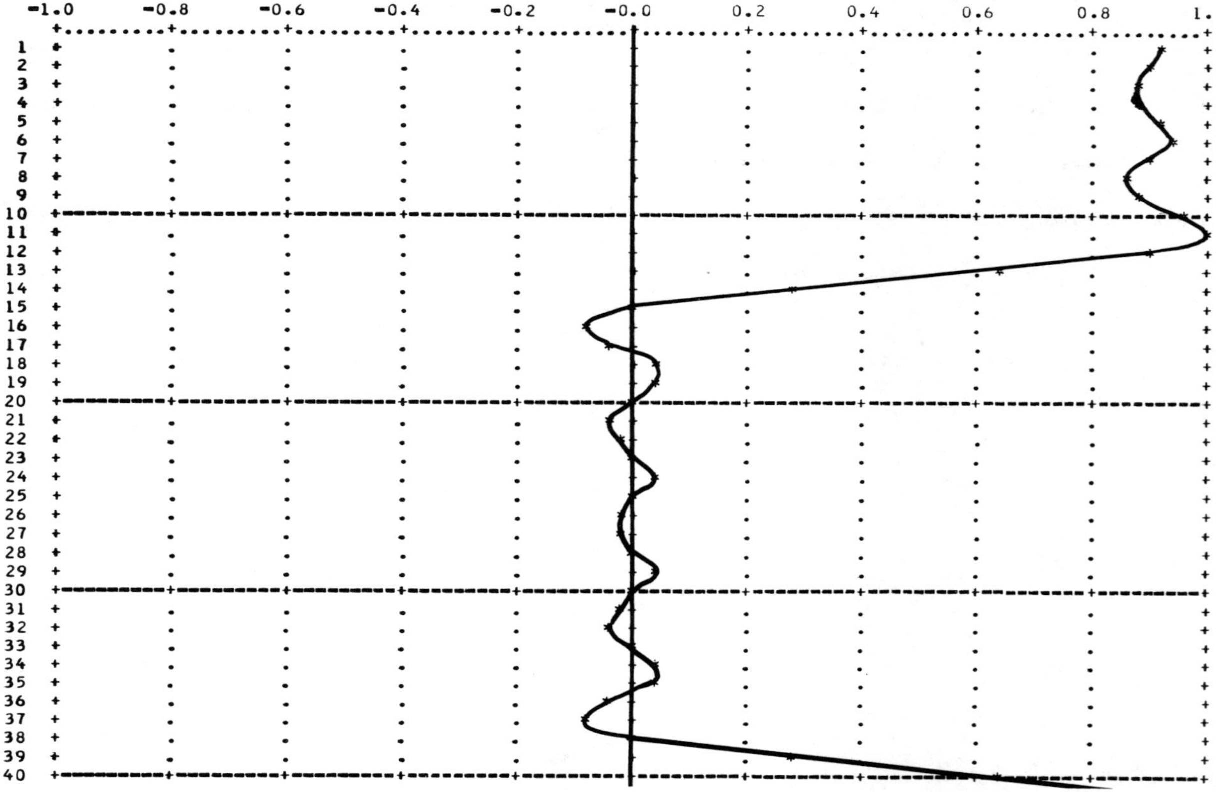

	TRUE VALUE
1	0.103E 01
2	0.991E 00
3	0.965E 00
4	0.984E 00
5	0.103E 01
6	0.104E 01
7	0.996E 00
8	0.948E 00
9	0.965E 00
10	0.105E 01
11	0.110E 01
12	0.991E 00
13	0.692E 00
14	0.308E 00
15	0.934E-02
16	-0.972E-01
17	-0.468E-01
18	0.353E-01
19	0.515E-01
20	0.380E-02
21	-0.385E-01
22	-0.273E-01
23	0.158E-01
24	0.349E-01
25	0.867E-02
26	-0.276E-01
27	-0.276E-01
28	0.867E-02
29	0.349E-01
30	0.158E-01
31	-0.273E-01
32	-0.385E-01
33	0.380E-02
34	0.515E-01
35	0.353E-01
36	-0.468E-01
37	-0.972E-01
38	0.934E-02
39	0.308E 00
40	0.692E 00

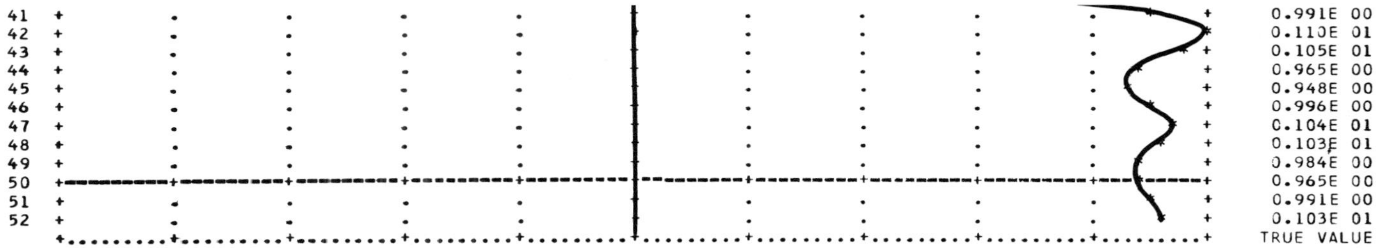


```
LIBRARY INPUT FUNCTIONS FUNCTIONAL TASK

USER PROGRAM NUMBER  1

INFORMATION PUT INTO ARRAY A

NUMBER OF SAMPLE POINTS IS   50

SAMPLING FREQUENCY OF DATA IS       600.0

INPUT IDENTIFICATION  SINE WAVE OF 10 HZ  WITH 60 HZ NOISE
```

```
LINE PLOTTER FUNCTIONAL TASK

INFORMATION TO BE PLOTTED CAME FROM ARRAY A

NUMBER OF DATA POINTS IN THE ARRAY IS   60

SAMPLING FREQUENCY OF THE DATA IS       600.0

DATA IS IN THE TIME DOMAIN

TIME INTERVAL BETWEEN SAMPLE POINTS IS    0.00167 SECONDS
```

Figure 4-23. Low-passed Time Series (Ideal Filter Experiment).

PRF = 10 HZ PLUS 60 HZ NOISE

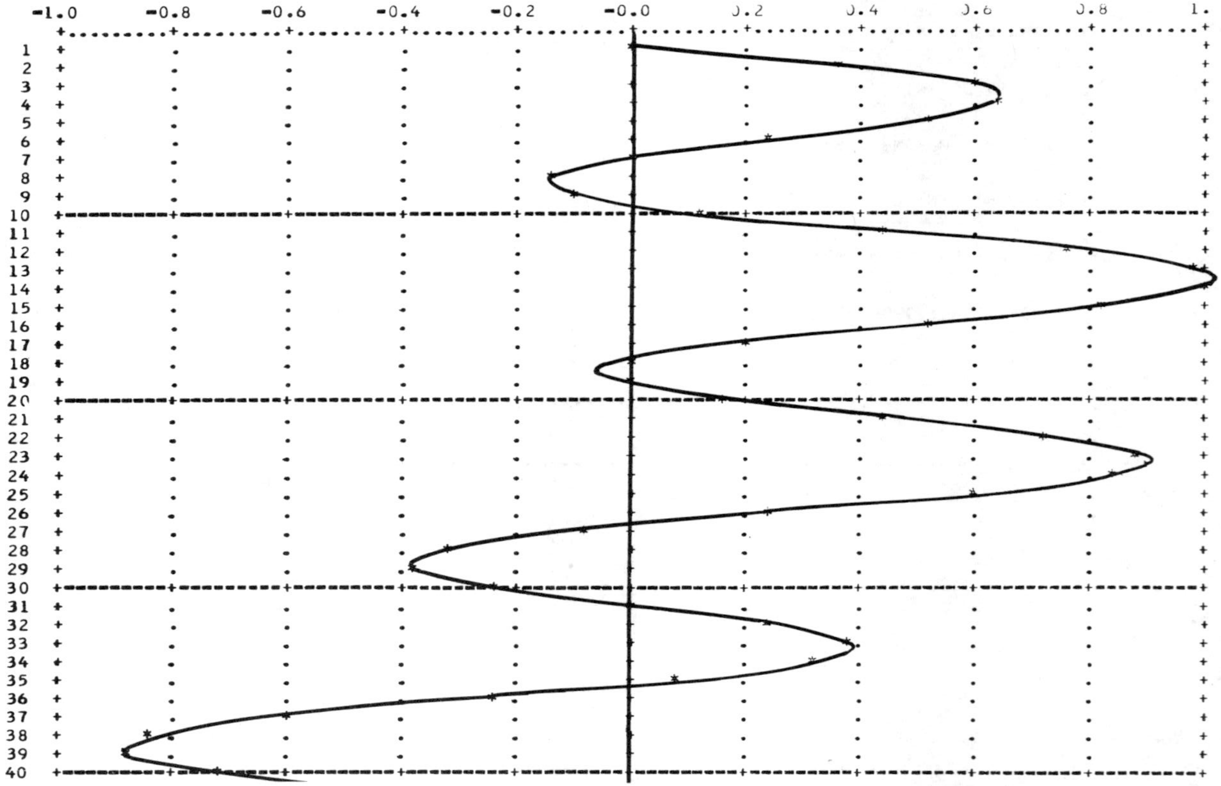

	TRUE VALUE
1	0.0
2	0.692E 00
3	0.116E 01
4	0.126E 01
5	0.995E 00
6	0.500E 00
7	0.161E-05
8	-0.282E 00
9	-0.208E 00
10	0.221E 00
11	0.866E 00
12	0.150E 01
13	0.190E 01
14	0.193E 01
15	0.158E 01
16	0.100E 01
17	0.407E 00
18	0.271E-01
19	-0.209E-05
20	0.326E 00
21	0.866E 00
22	0.140E 01
23	0.169E 01
24	0.162E 01
25	0.118E 01
26	0.500E 00
27	-0.181E 00
28	-0.642E 00
29	-0.743E 00
30	-0.483E 00
31	-0.695E-05
32	0.483E 00
33	0.743E 00
34	0.642E 00
35	0.181E 00
36	-0.500E 00
37	-0.118E 01
38	-0.162E 01
39	-0.169E 01
40	-0.140E 01

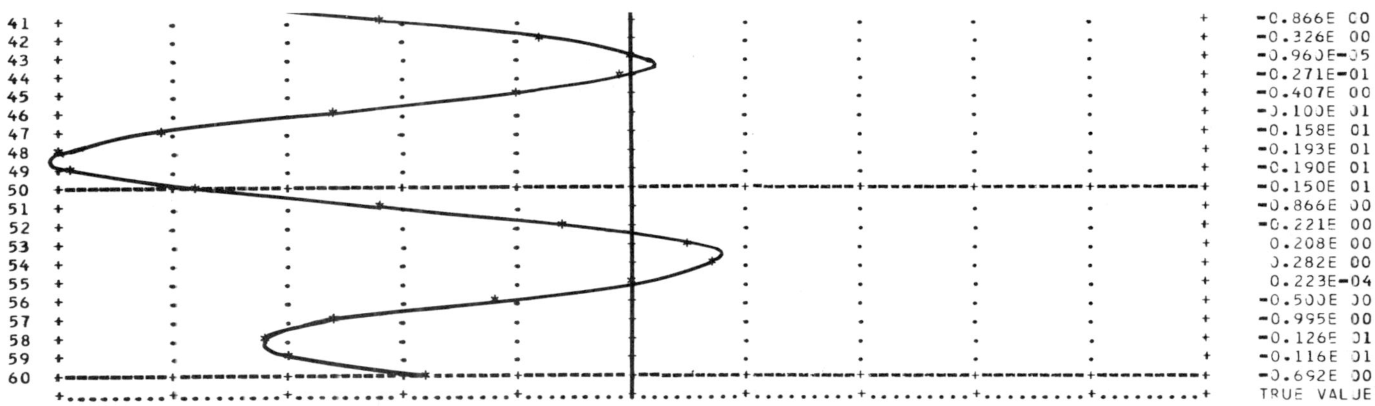

Figure 4-24. Synthesized 10- and 60-Hz Signal (Ideal Filter Experiment).

BEFORE FILTERING

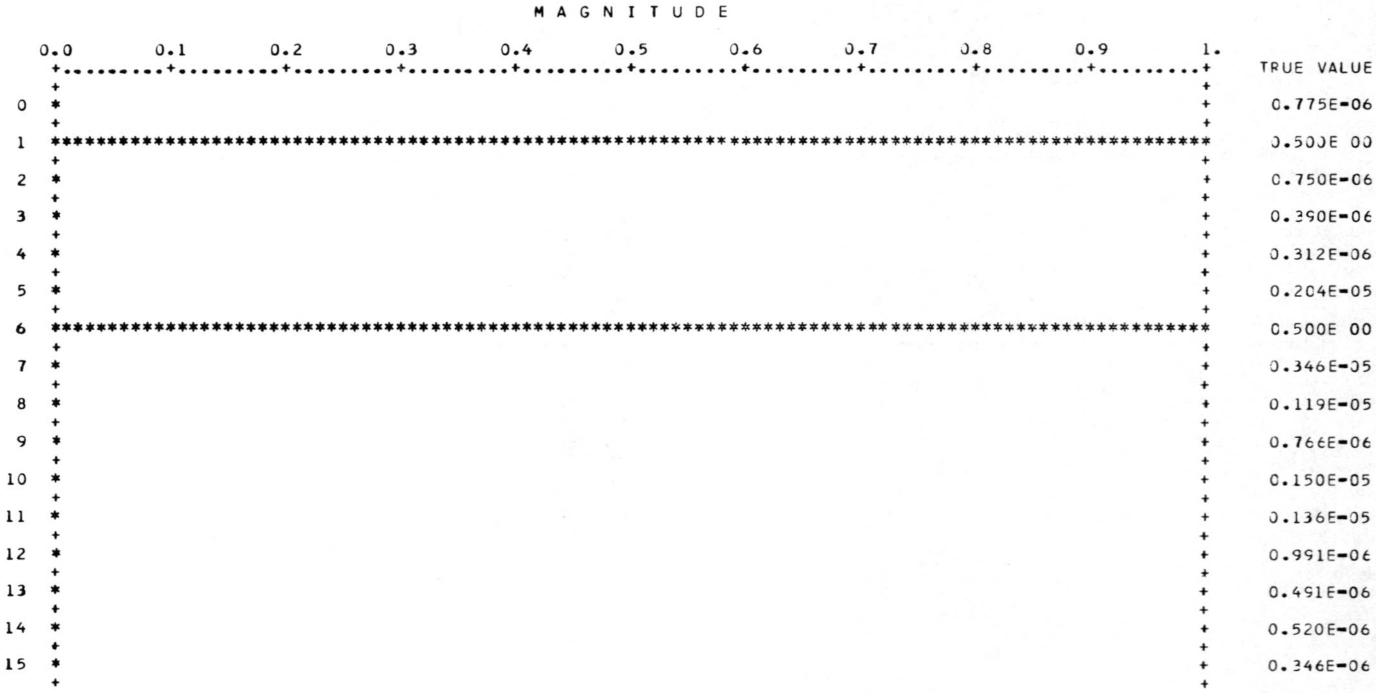

Figure 4-25. Spectra of Test Signal (Ideal Filter Experiment).

AFTER FILTERING

```
                                    M A G N I T U D E
      0.0       0.1       0.2       0.3       0.4       0.5       0.6       0.7       0.8       0.9       1.
       +.........+.........+.........+.........+.........+.........+.........+.........+.........+.........+   TRUE VALUE
       +                                                                                                   +
  0    *                                                                                                   +    0.775E-06
       +                                                                                                   +
  1    *****************************************************************************************************    0.500E 00
       +                                                                                                   +
  2    *                                                                                                   +    0.750E-06
       +                                                                                                   +
  3    *                                                                                                   +    0.390E-06
       +                                                                                                   +
  4    *                                                                                                   +    0.312E-06
       +                                                                                                   +
  5    *                                                                                                   +    0.204E-05
       +                                                                                                   +
  6    *                                                                                                   +    0.0
       +                                                                                                   +
  7    *                                                                                                   +    0.346E-05
       +                                                                                                   +
  8    *                                                                                                   +    0.119E-05
       +                                                                                                   +
  9    *                                                                                                   +    0.766E-06
       +                                                                                                   +
 10    *                                                                                                   +    0.150E-05
       +                                                                                                   +
 11    *                                                                                                   +    0.136E-05
       +                                                                                                   +
 12    *                                                                                                   +    0.991E-06
       +                                                                                                   +
 13    *                                                                                                   +    0.491E-06
       +                                                                                                   +
 14    *                                                                                                   +    0.520E-06
       +                                                                                                   +
 15    *                                                                                                   +    0.346E-06
       +                                                                                                   +
```

Figure 4-26. Spectra upon Notch Filtering (Ideal Filter Experiment).

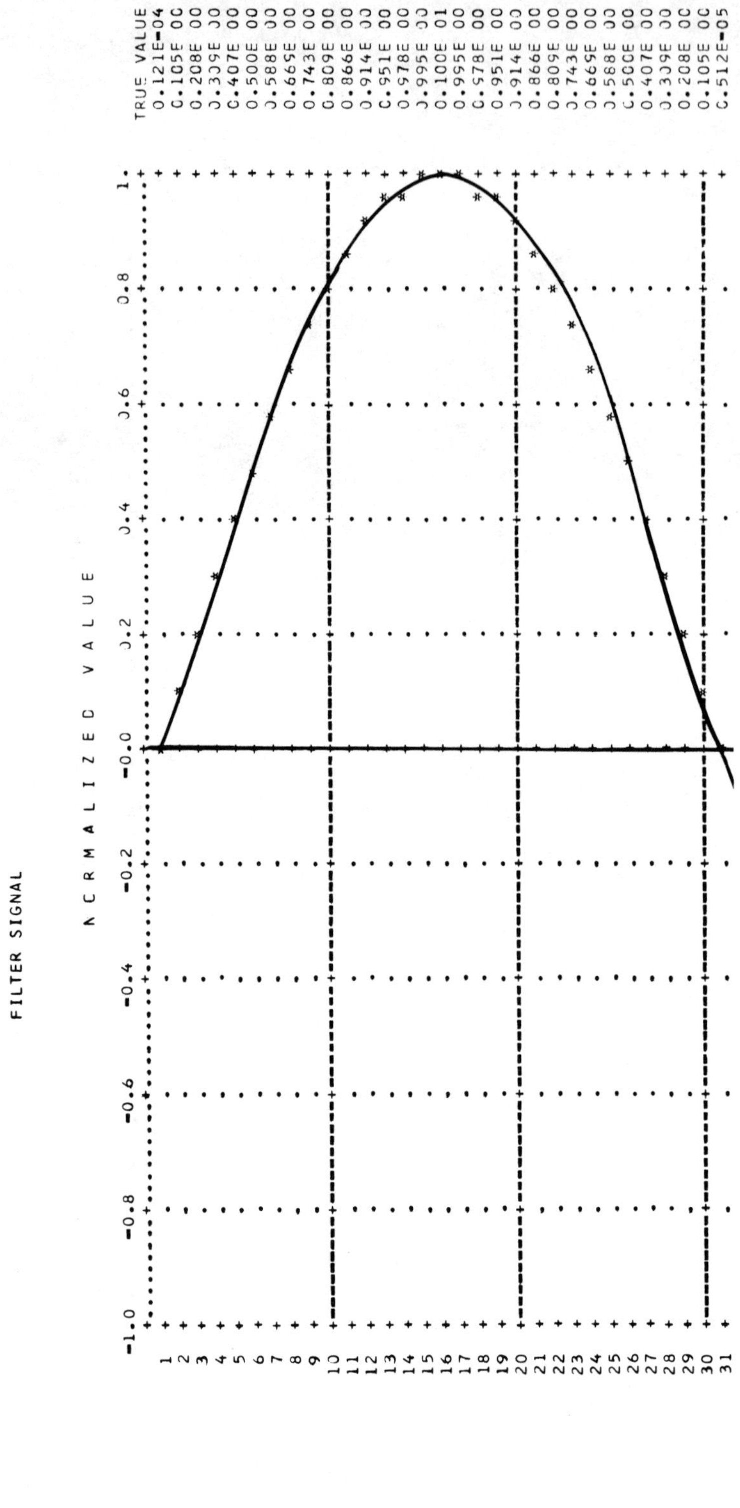
FILTER SIGNAL
NORMALIZED VALUE
-1.0 -0.8 -0.6 -0.4 -0.2 -0.0 0.2 0.4 0.6 0.8 1.
TRUE VALUE
0.121E-04
0.105E 00
0.208E 00
0.309E 00
0.407E 00
0.500E 00
0.588E 00
0.669E 00
0.743E 00
0.809E 00
0.866E 00
0.914E 00
0.951E 00
0.978E 00
0.995E 00
0.100E 01
0.995E 00
0.978E 00
0.951E 00
0.914E 00
0.866E 00
0.809E 00
0.743E 00
0.669E 00
0.588E 00
0.500E 00
0.407E 00
0.309E 00
0.208E 00
0.105E 00
0.512E-05

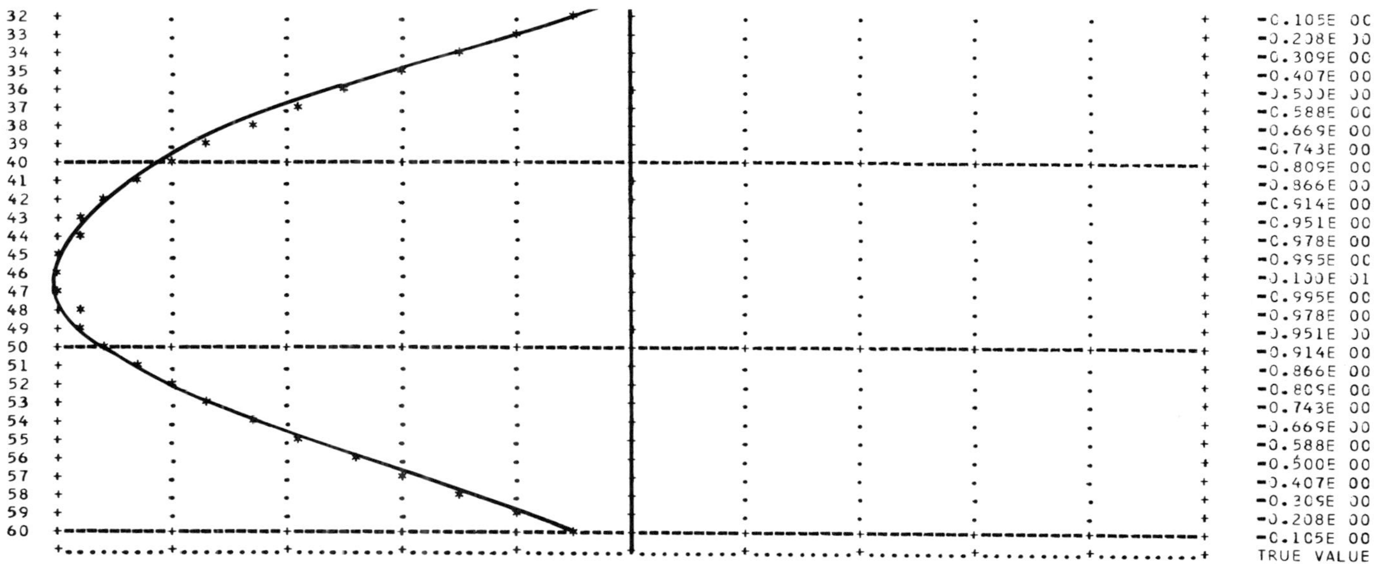

Figure 4-27. Time Series upon Notch Filtering (Ideal Filter Experiment).

sampling properties of digital filters (that is, sin x/x behavior) or attempt to emulate analog filter performance. Analog filter performance is accomplished through the transformation of an analog filter's transfer function—say, $H(s)$—into the discrete time-series domain by using the z transform—say, $H(z)$. Design procedures have been developed that will allow a designer to design digital versions of analog Butterworth, Chebyshev, and other like filters. Program DISCRETE will allow the SPECTRUM IV user to perform recursive filter operations.

Theory

Consider the input and output of a linear digital filter to be sampled every ΔT seconds. In addition, let the system have memory; that is, let it remember previous inputs and outputs. Let such a device be algebraically represented as follows: At some time $n\,\Delta T$

$$y(n\,\Delta T) = \sum_{i=0}^{R} \alpha_i x(n\,\Delta T - i\,\Delta T) - \sum_{i=1}^{N} \beta_i y\,(N\,\Delta T - i\,\Delta T) \tag{4.6a}$$

or

$$\sum_{i=0}^{N} \beta_i y\,(n\,\Delta T - i\,\Delta T) = \sum_{i=0}^{R} \alpha_i x\,(n\,\Delta T - i\Delta T) \tag{4.6b}$$

where R and N are the input and output memory lengths, respectively. (See Figure 4-28.) An alternative way of representing this result is through the so-called z transform. Define the scalar z in terms of the Laplace scalar s as follows:[b]

$$z = e^{s\,\Delta T} \tag{4.7a}$$

or equivalently,

$$z^{-1} = e^{-s\,\Delta T} \tag{4.7b}$$

Equation (4.7b) can be recognized, from the theory of Laplace transforms, to be a delay of ΔT seconds. Therefore, defining $Y(z)$ and $X(z)$ in the following manner,

$$Y(z) = \sum_{n=0}^{\infty} y(nT)z^{-n} \qquad \text{(output time series)} \tag{4.8}$$

$$X(z) = \sum_{n=0}^{\infty} x(nT)z^{-n} \qquad \text{(input time series)} \tag{4.9}$$

Equation (4.6b) can be rewritten for all n as

[b] Tables of z transforms can be found in Appendix B.

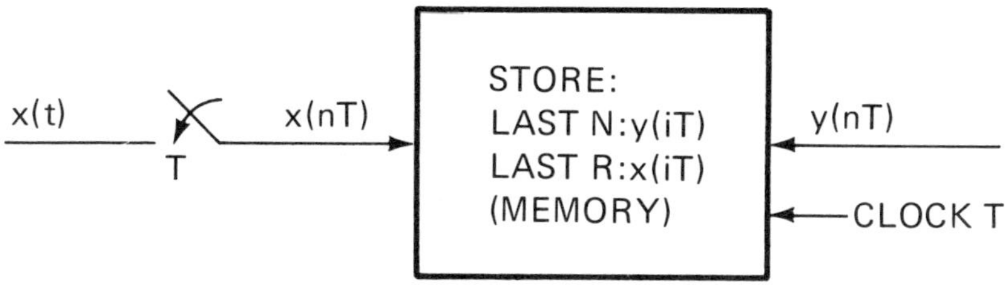

Figure 4-28. Digital Filter.

$$\sum_{i=0}^{N} \beta_i \sum_{n=0}^{\infty} y(n\,\Delta T - i\,\Delta T)z^{-n} = \sum_{i=0}^{R} \alpha_i \sum_{n=0}^{\infty} x(n\,\Delta T - i\,\Delta T)z^{-n}$$

or

$$Y(z) \sum_{i=0}^{N} \beta_i z^{-1} = X(z) \sum_{i=0}^{R} \alpha_i z^{-1}$$

which can be simplified to be

$$Y(z) = X(z)\ H(z) \tag{4.10}$$

where $H(z)$ is the transfer function of the digital filter in the z domain and it satisfies

$$H(z) = \sum_{i=0}^{R} \alpha_i z^{-i} \Big/ \sum_{i=0}^{N} \beta_i z^{-i} \tag{4.11}$$

In addition, $H(z)$ defines the system frequency-domain properties. The transfer function $H(z)$ has a direct interpretation in the frequency domain as follows: Define

$$H(z)\Big|_{\substack{\text{Steady}\\\text{State}}} = H(e^{s\,\Delta T})\Big|_{\substack{\text{Steady}\\\text{State}}} = H(e^{s\,\Delta T})\Big|_{s=jw} = H(e^{jw\,\Delta T}) \tag{4.12}$$

Digital filters are often classified in terms of their order. That is, they can be of order one ($N = 1$), two ($N = 2$), or order k ($N = k$). First-order filters offer exponential time-series behavior. Second-order filters can be configured to provide under, over, or critically damped time-series impulse responses. Filters of order two or greater can have resonant behavior.

Several popular filters—namely, the first and second-order digital filters and the digital resonator—will now be singled out for special consideration.

1. First-order filter

$$y(n\,\Delta T) = \beta_1 y(nT - \Delta T) + x(n\,\Delta T)$$

or

$$H(z) = \frac{1}{1 - \beta_1 z^{-1}}$$

The frequency domain of $H(z)$ becomes

$$H(e^{jw\,\Delta T}) = \underset{\text{(magnitude)}}{\left| H(e^{jw\,\Delta T}) \right|} \; \underset{\text{(phase)}}{\angle\phi(e^{jw\,\Delta T})}$$

where

$$|H(e^{jw\,\Delta T})| = 1/\sqrt{1 + \beta_1^2 - 2\beta_1 \cos(w\,\Delta T)}$$

$$\phi(e^{jw\,\Delta T}) = -\tan^{-1}[\sin w\,\Delta T/\cos(w\,\Delta T - \beta_1)]$$

2. Second-order filter

$$y(n\,\Delta T) = \beta_1 y(n\,\Delta T - \Delta T) + \beta_2 y(n\,\Delta T - 2\,\Delta T) + x(n\,\Delta T)$$

or

$$H(z) = \frac{1}{1 - \beta_1 z^{-1} - \beta_2 z^{-2}}$$

and

$$H(e^{jw\,\Delta T}) = |H(e^{jw\,\Delta T})| \angle\phi(e^{jw\,\Delta T})$$

where

$$|H(e^{jw\,\Delta T})| = \frac{1}{\sqrt{[1 - \beta_1 \cos(w\,\Delta T) - \beta_2 \cos(2w\,\Delta T)]^2 + [\beta_1 \sin(w\,\Delta T) + \beta_2 \sin(2w\,\Delta T)]^2}}$$

and

$$\phi(e^{jw\,\Delta T}) = \frac{-\tan^{-1}[\beta_1 \sin(w\,\Delta T) + \beta_2 \sin(2w\,\Delta T)]}{[1 - \beta_1 \cos(w\,\Delta T) - \beta_2 \cos(2w\,\Delta T)}$$

3. Digital resonators

Noting that a damped harmonic oscillator may be written as

$$H(s) = \frac{s + a}{(s + a)^2 + b^2}$$

then, for $z = e^{s\,\Delta T}$,

$$H(z) = \frac{1 - e^{-a\,\Delta T}[\cos(b\,\Delta T)]z^{-1}}{1 - 2e^{-aT}[\cos(b\,\Delta T)]z^{-1} + e^{-2aT} z^{-2}}$$

represents a digital resonator that satisfies the following difference equation:

$$y(n\,\Delta T) = e^{-asT}[\cos(b\,\Delta T)][2y(n\,\Delta T - \Delta T) - x(n\,\Delta T - \Delta T)]$$
$$-e^{-2a\,\Delta T}\,y(n\,\Delta T - 2\,\Delta T) + x(n\,\Delta T)$$

There are, of course, many other standard filter configurations, such as high-pass or low-pass or bandpass filters, Butterworth and Chebyshev filters, and so forth. It is beyond the scope of this book to treat them all; however, the interested reader can find a wealth of digital filter information, ranging from introductory to advanced, in the open literature.

Recursive digital filtering is accomplished under SPECTRUM IV control as shown in Figure 4-29.

Structure and Execution of Recursive Filter Program

Input. The input for this subroutine will consist of the primary information card needed to call it, followed by up to four groups of cards that will designate the various parameters of our filter. The primary information card will contain the eight-letter mnemonic necessary to call this routine, the identity(ies) of the array(s) involved with this routine, the format of the coefficients on the data cards, the number of sample points generated by the filter, the sampling frequency of the filter, and an integer to designate one of four options desired.

Option 1: Calculate the impulse response in the time domain of the filter.

Option 2: Derive the spectral frequency domain representation of the filter transfer function.

Option 3: Take an input signal and produce the filter's output response in the time domain.

Option 4: Perform option 3, place the input-output signals in the frequency domain, then derive a spectral representation of the digital filter transfer function over the frequencies $0 \leq f \leq f$ sample/2.

The following restrictions apply to the four options:

1. For options 3 and 4, the input signal must have the same sampling frequency and number of sample points as the filter, and it must exist in the time domain and be in the specified array.
2. For option 4, the input array must be C and the output must be placed in array B. Then the synthesized transfer function will be placed in array A, provided that arrays A and B are not under memory protection.

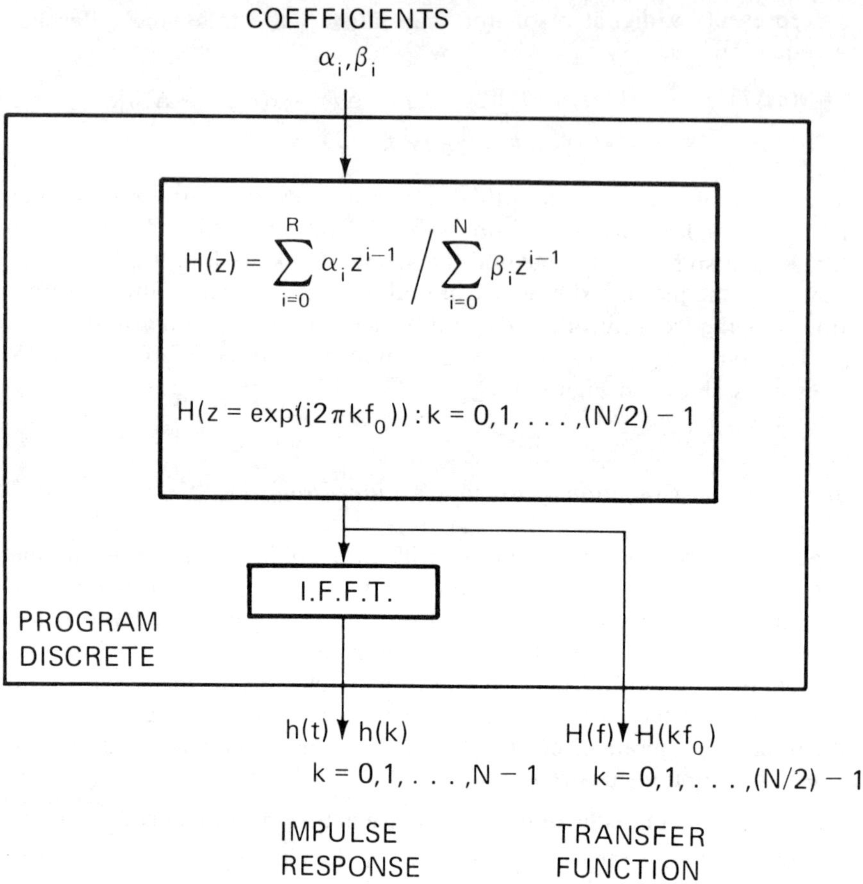

Figure 4-29. Program DISCRETE.

3. Sampling frequency must be specified to realize the filter.
4. Option parameter must be the integers 1 through 4.
5. The number of filter coefficients for system input-output memory α's, β's, and the number of initial conditions is limited to 20.
6. α_0 corresponding to system output memory of 0 seconds delay must be 0.0.

After the primary information card, our data are divided into groups that define various parameters of our recursive filter. The first card of each group will contain an eight-letter mnemonic designating that the following cards contain either coefficients of system output or input memory, initial input or output conditions, or a command to branch to a user-written subroutine. If the card does not designate a branch to a user-written subroutine, then the next one to three cards contain the numerical coef-

Table 4-5
Structure of a DISCRETE Call

Card	*Column Number*	*Description*	*Format or Contents*
Primary information card	108	Calls filter routine	DISCRETE
	15	Array to hold output	A1
	20	Array to hold input signal (if needed)	A1
	50	Format of input data	A1
	50-60	Number of sample points	I4
	61-72	Filter sampling frequency	F12.2
	80	Option parameter	I1
Secondary information cards for reading in values and coefficients	1-8	System output memory coefficients	MEMORY-0
	14-15	Number of coefficients	I2
	(OR)		
	1-8	System input memory coefficients	MEMORY-1
	14-15	Number of coefficients	I2
	(OR)		
	1-8	Initial system input values	
	14-15	Number of initial conditions	INITIALI I2
	(OR)		
	1-8	Initial system input values	
	14-15	Number of initial conditions	INITIAL0 I2

ficients of initial conditions, followed by a card with an end-of-file marker (see Table 4-5). The last card of the input deck contains the mnemonic *END to designate the end of input information to this routine.

If the user does not supply a special subroutine to define a filter structure, then the card sequence and information display shown in Table 4-6 must be provided. If a user-supplied subroutine is to be supplied, the cards and information shown in Table 4-7 must be supplied.

By inserting the mnemonic USER the user can branch to a subroutine called OWN. Using the third parameter, the user selects the portion of the subroutine that defines the filter:

```
SUBROUTINE OWN
   INTEGER SPL
   COMMON  REST(6148),TEMR(1024),TEMC(1024),FRN(20),
   FCN(20), FRD(20),FCID(20),PN(21),PD(21),REST1(82),
   NPOINT, REST2(5),SPL,REST3(2)
   GO TO (n1, n2, n3, ..., nm), SPL
n1    .
      :          User Program 1
      .
    GO TO 99                 .
                             :
                             .
```

Table 4-6
Recursive Filter from System-supplied Subroutine

Card	*Column Number*	*Description*	*Format or Contents*
Data cards containing initial conditions or coefficients		System output memory coefficients	(Up to 20 values)
	1-10	$y(nT) = 0.0$ always	7 F10.3
	11-20	$y(nT - T)$	or
	etc.	. . .	7 E10.3
	(OR)		
		System input memory coefficients	(Up to 20 values)
	1-10	$u(nT)$	7 F10.3
	11-20	$u(nT - T)$	or
	21-30	$u(nT - 2T)$	7 E10.3
	etc.	. . .	
	(OR)		
		Initial system input values	(Up to 20 values)
	1-10	$u(o)$	7 F10.3
	11-20	$u(-T)$	or
	21-30	$u(-2T)$	7E10.3
	etc.	. . .	
	(OR)		
		Initial system output values	(Up to 20 values)
	1-10	$y(o)$	7 F10.3
	11-20	$y(-T)$	or
	21-30	$y(-2T)$	7 E10.3
	etc.	. . .	
End-of-file cards	1-8	E-format end-of-file marker	EEEEEEEE
	(OR)		
	1-8	F-format end-of-file marker	FFFFFFFF
Final card of routine input	1-4	This designates no more input for this routine	*END

[a]User need input only those initial conditions or coefficients that are not all zero.

Table 4-7
Recursive Filter Derived from User-supplied Subroutine

Card	*Column Number*	*Description*	*Format or Contents*
Call to user subroutine	1-4	Branch to user subroutine	USER
	14-15	Maximum number of non-zero initial conditions or system memory coefficients of filter.	12
	19-20	Portion of user subroutine desired	12

```
n2   .              User Program 2
     .
     .
   GO TO 99
n3   .                    .
     .                    .
     .                    .
   GO TO 99
nm   .              User Program m
     .
     .
99 CONTINUE
   RETURN
   END
```

In the user program designated, the user may read in data, do calculations, call other subroutines, and so forth. However, eventually the user must put the filter system coefficients and/or initial conditions in the proper memory locations. Notice the structure of the COMMON statement required:

```
INTEGER SPL
COMMON  REST(6148),TEMR(1024),TEMC(1024),FRN(20),
FCN(20),FRD(20),FCID(20),PN(21),PD(21),REST1(82),NPOINT,
REST2(5),SPL,REST3(2)
```

All information that the program considers restricted from the user is contained in the arrays REST, REST1, REST2, and REST3. The arrays we will be concerned with for the digital filter are PN, PD, FRN, and FRD. It is the user's responsibility to see that the filter coefficients and initial conditions are placed in the proper array locations. The information should be put in as follows:

PD(1) = α_0	PN(1) = β_0	FRN(1) = $u(0)$	FRD(1) = $y(0)$
PD(2) = α_1	PN(2) = β_1	FRN(2) = $u(-T)$	FRD(2) = $y(-T)$
⋮	⋮	⋮	⋮
PD(20 = α_{19}	PN(20 = β_{19}	FRN(2) = $u(-19T)$	FRD(20) = $y(-19T)$

Again the user need put in only the nonzero coefficients of the filter; all other coefficients and initial conditions will be set to zero.

Output. The program will provide a print-out of all filter parameters inputted by the user, along with sampling, frequencies, number of sample points, identification of arrays involved, and information to designate which option is desired.

Example. Consider the first-order recursive low-pass filter given by

$$H(z) = \frac{(1 - a)z}{(z - a)} = \frac{(1 - a)}{(1 - az^{-1})}$$

where a denotes the half-power point or bandwidth of the low-pass filter. In block diagram form, $H(z)$ appears as shown in Figure 4-30. Consider n such filters placed in series (cascaded). Let the resulting filter be denoted $H_n(z)$, where

$$H_n(z) = \sum_{i=1}^{n} H(z) = \left[\frac{(1 - a)z}{z - a}\right] = \frac{(1 - a)^n z^n}{(z - a)^n}$$

The realization of such a filter can be found in Figure 4-31. In terms of input-output variables, say, x and y, $H_n(z)$ induces

$$y(k) - a\binom{\cdot \overset{n}{\cdot} \cdot}{1} y(k - 1) + a^2\binom{\cdot \overset{n}{\cdot} \cdot}{2} y(k - 2) + \cdots + (-a)^n y(k - n)$$

$$= (1 - a)^n x(k)$$

where (. . .) denotes a binomial coefficient. Using a design criterion of a 20-Hz system bandwidth, the parameter a for a fifth-order low-pass filter would be computed as follows:

$$a = \frac{1}{(2^{1/n} - 1)} \Big\{2^{1/n} - \cos(2\pi f_1 T)$$

$$- \sqrt{[2^{1/n} - \cos(2\pi f_l T)]^2 - [2^{1/n} - 1]^2}\Big\}$$

where $n = 5, f_1 = 20$ Hz, and T equals the sample interval that is chosen to be 5 msec (that is, sample frequency = 200 Hz). The computed value for a is 0.2304. A 50-point display of the filter's frequency-domain response is to be performed.

The card control sequence associated with this taks can be found in Figure 4-32. The single numerator and six (five nontrivial) denominator coefficients are supplied to the program in the manner prescribed in the text. The data are supplied in F format and each read operation is properly terminated. The *END card terminates the coefficient input operation. The DISCRETE operation is given the task of producing the filter's frequency-domain response (option 2). The magnitude frequency-domain response of the filter can be found in Figure 4-33. The frequency-domain

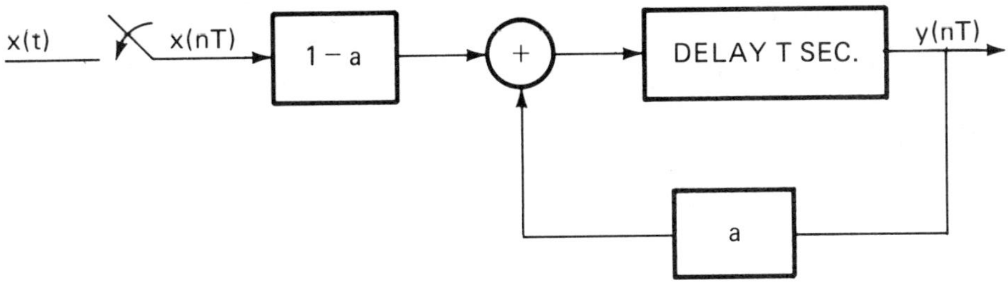

Figure 4-30. Low-Pass Filter.

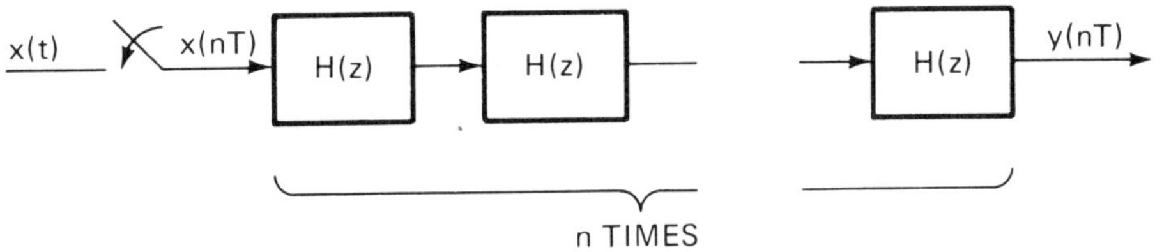

Figure 4-31. Cascaded Low-Pass Filters.

description of the derived filter can be noted to have a classical low-pass profile.

Example. A resonator is characterized by an impulse response of the form

$$h(t) = e^{-at} \cos(2\pi bt)$$

where $a > o$ for stability and $h(t)$ resonates at a frequency of b Hz. The Laplace transform of $h(t)$—namely, $H(s)$—is a transfer function satisfying

$$H(s) = \frac{s + a}{(s + a)^2 + b^2}$$

The discrete recursive filter representation of $h(t)$ is given through the z transformed $H(z)$, where

$$H(z) = \frac{1 - \exp(-aT)(\cos bT)z^{-1}}{1 - 2\exp(-aT)z^{-1} + \exp(-2aT)z^{-2}}$$

where T is the sampling rate.

Let a resonator be designed to operate at a frequency of $b = 20$ Hz, a damping of $\exp(-aT) = 0.998$, for a sampling rate of $T = 10^{-2}$ seconds/sample. Then

```
CARD          COLUMN                                                                        8Ø
              123456789Ø12      .         .         .         .         .         .         .
------------------------------------------------------------------------------------------------
1             DISCRETE      B                                   F      1ØØ       2ØØ.       2
2             MEMORY-I      1
3                  .27ØØ
4             FFFF
5             MEMORY-O      6
6                   Ø.Ø      1.152     -.531      .122     -.Ø14      .ØØ1
7             FFFF
8             *END
9             PLOTTER       B                                          5Ø
1Ø            FREQ   MAG          1   5Ø       THIS IS A 5-STAGE LOW-PASS FILTER   BF = 2ØHZ
11            TERM
                       .        .        .         .         .         .         .         .
```

Figure 4-32. Card Control Sequence for Recursive Low-pass Filter Experiment.

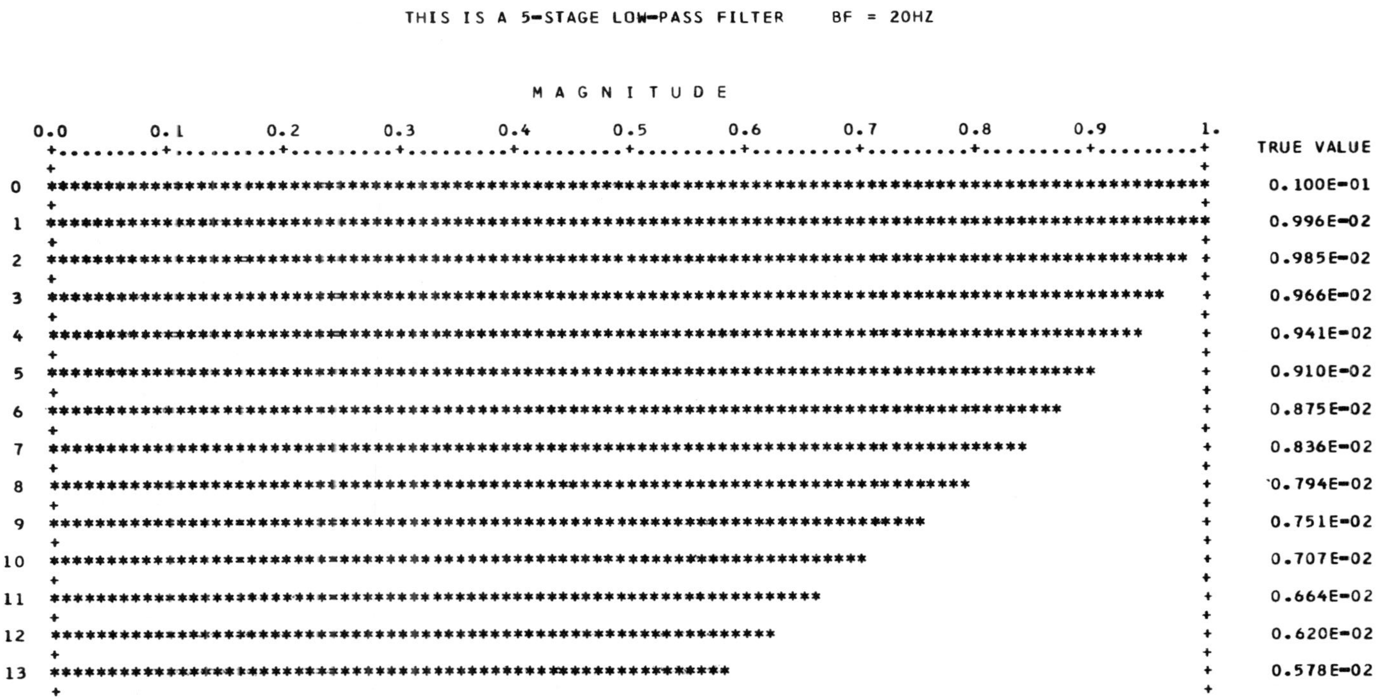

Figure 4-33. Single-pole, Low-pass Filter (Recursive Low-pass Filter Experiment).

```
14  *******************************************************                                                            +    0.538E-02
    +                                                                                                                  +
15  ***************************************************                                                                +    0.500E-02
    +                                                                                                                  +
16  ***********************************************                                                                    +    0.463E-02
    +                                                                                                                  +
17  ********************************************                                                                       +    0.429E-02
    +                                                                                                                  +
18  *****************************************                                                                          +    0.398E-02
    +                                                                                                                  +
19  **************************************                                                                             +    0.368E-02
    +                                                                                                                  +
20  ***********************************                                                                                +    0.341E-02
    +                                                                                                                  +
21  *********************************                                                                                  +    0.316E-02
    +                                                                                                                  +
22  *******************************                                                                                    +    0.294E-02
    +                                                                                                                  +
23  *****************************                                                                                      +    0.273E-02
    +                                                                                                                  +
24  ***************************                                                                                        +    0.254E-02
    +                                                                                                                  +
25  *************************                                                                                          +    0.237E-02
    +                                                                                                                  +
26  ***********************                                                                                            +    0.222E-02
    +                                                                                                                  +
27  **********************                                                                                             +    0.208E-02
    +                                                                                                                  +
28  *********************                                                                                              +    0.195E-02
    +                                                                                                                  +
29  *******************                                                                                                +    0.183E-02
    +                                                                                                                  +
30  *******************                                                                                                +    0.173E-02
    +                                                                                                                  +
31  *****************                                                                                                  +    0.163E-02
    +                                                                                                                  +
```

Figure 4-33 (Continued)

$$y(nT) = 2\exp(-aT)\cos(2\pi bT)y\,(nT - T) - \exp(-2aT)y(nT - 2T)$$
$$+ x(nT) - \exp(-aT)\cos(2\pi bT)x(nT - T)$$

Let a test signal $x(t) = [\cos(2\pi f_o t) + \cos(2\pi f_1 t) + \cos(2\pi f_2(t)]/2$ be generated for $f_o = 10$ Hz, $f_1 = 20$ Hz, $f_2 = 30$ Hz. Let $x(t)$ be sampled at a 10^{-2} seconds/sample rate and a 100-point FFT of $x(t)$—namely, $X(f)$—be generated. Let the magnitude spectra $X(f)$ be plotted. Furthermore, let $x(t)$ be processed by the digital resonator $h(t)$ and transformed into the frequency domain. Let the magnitude spectra of the resultant output be plotted.

The generation of $x(t)$ is accomplished in the user-supplied subroutine OWN, subprogram no. 1. The generation of $x(t)$ is accomplished in subprogram no. 1 and the filter coefficients are generated in subprogram no. 2.

The card control sequence used in this experiment can be found in Figure 4-34. The user-supplied subprogram OWN, used in conjunction with a USER call, is found in Figure 4-35. The generation of the filter coefficients is accomplished in accordance with the use rules of subprogram OWN. If nonzero initial conditions were required, they would be entered into this program by inserting the initial condition values into the FRD array. Again the user is directed to the discussion of the use of OWN, on pp. 10-14 for a detailed discussion of this feature. The multi-frequency input signal time series can be found in Figure 4-36 and its spectra in Figure 4-37. The result of filtering is found in Figure 4-38. The harmonic content of the output signal at 10 and 30 Hz is severely attenuated by the digital resonator.

D. Matched Filter

A signal-to-noise ratio is a measure of the power contained in a signal process to that contained in a noise process. Filters are often used to improve this mathematical measure. Here a noise-corrupted signal will be altered so that an improved signal-to-noise ratio can be achieved. If the temporal and spectral properties of a signal are known, and if the noise process can be characterized through a Fourier transform, then the signal-to-noise enhancement can be accomplished optimally. When the input signal process has a unique Fourier representation, the optimal filter is called a match filter. Therefore a certain degree of periodicity is required of the signal process. Such cases are typified by the injection of a periodic known—exactly signal into a system.

For example, a pulsed radar system is known to transmit a periodic pulse train. The detected return is a noise-corrupted version of the transmitted signal delayed in time. It is this temporal delay that allows the

```
                                                                                            8Ø
CARD        COLUMN
            123456789Ø12       .         .         .         .         .         .         .
------------------------------------------------------------------------------------------------
1           USER LIB      C                                             1ØØ       1ØØ.       1
2           THIS WILL CREATE THE 1Ø-2Ø-3Ø HZ WAVE
3           PLOTTER       C                                             1ØØ
4           TIME               1   1ØØ    THIS IS THE 1Ø-2Ø-3Ø HZ SINE WAVE COMBINATION
5           DISCRETE      B    C                              F         1ØØ       1ØØ.       3
6           USER          3    2
7           *END
8           SWITCH        A    C
9           FFT
1Ø          SWITCH        A    C
11          SWITCH        A    B
12          FFT
13          SWITCH        A    B
14          PLOTTER       C                                              5Ø
15          FREQ   MAG         1    5Ø    THIS IS THE INPUT SPECTRA  1Ø-2Ø-3Ø SINE WAVE
16          PLOTTER       B                                              5Ø
17          FREQ MAG           1    5Ø    OUTPUT OF RESONANCE FILTER TUNED TO 2Ø HZ
18          TERM
                   .         .         .         .         .         .         .         .
```

Figure 4-34. Card Control Sequence for Recursive Digital Filter Experiment.

```
FORTRAN IV G LEVEL  21                 OWN                DATE = 75156          16/19/49               PAGE 0001

            SUBROUTINE OWN
C
C    THE FOLLOWING FIVE STATEMENTS SHOULD BE INCLUDED IN ANY SUBROUTINE OWN
      REAL*8 BAN
      INTEGER DSO,E,F,TIME,FREQ,SPL
      COMMON REST(6148),TEMR(1024),TEMC(1024),FRN(20),FCN(20),FRD(20),
     1FCD(20),PN(21),PD(21),REST1(82),NPOINT,REST2(5),SPL,REST3(2)
      COMMON /LETTER/ F,E,MAR(3),LAIS(60),TIME,FREQ,IBAN,BAN,LN,NN,NP
C
C
      WRITE(LN,3) SPL
    3 FORMAT(10X,'USER PROGRAM NUMBER ',I2,/)
      GO TO (10,20),SPL
      GO TO 99
   10 PI2 = 8.0*ATAN(1.0)
      DO 11 K=1,NPOINT
      TEMR(K) = .5*SIN(PI2*(K-1)*10./100.) + .5*SIN(PI2*(K-1)*20./100.)
     1 + .5*SIN(PI2*(K-1)*30./100.)
   11 CONTINUE
      GO TO 99
   20 A = 1.0
      B = 20.
      T = .01
      PI2 = 8.0*ATAN(1.0)
      E1 = EXP(-A*T)
      E2 = EXP(-2.*A*T)
      E3 = COS(PI2*B*T)
      E4 = E1*E3*2.
      E5 = E1*E3
      PD(1) = 0.0
      PD(2) = E4
      PD(3) = -E2
      PN(1) = 1.0
      PN(2) = -E5
   99 CONTINUE
      RETURN
      END
```

Figure 4-35. Subroutine OWN (Recursive Digital Filter Experiment).

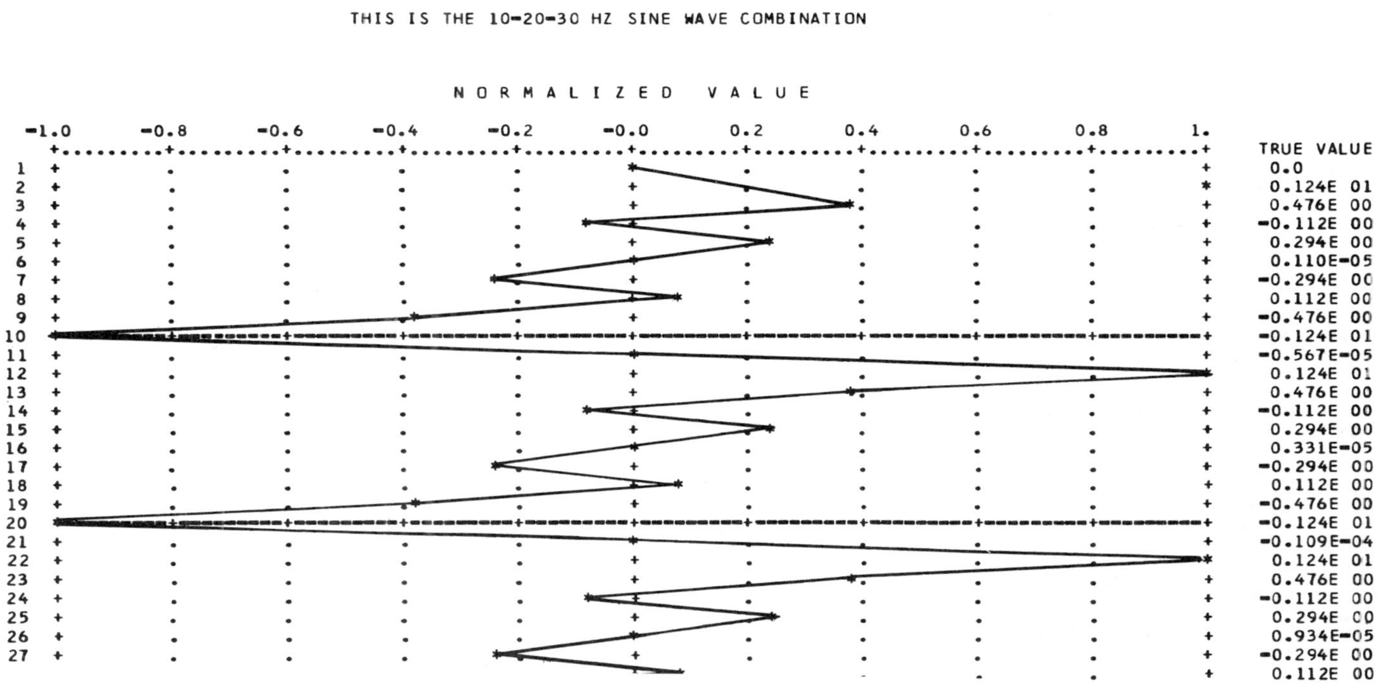

Figure 4-36. Input Signal Time Series (Recursive Digital Filter Experiment).

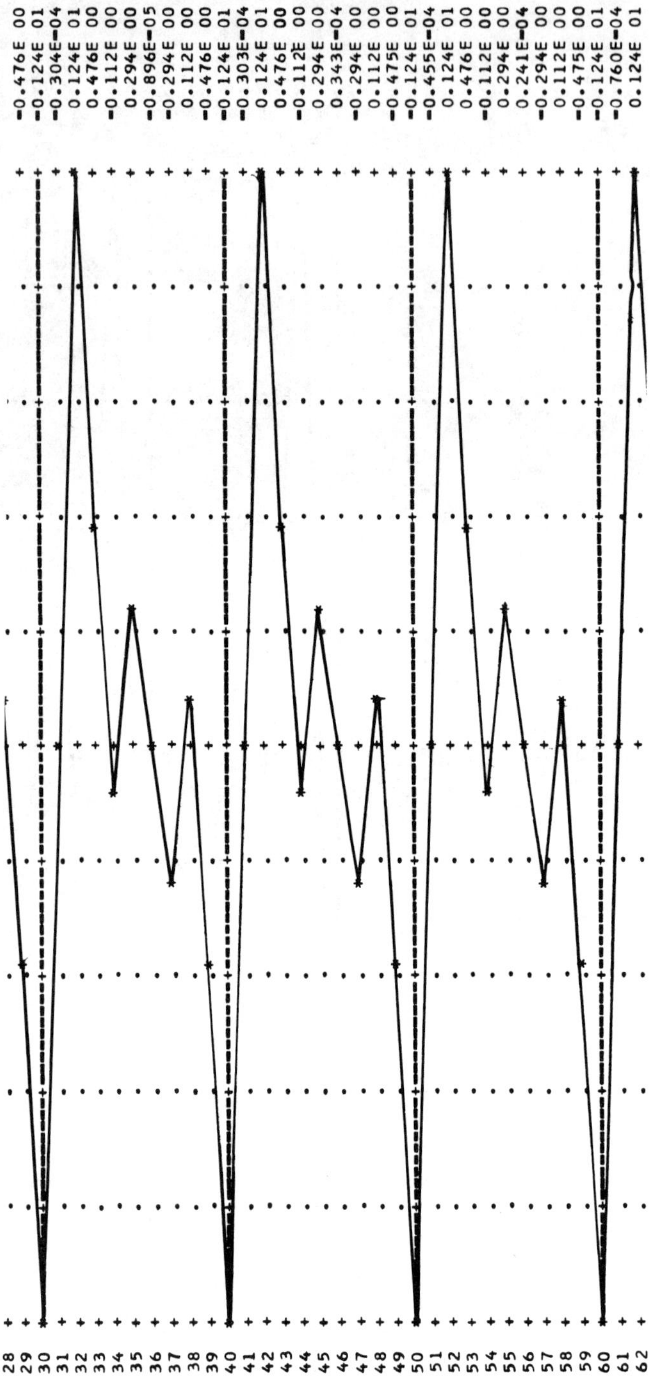
-0.476E 00
-0.124E 01
-0.304E-04
0.124E 01
0.476E 00
-0.112E 00
0.294E 00
-0.896E-05
-0.294E 00
0.112E 00
-0.476E 00
-0.124E 01
-0.303E-04
0.124E 01
0.476E 00
-0.112E 00
0.294E 00
0.343E-04
-0.294E 00
0.112E 00
-0.475E 00
-0.124E 01
-0.455E-04
0.124E 01
0.476E 00
-0.112E 00
0.294E 00
0.241E-04
-0.294E 00
0.112E 00
-0.475E 00
-0.124E 01
-0.760E-04
0.124E 01
28
29
30
31
32
33
34
35
36
37
38
39
40
41
42
43
44
45
46
47
48
49
50
51
52
53
54
55
56
57
58
59
60
61
62

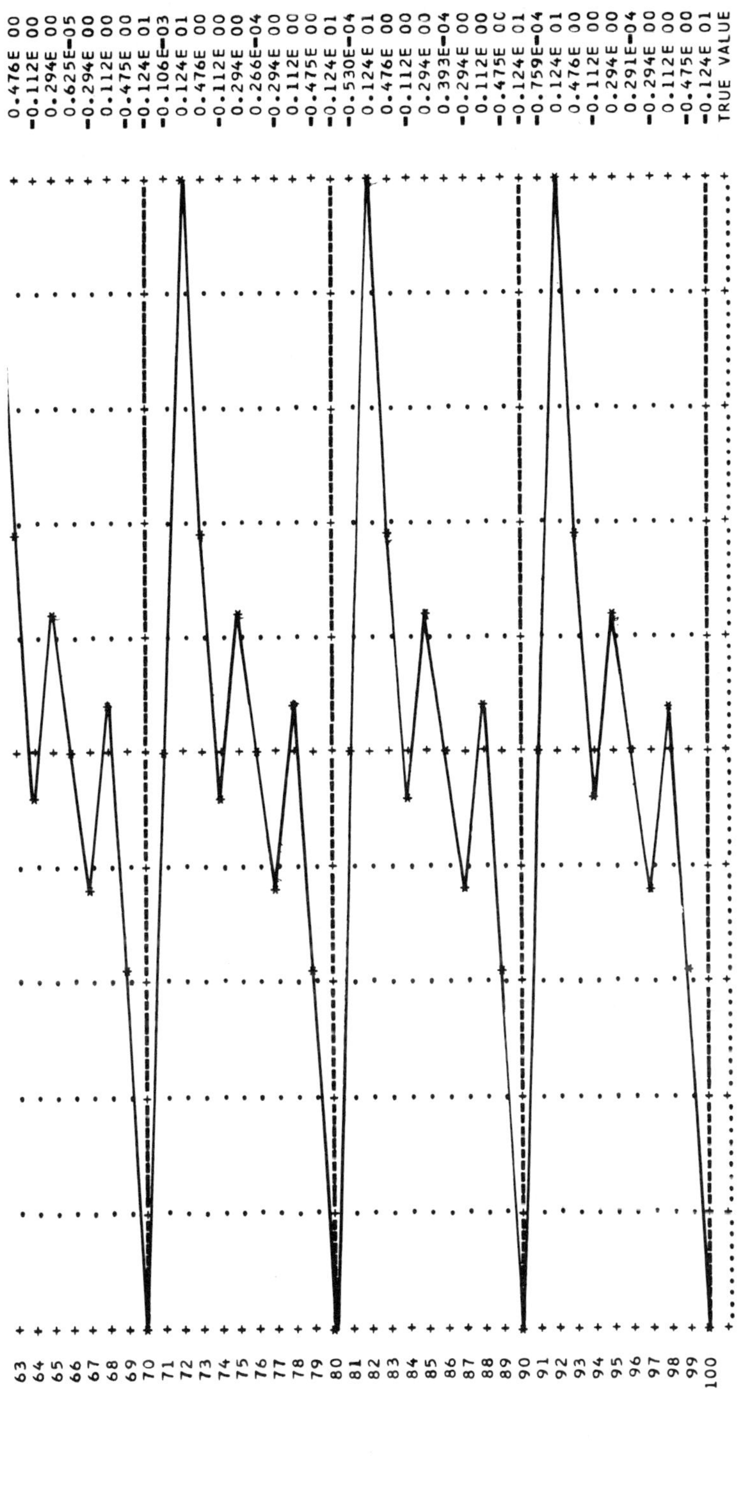

Figure 4-36 (Continued)

```
                         THIS IS THE INPUT SPECTRA  10-20-30 SINE WAVE


                                        M A G N I T U D E
      0.0       0.1       0.2       0.3       0.4       0.5       0.6       0.7       0.8       0.9        1.
       +.........+.........+.........+.........+.........+.........+.........+.........+.........+.........+   TRUE VALUE
       +                                                                                                   +
   0   *                                                                                                   +   0.117E-05
       +                                                                                                   +
   1   *                                                                                                   +   0.499E-06
       +                                                                                                   +
   2   *                                                                                                   +   0.425E-06
       +                                                                                                   +
   3   *                                                                                                   +   0.379E-06
       +                                                                                                   +
   4   *                                                                                                   +   0.474E-06
       +                                                                                                   +
   5   *                                                                                                   +   0.121E-05
       +                                                                                                   +
   6   *                                                                                                   +   0.123E-05
       +                                                                                                   +
   7   *                                                                                                   +   0.119E-05
       +                                                                                                   +
   8   *                                                                                                   +   0.932E-06
       +                                                                                                   +
   9   *                                                                                                   +   0.186E-05
       +                                                                                                   +
  10   *****************************************************************************************************   0.250E 00
       +                                                                                                   +
  11   *                                                                                                   +   0.257E-05
       +                                                                                                   +
  12   *                                                                                                   +   0.129E-05
       +                                                                                                   +
```

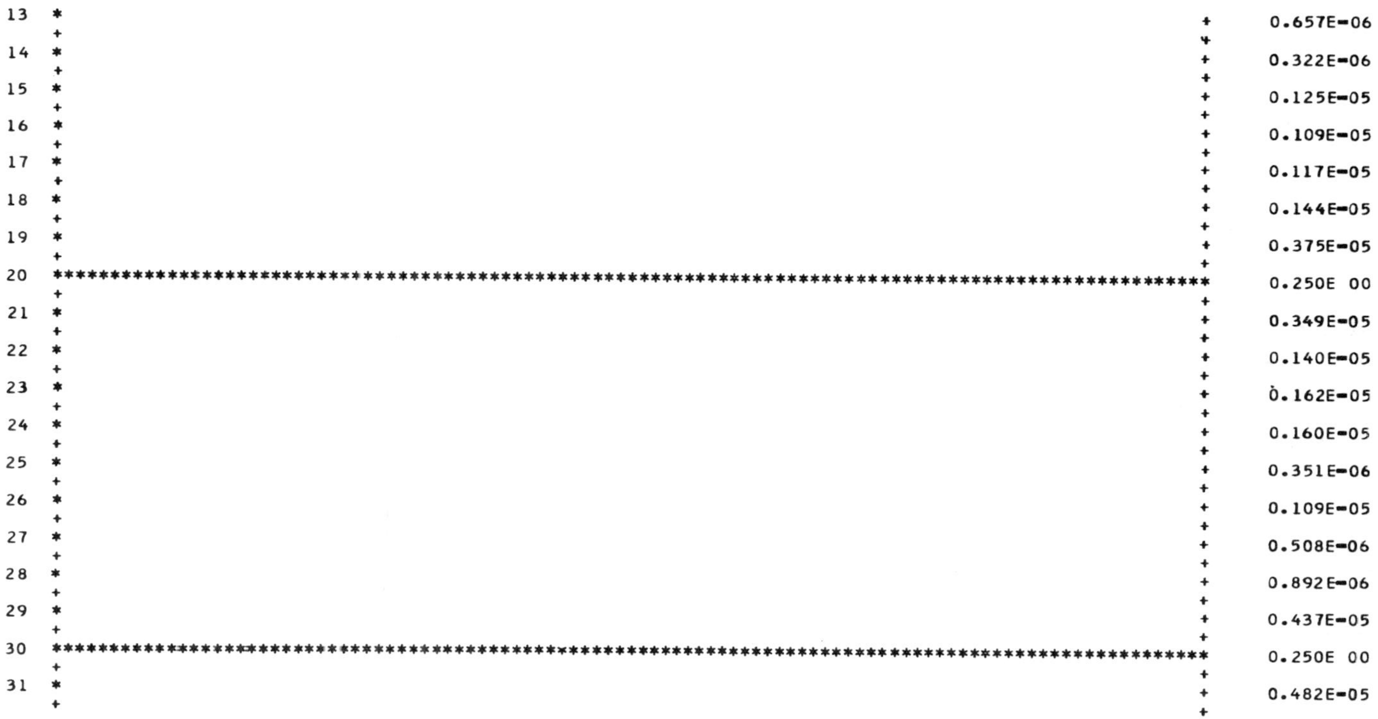

Figure 4-37. Input Spectra (Recursive Digital Filter Experiment).

```
32 *                                                  +   0.175E-05
   +                                                  +
33 *                                                  +   0.162E-05
   +                                                  +
34 *                                                  +   0.154E-05
   +                                                  +
35 *                                                  +   0.985E-06
   +                                                  +
36 *                                                  +   0.819E-06
   +                                                  +
37 *                                                  +   0.147E-05
   +                                                  +
38 *                                                  +   0.196E-05
   +                                                  +
39 *                                                  +   0.193E-06
   +                                                  +
40 *                                                  +   0.968E-06
   +                                                  +
41 *                                                  +   0.314E-06
   +                                                  +
42 *                                                  +   0.367E-06
   +                                                  +
43 *                                                  +   0.610E-06
   +                                                  +
44 *                                                  +   0.363E-06
   +                                                  +
45 *                                                  +   0.151E-05
   +                                                  +
46 *                                                  +   0.624E-06
   +                                                  +
47 *                                                  +   0.241E-06
   +                                                  +
48 *                                                  +   0.496E-06
   +                                                  +
49 *                                                  +   0.652E-06
   +....+....+....+....+....+....+....+....+....+....+  TRUE VALUE
```

Figure 4-37 (Continued)

```
                         OUTPUT OF RESONANCE FILTER TUNED TO 20 HZ

                                    M A G N I T U D E
     0.0       0.1       0.2       0.3       0.4       0.5       0.6       0.7       0.8       0.9       1.
      +.........+.........+.........+.........+.........+.........+.........+.........+.........+.........+   TRUE VALUE
      +                                                                                                   +
  0   ***                                                                                                 +   0.108E 00
      +                                                                                                   +
  1   ***                                                                                                 +   0.109E 00
      +                                                                                                   +
  2   ***                                                                                                 +   0.110E 00
      +                                                                                                   +
  3   ***                                                                                                 +   0.111E 00
      +                                                                                                   +
  4   ***                                                                                                 +   0.114E 00
      +                                                                                                   +
  5   ***                                                                                                 +   0.117E 00
      +                                                                                                   +
  6   ****                                                                                                +   0.121E 00
      +                                                                                                   +
  7   ****                                                                                                +   0.126E 00
      +                                                                                                   +
  8   ****                                                                                                +   0.132E 00
      +                                                                                                   +
  9   ****                                                                                                +   0.140E 00
      +                                                                                                   +
 10   ****                                                                                                +   0.127E 00
      +                                                                                                   +
 11   *****                                                                                               +   0.162E 00
      +                                                                                                   +
 12   *****                                                                                               +   0.179E 00
      +                                                                                                   +
 13   *****                                                                                               +   0.200E 00
      +                                                                                                   +
 14   ******                                                                                              +   0.228E 00
      +                                                                                                   +
```

Figure 4-38. Output Spectra (Recursive Digital Filter Experiment).

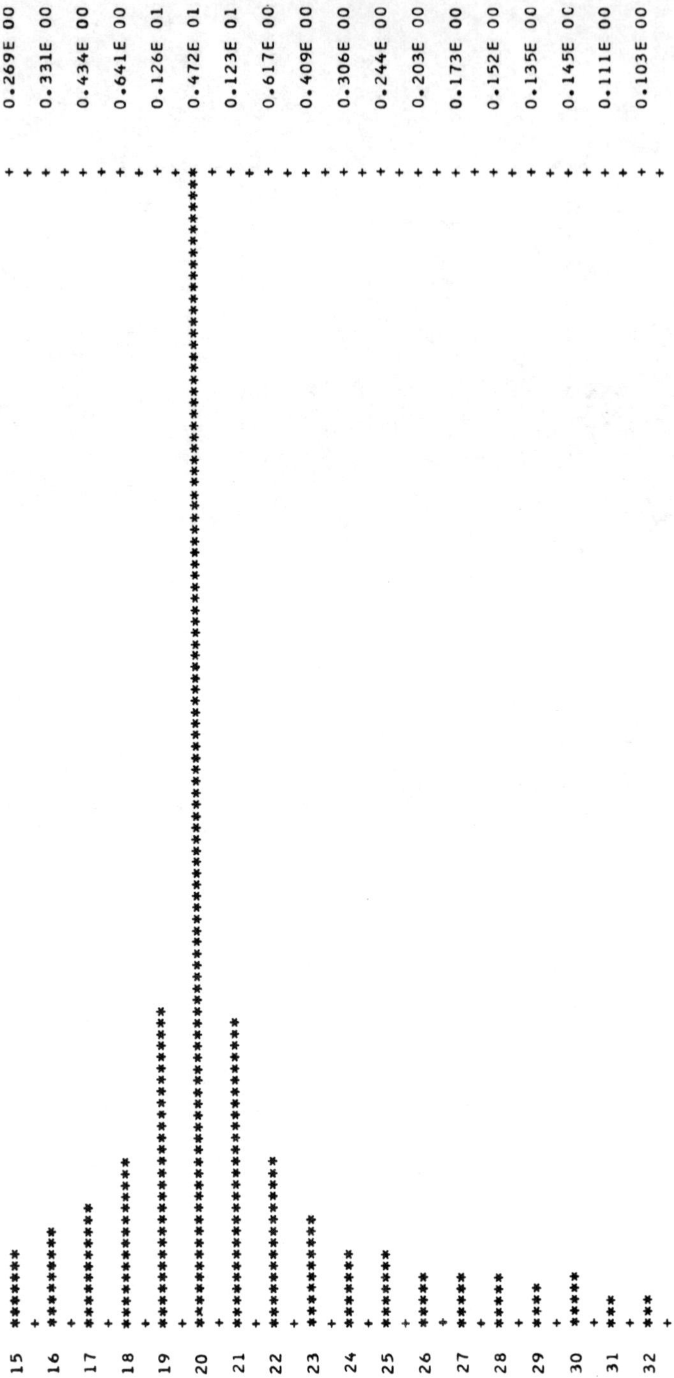
15 0.269E 00
16 0.331E 00
17 0.434E 00
18 0.641E 00
19 0.126E 01
20 0.472E 01
21 0.123E 01
22 0.617E 00
23 0.409E 00
24 0.306E 00
25 0.244E 00
26 0.203E 00
27 0.173E 00
28 0.152E 00
29 0.135E 00
30 0.145E 0C
31 0.111E 00
32 0.103E 00

```
33  ***                                                     +   0.955E-01
    +                                                       +
34  ***                                                     +   0.894E-01
    +                                                       +
35  ***                                                     +   0.842E-01
    +                                                       +
36  ***                                                     +   0.799E-01
    +                                                       +
37  ***                                                     +   0.761E-01
    +                                                       +
38  ***                                                     +   0.728E-01
    +                                                       +
39  ***                                                     +   0.701E-01
    +                                                       +
40  ***                                                     +   0.677E-01
    +                                                       +
41  ***                                                     +   0.656E-01
    +                                                       +
42  ***                                                     +   0.638E-01
    +                                                       +
43  ***                                                     +   0.624E-01
    +                                                       +
44  ***                                                     +   0.611E-01
    +                                                       +
45  ***                                                     +   0.601E-C1
    +                                                       +
46  ***                                                     +   0.593E-01
    +                                                       +
47  ***                                                     +   0.586E-01
    +                                                       +
48  ***                                                     +   0.582E-01
    +                                                       +
49  ***                                                     +   0.579E-01
    +.........+.........+.........+.........+.........+.........+.........+.........+.........+.........+   TRUE VALUE
```

Figure 4-38 (Continued)

radar to determine the range of a target. In general, the detected return is dominated, in an energy sense, by noise.

Therefore it is unknown, in general, whether a return was the result of signal-plus-noise or noise only. This is called a detection problem. Therefore it is essential that the existing signal-to-noise ratio of the given process be improved before performing a range analysis. A matched filter can be used to accomplish this objective. In practice, the output of the filter is used to measure the amount of signal energy in the return. If a signal is absent, then the output is low. The contrapositive is also true. Therefore, if a decision threshold is established, a signal will be considered present only if the filter output is equal to or greater than this prespecified threshold (see Figure 4-39). A matched filter operation can be performed under SPECTRUM IV control using program MATCH.

Theory

If the input to a linear system $h(t)$ is $s(t)$, where

$$s(t) = \sum_{i=-\infty}^{\infty} c_i e^{j2\pi fit} \tag{4.13}$$

and if the spectral representation of $h(t)$ is $H(f_n)$, $-\infty \leq f_n \leq \infty$, the power contained in the output process—say, $s_o(t)$ (see Figure 4-39)—where

$$\begin{aligned} s_o(t) &= s(t)*h(t) \\ &= \sum_{i=-\infty}^{\infty} [c_i H(f_i)] e^{j2\pi fit} \\ &= \sum_{i=-\infty}^{\infty} \tilde{c}_i e^{j2\pi fit} \end{aligned} \tag{4.14}$$

is given by

$$\begin{aligned} P_{s_0} &= \sum_{i=-\infty}^{\infty} |\tilde{c}_i|^2 \\ &= \sum_{i=-\infty}^{\infty} |c_i H(f_i)|^2 \end{aligned} \tag{4.15}$$

If a noise process whose power spectra is $G_n(f_i)$ is inputted into the same filter, the output power realized from a noise input only—say, P_{no} (see Figure 4-40)—is given by

$$P_{n_0} = \sum_{i=-\infty}^{\infty} |H(f_i)|^2 G_n(f_i) \tag{4.16}$$

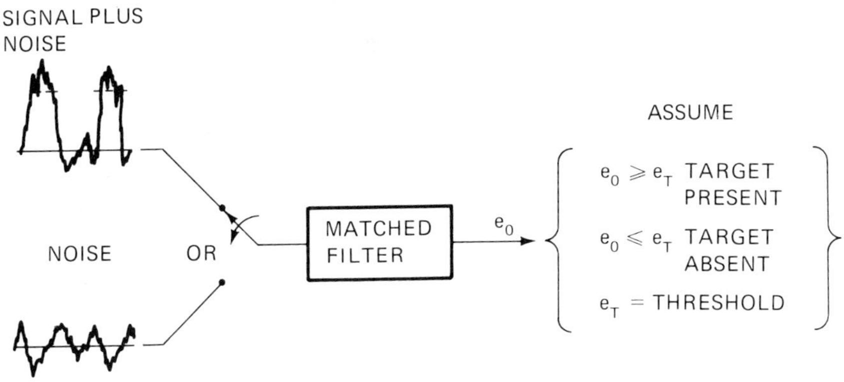

Figure 4-39. Matched Filter Application.

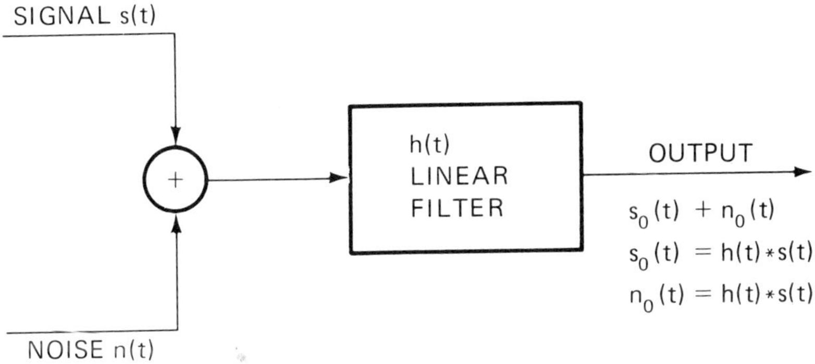

Figure 4-40. Noise Corrupted Linear System.

The signal-to-noise ratio realized at the system output, denoted γ, is given by

$$\gamma = \frac{P_{s_0}}{P_{n_0}} = \left[\sum_{i=-\infty}^{\infty} |H(f_i)c_i|^2\right] \Big/ \left[\sum_{i=-\infty}^{\infty} |H(f_i)|^2 G_n(f_i)\right] \qquad (4.17)$$

which we desire to maximize through the proper choice of linear filter function $h(t)$, or equivalently $H(f_i)$.

Using the Cauchy-Schwarz inequality, Equation (4.17) can be written as

$$\gamma = \left[\sum_{i=-\infty}^{\infty} |H(f_i) c_i|^2 \right] \Big/ \left[\sum_{i=-\infty}^{\infty} |H(f_i)|^2 G_n(f_i) \right] \tag{4.18}$$

$$\leq \left[\sum_{i=-\infty}^{\infty} |H(f_i)|^2 |c_i|^2 \right] \Big/ \left[\sum_{i=-\infty}^{\infty} |H(f_i)|^2 G_n(f_i) \right]$$

which is maximized when equality is established. This must be accomplished through the choice of H since c_i and G_n are known. Noting that if

$$H(f_i) = Kc_i{}^* e^{j2\pi f i t_o} \quad (K \text{ real}) \tag{4.19}$$

then

$$\begin{aligned} |H(f_i) c_i|^2 &= |K c_i c_i{}^* e^{j2\pi f i t_o}|^2 \\ &= |K|^2 |c_i c_i{}^*|^2 |e^{j2\pi f i t_o}|^2 \\ &= |K|^2 |c_i^2|^2 \\ &= |K|^2 |c_i|^2 |c_i|^2 \\ &= |H(f_i)|^2 |c_i|^2 \end{aligned} \tag{4.20}$$

and it follows

$$\sum_{i=-\infty}^{\infty} |H(f_i) c_i|^2 = \sum_{i=-\infty}^{\infty} |H(f)|^2 |c_i|^2 \tag{4.21}$$

Therefore the optimum filter becomes

$$H(f_i)_{\text{optimum}} = Kc_i^* \exp(j2\pi f_i t_o) \tag{4.22}$$

where K is a real constant filter gain and $\exp(j2\pi f_i t_o)$ represents a simple time delay of the form $\exp(st_o)$. The optimum filter is called the matched filter and can be generated if the spectral profile of the input signal $s(t)$ is known. Because the filter's magnitude profile "matches" the Fourier representation of the input signal process, the filter is logically called a matched filter. Note that the filter function is independent of the actual noise process residing in the system. The filter will have high gain at frequency locations occupied by high-signal energy and vice versa. The matched filter routine used in SPECTRUM IV assumes the following parameteric values:

$$\left. \begin{aligned} K &= 1 \\ t_o &= 0 \end{aligned} \right\} \tag{4.23}$$

which implies

$$H(f_i)_{\text{optimum (SPECTRUM IV)}} = c_i^* \tag{4.24}$$

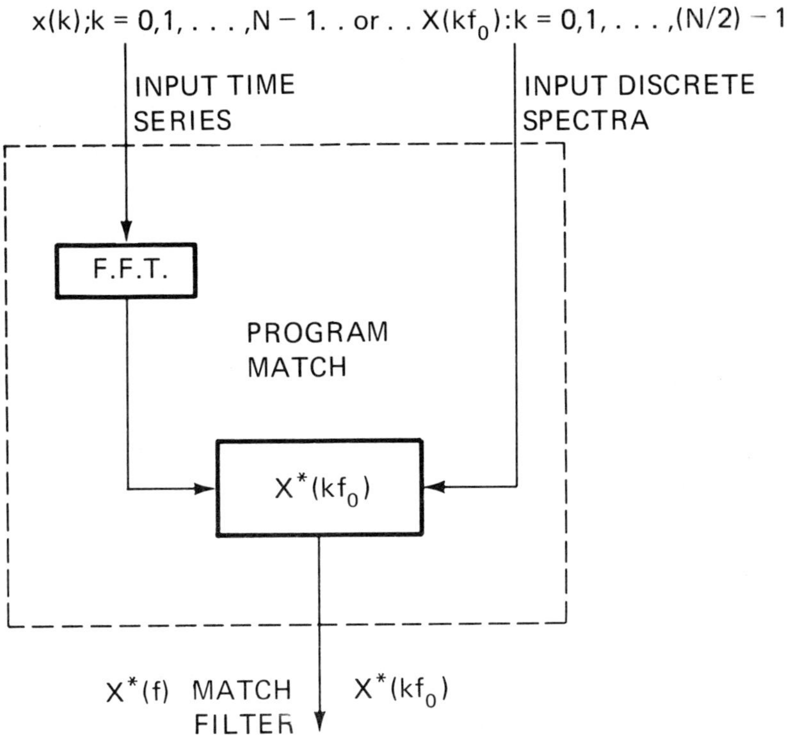

Figure 4-41. Program MATCH.

A matched filter is constructed under SPECTRUM IV control as shown in Figure 4-41.

Execution of MATCH

A matched filter is constructed through the use of the five-letter mnemonic MATCH. The only restriction imposed on the use of MATCH is that the Fourier representation of the signal process to be matched may not be zero. A Fourier representation of that signal is entered into a prespecified array, and the matched filter is returned to that array. The card control sequence required of such an operation is shown in Table 4-8. A MATCH operation is followed by a listing of the identifying parameters of transformed array. The matched filter is stored in the frequency domain.

Table 4-8
Structure of a MATCH Filter

Column Number	Description	Format or Contents
Primary information card		
1-5	Calls MATCH	MATCH
15	Array to be Matched (A, B, or C)	A1

Example. The a priori knowledge of a signal spectra can be used to define the spectral properties of a matched filter. The filter, when properly configured, will react to that signal in a manner that will maximize the signal-to-noise-ratio at the filter's output. To demonstrate this property, the following experiments are performed. A filter will be matched to a pulse train. Its ability to discriminate between a raised cosine, triangular wave, and pulse train will then be experimentally explored. The result of this experiment can be found in Figures 4-42 through 4-50.

The pulse train used in this example has a duty cycle of 0.25. The raised cosine and triangular wave, synthesized in user-supplied subprogram OWN as indirect addressed programs 20 and 10, are displayed in Figures 4-17 and 4-42, respectively. The card control sequence associated with this problem is found in Figure 4-42. Upon completing the requested convolutions, the signal array C is cleared to allow the next test signal to be entered into this previously protected register.

The matched filter created will optimally respond to a pulse of duty cycle 0.25. A visual inspection of the test signals considered implies that: the test pulse is maximally correlated, the raised cosine is less correlated, and the triangular wave is even less correlated to the pulse train used to define the matched filter. Therefore one would expect this behavior to be repeated when this test signal is convolved with the matched filter impulse response. This hypothesis is verified through experimentation, the result of which can be found in Figures 4-46, 4-48, and 4-50.

E. Wiener Filter

A noise process can be interpreted in the time domain as well as the sample space. In the time domain, a single record is investigated for all time. Such an experiment is diagrammed in Figure 4-51.

In the sample space, an arbitrarily large number of experiments are performed. At any given time t, a probability density function analysis can

```
CARD    COLUMN                                                                      8Ø
        1234567890123    .          .          .          .          .          .      .
----------------------------------------------------------------------------------------
1       LIBRARY      A                                              48      1ØØ.ØØ
2       PULSE OF DUTY CYCLE .25                      2  1.Ø  Ø.Ø       .25Ø
3       PLOTTER      A                                              48
4       TIME              1   48  PULSE OF DUTY CYCLE .25   MATCH FILTER SIGNAL
5       MATCH        A
6       SWITCH       A    B
7       USER LIB     C                                              48      1ØØ.ØØ      1
8       TRIANGULAR WAVE                                                   1.ØØØ  Ø.Ø
9       PLOTTER      C                                              48
1Ø      TIME              1   48  TRIANGULAR WAVE
11      CONVOLVE     B    C
12      PLOTTER      A                                              48
13      TIME              1   48  TRIANGLE THROUGH FILTER           WORST CORRELATION
14      ZERO-OUT     C
14      USER LIB     C                                              48      1ØØ.ØØ      2
15      RAISED COSINE                                                     1.ØØØ  Ø.Ø
16      PLOTTER      C                                              48
17      TIME              1   48  RAISED COSINE
18      CONVOLVE     B    C
19      PLOTTER      A                                              48
2Ø      TIME              1   48  RAISED COSINE THROUGH FILTER   GOOD CORRELATION
21      ZERO-OUT     C
22      LIBRARY      C                                              48      1ØØ.ØØ
23      THIS IS THE PULSE                            2  1.Ø  Ø.Ø       .25 1.ØØØ
24      PLOTTER      C                                              48
25      TIME              1   48  MATCH FILTER SIGNAL
26      CONVOLVE     B    C
27      PLOTTER      A                                              48
28      TIME              1   48  PULSE THROUGH FILTER   BEST CORRELATION
29      TERM
                 .          .          .          .          .          .          .      .
```

Figure 4-42. Card Control Sequence for Matched Filter Experiment.

```
FORTRAN IV G LEVEL  21              OWN              DATE = 75156        15/34/06              PAGE 0001

            SUBROUTINE OWN
      C
      C  THE FOLLOWING FIVE STATEMENTS SHOULD BE INCLUDED IN ANY SUBROUTINE OWN
            REAL*8 BAN
            INTEGER DSO,E,F,TIME,FREQ,SPL
            COMMON REST(6148),TEMR(1024),TEMC(1024),FRN(20),FCN(20),FRD(20),
           1FCD(20),PN(21),PD(21),REST1(82),NPOINT,REST2(5),SPL,REST3(2)
            CCMMON /LETTER/ F,E,MAR(3),LAIS(60),TIME,FREQ,IBAN,BAN,LN,NN,NP
      C
      C
            WRITE(LN,3) SPL
          3 FORMAT(10X,'USER PROGRAM NUMBER ',I2,/)
            GO TO (10,20),SPL
            GO TO 99
         10 N8 = NPOINT/8
            N7 = 7*N8+1
            DO 11 J=1,N8
            TEMR(J) = (7-J)/6.0
            TEMR(N7) =(N7-43)/6.0
            N7 = N7+1
         11 CONTINUE
            GO TO 99
         20 N8 = NPOINT/8
            N7 = 7*N8+1
            PI = 4.0*ATAN(1.0)
            DT = 1.0/12.0
            DO 21 K=1,N8
            TEMR(K) = COS((K-1)*DT*PI)
            TEMR(N7) =COS((43-N7)*DT*PI)
            N7 = N7+1
         21 CONTINUE
         99 CONTINUE
            RETURN
            END
```

Figure 4-43. Subroutine OWN (Matched Filter Experiment).

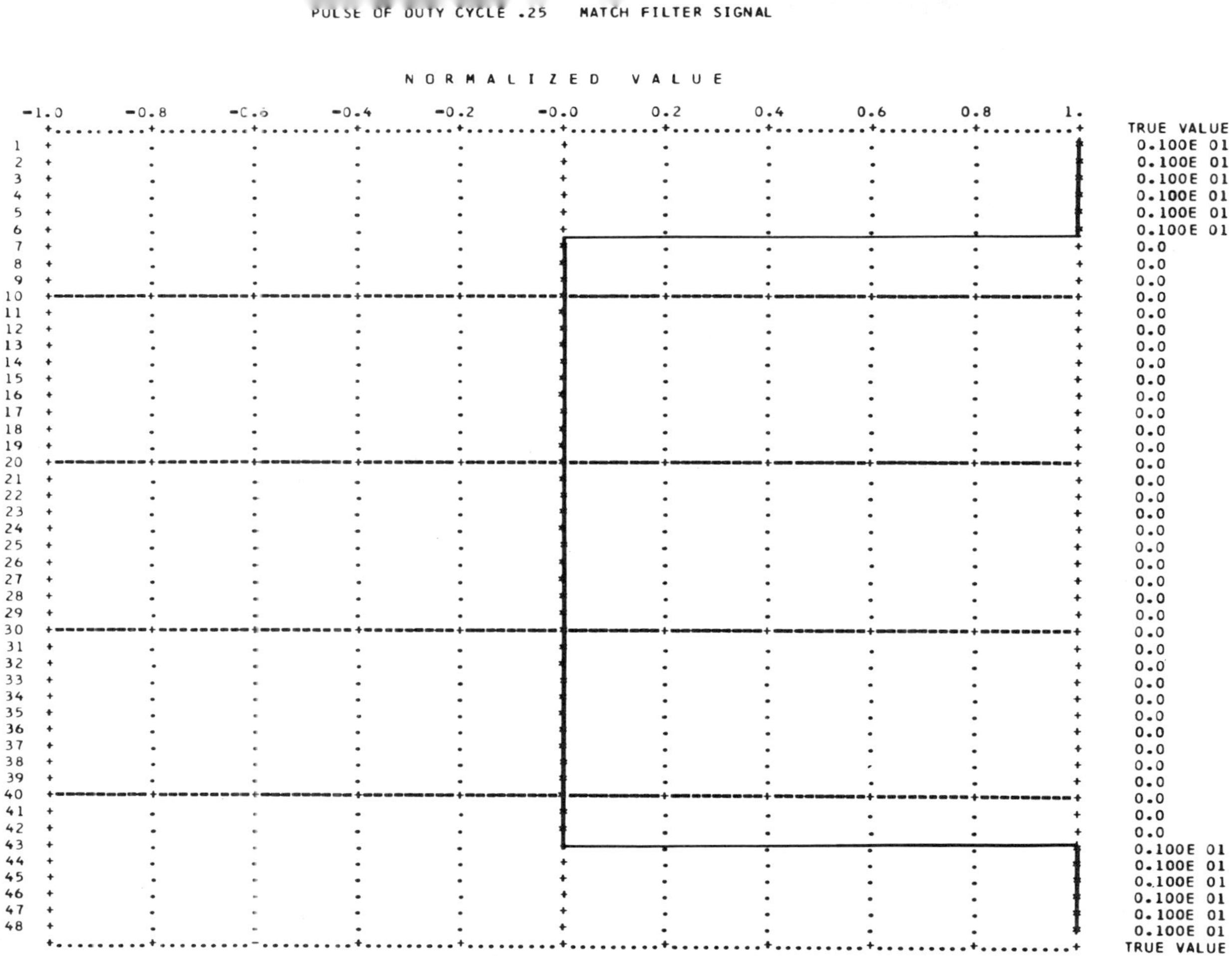

Figure 4-44. Reference Time Series (Matched Filter Experiment).

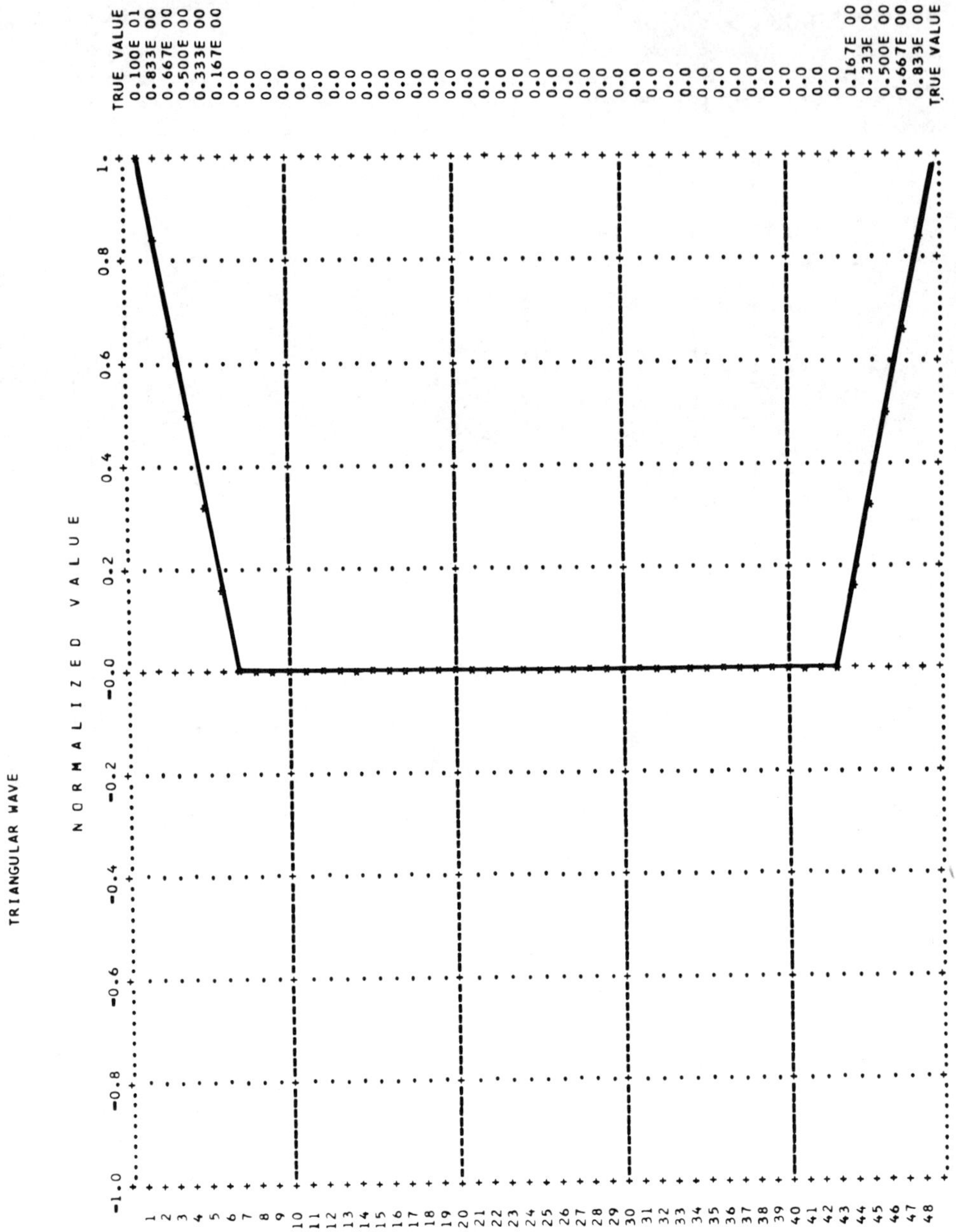

Figure 4.45 Triangular Test Signal (Matched Filter Experiment).

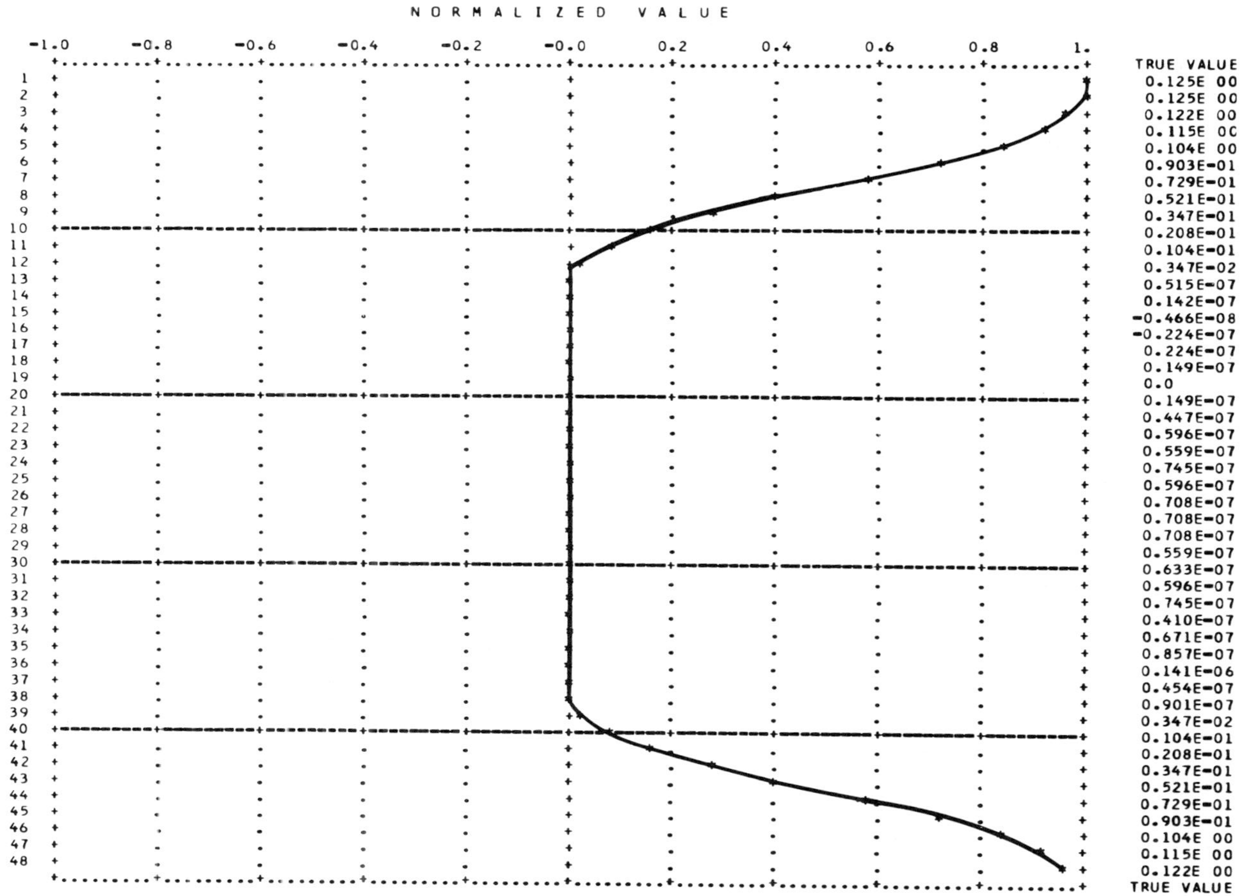

Figure 4-46. Triangular Wave Through a Matched Filter (Matched Filter Experiment).

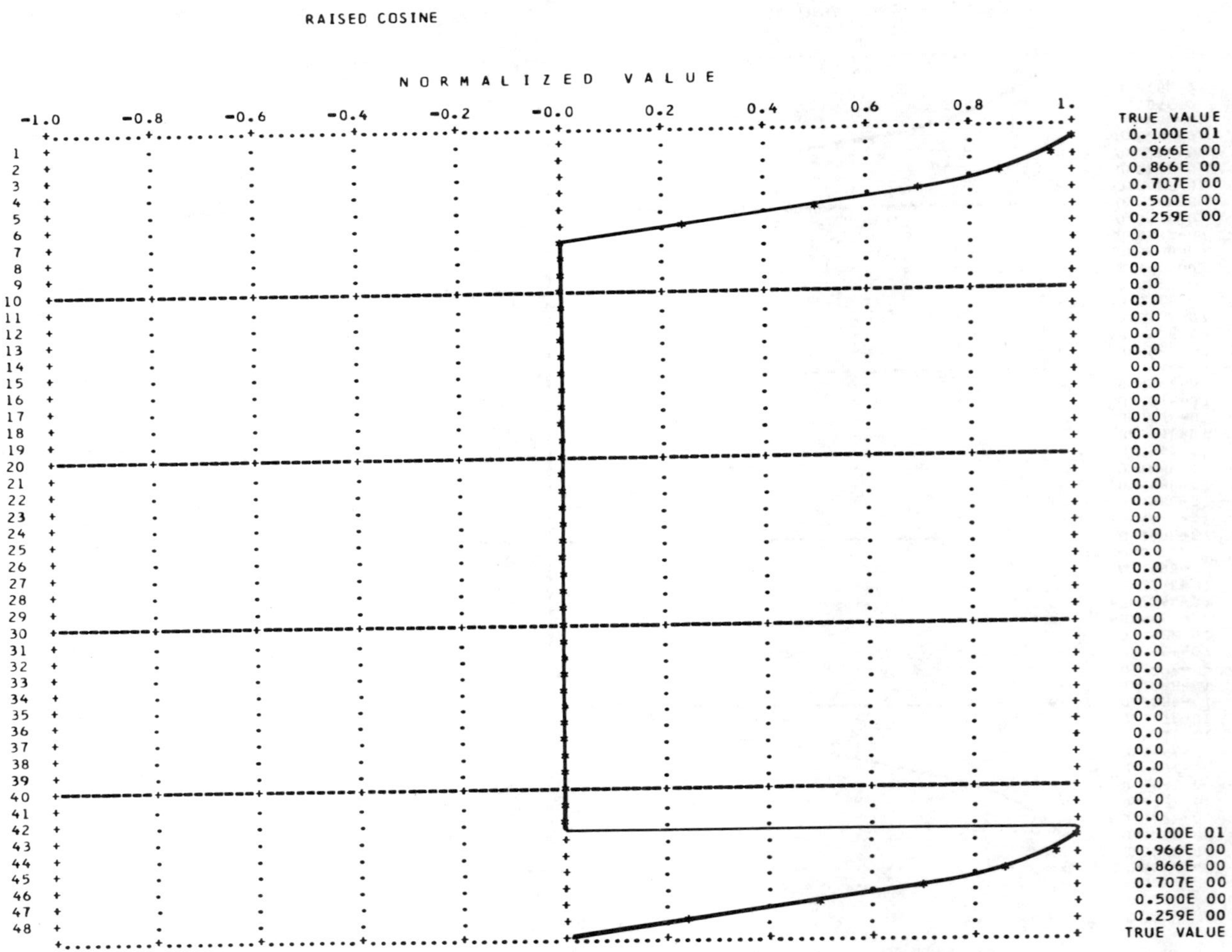

(Matched Filter Experiment)

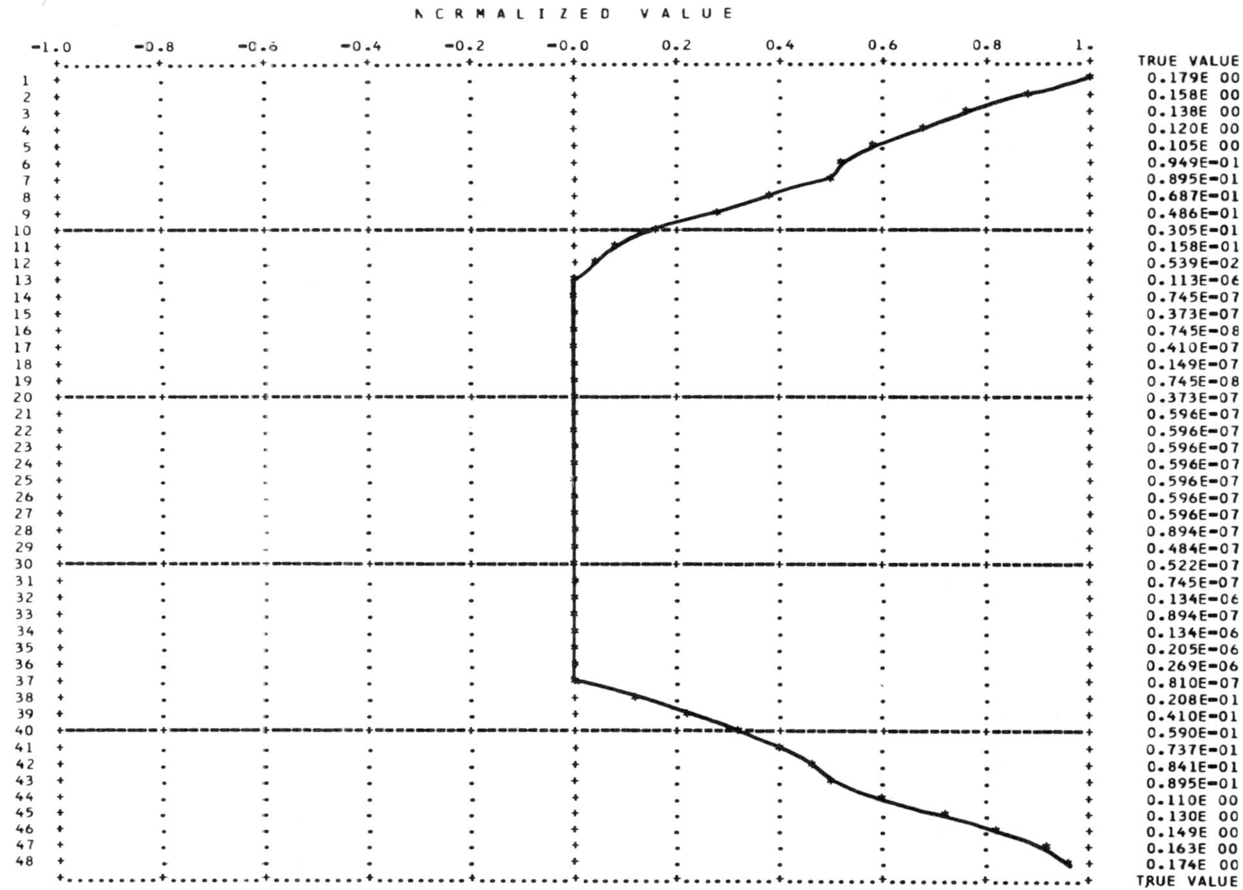

Figure 4-48. Raised Cosine Through a Matched Filter (Matched Filter Experiment).

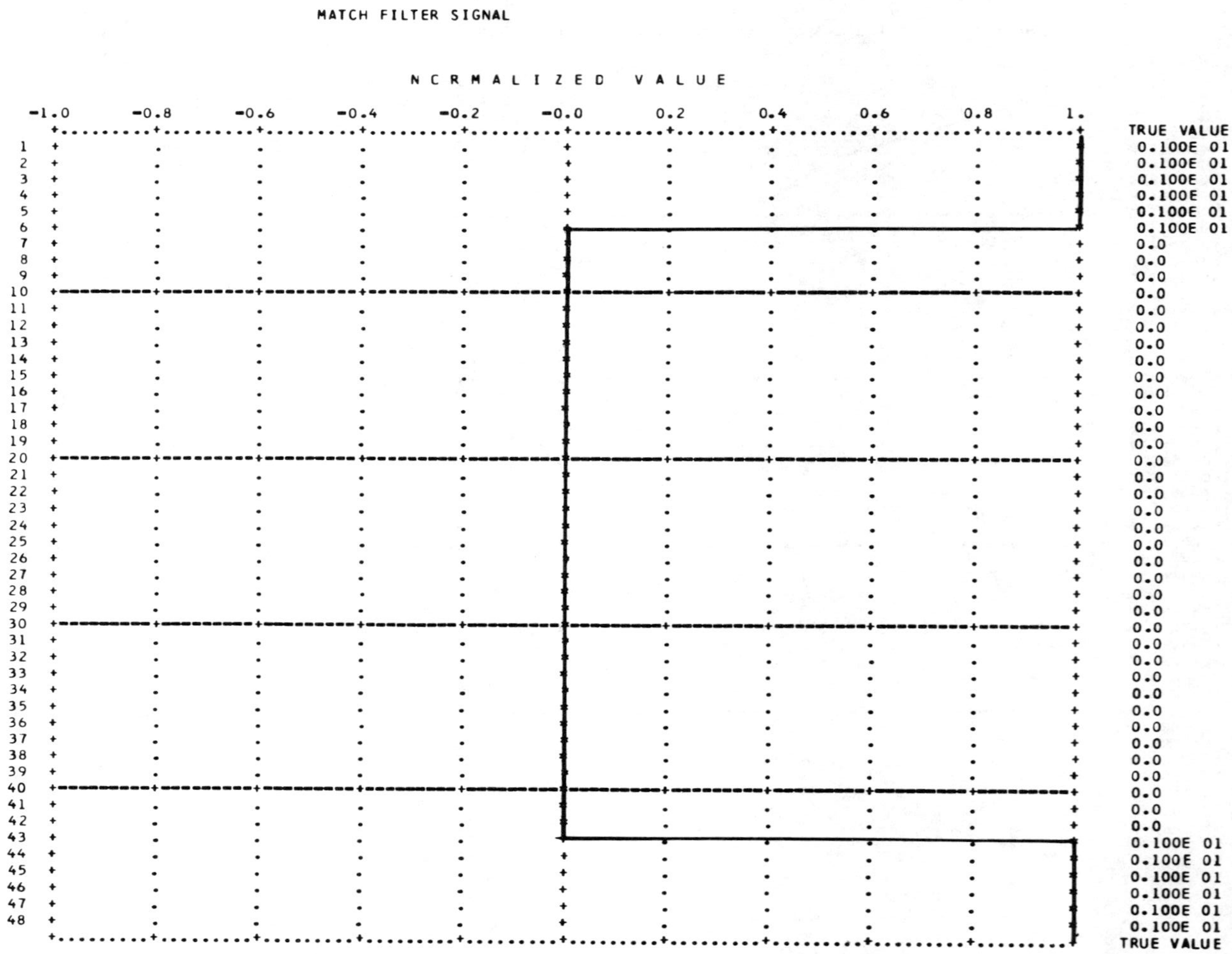

Figure 4-49. Test Pulse Signal (Matched Filter Experiment).

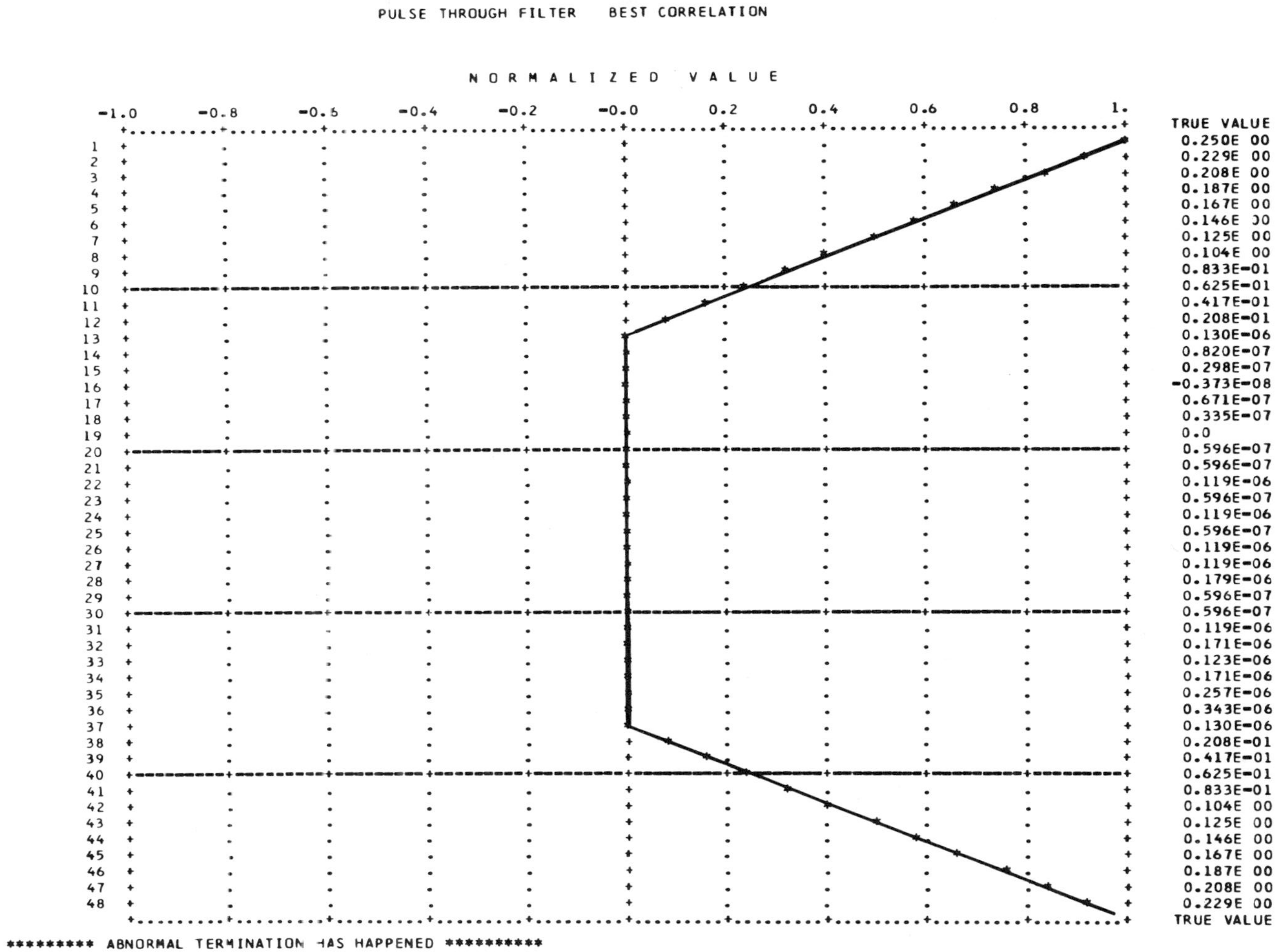

Figure 4-50. Pulse Through a Matched Filter (Matched Filter Experiment).

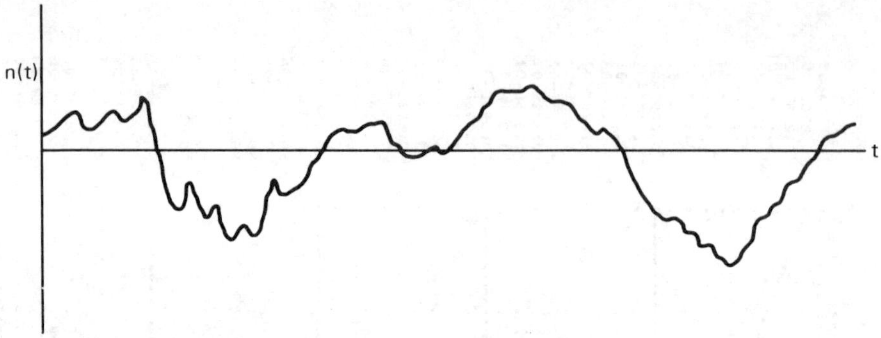

Figure 4-51. Temporal Noise Record.

be formed. The probability density function, denoted $p[\bar{n}(t)]$, is a continuous histogram of the event n at time t. The probability density function satisfies the following axiomatic properties:

$$0 \leq p[n(t)]$$
$$1 = \int p[n(t)]\, dn(t) \tag{4.25}$$

A sample space experiment is diagrammed in Figure 4-52. Statistics derived from such tests are called ensemble statistics.

Without loss of generality, let $n(t)$ be a zero mean process. Then the mth time and ensemble moments, denote $\bar{n}^m(t)$ and $\mathscr{E}[n^m(t)]$, respectively, are given by

$$\bar{x}(t) = \frac{1}{T}\int_T x^m\,(t)\,dt \qquad \text{as } T\to\infty \tag{4.26}$$

and

$$\mathscr{E}[x^m(t)] = \int x^m(t)p[x(t)]\,dx(t) \tag{4.27}$$

If all time and ensemble statistics are equal, the process is said to be ergodic. An ergodic process is also known to be stationary. That is, $\bar{x}^m(t) = \mathscr{E}[x^m(t)]$ independent of the time t. A process is said to be weak-sense ergodic if the autocorrelation and autocovariance values of the process $n(t)$ are the same. That is, the autocorrelation

$$R_n(\tau) = \frac{1}{T}\int n(t)n(t+\tau)\,dt \tag{4.28}$$

equals the autocovariance function, denoted $\phi_n(\tau)$

$$\phi_n(\tau) = \mathscr{E}(n(t)n(t+\tau)) \tag{4.29}$$

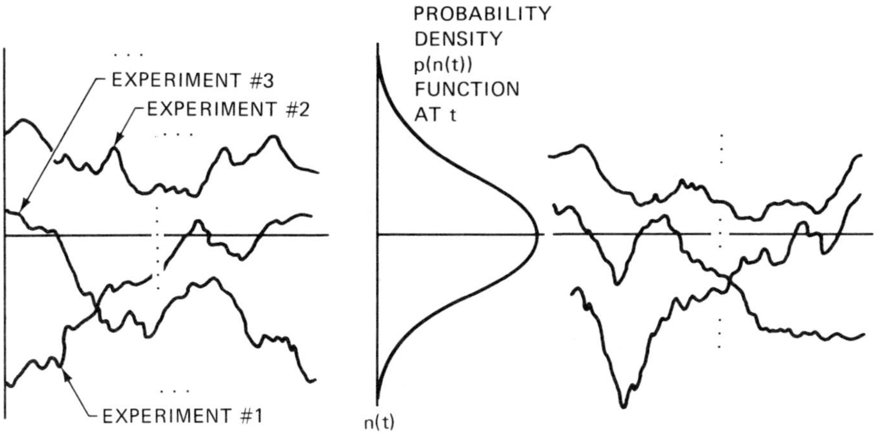

Figure 4-52. Sample Space Experiment.

Weak-sense ergodic processes play an important role in the study of linear systems corrupted by noise. Time-domain statistics, such as autocorrelation, can be obtained easily by analyzing a single time-domain record with an analog or digital instrument. However, if the same statistics were to be generated in the ensemble domain, an arbitrarily large number of simultaneous experiments would need to be performed, which is usually unrealistic. Since theoretical models of noise-corrupted processes usually specify system statistics in the ensemble domain, the importance of the ergodic hypothesis becomes self-evident. Under the ergodic hypothesis (usually one only requires a weak ergodic assumption), physically realizable time-domain statistics can be used to represent often unobtainable ensemble domain statistics.

Wiener's problem is a very useful and interesting problem of linear random systems. This study produces a filter theory that is applicable to a wide class of problems. The problem is as follows: Given the noisy linear system found in Figure 4-53, define the optimum filter.

The theory is used to define an optimum filter $s(t)$ that minimizes the mean squared error σ_e^2, where

$$\sigma_e^2 = \mathscr{E}(e(t)^2) \tag{4.30}$$

under the assumption that

1. the observer $i(t)$ is given
2. $n(t)$ is an ergodic noise process
3. a steady-state estimate of $x(t)$—namely, $\hat{x}(t)$—is requested (steady state→frequency domain)

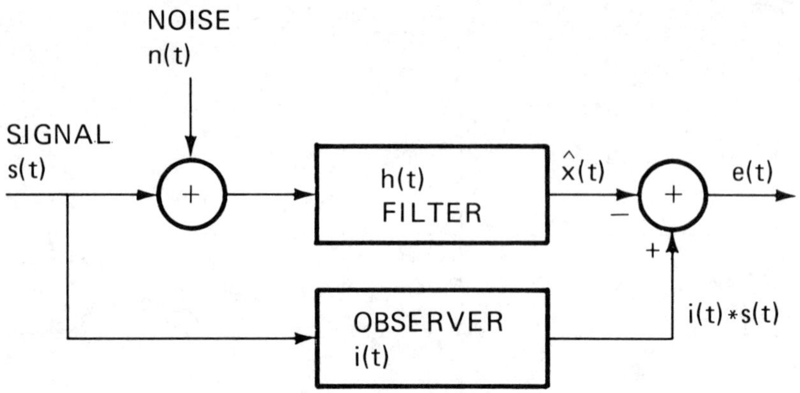

Figure 4-53. The Problem of Wiener.

The system observer $i(t)$ is defined as follows:

$$i(t) = 1(t - \sigma) \tag{4.31}$$

where $1(\lambda)$ is the unit step function. It is defined as follows:

$$1(\lambda) = \begin{Bmatrix} 1 \text{ if } \lambda \geq 0 \\ 0 \text{ otherwise} \end{Bmatrix} \tag{4.32}$$

If σ of Equation (4.31) equals zero, then $s(t)$ is observed without delay or distortion. If σ is a real number less than zero, then the observer will pass an undistorted but delayed version of $s(t)$. If σ is a real number greater than zero, the observer will pass an undistorted but predicted version of $s(t)$. The Laplace transform of $1(t + \sigma)$ is given by the delay theorem of operational calculus. It satisfies

$$1(t + \sigma) \underset{\mathscr{L}^{-1}}{\overset{\mathscr{L}}{\rightleftarrows}} \exp(\sigma s) \tag{4.33}$$

Therefore the filter that evolves from a Wiener analysis either will estimate, in a minimum expected least squares error sense $s(t)$ if $i(t) = 1(t)$, or will estimate a delayed (smoothed) version of $s(t)$—namely, $s(t + \sigma)$—if $i(t) = 1(t + \sigma)$, $\sigma < 0$. If $\sigma < 0$, then the estimate will be the predicted value of $s(t + \sigma)$, σ seconds into the future.

Wiener's minimal average mean square error filter has many applications. It has been sucessfully used in communication, radar, sonar, and telecommunications. The Wiener filter has also been successfully employed in speech recognition and biological signal enhancement systems.

Physical realizability is a problem associated with the Wiener filter. If a Wiener filter is to be constructed using analog devices, the resultant filter would be unstable. A modification of the Wiener problem, called the realizable suboptimal Wiener filter, will rectify this problem. Using digital filtering methods, the problem of filter instability can be bypassed. Program WIENER will allow the user to derive a Wiener filter under SPECTRUM IV control.

Theory

Recall that an ergodic process has equal time and ensemble moments (ensemble averages denoted $\mathscr{E}$). Then

$$R_y(\tau) = \mathscr{E}[y(t)\, y(t + \tau)] \tag{4.34}$$

where R_y denotes the autocorrelation of $y(t)$. It is also known that correlation and power spectral densities form a Fourier transform pair. That is,

$$R_y(\tau) = \mathscr{F}^{-1} G_y(w) \triangleq \frac{1}{2\pi i}\int_{-i\infty}^{i\infty} G_y(w)\, e^{j\omega\tau}\, d\omega \tag{4.35}$$

However, a special case of extreme importance occurs when $\tau = 0$. Consider $y(t)$ to be a zero mean process, then

$$R_y(0) = \mathscr{E}[y(t)\ y(t)] = \mathscr{E}[y^2(t)] \triangleq \sigma_y^2. \tag{4.36}$$

where σ_y^2 denotes the variance of y, but $R_y(0)$ also equals

$$R_y(0) = \frac{1}{2\pi j}\int_{-j\infty}^{j\infty} G_y(\omega)\, d\omega \tag{4.37}$$

In practice $G_y(\omega) = Y(\omega)Y(-\omega)$ if $y(t)$ is periodic and deterministic, and $G_y(\omega) = \mathscr{E}(Y(\omega)Y(-\omega))$ if $y(t)$ is a random process.

Then the error variance of the system under consideration can be written as

$$\sigma_e^2 = \mathscr{E}(e^2(t)) = \mathscr{E}\left[\frac{1}{2\pi j}\int_{-j\infty}^{j\infty} G_e(\omega)\, d\omega\right]$$

$$= \mathscr{E}\left[\frac{1}{2\pi j}\int_{-j\infty}^{j\infty} E(\omega)E(-\omega)\, d\omega\right] \tag{4.38}$$

$$E(\omega) = S(\omega)I(\omega) - H(\omega)[S(\omega) + N(\omega)]$$

$$= S(\omega)[I(\omega) - H(\omega)] - N(\omega)H(\omega)$$

then

$$E(\omega)E(-\omega) = S(\omega)S(-\omega)[I(\omega) - H(\omega)][I(-\omega) - H(-\omega)]$$
$$- S(\omega)[I(\omega) - H(\omega)]N(-\omega)H(-\omega)$$
$$- S(-\omega)[I(-\omega) - H(-\omega)]N(\omega)H(\omega)$$
$$+ N(\omega)N(-\omega)H(\omega)H(-\omega) \qquad (4.39)$$

Suppose further that the signal processes $s(t)$ and $n(t)$ are uncorrelated. Then

$$R_{sn}(\tau) = 0 \Rightarrow \mathscr{E}[G_{sn}(\omega)] = \mathscr{E}[S(\omega)N(-\omega)] = 0$$
$$R_{ns}(\tau) = 0 \Rightarrow \mathscr{E}[G_{ns}(\omega)] = \mathscr{E}[N(\omega)S(-\omega)] = 0 \qquad (4.40)$$

then $\mathscr{E}[E(\omega)E(-\omega)]$ becomes

$$G_e(\omega) = \mathscr{E}[E(\omega)E(-\omega)] = \mathscr{E}\{S(\omega)S(-\omega)[I(\omega)-H(\omega)][I(-\omega)-H(-\omega)]\}$$
$$+ \mathscr{E}[N(\omega)N(-\omega)H(\omega)H(-\omega)]$$
$$= G_s(\omega)[I(\omega) - H(\omega)][I(-\omega) - H(-\omega)]$$
$$+ G_n(\omega)H(\omega)H(-\omega) \qquad (4.41)$$

Example. If $I(s) = 1$, $R_n(\tau) = \sigma_{N^2}\delta(\tau) \Rightarrow G_n(\omega) = \sigma_{N^2}$ and $s(t) \Rightarrow S(\omega) = 1/s$, for $s = j\omega$, then $S(\omega)S(-\omega) = (1/j\omega)(1/-j\omega) = 1/\omega^2$. Let $h(t)$ be assumed to be a first-order filter such that $h(t) = a \exp(-at)$, then $H(s) = a/(s + a)$ or $H(\omega) = a/(j\omega + a)$.

Therefore

$$G_e(\omega) = \frac{1 + \sigma_{N^2}a^2}{w^2 + a^2}$$

$$\sigma_e = \frac{1}{2\pi j}\int_{-j\infty}^{j\infty} G_e(\omega)\, d\omega$$

$$= \frac{}{2\pi j}\int_{-j\infty}^{j\infty} \left(\frac{1 + \sigma_{N^2}a^2}{\omega^2 + a^2}\right) d\omega = \frac{1 + \sigma_{N^2}a^2}{2a}$$

What is the optimum choice of a, say a^*, which minimizes the error variance σ_e ? It can be obtained easily from a direct derivative test:

$$\left.\frac{\partial \sigma_{e^2}}{\partial a}\right|_{a=a^*} = \frac{\sigma_{N^2}}{2} - \frac{1}{2a^2} = 0$$

or

$$a = 1/\sigma_{N^2}$$

Using an analogous derivative argument, the optimum filter—say, $H^o(\omega)$—for a prespecified $G_s(\omega)$ and $G_n(\omega)$, is given by

$$H^o(s)\bigg|_{s=j\omega} = \frac{I(s)G_s(s)}{G_s(s) + G_n(s)}\bigg|_{S=j\omega} \qquad \text{(The Wiener Filter)} \qquad (4.42)$$

The filter's structure may be argued as follows. For simplicity, consider $I(s)=1$: estimation problem.

1. No noise: If $n(t) = 0$ for all time, $G_n(\omega) = 0$ for all ω and

   $$H^o(w) = 1$$

   or the optimal squares estimate of the input $s(t)$ is the output $x(t) = s(t) + n(t) = s(t)$.
2. White noise: If the noise process is white, its power spectrum $G_s(\omega)$ is "flat" (constant for all frequency, say, N). Then the relative gain of the filter is decreased as a function of N. If the noise process is strong, N is large, and the relative gain of the filter is reduced. Intuitively it implies that one turns the receiver gain down in the presence of a strong sinal.
3. Narrow-band noise: If the noise spectra is narrow band and has a spectra reasonably disjointed from the signal spectra $G_s(\omega)$, the Wiener filter has high gain in the frequencies covered by signal energy and low gain in the regions of high energy.

Subprogram WIENER of SPECTRUM IV will produce a Wiener filter from user-supplied noise, signal, and delay information—that is, $i(t)$. The computation process is shown in Figure 4-54.

Execution of WIENER

A Wiener filter can be constructed under SPECTRUM IV control by using the six-letter mnemonic WIENER. The use of WIENER requires two control cards, which supply the user-supplied data to SPECTRUM IV. This information is used to characterize the expected noise and signal processes. In addition, the observer characteristics are supplied through user-supplied data. In general, for $i(t + \sigma)$, equivalently $I(s) = \exp(\sigma s)$,

$\sigma = 0$ estimation

$\sigma > 0$ prediction

$\sigma < 0$ smoothing

Restrictions imposed on the use of WIENER are:

1. The expected Fourier representation of the noise process must be entered into array C—that is, $N(lf_o)$.

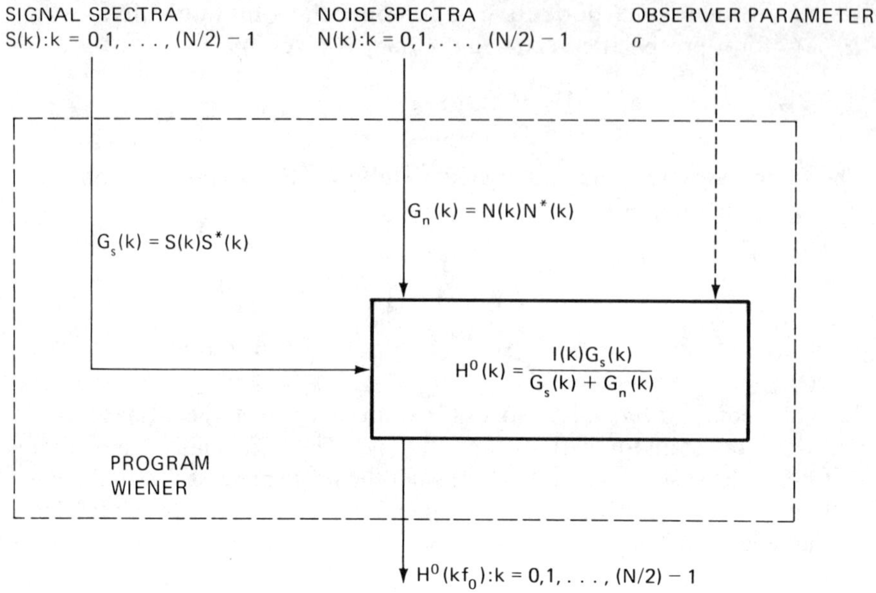

Figure 4-54. Program WIENER.

2. The expected Fourier representation of the signal to be estimated, smoothed, or predicted must reside in array B—that is, $S(lf_o)$.
3. Since the produced Wiener filter is returned to array A, array A must be free of memory protection.
4. Arrays B and C cannot be the null arrays.
5. Arrays B and C must contain the same number of data values.
6. Arrays B and C must be generated with the same sample frequency.

The card control for WIENER is shown in Table 4-9.

Under SPECTRUM IV control, labels indicating the parameter associated with the WIENER operation are outputted. The derived filter resides in array A and is in the frequency domain. Since there is a potential divide fault in a WIENER operation, the divide interpolation method outlined in Section A of this chapter is used. The success of any divide fault rectification process is outputted by SPECTRUM IV automatically. The filter derived by program WIENER is memory-protected (that is, it is in array A).

Example. With respect to the previously considered system constraints, a Wiener filter has been shown to be optimal. The following experiment is performed to demonstrate the capabilities of the Wiener filter.

Table 4-9
Structure of a WIENER Call

Column Number		*Description*	*Format or Contents*
Primary information card			
	1-6	Calls WIENER	WIENER
Secondary information card			
	1-10	Define $\sigma = 0$ estimation $\sigma > 0$ prediction $\sigma < 0$ smoothing	F10.5

A filter will be created to produce the best estimate of an input pulse train in the presence of noise. Recall that an estimate implies that the previously considered time delay equals zero (that is, SEC = 0). The results of experimentation are summarized in Figures 4-55, 4-56, and 4-57.

Figure 4-55 contains the control card sequence; note that a Wiener with zero time delay is requested. Several subtle card control operations are required by the problem under consideration. After the Wiener filter is constructed, it is moved into array B for future convolution. Finally, array C, the signal array, is cleared after use to remove the memory protection assigned that array. This will facilitate the reuse of array C.

The utility of a Wiener filter can be observed by comparing Figures 4-56 and 4-57. The effects of additive noise can be reduced significantly through the proper use of a Wiener filter. That is, the time-series estimate of the input process is a good representation of an uncorrupted pulse train.

F. Hanning Filter

We have noted that leakage is one of the error sources found in a DFT. The problem of leakage was characterized by a time-series input record having a fundamental period differing from the DFT sampling interval by some noninteger value. The leakage would disappear, however, if these two time intervals were related by an integer. Therefore the problem can be minimized if the input time series is made to "appear" periodic in the DFT sampling interval. Such a condition can be produced by inserting a periodicity-inducing filter between the input time series and a DFT operation. Some of the more popular periodicity-inducing filters are those of Hanning, Hamming, and Blackman. Program HANNING will allow the user to perform a Hanning operation on a time series.

```
CARD          COLUMN                                                                                   8Ø
              123456789Ø12         .          .          .          .          .          .          .
---------------------------------------------------------------------------------------------------------
1             LIBRARY       A                                                     48       1ØØ.ØØ
2             PULSE OF DUTY CYCLE .25                              2  1.Ø  Ø.Ø        .25Ø
3             FFT           A
4             SWITCH        A    B
5             LIBRARY       A                                                     48       1ØØ.ØØ
6             THIS IS UNIFORM NOISE  AMP = 1.Ø                     5  Ø.Ø  Ø.Ø        .ØØØ1.ØØØ  Ø.Ø
7             FFT           A
8             SWITCH        A    C
9             WIENER        B    C
1Ø            Ø.ØØØ
11            ZERO-OUT      C
12            SWITCH        A    B
13            ZERO-OUT      A
14            LIBRARY       C                                                     48       1ØØ.ØØ
15            PULSE + NOISE  AMP = 1.Ø                             4  1.Ø  Ø.Ø        .25 1.ØØØ
16            PLOTTER       C                                                     48
17            TIME               1   48   THIS IS THE .25 DUTY PULSE IN UNIFORM NOISE AMP=1.
18            CONVOLVE      B    C
19            PLOTTER       A                                                     48
2Ø            TIME               1   48   SIGNAL PLUS NOISE CONVOLVED WITH WIENER FILTER
21            TERM
                         .          .          .          .          .          .          .          .
```

Figure 4-55. Card Control Sequence for Wiener Filter Experiment.

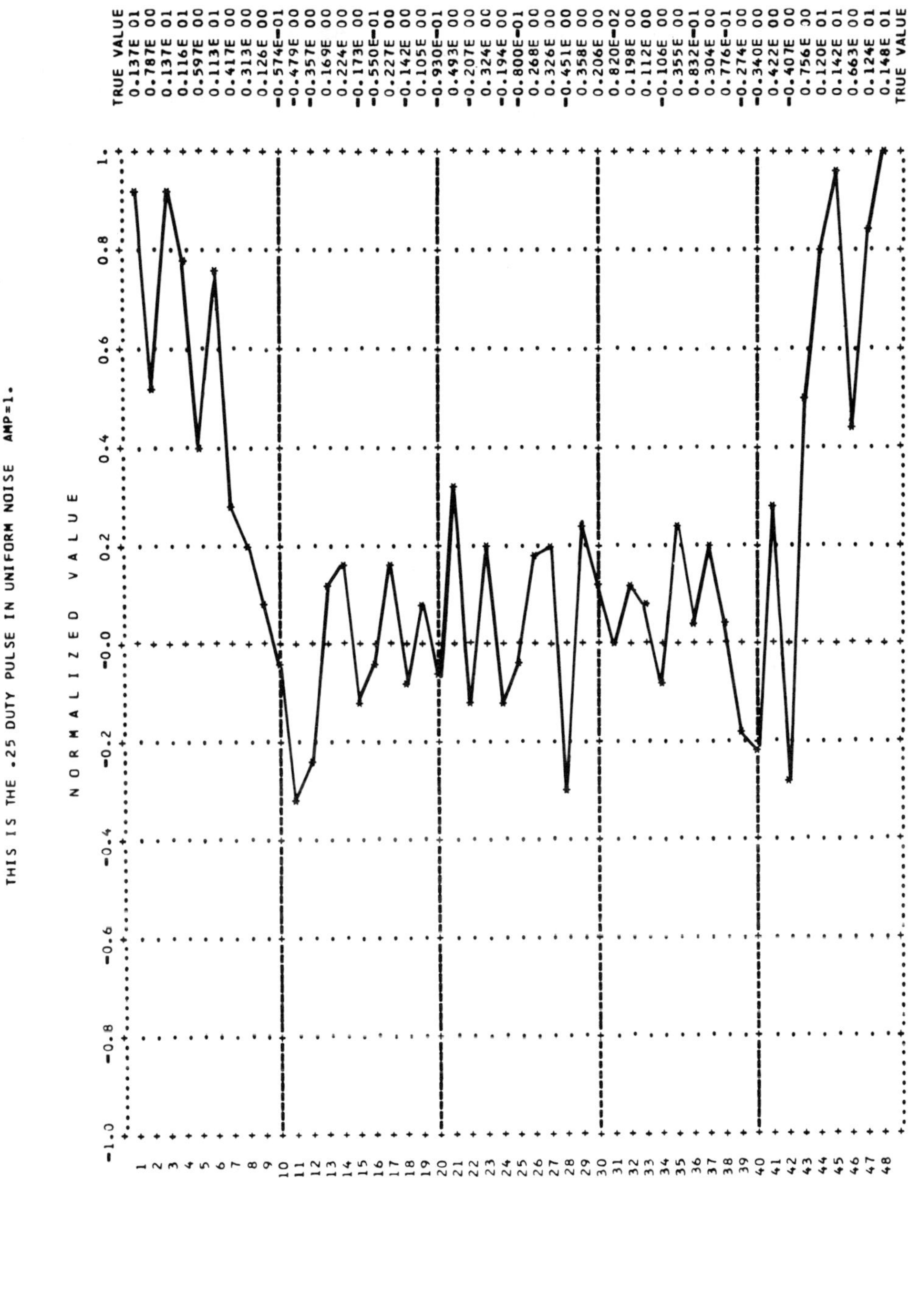

Figure 4-56. Signal-plus-noise (Wiener Filter Experiment).

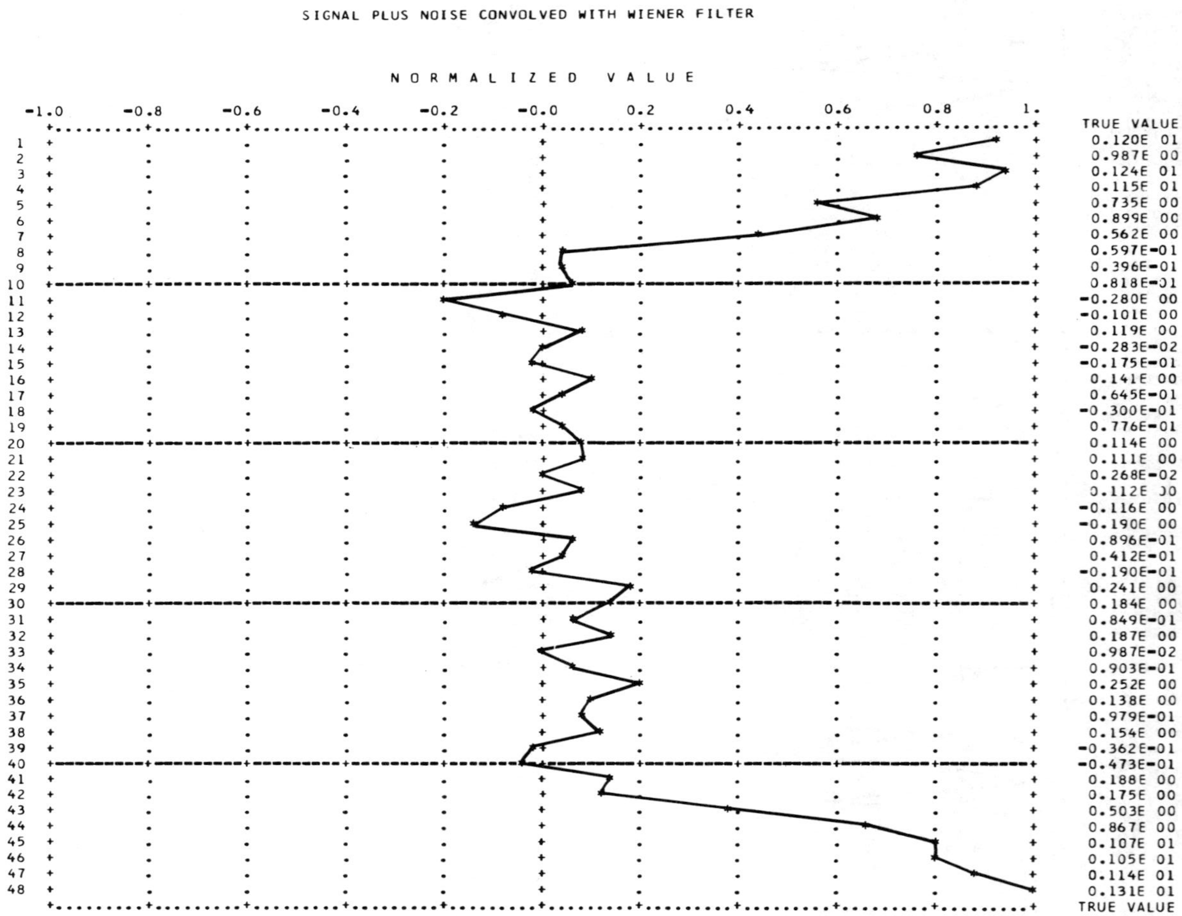

Figure 4.17 Filter Time-series Estimate (Wiener Filter Experiment)

Theory

Consider a signal $x(t)$ to be observed over an interval T. Let the observed value of $x(t)$ be denoted $y(t)$. Consider the two following observation philosophies:

1. Uniform window $\left[\prod(t/T)\right]$

$$y(t) = x(t) \cdot \left[\prod(t/T)\right] \tag{4.43}$$

where

$$\prod(t/T) = \begin{Bmatrix} 1 \text{ if } 0 \leq t \leq T \\ 0 \text{ otherwise} \end{Bmatrix} \tag{4.44}$$

The uniform window is exemplified in Figure 4-58. Note that the $y(t)$ is periodic if and only if $x(t)$ is periodic in T. If $x(t)$ does not have this periodicity, the resultant DFT of $y(t)$ will suffer from leakage. Consider now another window philosophy, that of Hanning.

2. Hanning window $[H(t/T)]$

$$y(t) = x(t) \times [H(t/T)]$$

where

$$H(t/T) = \begin{Bmatrix} 1/2[1 - \cos(2\pi t/T)] \; if \; 0 \leq t \leq T \\ \\ 0 \text{ otherwise} \end{Bmatrix}$$

The Hanning window is exemplified in Figure 4-59.

A nonperiodic signal $x(t)$ can be made to look "almost" periodic because the Hanning weight forces $y(t)$ to have a common value zero at the

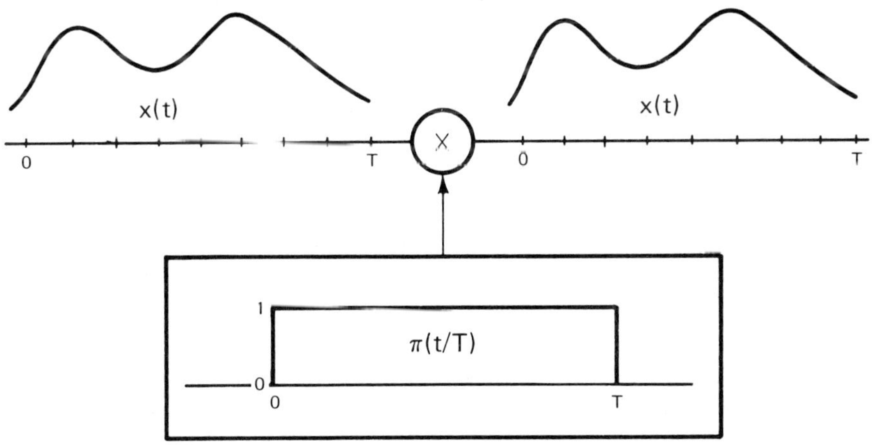

Figure 4-58. Uniform Window.

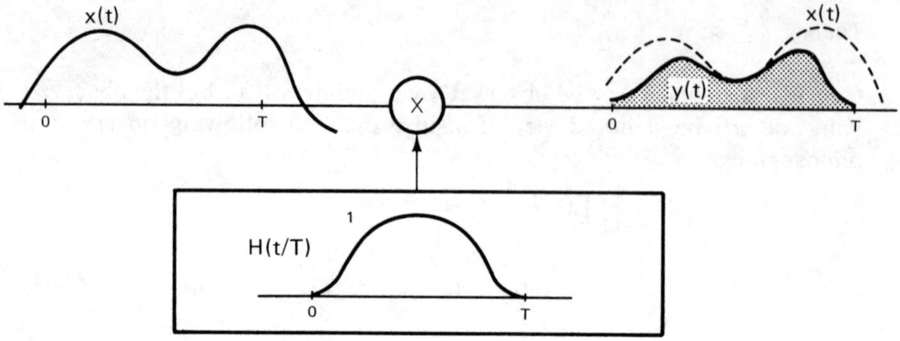

Figure 4-59. Hanning Window.

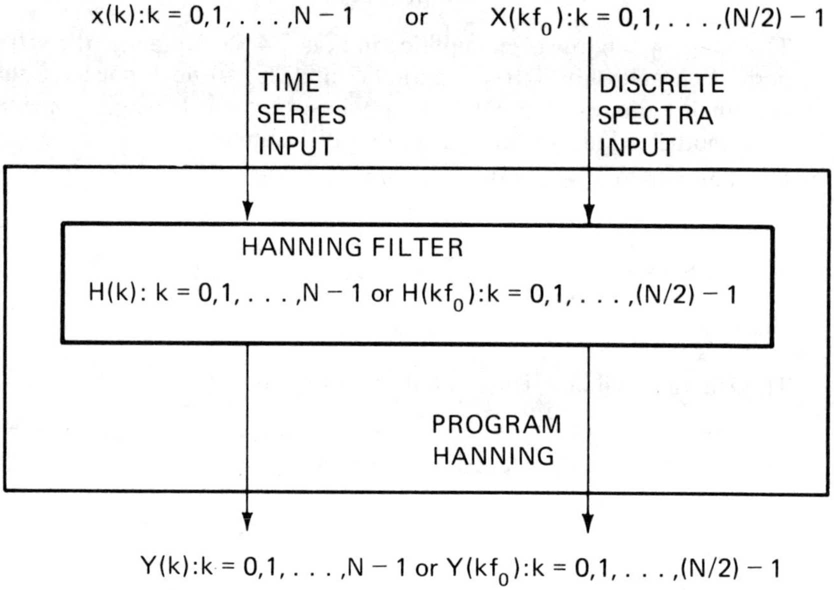

Figure 4-60. Program HANNING.

Table 4-10
Structure of a HANNING Call

Column Number	*Description*	*Format or Contents*
Primary information card		
1-7	Calls HANNING	HANNING
15	Array to be filtered (A, B, or C)	A1

```
CARD        COLUMN                                                               8Ø
            123456789Ø12        .        .        .        .        .        .    .
-----------------------------------------------------------------------------------
1           LIBRARY      A                                          5Ø     1ØØØ.
2           RANDOM A-PERIODIC SIGNAL                    8  1Ø.   Ø.     5.Ø   1.   Ø.
3           PLOTTER      A                                          5Ø
4           TIME                1    5Ø   SIGNAL SPECTRA BEFORE HANNING WINDOW CONVOLUTION
5           HANNING      A
6           PLOTTER      A                                          5Ø
7           TIME                1    5Ø   RESULTS OF ONE HANNING CONVOLUTION
8           HANNING      A
9           HANNING      A
1Ø          HANNING      A
11          HANNING      A
12          PLOTTER      A
13          TIME                1    5Ø   RESULTS OF 5 HANNING CONVOLUTIONS
14          TERM
                  .        .        .        .        .        .        .        .
```

Figure 4-61. Card Control Sequence for Hanning Experiment.

SIGNAL SPECTRA BEFORE HANNING WINDOW CONVOLUTION

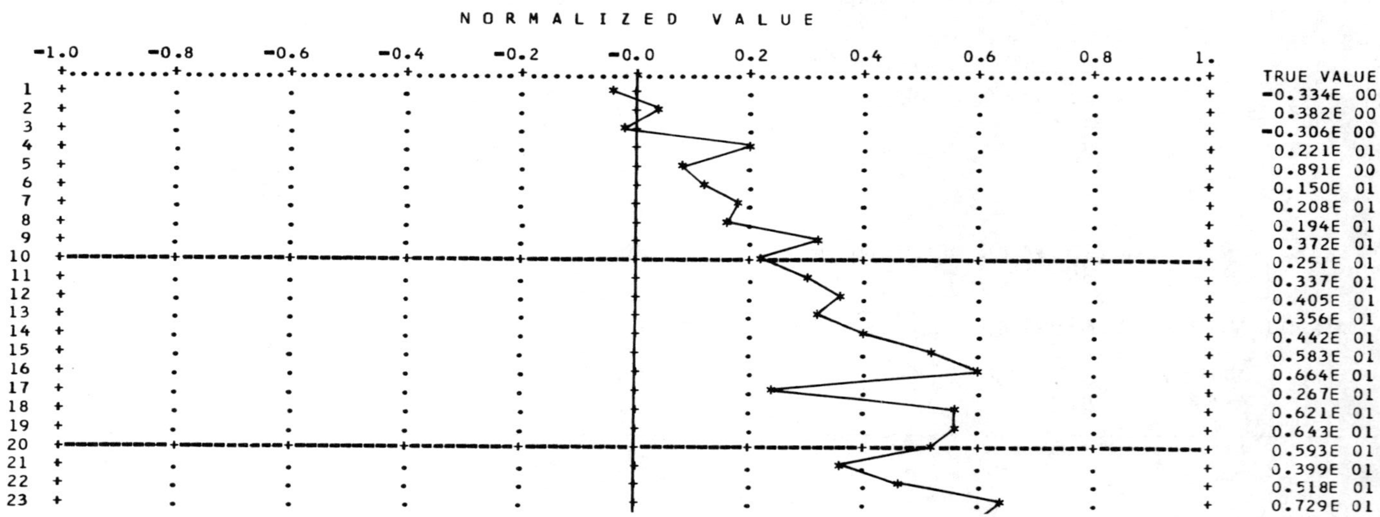

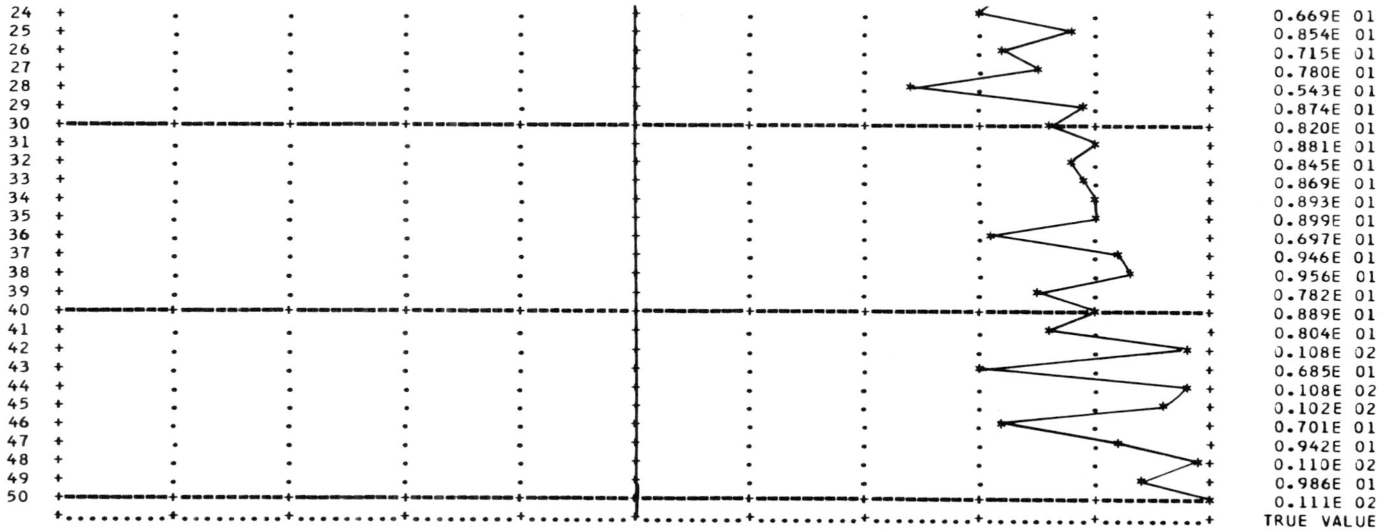

Figure 4-62. Aperiodic Test Signal (Hanning Experiment).

RESULTS OF ONE HANNING CONVOLUTION

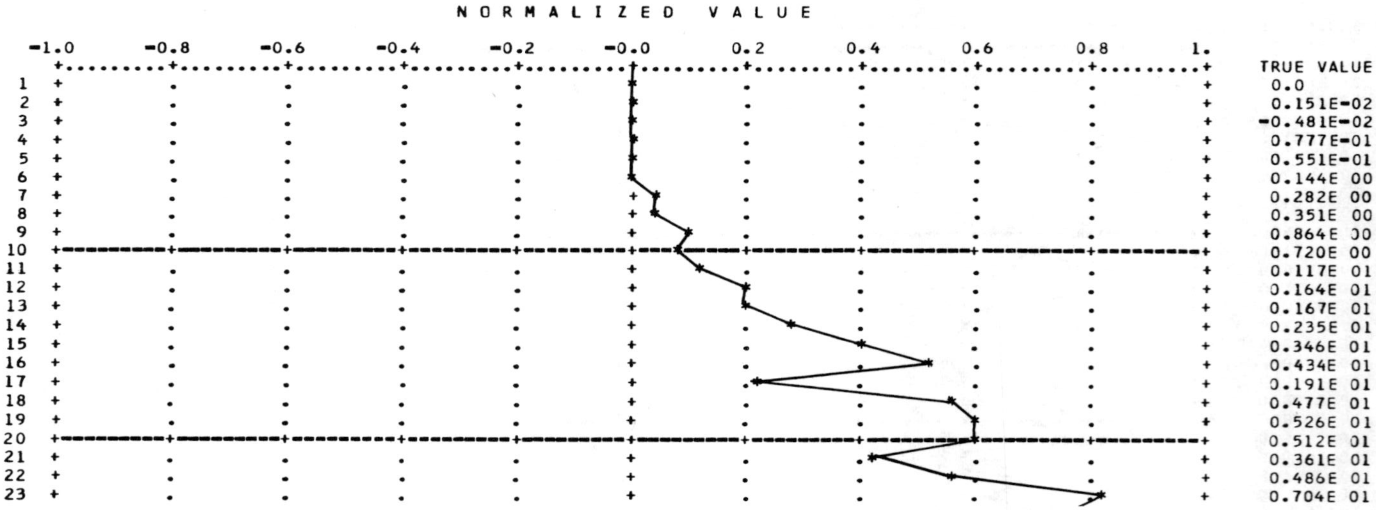

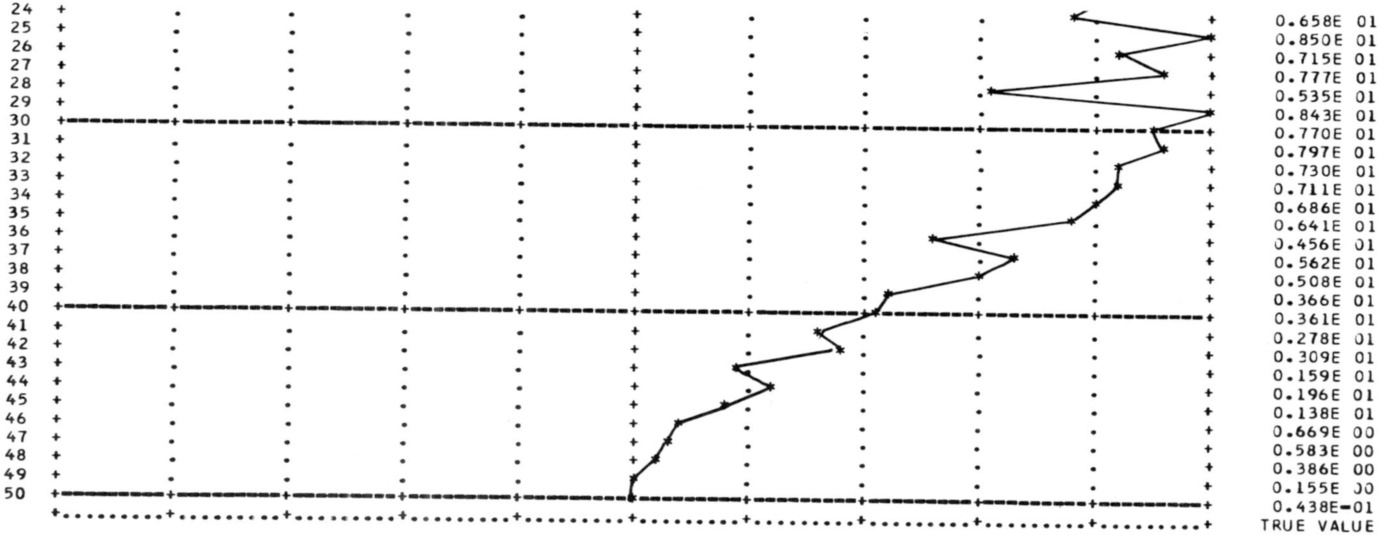

Figure 4-63. Result of a HANNING Operation.

RESULTS CF 5 HANNING CONVOLUTIONS

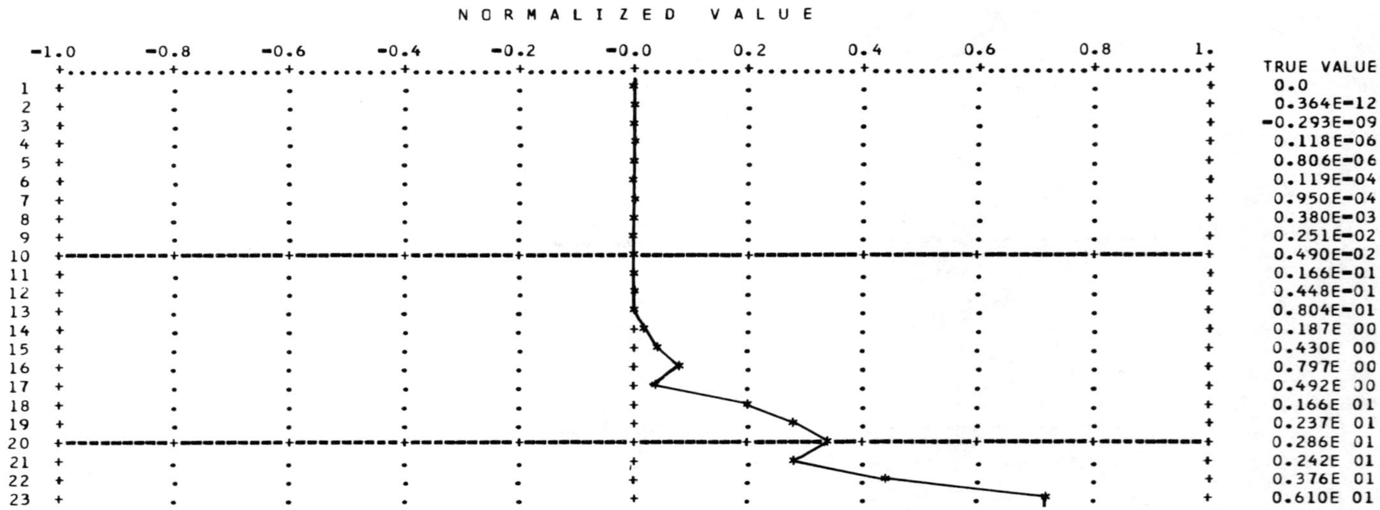

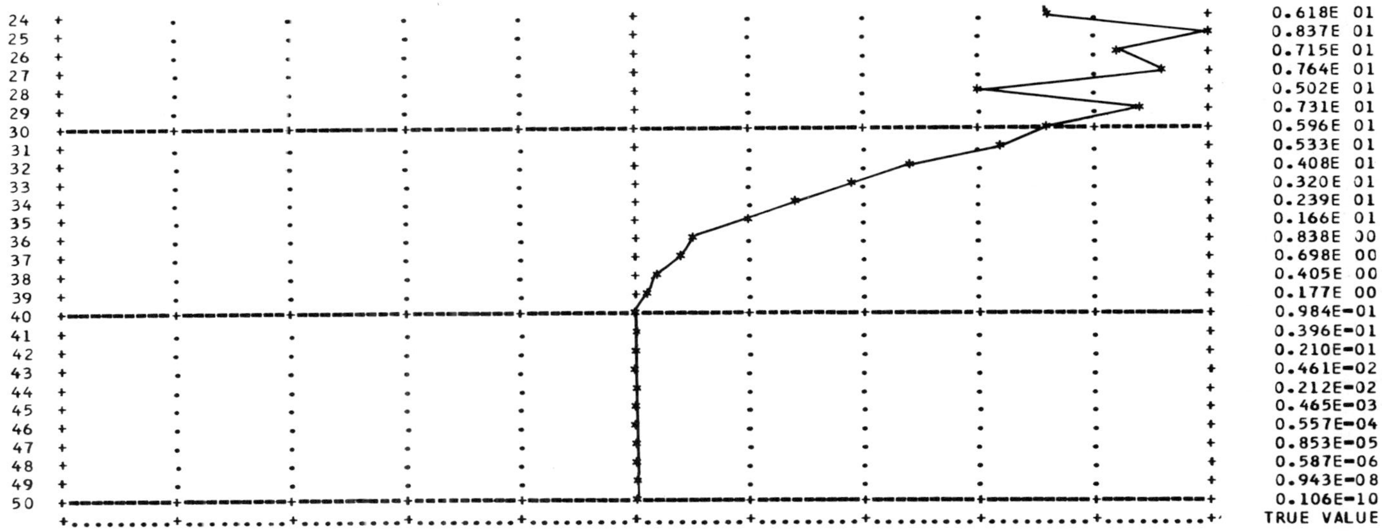

Figure 4-64. Result of Five Cascaded HANNING Operations.

boundary times $t = 0$ and T. Its weighing policy also attenuates the signal heavily about these boundary times. Therefore, a nonperiodic signal $s(t)$ appears at the output as a nearly periodic signal $y(t)$.

A HANNING operation is accomplished by SPECTRUM IV in a straightforward manner. The Hanning profile and input series are multiplied together, sample by sample. In block diagram form, a HANNING operation appears in Figure 4-60.

Execution of HANNING

A HANNING operation is initiated with the seven-letter mnemonic HANNING. Program HANNING will cause the spectra of a prespecified time-series array to be modified in a Hanning filter sense. The only restriction imposed on a HANNING operation is that the array to be modified cannot be the null array.

The card control required of a HANNING operation is shown in Table 4-10. A HANNING operation will be followed by a print-out of the array-defining parameters. A HANNING operation will not establish any memory protection on the array operated upon.

Example. A noisy sinusoidal signal was generated. The sampling interval for the problem was 50 msec in length. The fundamental period of the sythesized sinewave was one fifth (1/5) of that, or 10.0 msec. Additive Gaussian noise, mean value 0 and variance 1, was added to the sythesized pure sine wave to induce aperiodic behavior in the tested time series. The input time series is graphically displayed after the completion of one HANNING operation and again after four more successive HANNING operations. The card control sequence required of this operation can be found in Figure 4-61. The result of such an action can be found in Figures 4-62 through 4-64. The original time series is ''grossly'' aperiodic in the sample interval. This condition is significantly improved after performing a HANNING operation. The time series becomes almost completely periodic after five HANNING operations are completed. The user should note that the periodic behavior was achieved at the expense of distorting the original time series severely. The user should be cautioned that the periodicity-inducing methods, such as HANNING, usually are considered effective when analyzing nearly periodic signal sources. That is, the signal to be analyzed should exhibit strong periodic behavior if a HANNING operation is to be successful. If the signal did not have this property, the signal would be a distorted version of itself after being subjected to a HANNING operation.

5 SPECTRUM IV Support

The work found in the next several sections is a hybrid, representing a collection of SPECTRUM IV service and support routines. These methods will not perform spectral or time-series analysis by themselves. However, they will allow the previously discussed spectral methods to be expeditiously serviced or cosmetically enhanced. In some cases the techniques found in this chapter are necessary if multiple spectral or time-series events are to be processed in one SPECTRUM IV program. The four sections of this chapter are:

A. Special Functions
B. Software Control
C. Disk Storage
D. Diagnostics and System Information

The subject matter of each topic will be developed next. Unlike the previous chapters, the text associated with each new operation will not be followed by an example problem. But most of the ideas developed in this chapter are exemplified either in the subject chapters or in the example problems found at the end of the book.

A. Special Functions

The execution of a SPECTRUM IV program is sometimes followed by non-time-series operations. These operations may be either analytic or cosmetic. An analytic operation serves a mathematical purpose, whereas a cosmetic operation will serve only to make a data set more presentable. In some cases a SPECTRUM IV analysis requires the support of a peripheral analytic operation. For example, in general a coherence operation requires that the data records be ensemble averaged. In other applications, analytic methods are needed to measure the statistical properties of a given data record. Here analytic methods are used to compute the mean and variance of a signal process.

At other times a data record is to be edited or rescaled to make it more aesthetically pleasing. Such modifications may be dictated by the customs of a discipline or the personal tastes of the user. For example, control and communication engineers are often interested in displaying data in logarithmic units. In sciences where the signal sources vary from subject to subject or test to test, data are often presented in normalized form. If a signal record is noisy, the scientist may wish to remove highly irregular data values, which is called despiking. Finally, for the sake of analysis, a user may wish to display only the nontrivial values of a data set for cosmetic purposes.

SPECTRUM IV allows a user to perform the following analytic and cosmetic data array operations:

Analytic operations	
1. Ensemble average	FREQ-AVG
2. Statistical editor	EDITOR
Cosmetic operations scaling	
1. Normalization	NORMAL
2. Scaling	SCALE
3. Decibel Conversion	DB-SCALE
Alteration	
1. Magnitude Edit	FUZZ OUT

In this section, the preceding array-modification methods are developed. They support the time-series and spectral analysis methods found in SPECTRUM IV.

Ensemble Averaging

Ensemble averaging in the frequency domain means that a number of spectral records are averaged together, harmonic by harmonic. Ensemble averaging can be used to enhance a spectral analysis. Many of the spectral techniques discussed in this book explicitly or implicitly require ensemble averaging. If there is a measurable degree of aperiodicity, ensemble averaging can be used to improve the user's knowledge of a system. The spectral averaging of many experiments will accent repetitive features and deaccentuate nonrepetitive features. In other cases, such as the generation of a coherence function, ensemble averaging must be performed in the frequency domain. Ensemble averaging can be performed under SPECTRUM IV control using program FREQ-AVG.

Program FREQ-AVG is a conditional controller. This routine allows SPECTRUM IV operations to be executed without interference. Once completed, control is returned to FREQ-AVG. This control exchange process will occur N times in an N ensemble-averaging operation. The following terms are associated with a FREQ-AVG execution:

DATA SET	An array of data residing in the FREQ domain to be averaged

INTERMEDIATE OPERATIONS	Other SPECTRUM IV operations that perform input-output, time-series and spectral analysis (for example, F.F.T., CONVOLVE, PRINT)
AVERAGING ARRAY	The array that acts as an accumulator for the purposes of averaging
ENTERING ARRAY	The array that is to be added to the averaging array

Two cards are necessary to execute a FREQ-AVG operation. These cards establish the number of data sets, record sizes, and sampling frequency in an ensemble average. The cards also request that a FREQ-AVG operation be executed, and they specify certain output options. These control cards are followed by one special-purpose card per data set. Called the data set card, it specifies where the ENTERING ARRAY is located and the number of INTERMEDIATE OPERATIONS associated with that data set.

In practice, the ensemble information may be generated "on-line" or "off-line." When the ensemble average of a single array is required—such as in the smoothing of aperiodic FFT records—the ensembling may be accomplished on-line. For example, suppose 20 FFT records are to be averaged. The user would interleaf 20 FFT and data set cards. Thus each FFT operation would be entered into the accumulator immediately. In other operations, such as coherence, several data arrays are to be averaged. Here a different strategy must be used. Now the data would be processed off-line. The data, derived from each experiment, would be stored on punch cards (using PUNCH) or, if available, disk (using DISK OUT). Data designated to belong to a common array then would be reentered from punch card on disk and ensemble averaged. For example, suppose a coherence function is to be generated over 20 experiments. The required cross- and auto-power spectral densities would be computed and stored 20 times. After completion, the 20 cross-input auto-, and output auto-power spectral densities are individually analyzed in an ensemble-averaging sense.

The following restrictions are associated with a FREQ-AVG operation:

1. Once a FREQ-AVG operation starts, the array acting as the accumulation must not be changed by an INTERMEDIATE OPERATION. Any attempt to do so will cause an error message to be printed. How-

ever, the contents of the accumulator can be listed, plotted, or written onto disk.

2. Once all intermediate operations are completed, arrays must reside in the following locations:
   Array A = Averaging array in the FREQ domain
   Array B or C = Array to be entered into the ensemble average
3. All data records must be the same length.
4. All data records must have the same sampling frequency.
5. An operation is not to be performed on the null array.

The control card structure associated with a FREQ-AVG operation is shown in Table 5-1, and the card structure for a FREQ-AVG operation for on-line and off-line applications are summarized in Table 5-2.

The output derived from a FREQ-AVG operation consists of the identification of record size, sampling frequency, and the number of data set considered. For an example of FREQ-AVG utilization, see the discussion of COHERNCE in Chapter 3.

Table 5-1
Structure for a FREQ-AVG Call

Column Number	*Description*	*Format or Contents*
Primary information card		
1-8	Calls FREQ-AVG	FREQ-AVG
80	Output optional parameter (0, 1, 2)	I1
	Option 0: For each data set the INTERMEDIATE OPERATION will output its preassigned standard message.	
	Option 1: No output message is generated	
	Option 2: A one-line message is generated for each INTERMEDIATE OPERATION performed	
Secondary information card		
3-5	Number of data sets to be averaged	I3
7-10	Number of data points in each data set	I4
16-25	Sampling frequency	F10.1
Data set card		
1-2	Number of INTERMEDIATE OPERATIONS to follow	I2
5	ENTERING ARRAY designation	B or C

Table 5-2
Card Structure for a FREQ-AVG Operation

ON-LINE: PRIMARY CARD
SECONDARY CARD
DATA SET CARD (NO. 1)
(1)
(2)
.
. M INTERMEDIATE OPERATIONS
.
(m)

DATA SET CARD (NO. 2)
(1)
(2)
.
. h INTERMEDIATE OPERATIONS
.
(h)
.
.
.
DATA SET- CARD (NO. N)
(1)
(2)
.
. k INTERMEDIATE OPERATIONS
.

OFF-LINE:

PRIMARY CARD	
SECONDARY CARD	
DATA SET CARD	(DATA TYPE NO. 1, RECORD NO. 1)
CALL DATA RECORD	INTERMEDIATE OPERATION
DATA SET CARD	(DATA TYPE NO. 1, RECORD NO. 2)
CALL DATA RECORD	INTERMEDIATE OPERATION
.	
.	
.	
DATA SET CARD	(DATA TYPE NO. 1, RECORD k)
CALL DATA RECORD	INTERMEDIATE OPERATION
STORE ENSEMBLE	
AVERAGE OFF-LINE	
DATA SET CARD	(DATA TYPE NO. 2, RECORD NO. 1)
CALL DATA RECORD	INTERMEDIATE OPERATION
.	
.	
.	
DATA SET CARD	(DATA TYPE NO. M, RECORD NO. m)
CALL DATA RECORD	INTERMEDIATE OPERATION
STORE ENSEMBLE	
AVERAGE OFF-LINE	

Statistical Editor

A user of SPECTRUM IV is generally interested in the quantitative properties of data array. The routines of SPECTRUM IV will allow the user to perform many interconnected time-series and spectral operations. However, the user may also wish to specify some of the statistical parameters of a data array. In particular, a scientist is often interested in computing the mean and variance of a data record, especially if the data record is noise-corrupted. A second extremely useful data test is called despiking. Here any data value that is outside the prespecified data range is considered bogus. That is, if a range of values is given in which the data are assumed to be valid, the poorly instrumented or excessively noisy data will be excluded from the data set. This is especially useful when experimentally derived data records are studied. For example, suppose a valid data value lies between +1 and +5. If a missing data record assumes a value of zero, then using the previously considered test, the absent records could be ignored. Using the six-letter mnemonic EDITOR will allow the user to perform a statistical analysis as well as to establish limits of confidence on a data array. The following restrictions are imposed on the use of EDITOR:

1. The array to be analyzed must be in the time (TIME) domain.
2. The difference between the upper and lower limit of the data confidence interval must be greater than 0.001.
3. The array to be analyzed must not be the null array.

The control cards required of such an operation are listed in Table 5-3.

The output following an EDITOR operation contains the array-identifying parameters. The mean and variance values of the time series analyzed are listed, and the maximum and minimum values of the admissible data range are computed and listed. Finally, the sample numbers that exceed the prespecified confidence limits are outputted.

Cosmetic Special Functions

The presentation media of time-series data and spectral data vary among disciplines. There are studies where only the shape or character of a signal is important, such as in many biological sciences where signal levels vary significantly from output of subject. Therefore the data base associated with the signals is often presented in normalized units. Communication, filter, and control operations are often interpreted in terms of a decibel metric. This will allow many decades of change in a particular variable to be compressed into an interpretable data range. Sciences such as societal studies often require that the data be interpreted without any cosmetic

Table 5-3
Structure for an EDITOR Call

Column Number		*Format or Contents*
Primary information card		
1-6	Calls EDITOR	EDITOR
15	Array to be analyzed (A, B, or C)	A1
Secondary information card		
1-10	Lower limit of acceptable data range	F10.3
11-20	Upper limit of acceptable data range	F10.3

alteration. Under SPECTRUM IV control, there is a family of scaling operations available to the user. They belong to either the scaling group or the alteration group. Scaling operations allow the user to perform a prespecified nonzero mathematical operation on an array. Alterations, however, will radically alter the contents of an array by nulling all or a portion of a given array. In particular, the modification routines found in SPECTRUM IV are:

1. Scaling
   S1: NORMAL: Normalizes data to be bounded between +1 and −1
   S2: SCALE: Divides or multiplies all the elements of an array by a prespecified number.
   S3:DB-SCALE: Converts array data into a decibel measure.
2. Alterations
   A1: FUZZ OUT: Zeroes all elements of an array that are considered insignificant

1. Scaling Operations

A common restriction imposed on the use of all scaling operations is that the array to be modified cannot be the null array. If a normalization, multiply, divide, or dB rescale is attempted on the null array, an error will result. The structures of the three scaling programs follow.

S1: Normalization. Normalization of a prespecified array to a range of +1 to −1 is executed through the six-letter mnemonic NORMAL. The card structure associated with this operation is shown in Table 5-4. Upon executing the NORMAL program, SPECTRUM IV automatically labels

Table 5-4
Structure for a NORMAL Call

Column Number	*Description*	*Format or Contents*
Primary information card		
1-6	Calls NORMAL	NORMAL
15	Array to be normalized (A, B, or C)	A1

the identification parameter associated with the modified array. The normalizing coefficient also is supplied to the user.

S2: Scaling operation. The scaling of an array is accomplished by using the five-letter mnemonic SCALE. A designated array can be multiplied or divided by a prespecified constant by using the four-letter mnemonic MULT (multiply) or DIVD (divide). Restrictions on the use of SCALE are:

1. The division of multiply scale factor cannot be zero.
2. The correct mnemonic, MULT or DIVD, must be used.

The control card structure of a SCALE operation is shown in Table 5-5.

Under SPECTRUM IV control, a SCALE operation is followed by an automatic labeling of array parameters. Information identifying the scaling operation requested is also displayed.

S3: Decibel Conversion. A decibel inversion of a data array is accomplished by using the eight-letter mnemonic DB-SCALE. As a convenience to the user, three decibel conversion routines are provided as options of DB-SCALE. These options reflect the defining conventions associated with a decibel operation. They are given in terms of the following options:

Option 1. (POWER)
$10 \log_{10}$ (data values in power units)

Option 2. (VOLTAGE)
$20 \log_{10}$ (data values in voltage units)

Option 3. (CURRENT)
$20 \log_{10}$ (data values in current units)

Since a decibel measure is used most often in an electrical or electronic application, program DB-SCALE is written in terms of the measurement units of this science. If the user is interested in displaying the data only in logarithmic units, OPTION 1 is to be used. The logarithmic scale factor found in OPTION 1 can be removed through the DIVD option of program SCALE. The restriction imposed on the use of DB-SCALE is that one of

Table 5-5
Structure for a SCALE Call

Column Number	*Description*	*Format or Contents*
Primary information card		
1-5	Calls SCALE	SCALE
15	Array to be scaled (A, B, or C)	A1
Secondary information card		
1-4	Operation requested MULT = multiply; DIVD = divide	MULT or DIVD
11-20	Multiplication factor	E10.3
21-30	Division factor 10^{-10}	E10.3

Table 5-6
Structure for a DB-SCALE Call

Column Number	*Description*	*Format or Contents*
Primary information card		
1-8	Calls DB-SCALE	DB-SCALE
15	Array to be altered (A, B, or C)	A1
Secondary information card		
1-8	Option mnemonic POWERbb CURRENT CURRENT	A8

the allowable decibel options must be used and identified with the proper mnemonic.

Since the logarithm of an argument near or less than zero may create a numerical fault, SPECTRUM IV will take any array entry that has a value less than 10^{-50} and assign it the value -500 (option 1) or -1000 (option 2 or 3). The control card structure of DB-SCALE is shown in Table 5-6. Under SPECTRUM IV control, a DB-SCALE operation will be followed by a listing of the array defining parameters.

2. Alterations

A1: Fuzz out. For the selective zeroing of portions of a prespecified array, the eight-letter mnemonic FUZZbOUT is used. Program FUZZ OUT will set to zero any array element whose absolute value is less than the user-supplied test parameter ALFUZZ. The system default value for ALFUZZ is 10^{-3}. The card control for a FUZZ OUT operation is shown in Table 5-7. Under SPECTRUM IV control, a FUZZ OUT operation will be followed by a listing of the array-defining parameters.

B. Software Control

Utility Functions

During the execution of a SPECTRUM IV program, the user often finds need for an array management policy. An array management routine should allow the user to:

1. *Correct the contents of an array during the execution cycle of a program*. This, for example, will allow a user to add a 60-Hz component to a previously defined frequency-domain record.
2. *Switch the contents of one prespecified array into another*. Since many of the routines found in SPECTRUM IV require that data be presented to the algorithm in a prespecified location, the ability to transfer data from one array to another is indispensable.
3. *Clear the contents of all or one of the system arrays*. A user may wish to nest several unique and independent experiments together and then execute all under SPECTRUM IV. Therefore the user can solve several problems during the execution of one "batch" operation. It is desirable to clear the contents of working arrays A, B, and C between individual programs to insure their isolation. In addition, it is also desirable to null the contents of a particular array and thereby release it for acceptance of additional data. The clearing operations found in SPECTRUM IV also serve to remove any memory protection that may have been assigned to an array or arrays. Therefore a clearing operation will allow a user to re-enter a previously protected array.

These methods, techniques, and services are developed in this section in the following order: (1) CORRECT, (2) SWITCH, (3) CLEAR-AL, and (4) ZERO-OUT.

Correct and Edit: CORRECT. A user may wish to change or modify the contents of a particular array, perhaps to remove undesirable portions of a data record. For example, the user may discover in a post-experiment

Table 5-7
Structure for a FUZZ OUT Call

Column Number	*Description*	*Format or Contents*
Primary information card		
1-8	Calls FUZZ OUT	FUZZbOUT
15	Array to be modified (A, B, or C)	A1
Secondary information card		
11-20	Test parameter ALFUZZ	E10.3

analysis that a periodic noise source corrupted the reduced data. In the time domain such a noise process could take the form of a periodic "spike" due to a sampling or switching operation. In the frequency domain the noise source could take the form of line frequency (multiples of 60 Hz) interference. The removal of such a noise source, whether it resides in the time or frequency domain, can be accomplished under SPECTRUM IV control. Program CORRECT will allow the user to modify the contents of a single location or a range of array elements. Besides removing unwanted sample values, program CORRECT can be used as an interesting experimental tool. If the user is interested in what effect 60-Hz noise would have on system performance, program CORRECT can be used as the test vehicle. Here the user would enter a nonzero value to all frequency-domain data records to be analyzed. By executing over these synthesized data records, the experimenter will be able to predict what effect such noise disturbance would have on system performance.

Program CORRECT is structurally identical to a READ IN operation. It is initiated by using the seven-letter mnemonic CORRECT. It differs functionally from a READ IN operation in that it can process only one data record at a time (a READ IN operation can be performed over two arrays simultaneously), and the optional parameters found in a READ IN operation must now be specified. The number of points to be serially corrected must also satisfy the algebraic equation

$$\text{NPOINT}=\text{NM}=\text{NSTART}-\text{NSTOP}+1$$

The card control sequence required is shown in Table 5-8. To complete a CORRECT operation, the end-of-file and data cards, described in the discussion of READ IN in Chapter 1, must be supplied.

Exchange Array Contents: SWITCH. Often the user of SPECTRUM IV

Table 5-8
Structure for a CORRECT Call

Column Number	*Description*	*Format or Contents*
Primary information card		
1-7	Calls CORRECT	CORRECT
15	Array to be corrected	A1
57-60	Number of points in serial correction (NPOINT)	I4
Secondary information card		
20	Format of array to be corrected	E or F
27-30	Domain of array to be corrected	E or F
37-40	NM	I4
47-50	NSTART	I4
57-60	NSTOP	I4

will require that the contents of a particular array be relocated. Some SPECTRUM IV operations have inflexible array rules attached to their use. Some of these rules require that the input array(s) be found in prespecified locations. Other operations will return data to array A automatically. Unless there were a means of transferring data arrays, some nested operations would be prohibited under SPECTRUM IV control. Program SWITCH allows the user complete versatility in how the data arrays may be exchanged. The only restriction on the use of SWITCH is that an array cannot be exchanged with itself. The mechanics of a SWITCH operation are straightforward. Given two arrays, say, A1 and A2, SWITCH will insert the contents of A1 into A2 and A2 into A1. Such a task is initiated by the six-letter mnemonic SWITCH. The control card sequence required by this operation is shown in Table 5-9. A SWITCH operation is followed by a listing of the identification parameters that characterize the contents of arrays A1 and A2.

Clear All Arrays: CLEAR-AL. It is often required or desired to null the contents of all SPECTRUM IV working arrays. These arrays may be zeroed during any SPECTRUM IV execution cycle. However, generally they are zeroed at the beginning of each independently nested problem. Program CLEAR-AL will allow the user to zero the contents of working arrays A, B, and C simultaneously. In addition, a CLEAR-AL operation will remove any memory protection these arrays may have had before this operation.

Table 5-9
Structure for a SWITCH Call

Column Number	*Description*	*Format or Contents*
Primary information card		
1-6	Calls SWITCH	SWITCH
15	Data array to be transferred A1 (A, B, or C)	A1
20	Destination of A1, namely, A2 (B, C, or A)	A2

Table 5-10
Control Card Structure for CLEAR-AL

Column Number	*Description*	*Format or Contents*
Primary information card		
1-8	Calls CLEAR-AL	CLEAR-AL

A CLEAR-ALL task is initiated by the eight-letter mnemonic CLEAR-AL. The control card structure for such an operation is shown in Table 5-10.

Clear an Array: ZERO-OUT. Often the user of SPECTRUM IV will be required to clear the contents of an array if that array is needed for input purposes. You will recall that some of the routines used in SPECTRUM IV will return data to a prespecified array location. These returned data are generally in some form of memory protection. Therefore, before that array location can be reused, it must have its protection removed. Removal can be accomplished several ways. If the data are no longer of any use, however, it is suggested that they be removed with this clear operation.

The selective clearing of array A or B or C can be accomplished by using the eight-letter mnemonic ZERO-OUT. The control card structure required by this operation is shown in Table 5-11.

C. Disk Storage

SPECTRUM IV is constructed to run on medium to large general-purpose computing systems. Typically, these systems include mass storage devices, which may appear in the form of magnetic tapes or "floppy,"

Table 5-11
Structure for a ZERO-OUT Call

Column Number	Description	Format or Contents
Primary information card		
1-8	Calls ZERO-OUT	ZERO-OUT
15	Array to be cleared (A, B, or C)	A1

fixed-head, or moving-head disks. SPECTRUM IV is written to make use of a disk storage device whenever it is made available to the user. Under such conditions, the user may be able to use the data storage and manipulation powers of a disk device. SPECTRUM IV allows the user to perform disk operations through the use of FORTRAN IV verbs.[a] However, the existence of a disk is not a prerequisite of SPECTRUM IV. The software system will work from a source listing without disk support.

The following commands are admissible under SPECTRUM IV's disk option:

DISK IN	Loads a data record from disk into one of the operating arrays (A, B, or C)
DISK OUT	Loads onto the disk a record residing in an operating array (A, B, or C)
INITIAL	Places the disk into a ready status for further input or output operations. Prints the rules governing a disk operation.
DIRECTORY	Systematically lists all information identifying the content of signals residing on the disk. The format of the information follows.

Disk Information: Record Number

1	2	3· · ·	
Number of signals on disk	Identification for signal 1	Signal record 1	. . . .

[a] SPECTRUM IV was designed to work with an IBM 2314 disk. Users may find that the existing software system may or may not work on their resident computer. If not, simple

2N	2N + 1
Identification for signal N	Signal record N

where the identification code for signal k is given by

IDENTIFICATION	DOMAIN	NPOINT	FREQUENCY
80 A1	A4	I4	F10.1

where IDENTIFICATION = alphanumeric message identifying the experiment or signal source

DOMAIN = TIME or FREQ

NPOINT = record size

FREQUENCY = sampling frequency

For a time-domain signal, all sample values in a time series are stored in the kth signal record location. For a frequency-domain signal, only the positive harmonics (real and imaginary) are stored in the kth signal record location.

The following rules have been established to add programming efficiency to disk operations.

Read from Disk: DISK IN. The execution of a DISK IN operation is accomplished by using the seven-letter mnemonic DISKbIN. To retrieve a data record from disk, the user must specify what record is desired. In addition, the user must specify the record size and sampling rate associated with that record. This information is available by consulting the DIRECTRY. The following restrictions are imposed on the use of DISK IN:

1. The number of sample points and sampling frequency specified on the primary information card must agree with identification parameters of the requested signal.
2. The array to receive the disk-resident data must be free of memory protection.
3. The domain of the data record must be specified.

The control card sequence required of a DISK IN operation is shown in Table 5-12.

---

changes in the disk-handling routine are required. This service usually can be obtained from a system's programmer who is familiar with that particular operating system.

Table 5-12
Structure for a DISK IN Call

Column Number	*Description*	*Format or Contents*
Primary information card		
1-7	Call DISK IN	DISKbIN
15	Destination array (A, B, or C)	A2
27-30	Domain of data record (TIME or FREQ)	A4
57-60	Number of sample points (NPOINT)	I4
61-72	Sampling frequency	F12.2
77-80	Signal record number (i.e., *k*th signal)	I4

SPECTRUM IV outputs to the user all identification parameters associated with a DISK IN operation. In addition, this information is copied into the DOMAIN STATUS OPERATOR (DSO) for the designated array.

Write on Disk: DISK OUT. A DISK OUT operation can be executed by using the eight-letter mnemonic DISKbOUT. To transfer data from a working array to the disk, two control cards are needed. The first is the primary information card discussed in Table 5-12. The parameters on this card are compared to the identification parameters of the array data. If all tests are successful, the array-identification parameters are transferred to the disk. After this operation is complete, the data itself is transferred to the disk.

If the record stored in array A, B, or C is in the time domain, the complete time series is transferred. If the data are in the frequency domain, only the real and imaginary positive harmonics are transferred. Restrictions on the use of DISK OUT are:

1. The number of data points and sampling frequency of the requested transfer must agree with the parameters associated with the array-resident data.
2. The transfer array cannot be the null array.
3. The identification label associated with the signal or experiment must be left justified. In addition, the first four entries of the identification label cannot be blanks.

The user may need to save the contents of the temporary arrays TEMR and TEMC. This, for example, will allow the user to store the results of a COHERNCE operation, which is always stored in a temporary array, on disk for future use or display. Also, signal sources created in subprogram OWN through a USER LIB operation can be stored in a disk file because

Table 5-13
Structure for DISK OUT Call

Column Number	*Description*	*Format or Contents*
Primary information card		
1-8	Calls DISK OUT	DISKbOUT
15	Array to be transferred to disk	A1
57-60	Number of sample points in record (NPOINT)	I4
61-72	Sampling frequency	F12.2
80	Optional parameter	0 = Default 1 = Temp Array
Secondary information card		
1-80	Array contents identification; description of experiment or signal source	20A4

they are created in temporary arrays. This option is exercised by adding a control parameter to a standard DISK OUT call. To complete a valid data transfer, the information about domain, number of sample points, and so forth, also must be passed to the disk. The user specifies these parameters by referring to one of the three working arrays—A, B, or C. Upon specifying one of these arrays in a DISK OUT call, using the optional parameter, SPECTRUM IV will assign the attributes of the labeled array to the temporary array to be transferred. For example, in a COHERNCE task, the temporary array holds the results of a COHERNCE operation. Since the contents of the temporary array is consistent with the array-identification parameters of A, B, or C, a DISK OUT using the optional parameter can be executed with any of these three identifying parameter sets. The card control sequence for a DISK OUT operation is shown in Table 5-13.

SPECTRUM IV automatically outputs all parameters associated with the transfer operation. SPECTRUM IV assigns a signal identification number to the record to be transferred. This number is automatically listed by SPECTRUM IV. The user may request a DIRECTRY operation after completing a DISK OUT operation. The use of DIRECTRY can be used to verify a successful data transfer.

List Contents of Disk: DIRECTRY. A SPECTRUM IV directory listing may be requested through the eight-letter mnemonic DIRECTRY. DIRECTRY supplies the user with a documentation of the signal records currently stored on disk. The control card structure associated with a DIRECTRY operation is shown in Table 5-14.

Table 5-14
Structure for a DIRECTRY Call

Column Number	Description	Format or Contents
Primary information card		
1-8	Calls DIRECTRY	DIRECTRY

SPECTRUM IV automatically outputs, in tabular form, the domain, the number of sample points, the alphanumeric eight-letter identification, and the record numbers of all signals stored on the system disk.

Initialize Disk: INITIAL. A disk initialization operation is accomplished through the seven-letter mnemonic INITIAL. This routine initializes the disk data-storage software system. The control card structure for a INITIAL operation is shown in Table 5-15.

SPECTRUM IV automatically places a zero into the first record location on the disk, indicating to the system that no data records are currently on disk. As a convenience to the user, a listing of the programming requirements associated with the disk operations is also produced. It is suggested that if disk operations are to be used, the first SPECTRUM IV operation requested be INITIAL.

D. Diagnostics and System Information

Error diagnostics should appear in two forms, narrative and numerical. A narrative diagnostic is a message generated by the software system that states the nature of an encountered error and suggests possible remedies. A numerical diagnostic will provide a numerical listing, or dump, of the contents of critical SPECTRUM IV arrays before terminating the execution cycle. Such information, whether it be in narrative, numerical, or both, will assist the user in debugging a SPECTRUM IV program. The diagnostic and information routines found in SPECTRUM IV are:

ERR-LIST narrative
STATUS numerical.

Error Messages: ERR-LIST. SPECTRUM IV is a special analysis software system supported by an error-diagnostic package. The internal error-detection system used in SPECTRUM IV will insure that all system software format and logical prerequisites are satisfied. If an error is detected, SPECTRUM IV automatically terminates the program being

Table 5-15
Structure for an INITIAL Call

Column Number	*Description*	*Format or Contents*
Primary information card		
1-7	Calls INITIAL	INITIAL

Table 5-16
Structure for an ERR-LIST Call

Column Number	*Description*	*Format or Contents*
Primary information card		
1-8	Calls ERR-LIST	ERR-LIST

executed and outputs an error message, a verbal description of the nature of the error and recommended corrective procedures. Thirty-four formal messages are in the SPECTRUM IV error-diagnostic library (a listing of these error messages can be found in Appendix C). As a convenience to the user, a catalog of these errors can be listed by using the eight-letter mnemonic ERR-LIST. The card structure for this task is shown in Table 5-16.

System Status: STATUS. To assist the user in debugging a potentially complex program, a numerical diagnostic routine has been incorporated into SPECTRUM IV. This program will allow the user to display a comprehensive list of the salient parameters and data values in a SPECTRUM IV execution. The output includes control and identification parameters as well as the contents of the system data and temporary arrays (a listing of control parameters and their meanings can be found in Appendix D). By analyzing the "dumped" data, the user can more intelligently discover an error that may be located in a program. This invaluable error-diagnostic capability is called by the six-letter mnemonic STATUS. The card control sequence required for such an operation is shown in Table 5-17.

The calling sequence associated with program STATUS is somewhat unique. The numerical diagnostic output belonging to a STATUS operation can be initiated through voluntary or involuntary mechanisms. If the user were interested in terminating a SPECTRUM IV program at a prespecified point in that program, the execution of STATUS would be voluntary. However, the user may wish to have STATUS called any time a SPECTRUM IV system error interrupted the execution of a program (for an

Table 5-17
Structure for a STATUS Call

Column Number	*Description*	*Format or Contents*
Primary information card		
1-6	Calls STATUS	STATUS

example of a STATUS case see the example on page 201). Under such conditions, the use of STATUS is said to be involuntary. Independent of the use option chosen, the user is instructed to make a STATUS card the first card of the program deck. Doing so will equip the system to handle any future STATUS calls.

Once the program has been armed through the initial STATUS call, an involuntary data dump will occur automatically if any SPECTRUM IV programming error is encountered during execution. The program will be terminated at that point. Finally, a voluntary data dump will occur if a second STATUS card is encountered during the execution of a program that has been initialized with a STATUS card.

6 Example Problems

The following set of example problems is offered as a guide to the user. The problems make use of multiple SPECTRUM IV operations and thereby will serve as a comprehensive summary of the time-series and spectral methods discussed in this book. The sample problems cover a wide range of technological questions, including classical communication, detection, and statistical signal analysis as well as biological and societal system analysis. In addition, a detailed discussion of how to use subroutine USER LIB is included to familiarize the user with the mechanical techniques of generating special mathematical functions with USER LIB.

A. Use of USER LIB

The user of SPECTRUM IV will supply signal data to the system from cards, disk (where applicable) system library, or user-supplied subprogram. The user-supplied subroutine OWN is created by the user whenever the signal is to be characterized in a mathematical sense and the particular function desired does not reside in LIBRARY. This option, which is called through a USER LIB operation, has been used throughout this book. For completeness, several typical deterministic and random signals are constructed in a subroutine OWN format. They are to act as programming guides to subprogram OWN. The user should find no difficulty in expanding these examples into more complex and exotic signal synthesis routines.

1. An IMPULSE (see Figure 6-1)

TEMR(1)=A
TEMR(J)=0.0,J=2, . . . ,NPOINT

2. A TRIANGULAR wave (see Figure 6 2)

Let τ=duty cycle
N=(τ/2)* NPOINT

TEMR(L)=0.0 , L=N+2, . . . ,NPOINT+1−N
TEMR(J)=A* (N+1−J) /N , J+1, . . . ,N
TEMR(K)=A* (K−((NPOINT+1))/N,K=(NPOINT+1)−N, . . ., NPOINT

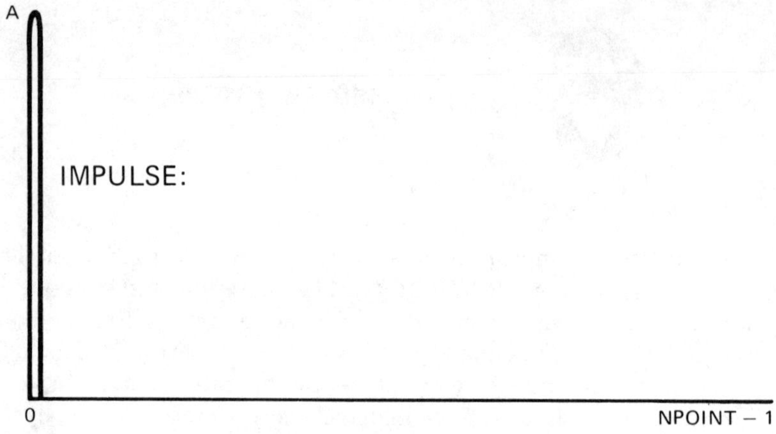

Figure 6-1. An Impulse Function.

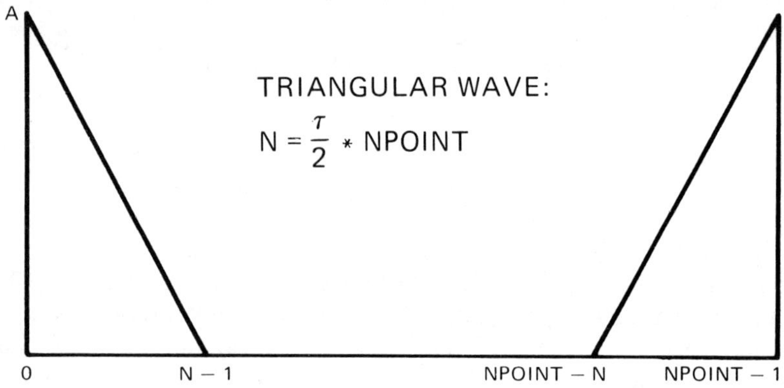

Figure 6-2. A Triangular Wave.

3. A SINE or COSINE wave

   Let P12 $=2\pi$

   i.e., P12 =8.0*ATAN(1)

   Let SAMP=sampling frequency as specified

   Let FR=frequency of wave to be synthesized

   TEMR(J)=SIN(P12*(J−1)*FR/SAMP) j=1, . . . ,NPOINT

   or TEMR(J)=COS(P12*(J−1)*FR/SAMP)

4. AN EXPONENTIAL (see Figure 6-3)

   Let DT=1/sampling frequency

   TEMR(J)=AMP*EXP(−(J−1)*DT) J=1, . . . ,NPOINT

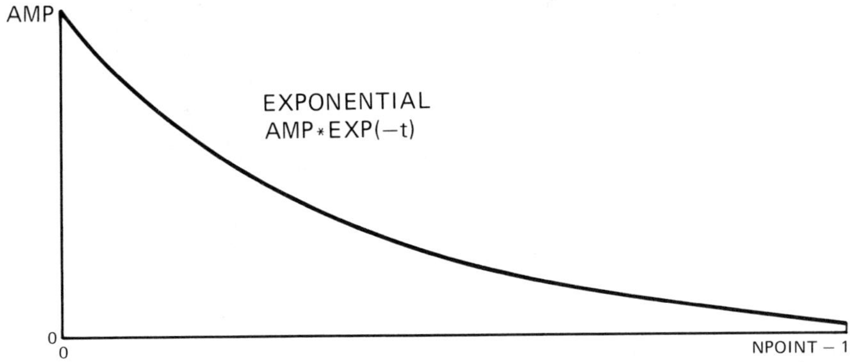

Figure 6-3. An Exponential.

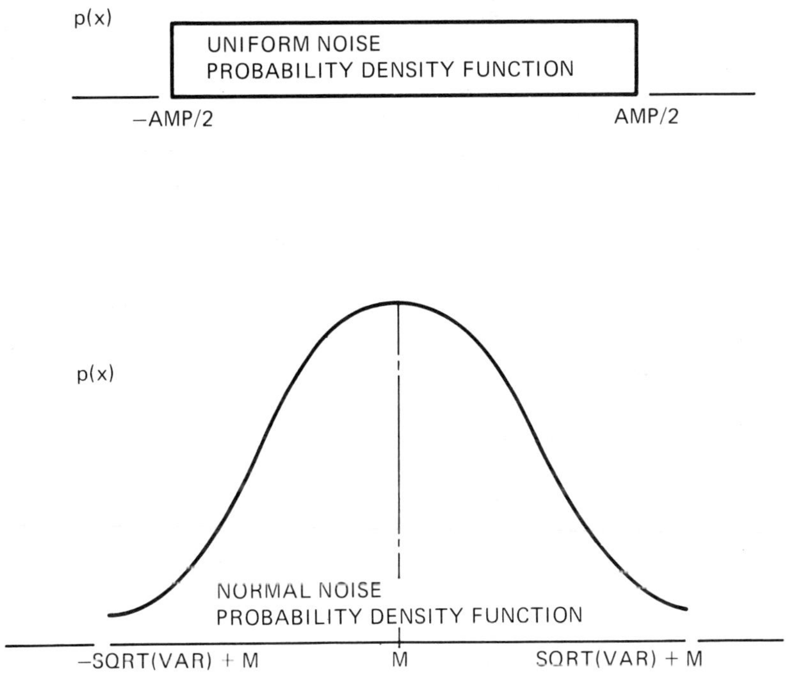

Figure 6-4. A Noise Source.

5. A NOISE SOURCE (see Figure 6-4)

   Let ISEED=65549 (initializes noise generator)

   UNIFORM NOISE mean=0.0, variance=AMP/12

```
TEMR(J)=AMP*RANDU(ISEED)-.5*AMP   J=1, . . .
        ,NPOINT

NORMAL NOISE      mean=M, variance=VAR
       SUM=0.0
       DO*I=1, 12
      *SUM=SUM+RANDU(ISEED)
       SUM=SUM-6.0
    TEMR(J)=SUM*SORT(VAR)+M
```

B. Radar Match Filtering

Pulsed radar systems are used to acquire and/or measure the parameters of a target. During the acquisition phase, a radar system searches for a target. In the absence of a target, the radar receives only noise. When the radar antenna is pointing at a target, the radar will receive a portion of the transmitted signal in the presence of additive noise. Unfortunately, the energy in the noise process is often greater than the energy in the signal process. Therefore, to detect the presence of a target in a radar reception, the signal-to-noise ratio of the input signal process must be improved. Since the potential signal contribution in a radar reception is known, except for magnitude and distributed delays, a matched filter can be used to accomplish this task.

The output of a matched filter is defined to be the convolution of the filter's impulse response and an input signal process. The energy present at the output of the matched filter should be high if the signal process to which the filter is matched is present at the input. Contrapositively, the filter output will be low if this signal is not present. In practice, a threshold is established internal to the radar system. This threshold will compare the energy in the filter's output to this number. If this value is exceeded, a target is assumed to be present. To exemplify this technique, let it be assumed that the radar transmission is a pulse of duty cycle 0.1. Let a matched filter be derived under SPECTRUM IV control and tested against signal-plus-noise and noise-only inputs.

The card control sequence for this experiment can be found in Figure 6-5. The problem requires that the radar pulse train be generated in the system library, transformed, and then operated on by program MATCH. Then the magnitude profile of the matched filter is plotted. Note that it has a $\sin(x)/x$ character. An inverse transform is used to synthesize the matched-filter impulse response. The impulse response is stored in array B for future convolution. A signal-plus-noise time series is then generated in the system library and transferred to array C (the synthesized signal could have been

```
CARD      COLUMN                                                                      8Ø
          123456789Ø12       .         .         .         .         .         .         .
----------------------------------------------------------------------------------------------
1         LIBRARY       A                                           6Ø     1ØØØ.
2         RADAR PULSE TRAIN                           2  1Ø.   Ø.        .1
3         FFT
4         MATCH         A
5         PLOTTER       A                                           3Ø
6         FREQ   MAG         1   3Ø    MAGNITUDE OF MATCHED FILTER
7         SWITCH        A    B
8         LIBRARY       A                                           6Ø     1ØØØ.
9         RADAR PULSE TRAIN PLUS NOISE                9   1.   Ø.        .1   1.   Ø.
1Ø        PLOTTER       A                                           6Ø
11        TIME               1   6Ø    THIS IS A PULSE + NOISE N(Ø.Ø,1.Ø)
12        SWITCH        A    C
13        CONVOLVE      B    C
14        EDITOR        A
15          -1ØØ.      1ØØ.
16        PLOTTER       A                                           6Ø
17        TIME               1   6Ø    OUTPUT OF MATCHED FILTER FOR SIGNAL + NOISE
18        ZERO-OUT      A
19        ZERO-OUT      C
2Ø        LIBRARY       C                                           6Ø     1ØØØ.
21        NOISE ONLY                                 1Ø                       1.   Ø.
22        PLOTTER       C                                           6Ø
23        TIME               1   6Ø    THIS IS NOISE ONLY N(Ø.Ø,1.Ø)
24        CONVOLVE      B    C
25        PLOTTER       A                                           6Ø
26        TIME               1   6Ø    OUTPUT FROM MATCHED FILTER WITH NOISE ONLY
27        EDITOR        A
28          -1ØØ.      1ØØ.
29        TERM
                     .         .         .         .         .         .         .         .
```

Figure 6-5. Card Control Sequence for Radar Detection Experiment.

loaded directly into array C). Then the two time-domain signals are convolved and analyzed using program EDITOR. Program EDITOR (see Section A of Chapter 5) will interpret a time series in terms of mean values, variances, and minimum/maximum data values. The variance value of this computation will specify the amount of statistical energy in the investigated time series. The data in array A, being and protected of no future use, are nulled using ZERO-OUT. The matched-impulse response, which originated in array B, now resides in the frequency domain. The frequency-domain image of the matched filter is returned to the cleared array A, inverse transformed, and returned to array B, thereby reconstructing the matched-filter impulse response. Since the input time-series array C is also no longer needed and protected, it is nulled. A new time series consisting of a noise record only is then entered into the cleared array C. The time-domain signals are convolved and analyzed as before. The results of this experiment can be found in Figures 6-6 through 6-10. It is interesting to note that when a signal was present, the output variance was 0.19941. With only noise present, the output variance dropped to 0.09845.

C. Societal Models

Societal models generally represent a highly interconnected system of social forces, which may be natural and/or manufactured. The forces interact to create growth and recession, order or chaos, change or stagnation. If the model being used is a reasonable representation of the actual societal system under study, the social scientist can perform meaningful experiments on that model. These experiments can be used to test various control and decision policies through simulation. By observing the results of these tests, the scientist often can detect cause-effect relationships. Such information will allow the researcher to understand better the workings of a highly complex and interactive social process.

One of the more interesting societal models currently under investigation is due to the research of Jay Forrester [11]. This model, the "World Dynamic Model," is a nonlinear time-varying description of how world population, pollution, food supply, natural resources, and capital investment interrelate. The user can enter a set of initial conditions and decision policies into the model, execute the program, and analyze the impact of these a priori policies. However, the tools of time-series and discrete spectral analysis can be used to perform this analysis in a flexible and efficient manner. In particular, the cross-correlation method in this book can prove to be a very effective societal data-analysis routine.

Using the Forrester model, a data set representing the experimentally derived values of population, capital investment, quality of life, natural resources, and capital investment fraction in agriculture from 1972 to 2172 was developed. The data were stored on punch cards for future analysis under SPECTRUM IV control. The results of this experiment can be found in Figures 6-11 through 6-15. For the given set of initial conditions and decision rules, the data displayed the following character:

1. World population monotonically increases to the year 2020, then monotonically decreases.
2. Natural resources are continually being depleted, but the rate at which they are being consumed slows drastically near the year 2127. At that time population has attained its smallest value.
3. The population profile is similar to the pollution profile.
4. Capital investment seems to follow a population-type curve.
5. Changes in capital investment in agriculture fraction appear before those found in 1, 3, and 4.

The card-based data set was entered into the SPECTRUM IV software system and then operated on by program CROSS-C (cross-correlation). The result of such an operation was normalized by using program NORMAL. The following cross-correlation tests were performed:

1. Capital investment versus population
2. Capital investment versus natural resources
3. Capital investment versus pollution
4. Capital investment versus capital investment in agriculture fraction

The results of these tests can be found in Figures 6-16 through 6-19, and they can be summarized as follows:

1. Capital investment leads population by approximately 10 years. The correlation of these 2 parameters remains high for all time but decreases with time.
2. Capital investment leads natural resources by approximately 36 years. These parameters are strongly correlated and appear to have periodic behavior with a period of approximately 160 years.
3. Capital investment lags pollution by approximately 8 years. The parameters are not as strongly correlated as those found in test 1.
4. Capital investment and capital investment in agriculture have a cross-correlation analysis similar to that found between capital investment and natural resources. The difference in the lag time is now approximately 20 years versus 36 years.

MAGNITUDE OF MATCHED FILTER

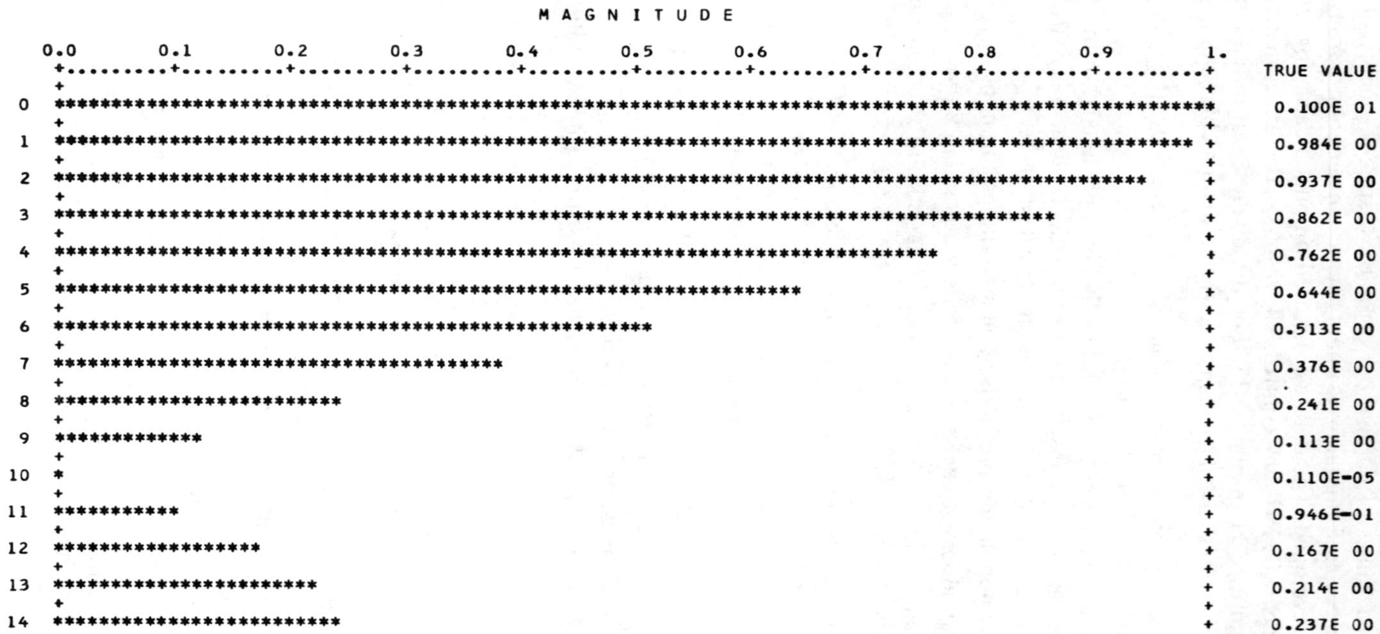

Figure 6-6. Magnitude Profile of a Matched Filter (Radar Detection Experiment).

THIS IS A PULSE + NOISE N(0.0,1.0)

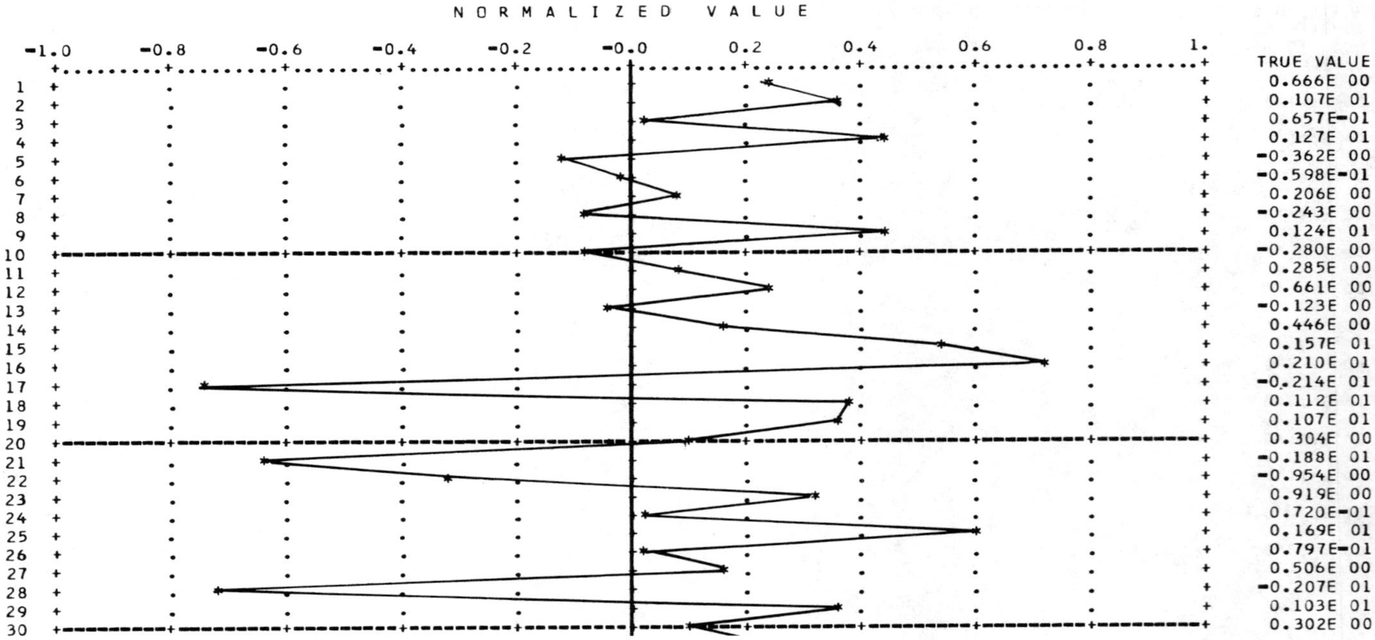

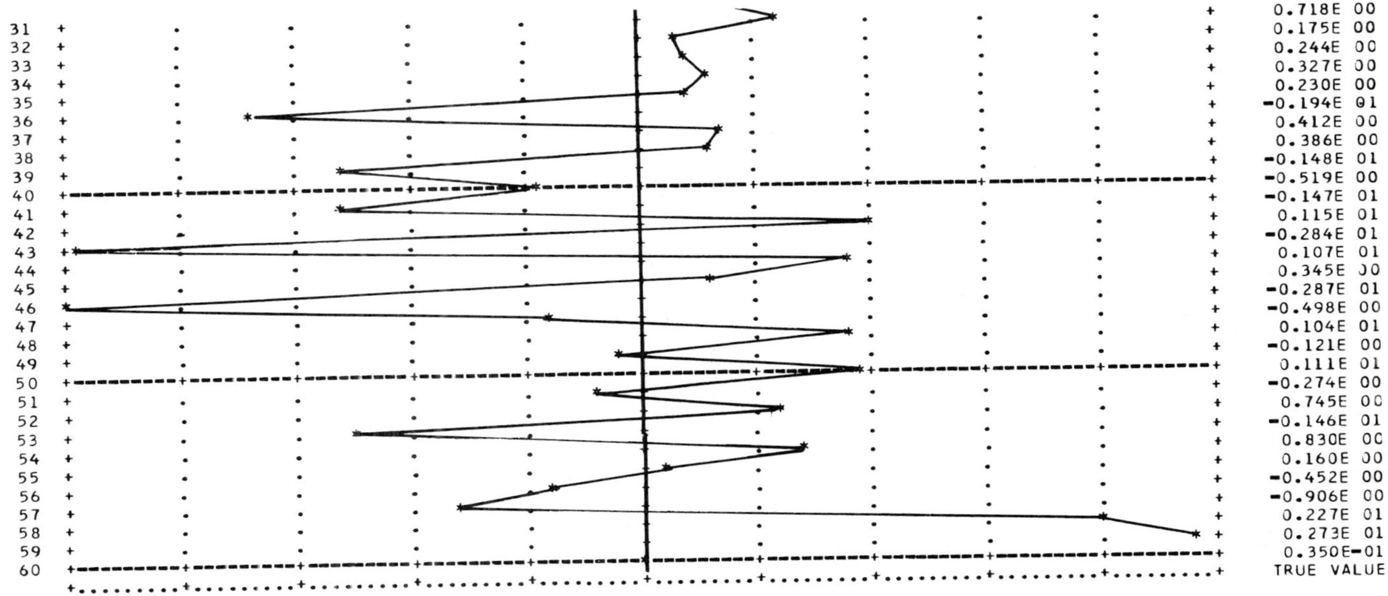

Figure 6-7. Signal-plus-Noise (Radar Detection Experiment).

OUTPUT OF MATCH FILTER FOR SIGNAL + NOISE

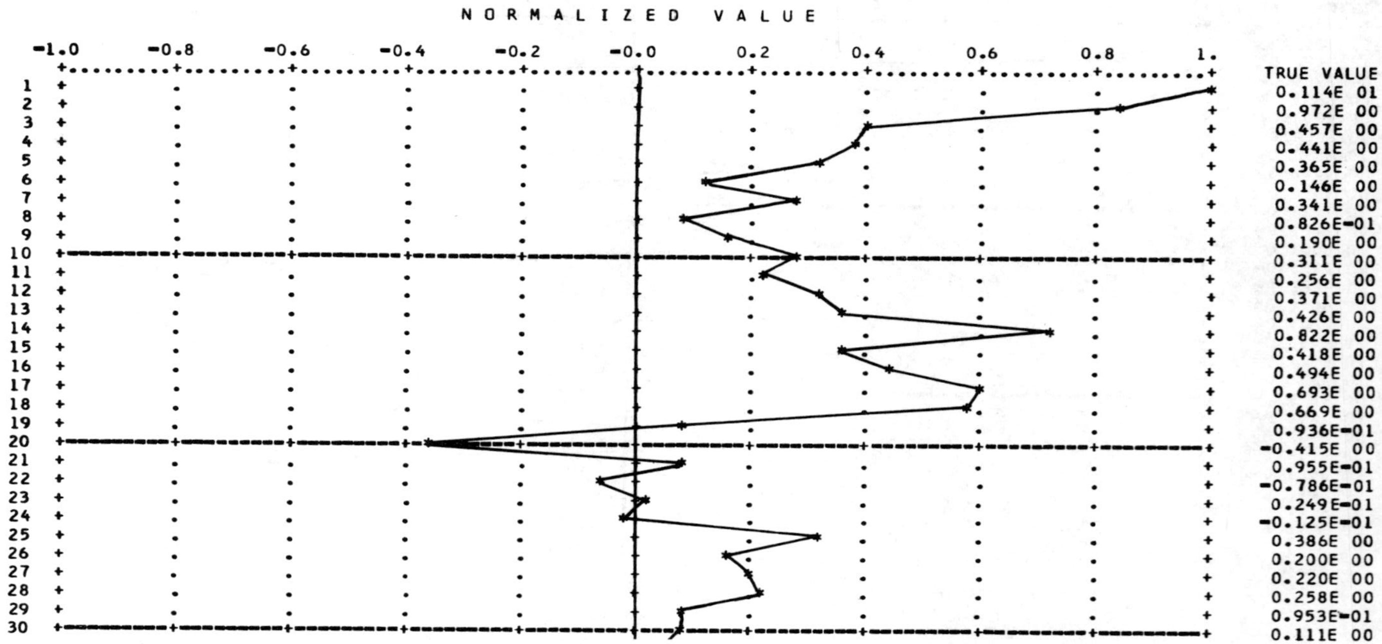

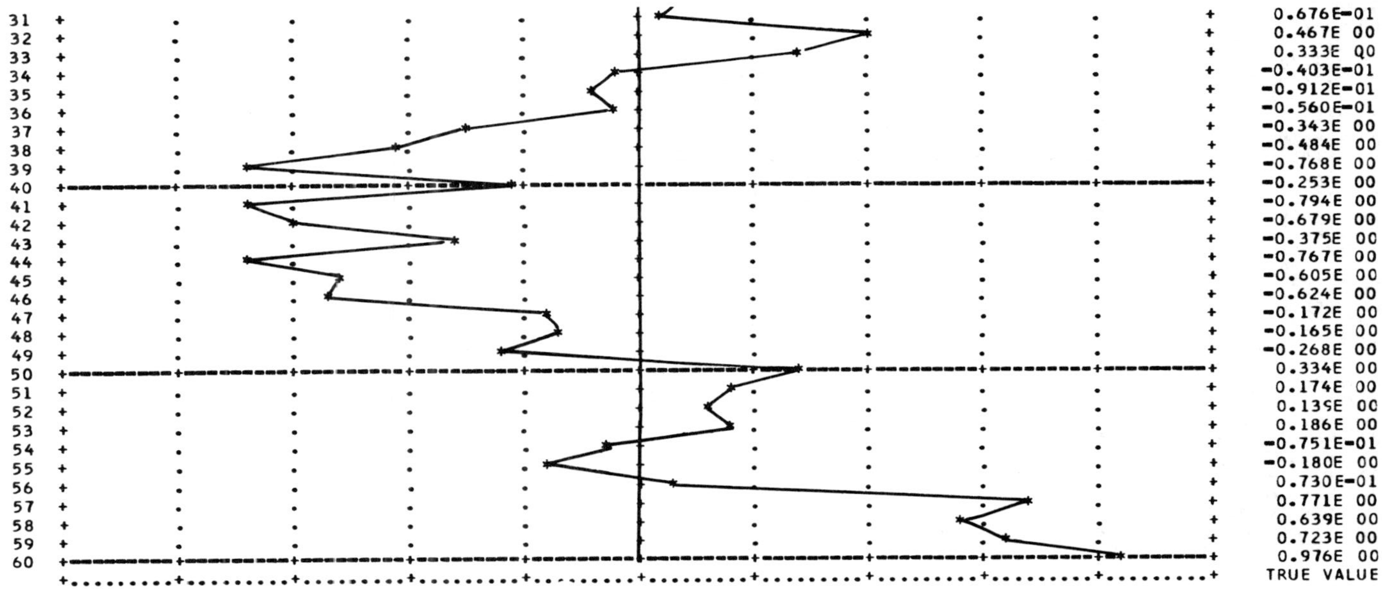

Figure 6-8. Output of a Matched Filter (Radar Detection Experiment).

THIS IS NOISE ONLY N(0.0,1.0)

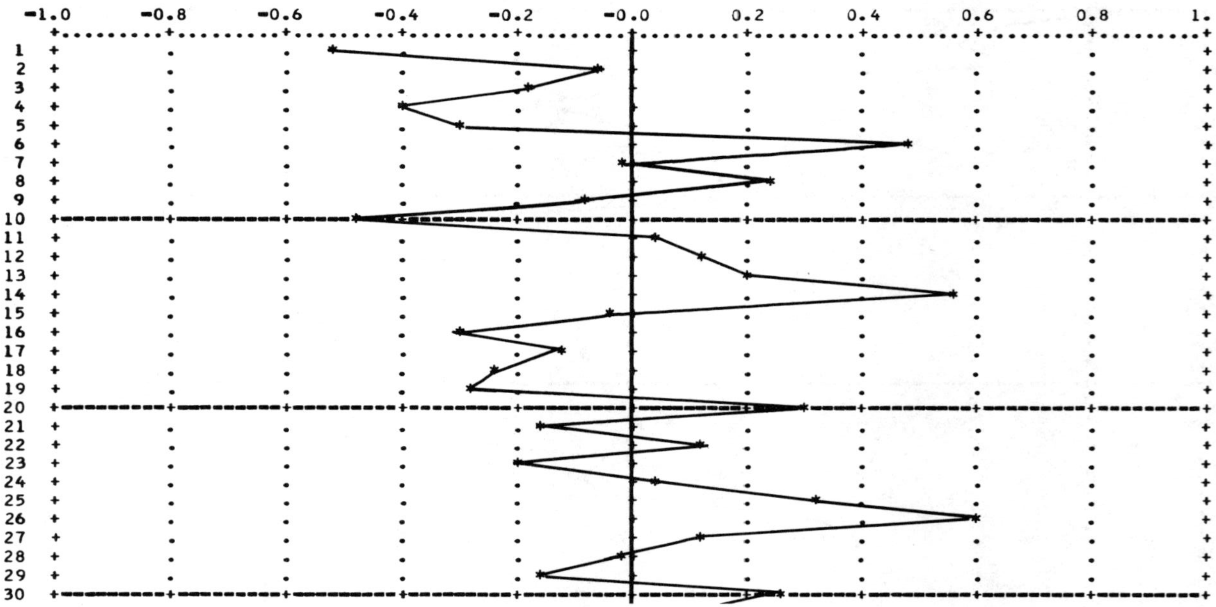

	TRUE VALUE
1	-0.141E 01
2	-0.181E 00
3	-0.503E 00
4	-0.113E 01
5	-0.836E 00
6	0.134E 01
7	-0.323E-01
8	0.701E 00
9	-0.214E 00
10	-0.135E 01
11	0.146E 00
12	0.336E 00
13	0.588E 00
14	0.154E 01
15	-0.152E 00
16	-0.834E 00
17	-0.376E 00
18	-0.646E 00
19	-0.779E 00
20	0.836E 00
21	-0.485E 0C
22	0.348E 00
23	-0.583E 00
24	0.154E 00
25	0.923E 00
26	0.169E 01
27	0.337E 00
28	-0.818E-01
29	-0.479E 00
30	0.723E 00

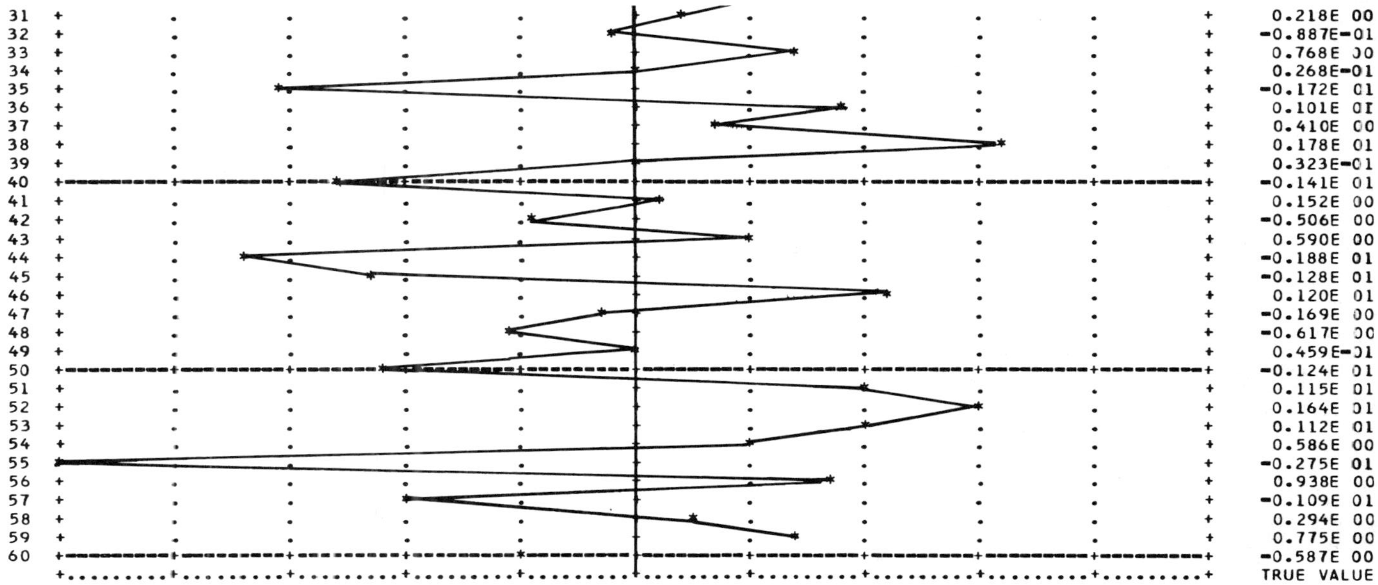

Figure 6-9. Noise Only (Radar Detection Experiment).

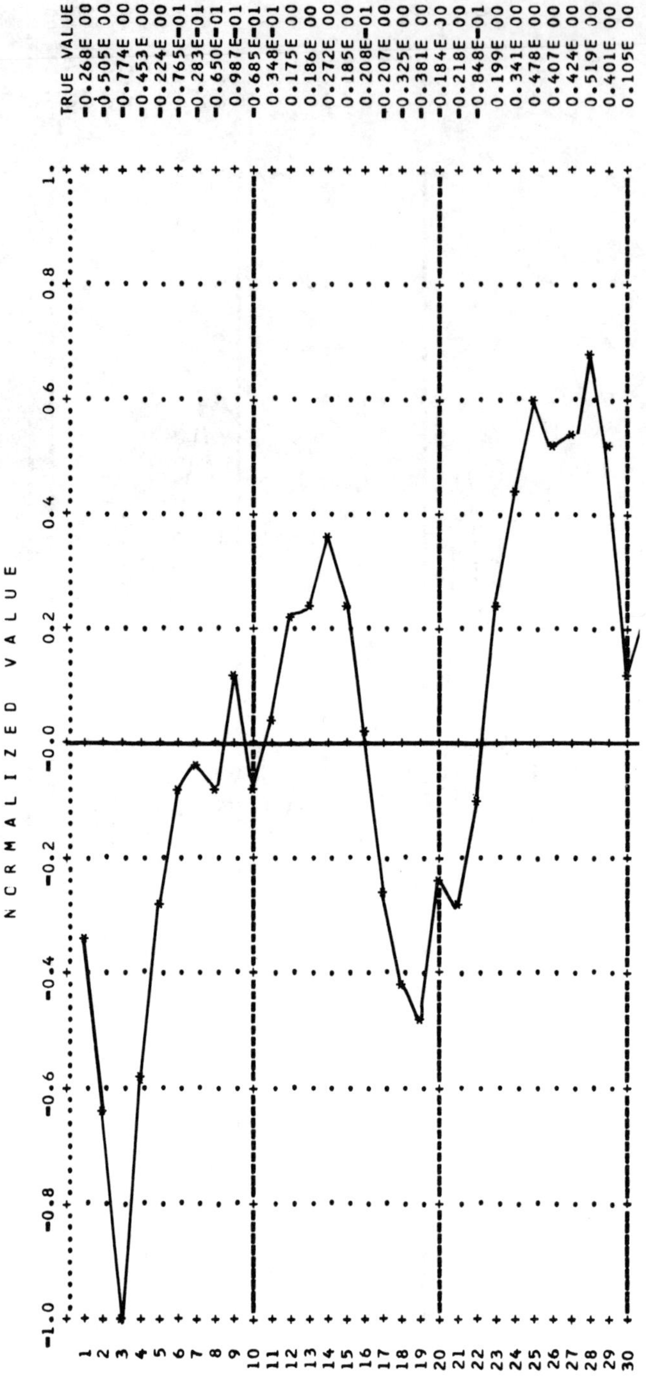

OUTPUT FROM MATCHED FILTER WITH NOISE ONLY

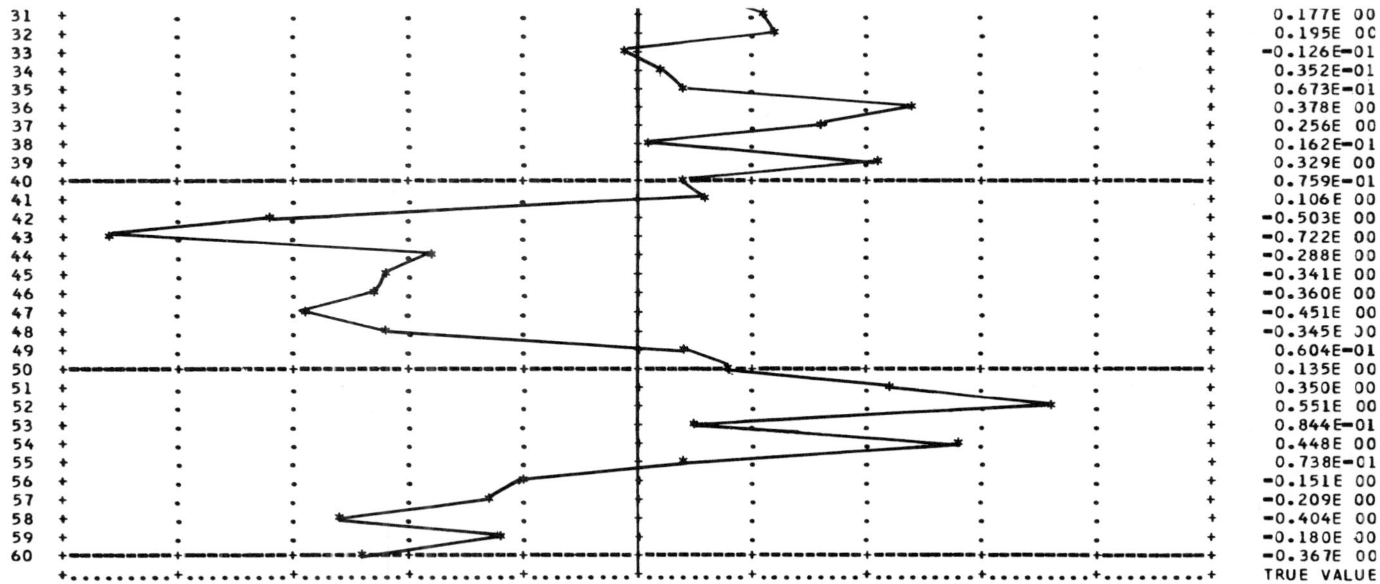

Figure 6-10. Output of a Matched Filter (Radar Detection Experiment).

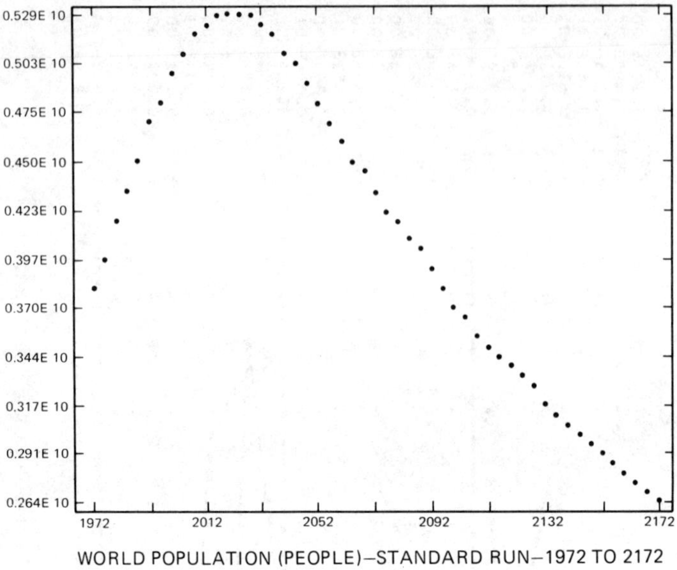

Figure 6-11. World Population (People)—Standard Run, 1972-2172.

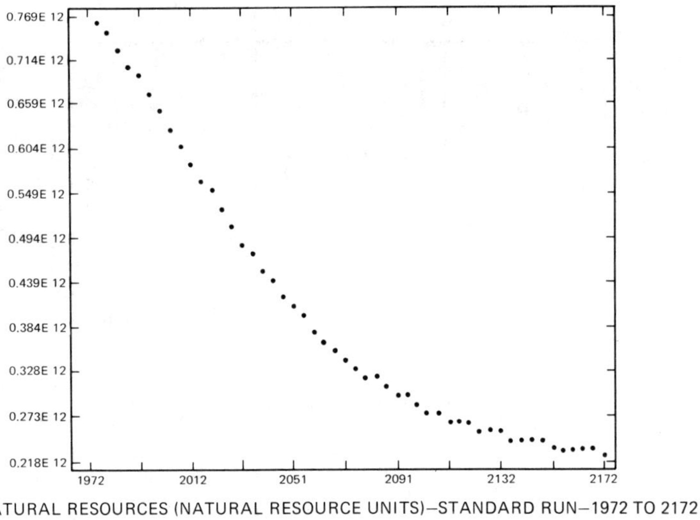

Figure 6-12. Natural Resources (Natural Resource Units)—Standard Run, 1972-2172.

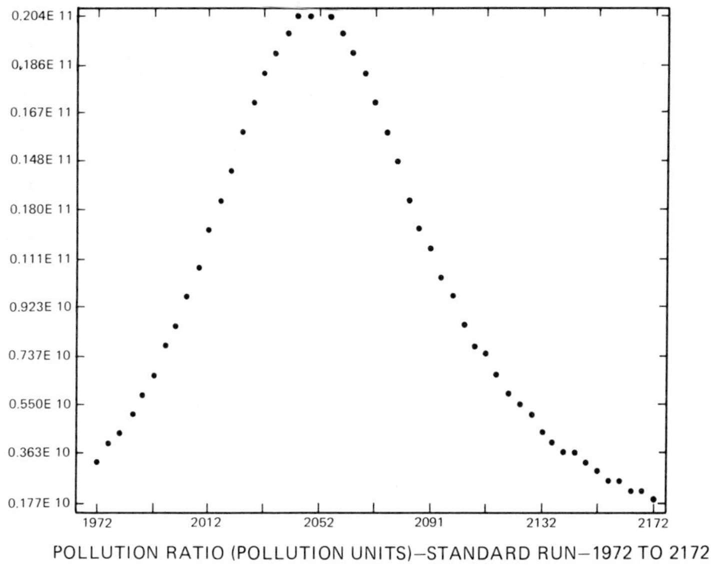

Figure 6-13. Pollution Ratio (Pollution Units)—Standard Run, 1972-2172.

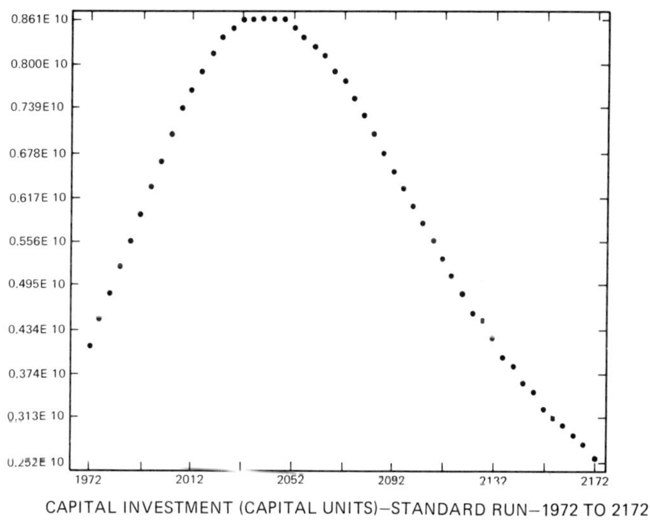

Figure 6-14. Capital Investment (Capital Units)—Standard Run, 1972-2172.

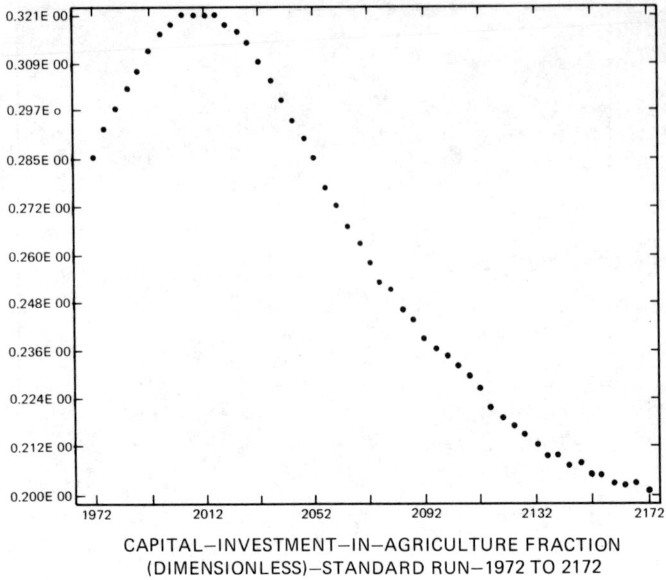

Figure 6-15. Capital-Investment-in-Agriculture Fraction (Dimensionless)—Standard Run, 1972-2172.

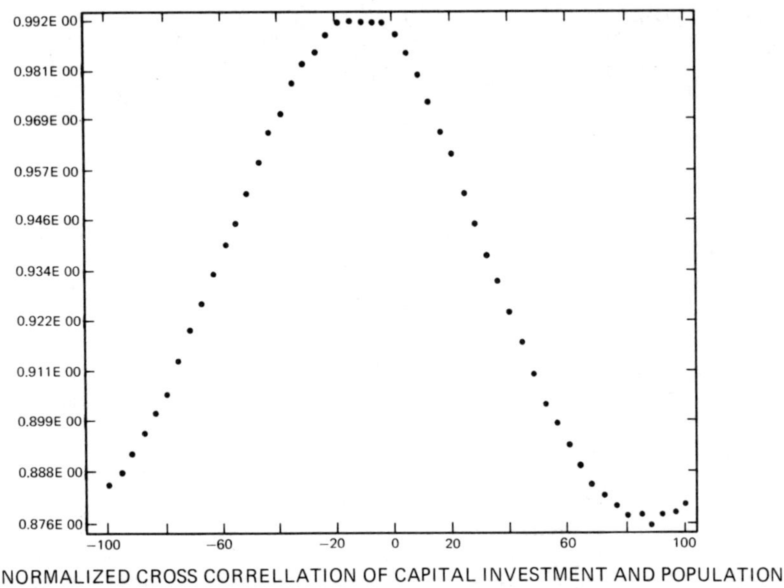

Figure 6-16. Normalized Cross-Correlation of Capital Investment and Population.

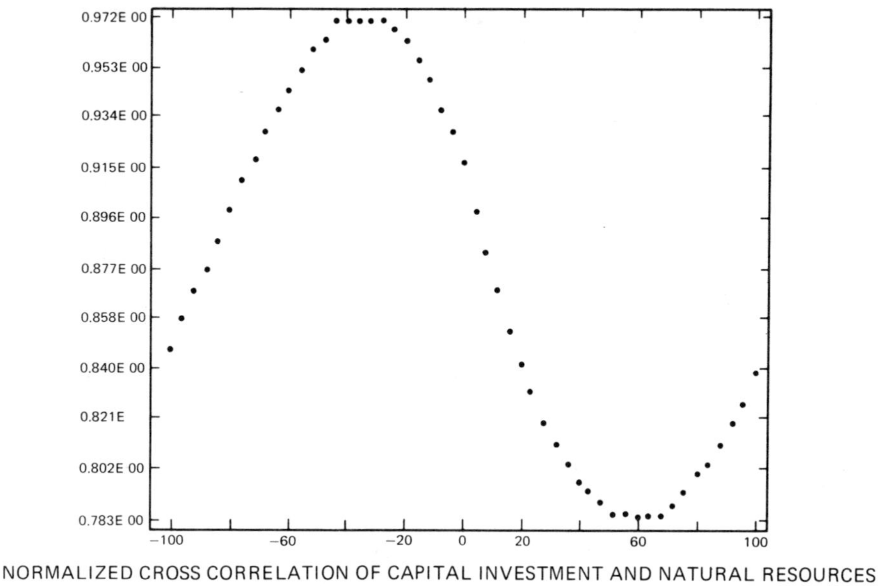

Figure 6-17. Normalized Cross-Correlation of Capital Investment and Natural Resources.

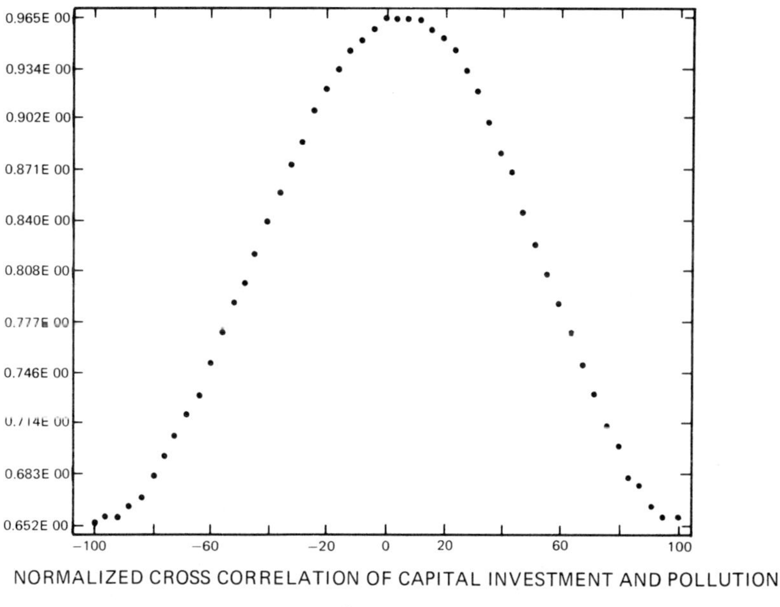

Figure 6-18. Normalized Cross-correlation of Capital Investment and Pollution.

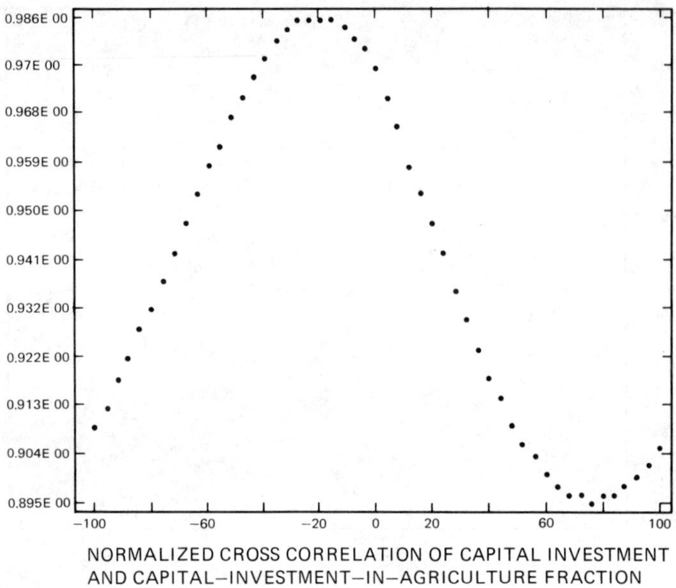

Figure 6-19. Normalized Cross-correlation of Capital Investment and Capital-investment-in-agriculture Fraction.

D. Electrocardiogram Analysis Using a Digital Filter

Digital filters have been used to process an electrocardiogram (EKG) signal process (see reference [5]). If the signal process is corrupted with 60-Hz line frequency noise, the analysis of the EKG trace can be made unnecessarily difficult. In general, an EKG trace would appear as shown in Figure 6-20.

The five points found in Figure 6-20 represent the three phases of heart action. At point *P*, the sinoatial node (pacemaker) of the heart transmits a nerve impulse to all sections of the heart in order to stimulate the pumping action. During the *QRS* phase, heart muscles actually contract to pump blood. Finally, point *T* denotes the bioelectric signal indicating that the heart is relaxing.

In this example, a 60-Hz noise component was added to the author's EKG trace to partially mask points *P* and *T*. A reproduction of the uncorrupted trace is found in Figure 6-21. The noise-corrupted EKG trace is to be processed through a digital filter bank, which is composed of three cascaded second-order digital filters. They are configured to reject a 60-Hz component without significantly distorting other frequency components. In particular, the three filters synthesized satisfy the following discrete equations:

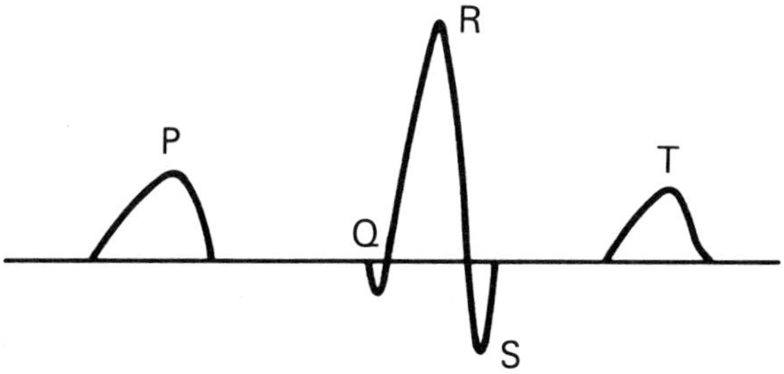

Figure 6-20. Sample EKG Trace.

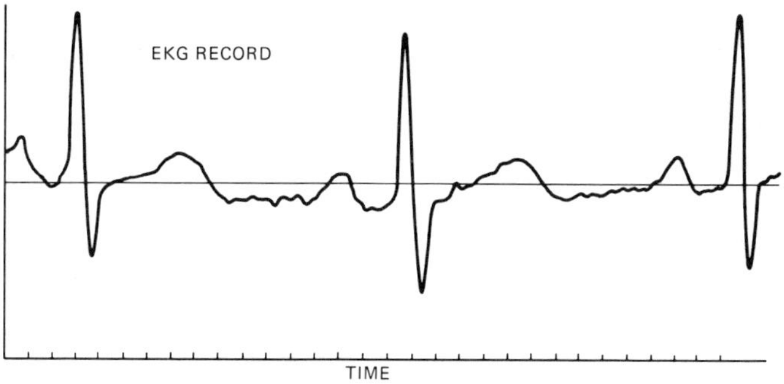

Figure 6-21. Uncorrupted EKG Trace.

Filter 1

$$y_1(k) - u_1(k) + 1.80193774u_1(k-1) + u_1(k-2) - 1.807962y_1(k-1) - 0.9866349y_1(k-2)$$

Filter 2

$$y_2(k) = u_2(k) + 1.80193774u_2(k-1) + u_2(k-2) - 1.761502y_2(k-1) - 0.9556235y_2(k-2)$$

Filter 3

$$y_3(k) = u_3(k) + 1.80193774u_3(k-1) + u_3(k-2) - 1.770923y_3(k-1) - 0.9866349y_3(k-2)$$

Using a sample rate of 140 samples per second, the data were processed through the digital filter system. Figure 6-22 is a block diagram description of the experiment.

The card control sequence belonging to this experiment can be found in Figure 6-23. The digitized data representing the sample values of the uncorrupted wave, sampled at a 140 sample/second rate, are read into the

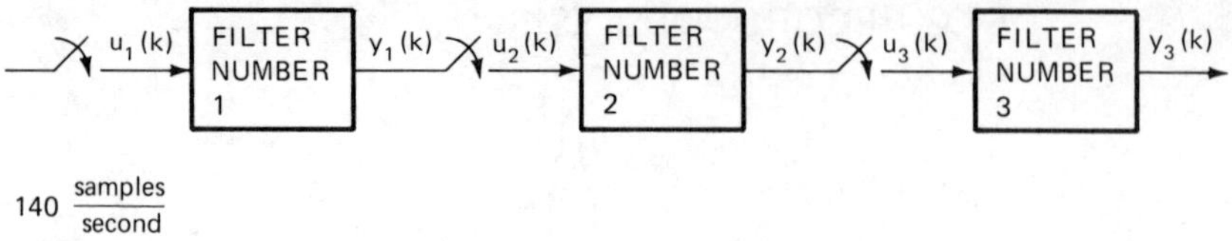

Figure 6-22. EKG Filter.

sytem. This is accomplished through a READ IN call. Also note that, upon transforming the uncorrupted time series, a 60-Hz noise component is added through a CORRECT operation. This operation will insert the complex number $1.0+j0.0$ into the 60-Hz location of the spectral record representing the original time series. You may recall that this complex number, located at 60-Hz, represents a signal $\cos(2\pi 60t)$. Finally, the 60-Hz line has been identified as the sixty-first storage location because the frequency resolution belonging to the performed FFT on the time series is 1 Hz. The first location is occupied by 0 Hz, the second by 1 Hz, and so on. The remaining cards are used to construct the digital filter in the manner prescribed by program DISCRETE, and to complete the example. The uncorrupted EKG time series can be found in Figure 6-24 and its spectra in Figure 6-25. The spectra belonging to the noise-corrupted EKG time series is displayed in Figure 6-27. Note how EKG points *P* and *T* are masked by the additive noise. The filtering operation is accomplished by using program DISCRETE, option 3. Option 3 convolves the declared input signal with the created filter function to produce and output time series. The result of filtering the noise-corrupted input EKG with the filter system can be found in Figure 6-28. The filtered waveform found in Figure 6-28 is a reasonable reproduction of the original uncorrupted EKG signal found in Figure 6-24. Finally, the spectra of the filtered EKG signal is presented in Figure 6-29. The reader will note a severe attentation of the strong 60-Hz component associated with noise-corrupted input.

E. Communications

A large class of classical analog communication systems is categorized either as AM (amplitude modulation) or as FM (frequency modulation) systems. Three AM/FM experiments are performed under SPECTRUM IV control to exhibit some of the salient features of these modulation methods. In particular, the problems studied are:

1. An AM DSB/woc (double sideband without carrier) signal characterized by

$$x(t) = \sin(\omega_m t)\cos(\omega_c t)$$

where ω_m and ω_c are the modulating and carrier frequencies, respectively. In addition,

$$\omega_m = 2\pi f_m \, (f_m = \text{modulating frequency in Hz})$$

$$\omega_c = 2\pi f_c \, (f_c = \text{carrier frequency in Hz})$$

2. A narrow-band FM signal characterized by

$$x(t) = \cos[\omega_c t + \beta \sin(\omega_m t)]$$

where β is the modulation index. For a narrow-band FM transmission, $\beta \leq 0.5$.

3. A wide-band FM signal characterized by

$$x(t) = \cos^3\omega_c t + \beta \sin(\omega_m t)]$$

where $\beta \geq 0.5$. In particular, let

$$f_m = 2Hz$$

$$f_c = 25Hz$$

$$\beta_{\text{narrow band}} = 0.5$$

$$\beta_{\text{wide band}} = 5$$

The construction of the test signals is accomplished in a user-supplied subroutine.

The result of this test can be found in Figures 6-30 through 6-34. The card control sequence required by the problem can be found in Figure 6-30. A source listing of the user-supplied subroutine OWN can be found in Figure 6-31. The AM DSB/woc transmission magnitude spectra, found in Figure 6-32, exhibits the upper and lower sidebands. Note that the AM carrier, defined to be 25 Hz, is absent. Thus this particular transmission is called "AM double sideband without carrier."

The narrow-band FM experiment produces a magnitude spectra, found in Figure 6-33, which possesses few sidebands tightly grouped about the unmodulated carrier frequency of 25 Hz. The fact that but a few frequencies are required to completely characterize the transmitted signal defines this FM strategy to be narrow-band.

The wide-band FM magnitude spectra, found in Figure 6-34, is characterized by many nontrivial sidebands distributed about the unmodulated carrier frequency of 25 Hz. The fact that a wide range of frequencies is required to characterize the transmitted signal defines this FM strategy to be wide-band.

```
CARD      COLUMN                                                          8Ø
          123456789Ø12     .          .          .          .          .          .

1         READ IN      A          TIME                  F        14Ø         14Ø.
2                          F      TIME
3              1         1.1        1.2        1.5        1.8        1.8        1.9
4              2         1.3         .6         .5        .45         .3         .1
5              3          .Ø         .Ø         .Ø         .Ø         .5        1.Ø
6              4         3.Ø        5.Ø        7.Ø        7.Ø        4.5        Ø.Ø
7              5        -3.Ø       -3.Ø       -2.Ø       -1.Ø        -.2        -.2
8              6         -.2        -.2        -.1        -.1         .Ø         .3
9              7          .4         .4         .4         .4         .4         .5
1Ø             8          .6         .6         .6         .7         .8         .9
11             9         1.Ø        1.Ø        1.Ø        1.1        1.1        1.2
12            1Ø         1.2        1.2        1.1         .7         .3         .Ø
13            11         -.3        -.4        -.6        -.7        -.7        -.7
14            12         -.7        -.6        -.6        -.6        -.6        -.6
15            13         -.5        -.5        -.4        -.5        -.6        -.7
16            14         -.9        -.8        -.7        -.7        -.6        -.5
17            15         -.6        -.7        -.8        -.8        -.9        -.8
18            16         -.7        -.6        -.5        -.2        -.1         .Ø
19            17          .1         .2         .3         .3         .1        -.1
2Ø            18         -.7       -1.Ø       -1.Ø       -1.1       -1.1       -1.1
21            19        -1.1       -1.1       -1.1       -1.Ø        -.8        -.4
22            2Ø         1.Ø        2.4        6.Ø        4.Ø        3.Ø        Ø.Ø
23            21        -4.6       -3.Ø       -1.Ø        -.8        -.8        -.7
24            22         -.7        -.7        -.5        -.4        -.4        -.3
25            23         -.2        -.2        -.2        -.1        Ø.Ø         .1
26            24          .2         .3
27        FFFF
28        PLOTTER      A                                           8Ø
29        TIME                 1   8Ø    THIS IS PART OF THE ELECTROCARDIOGRAM
3Ø        FFT
31        PLOTTER      A                                           7Ø
32        FREQ   MAG           1   7Ø    THIS IS THE ELECTROCARDIOGRAPHIC SPECTRUM
33        CORRECT      A          FREQ                  F          1
34                         F      FREQ       1         61         61
35             1         1.Ø      Ø.Ø
36        FFFF
37        PLOTTER      A                                           7Ø
38        FREQ   MAG           1   7Ø    THIS IS THE CORRUPTED EKG SPECTRA
```

```
IFFT
PLOTTER        A                                                 8Ø
TIME                   1    8Ø    THIS IS PART OF THE 6Ø HZ CORRUPTED EKG
SWITCH         A       C
DISCRETE       B       C                               F         14Ø        14Ø.        3
MEMORY-O       3
        .Ø-1.8Ø79621-.98663491
FFFF
MEMORY-I       3
        1.Ø1.8Ø193774        1.Ø
FFFF
*END
SWITCH         B       C
ZERO-OUT       B
DISCRETE       B       C                               F         14Ø        14Ø.        3
MEMORY-O       3
        .Ø-1.7615Ø23-.95562356
FFFF
MEMORY-I       3
        1.Ø1.8Ø193774        1.Ø
FFF=
*END
SWITCH         B       C
ZERO-OUT       B
DISCRETE       B       C                               F         14Ø        14Ø.        3
MEMORY-O       3
        .Ø-1.77Ø9229-.9866349
FFFF
MEMORY-I       3
        1.Ø1.8Ø193774        1.Ø
FFFF
*END
PLOTTER        B                                                 8Ø
TIME                   1    8Ø    THIS IS THE FILTERED ELECTROCARDIOGRAM
SWITCH         A       B
FF‾
PLOTTER        A                                                 7Ø
FREQ    MAG            1    7Ø    THIS IS THE SPECTRA OF THE FILTERED EKG
TERM
        .        .        .        .        .        .        .        .
```

Figure 6-23. Card Control Sequence for EKG Example.

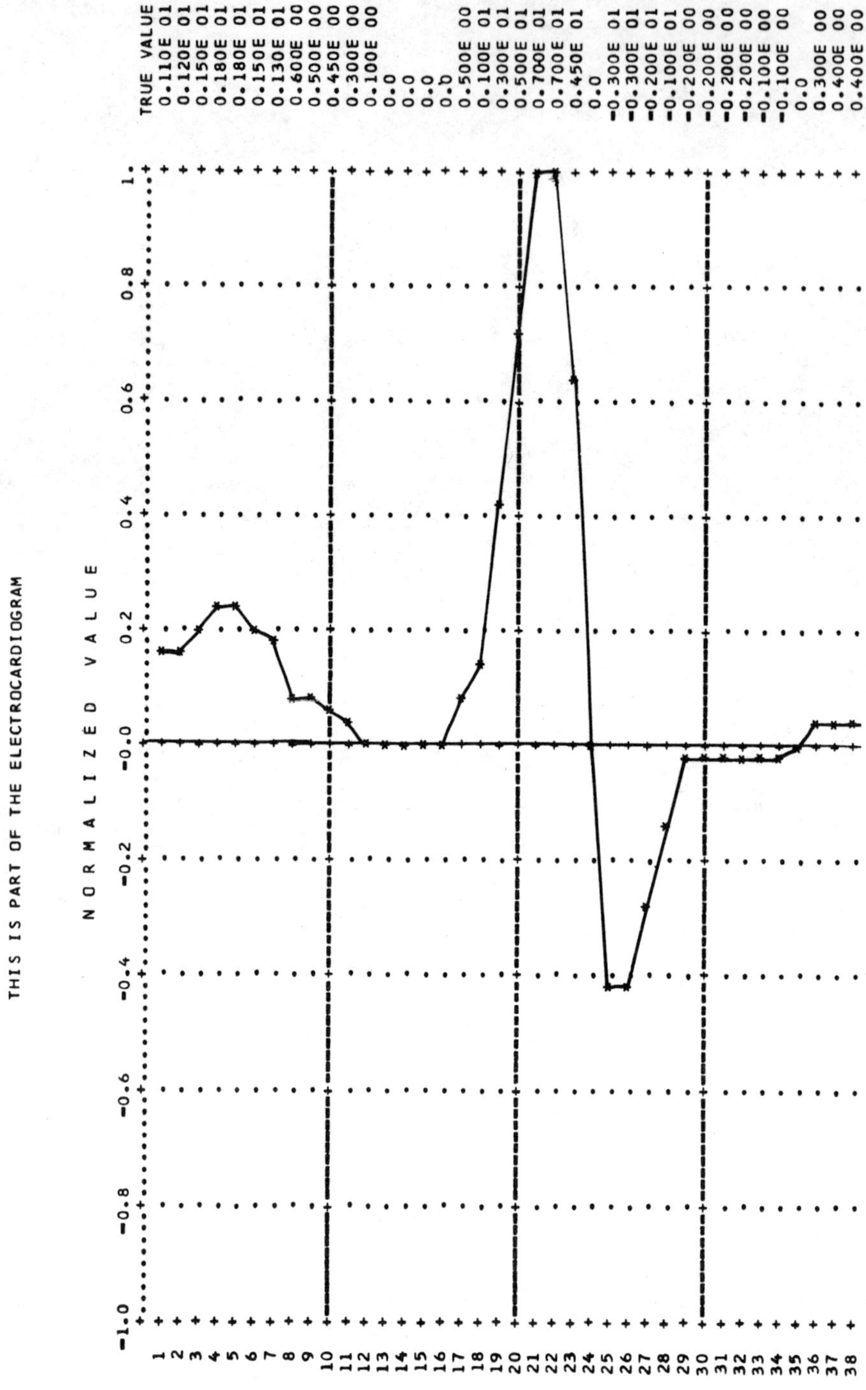
THIS IS PART OF THE ELECTROCARDIOGRAM
NORMALIZED VALUE
-1.0
-0.8
-0.6
-0.4
-0.2
-0.0
0.2
0.4
0.6
0.8
1.
TRUE VALUE
0.110E 01
0.120E 01
0.150E 01
0.180E 01
0.180E 01
0.150E 01
0.130E 01
0.600E 00
0.500E 00
0.450E 00
0.300E 00
0.100E 00
0.0
0.0
0.0
0.0
0.500E 00
0.100E 01
0.300E 01
0.500E 01
0.700E 01
0.700E 01
0.450E 01
0.0
-0.300E 01
-0.300E 01
-0.200E 01
-0.100E 01
-0.200E 00
-0.200E 00
-0.200E 00
-0.200E 00
-0.100E 00
0.0
0.300E 00
0.400E 00
0.400E 00
1
2
3
4
5
6
7
8
9
10
11
12
13
14
15
16
17
18
19
20
21
22
23
24
25
26
27
28
29
30
31
32
33
34
35
36
37
38

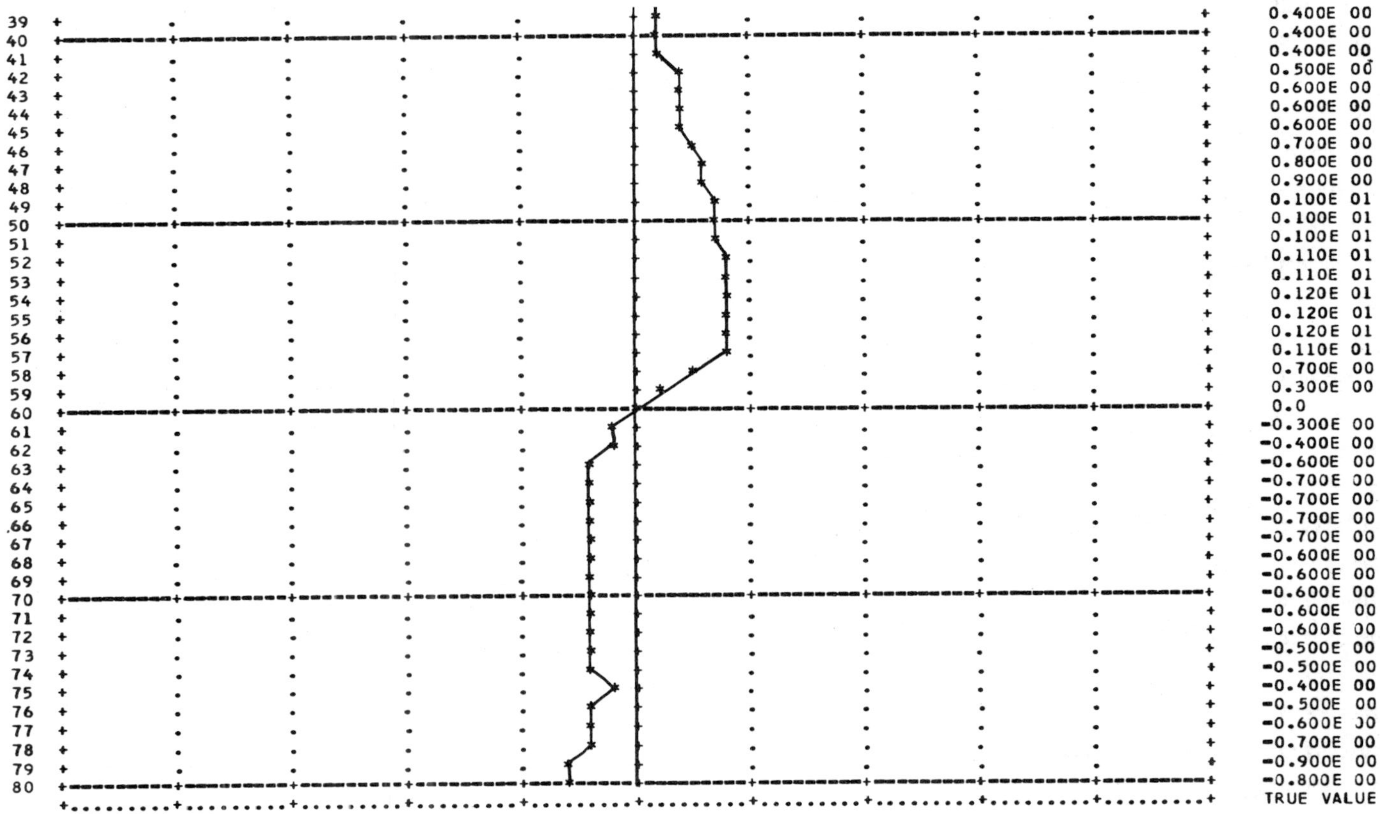

Figure 6-24. EKG Record (EKG Example).

THIS IS THE ELECTROCARDIOGRAPHIC SPECTRUM

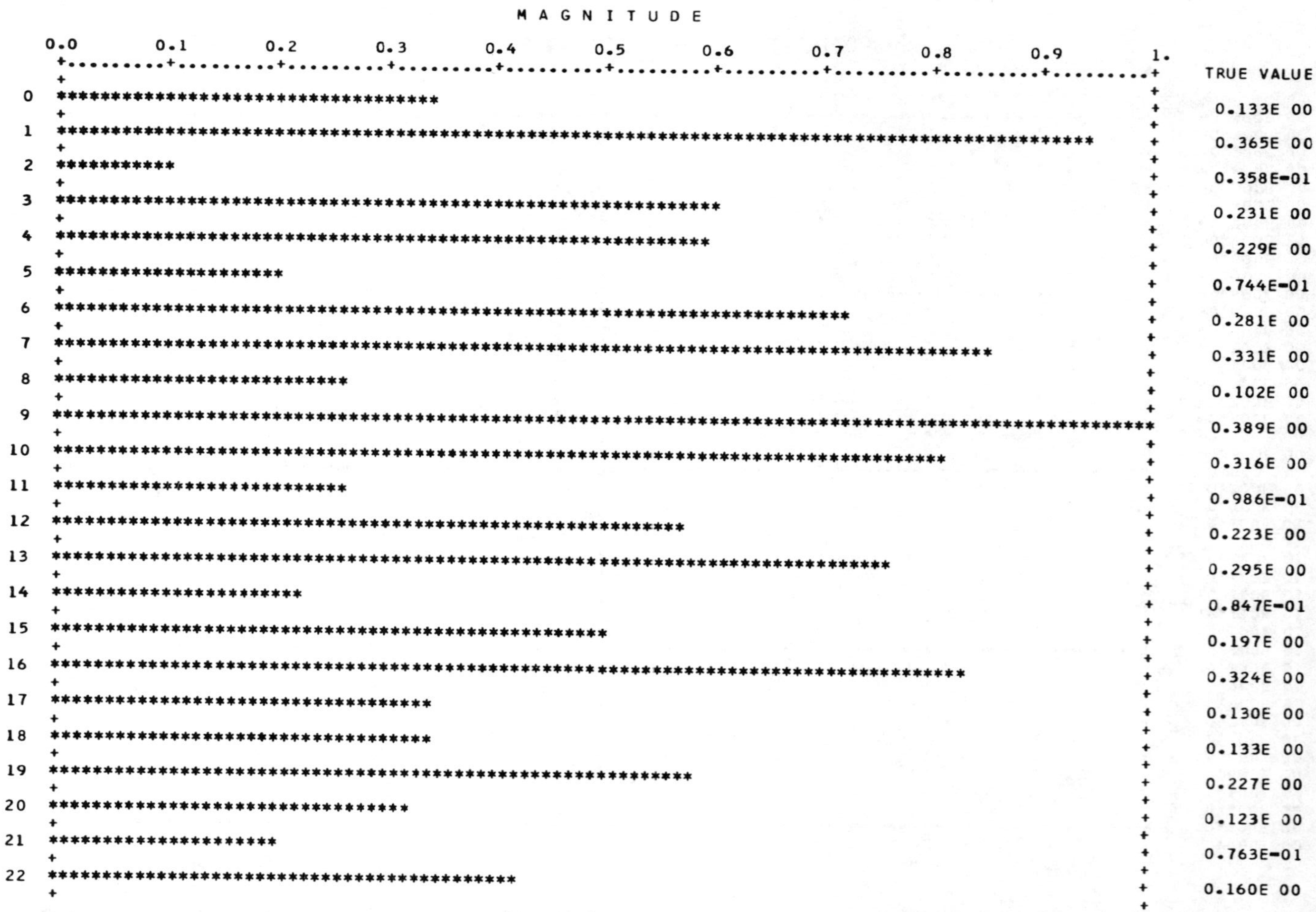

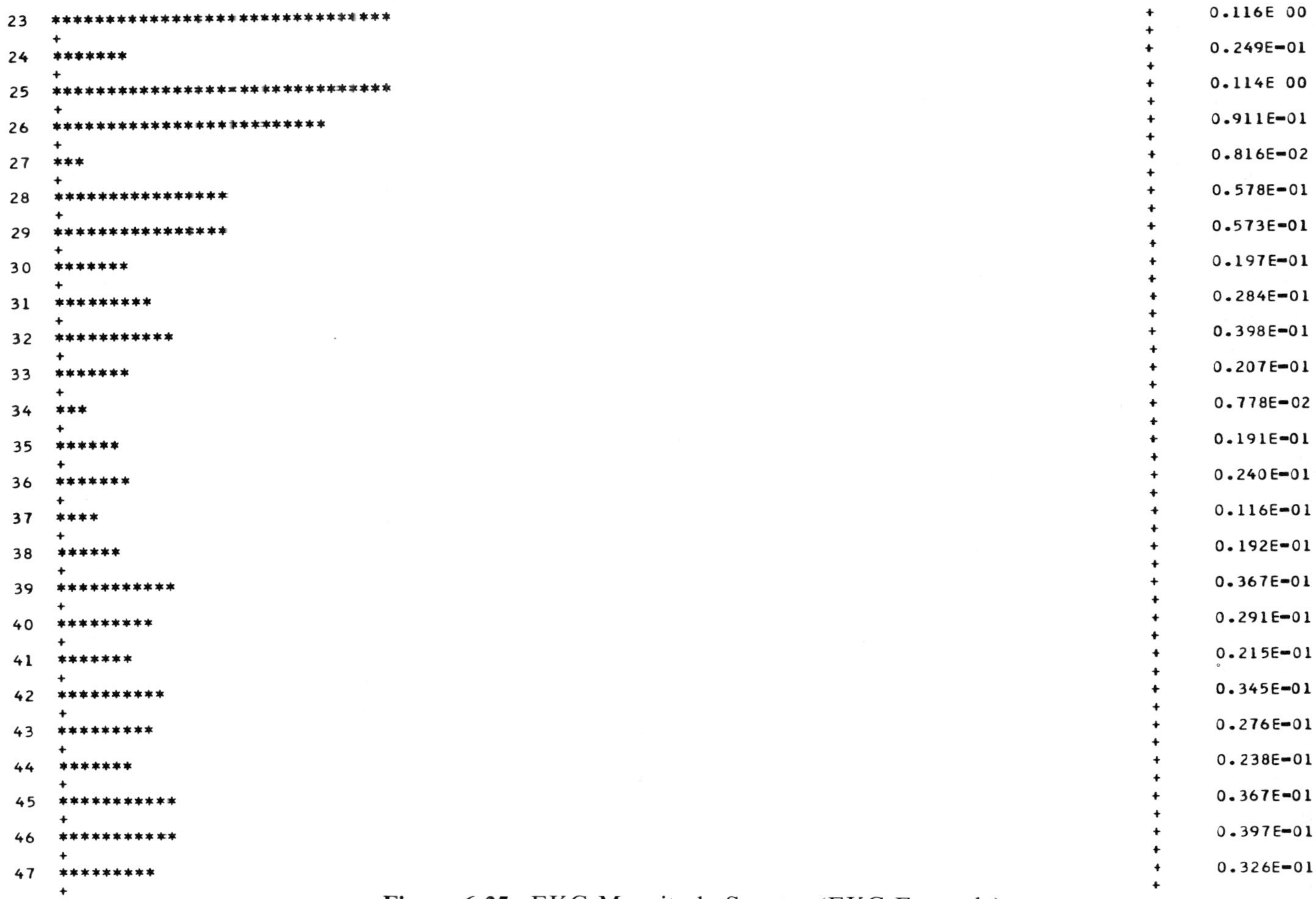

Figure 6-25. EKG Magnitude Spectra (EKG Example).

```
48  *********                                  +   0.300E-01
    +                                          +
49  *********                                  +   0.305E-01
    +                                          +
50  *******                                    +   0.250E-01
    +                                          +
51  **********                                 +   0.330E-01
    +                                          +
52  *********                                  +   0.308E-01
    +                                          +
53  *********                                  +   0.306E-01
    +                                          +
54  *********                                  +   0.315E-01
    +                                          +
55  *******                                    +   0.219E-01
    +                                          +
56  *********                                  +   0.274E-01
    +                                          +
57  **********                                 +   0.337E-01
    +                                          +
58  *******                                    +   0.235E-01
    +                                          +
59  ******                                     +   0.187E-01
    +                                          +
60  *********                                  +   0.273E-01
    +                                          +
61  ******                                     +   0.191E-01
    +                                          +
62  *****                                      +   0.119E-01
    +                                          +
63  *****                                      +   0.175E-01
    +                                          +
64  ******                                     +   0.188E-01
    +                                          +
65  *****                                      +   0.130E-01
    +                                          +
66  *****                                      +   0.149E-01
    +                                          +
67  *****                                      +   0.165E-01
    +                                          +
68  ***                                        +   0.405E-02
    +                                          +
69  *****                                      +   0.148E-01
    +.........+.........+.........+.........+..+   TRUE VALUE
```

Figure 6-25 (Continued)

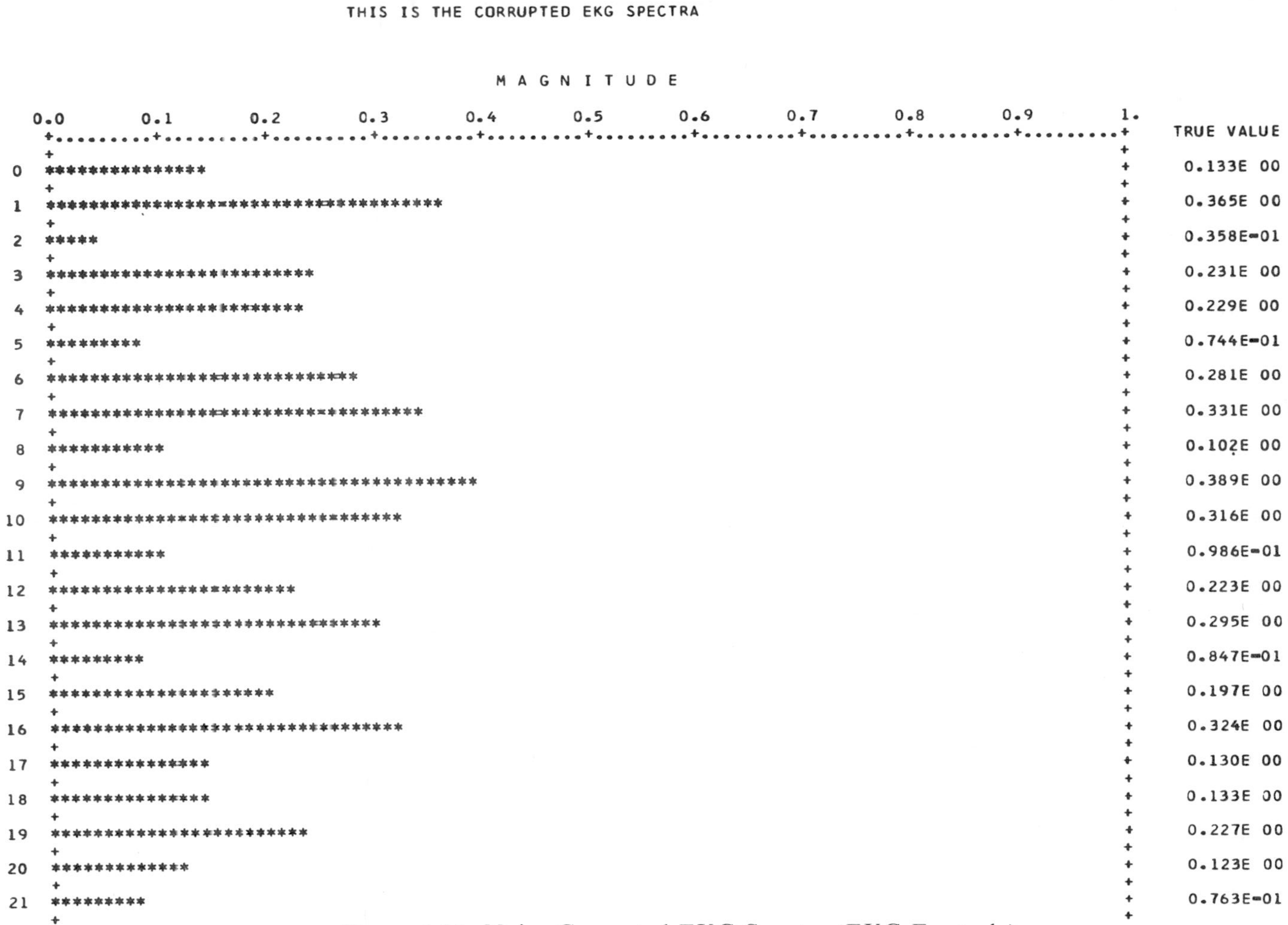

Figure 6-26. Noise-Corrupted EKG Spectra (EKG Example).

```
22  *****************                                    +   0.160E 00
    +                                                    +
23  *************                                        +   0.116E 00
    +                                                    +
24  ***                                                  +   0.249E-01
    +                                                    +
25  *************                                        +   0.114E 00
    +                                                    +
26  ***********                                          +   0.911E-01
    +                                                    +
27  **                                                   +   0.816E-02
    +                                                    +
28  *******                                              +   0.578E-01
    +                                                    +
29  *******                                              +   0.573E-01
    +                                                    +
30  ***                                                  +   0.197E-01
    +                                                    +
31  ****                                                 +   0.284E-01
    +                                                    +
32  *****                                                +   0.398E-01
    +                                                    +
33  ***                                                  +   0.207E-01
    +                                                    +
34  **                                                   +   0.778E-02
    +                                                    +
35  ***                                                  +   0.191E-01
    +                                                    +
36  ***                                                  +   0.240E-01
    +                                                    +
37  ***                                                  +   0.116E-01
    +                                                    +
38  ***                                                  +   0.192E-01
    +                                                    +
39  *****                                                +   0.367E-01
    +                                                    +
40  ****                                                 +   0.291E-01
    +                                                    +
41  ***                                                  +   0.215E-01
    +                                                    +
42  *****                                                +   0.345E-01
    +                                                    +
43  ****                                                 +   0.276E-01
    +                                                    +
44  ***                                                  +   0.238E-01
    +                                                    +
45  *****                                                +   0.367E-01
    +                                                    +
46  *****                                                +   0.397E-01
    +                                                    +
```

```
47  *****                                                        +  0.326E-01
    +                                                            +
48  ****                                                         +  0.300E-01
    +                                                            +
49  *****                                                        +  0.305E-01
    +                                                            +
50  ****                                                         +  0.250E-01
    +                                                            +
51  *****                                                        +  0.330E-01
    +                                                            +
52  *****                                                        +  0.308E-01
    +                                                            +
53  *****                                                        +  0.306E-01
    +                                                            +
54  *****                                                        +  0.315E-01
    +                                                            +
55  ***                                                          +  0.219E-01
    +                                                            +
56  ****                                                         +  0.274E-01
    +                                                            +
57  *****                                                        +  0.337E-01
    +                                                            +
58  ***                                                          +  0.235E-01
    +                                                            +
59  ***                                                          +  0.187E-01
    +                                                            +
60  *************************************************************   0.100E 01
    +                                                            +
61  ***                                                          +  0.191E-01
    +                                                            +
62  ***                                                          +  0.119E-01
    +                                                            +
63  ***                                                          +  0.175E-01
    +                                                            +
64  ***                                                          +  0.188E-01
    +                                                            +
65  ***                                                          +  0.130E-01
    +                                                            +
66  ***                                                          +  0.149E-01
    +                                                            +
67  ***                                                          +  0.165E-01
    +                                                            +
68  *                                                            +  0.405E-02
    +                                                            +
69  ***                                                          +  0.148E-01
    +.........+.........+.........+.........+.........+.........+  TRUE VALUE
```

Figure 6-26 (Continued)

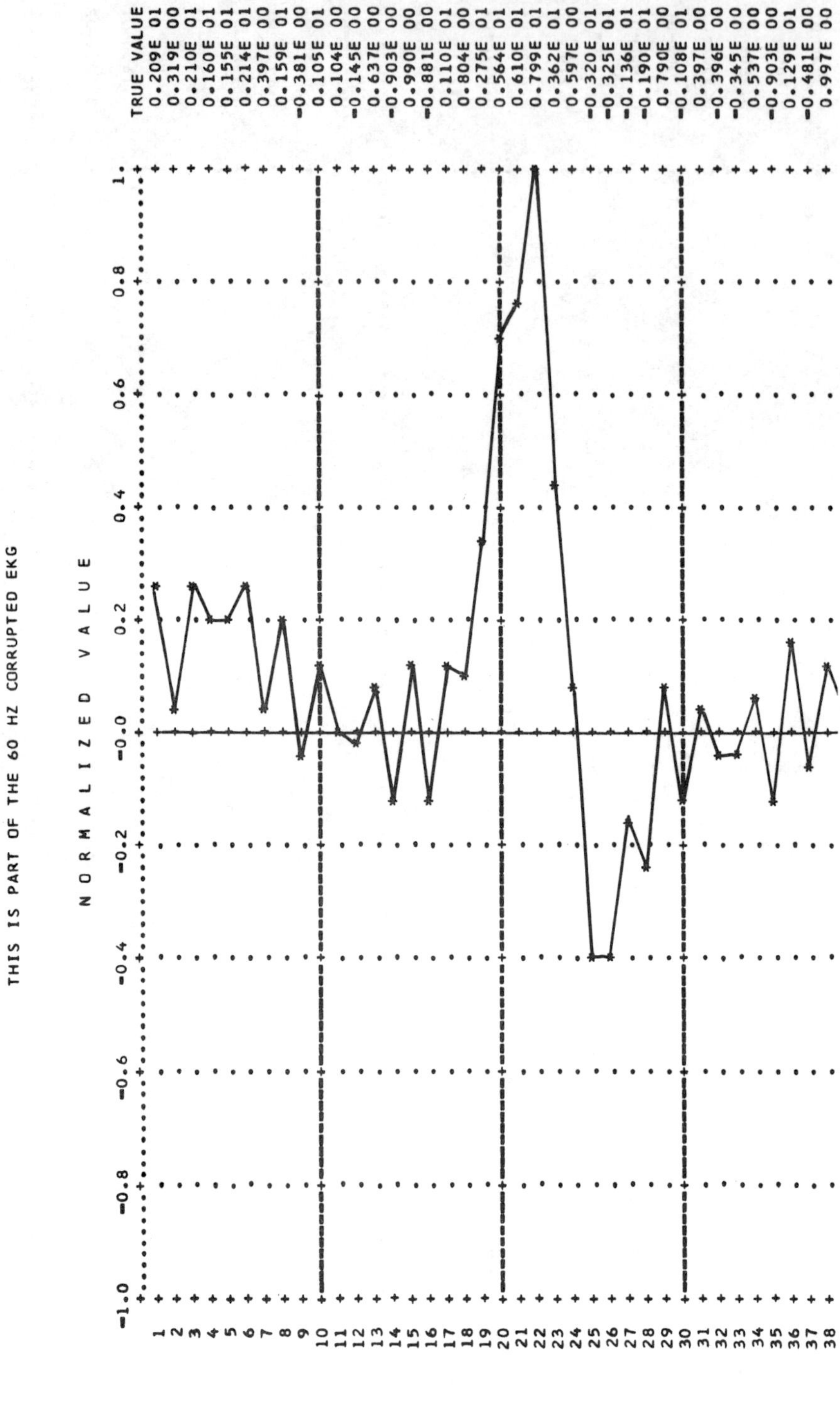
THIS IS PART OF THE 60 HZ CORRUPTED EKG
NORMALIZED VALUE
-1.0
-0.8
-0.6
-0.4
-0.2
-0.0
0.2
0.4
0.6
0.8
1.
TRUE VALUE
0.209E 01
0.319E 00
0.210E 01
0.160E 01
0.155E 01
0.214E 01
0.397E 00
0.159E 01
-0.381E 00
0.105E 01
0.104E 00
-0.145E 00
0.637E 00
-0.903E 00
0.990E 00
-0.881E 00
0.110E 01
0.804E 00
0.275E 01
0.564E 01
0.610E 01
0.799E 01
0.362E 01
0.597E 00
-0.320E 01
-0.325E 01
-0.136E 01
-0.190E 01
0.790E 00
-0.108E 01
0.397E 00
-0.396E 00
-0.345E 00
0.537E 00
-0.903E 00
0.129E 01
-0.481E 00
0.997E 00
1
2
3
4
5
6
7
8
9
10
11
12
13
14
15
16
17
18
19
20
21
22
23
24
25
26
27
28
29
30
31
32
33
34
35
36
37
38

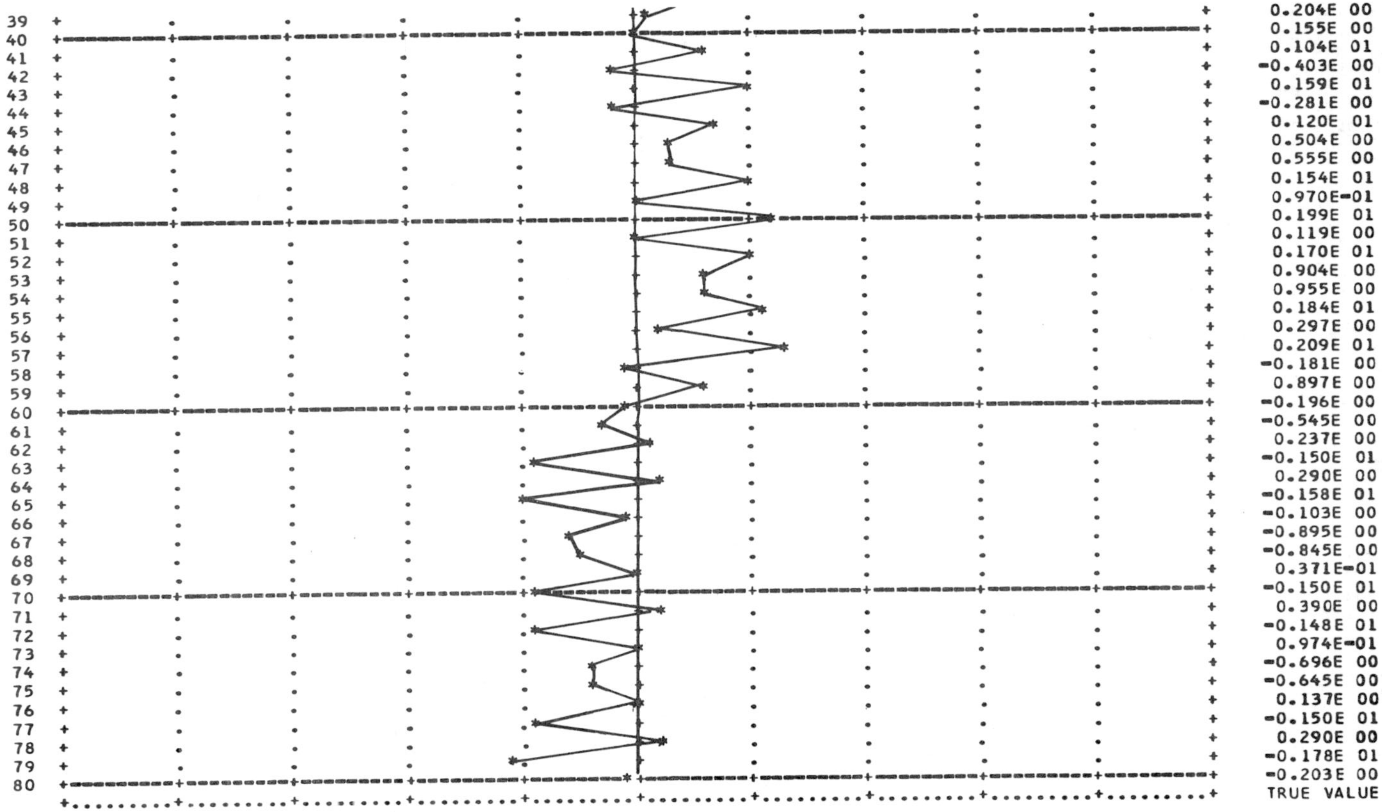

Figure 6-27. Noise-corrupted EKG Time Series (EKG Example).

THIS IS THE FILTERED ELECTROCARDIOGRAM

NORMALIZED VALUE

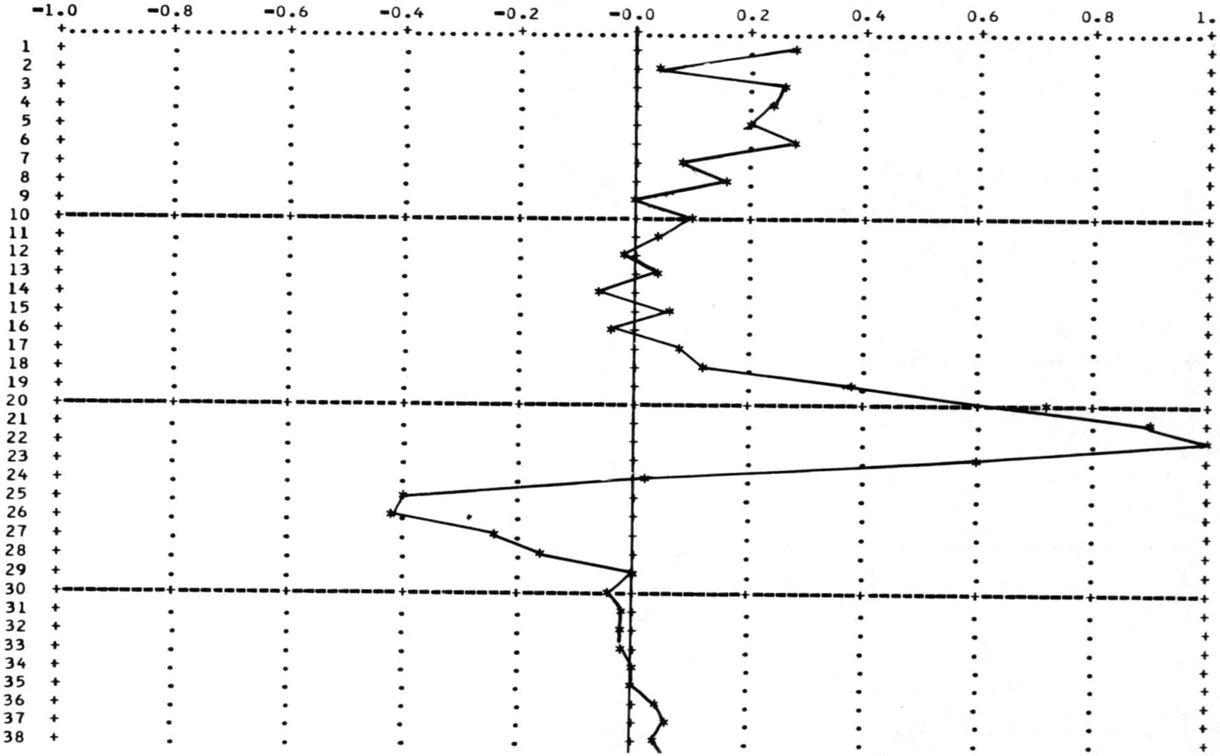

	TRUE VALUE
1	0.209E 01
2	0.456E 00
3	0.203E 01
4	0.176E 01
5	0.161E 01
6	0.211E 01
7	0.647E 00
8	0.136E 01
9	-0.759E-01
10	0.824E 00
11	0.247E 00
12	-0.969E-01
13	0.412E 00
14	-0.519E 00
15	0.514E 00
16	-0.410E 00
17	0.738E 00
18	0.993E 00
19	0.290E 01
20	0.543E 01
21	0.688E 01
22	0.760E 01
23	0.452E 01
24	0.204E 00
25	-0.306E 01
26	-0.326E 01
27	-0.190E 01
28	-0.126E 01
29	-0.596E-01
30	-0.288E 00
31	-0.199E 00
32	-0.157E 00
33	-0.187E 00
34	-0.228E-01
35	-0.539E-01
36	0.308E 00
37	0.457E 00
38	0.347E 00

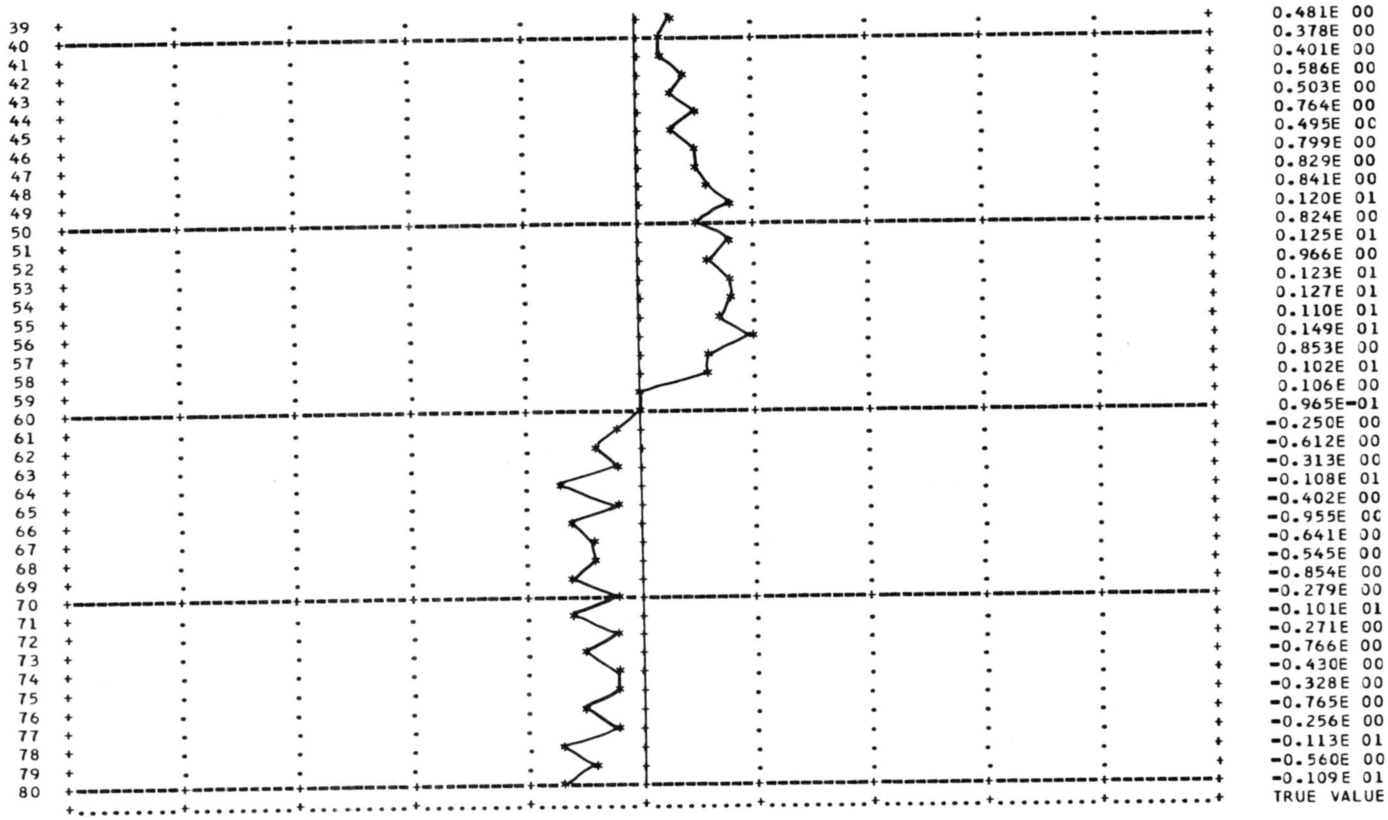

Figure 6-28. Filtered Noise-corrupted EKG Signal (EKG Example).

THIS IS THE SPECTRA OF THE FILTERED EKG

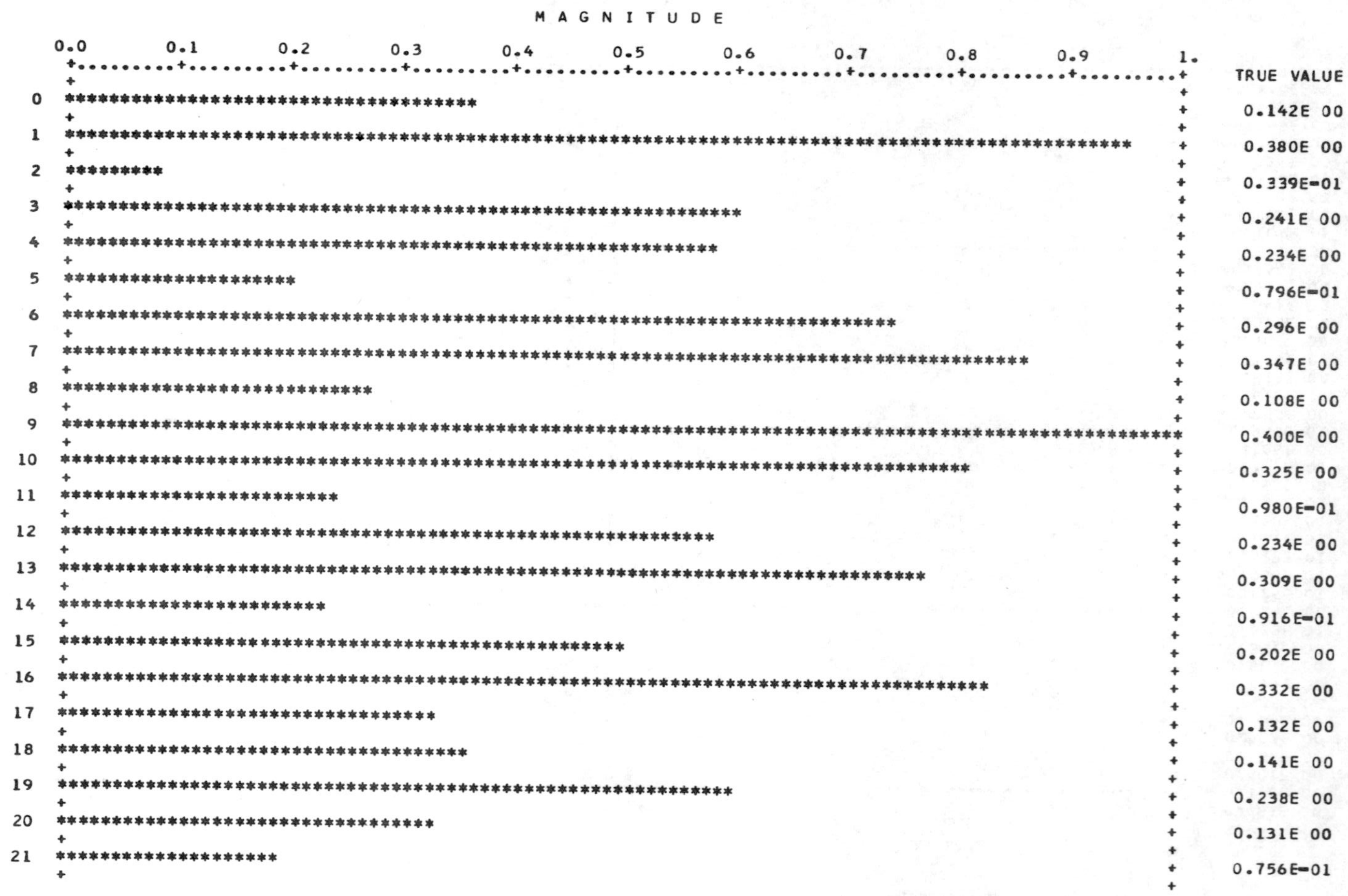

Figure 6-29. Magnitude Spectra of Filtered EKG Time Series (EKG Example).

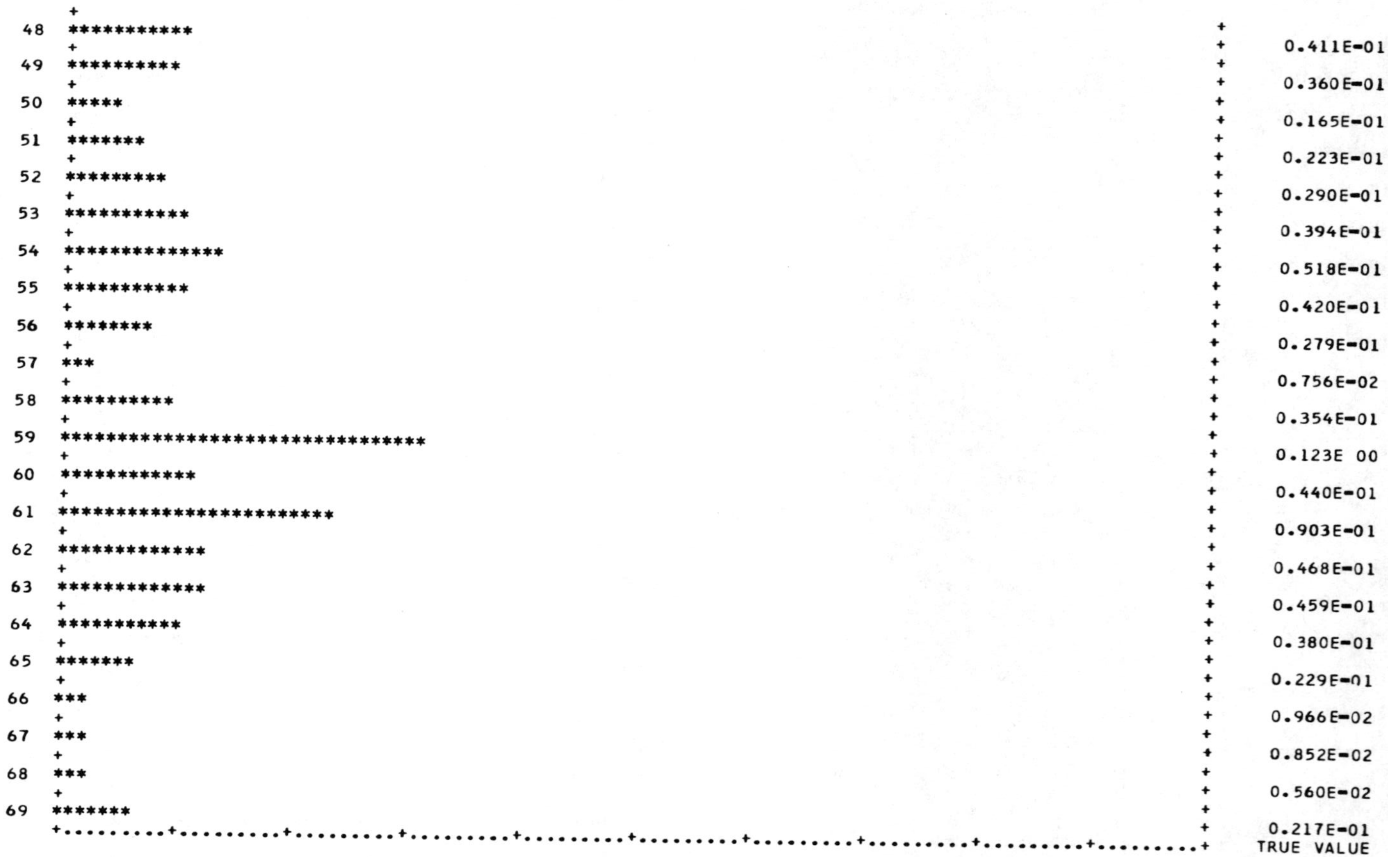

Figure 6-29 (Continued)

```
CARD        COLUMN                                                                   8Ø
            123456789Ø12      .       .       .       .       .       .       .
--------------------------------------------------------------------------------------
1           USER LIB     A          TIME                     1ØØ      1ØØ.      1
2           F(T) = SIN(WM*T)*COS(WC*T)
3           FFT
4           PLOTTER      A                                    5Ø
5           FREQ   MAG        1   5Ø    AM MODULATED SINE WAVE  FM=2   FC=25
6           USER LIB     A          TIME                     1ØØ      1ØØ.      2
7           F(T) = COS(WC*T + BSIN(WM*T))  B = 1/2
8           FFT
9           PLOTTER      A                                    5Ø
1Ø          FREQ   MAG        1   5Ø    FM MODULATION SINE WAVE  FM=2   FC=25  B=1/2
11          USER LIB     A          TIME                     1ØØ      1ØØ.      3
12          F(T) = COS(WC*T + BSIN(WM*T))  B=5
13          FFT
14          PLOTTER      A                                    5Ø
15          FREQ   MAG        1   5Ø    FM MODULATED SINE WAVE  FM=2  FC=25  B = 5
16          TERM
                  .       .       .       .       .       .       .       .
```

Figure 6-30. Card Control Sequence for Communication Experiment.

```
FORTRAN IV G LEVEL  21                 OWN                  DATE = 75156          16/04/50                  PAGE 0001

                 SUBROUTINE OWN
        C
        C  THE FOLLOWING FIVE STATEMENTS SHOULD BE INCLUDED IN ANY SUBROUTINE OWN
                 REAL*8 BAN
                 INTEGER DSO,E,F,TIME,FREQ,SPL
                 COMMON REST(6148),TEMR(1024),TEMC(1024),FRN(20),FCN(20),FRD(20),
                1FCD(20),PN(21),PD(21),REST1(82),NPOINT,REST2(5),SPL,REST3(2)
                 COMMON /LETTER/ F,E,MAR(3),LAIS(60),TIME,FREQ,IBAN,BAN,LN,NN,NP
        C
        C
                 WRITE(LN,3) SPL
               3 FORMAT(10X,'USER PROGRAM NUMBER ',I2,/)
                 PI = 8.0*ATAN(1.0)
                 GO TO (10,20,30),SPL
                 GO TO 99
              10 DO 11 J=1,NPOINT
                 TEMR(J) = COS(PI*(J-1)*25./100.)*SIN(PI*(J-1)*2.0/100.)
              11 CONTINUE
                 GO TO 99
              20 BETA = .5
                 FM = 2.
                 GO TO 22
              30 BETA = 5.0
                 FM = 2.0
              22 DO 21 J=1,NPCINT
                 DPT =       BETA*SIN(PI*(J-1)*FM/100.)
                 TEMR(J) = COS(PI*(J-1)*25./100.+DPT)
              21 CONTINUE
              99 CONTINUE
                 RETURN
                 END
```

Figure 6-31. Subroutine OWN (Communication Experiment).

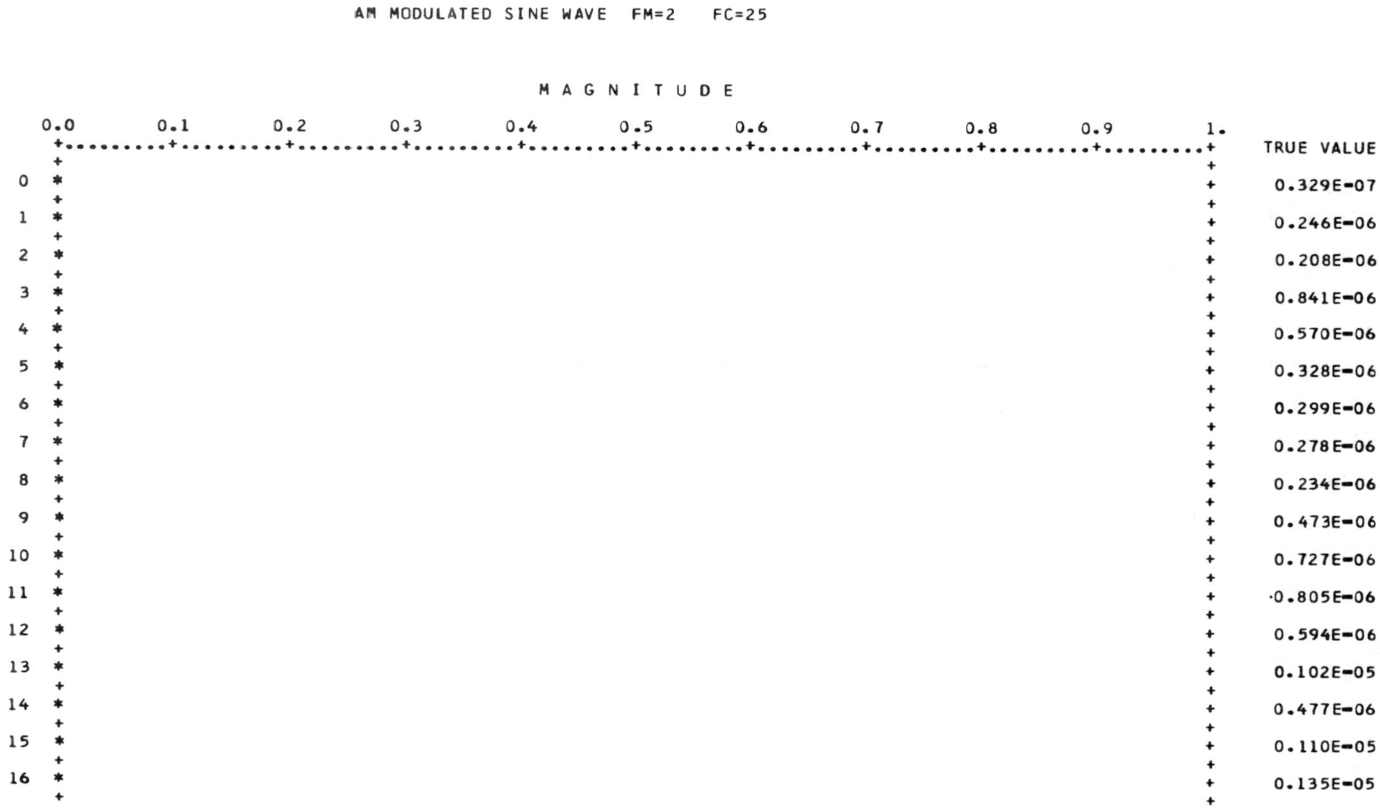

Figure 6-32. AM DSB/woc (Communication Experiment).

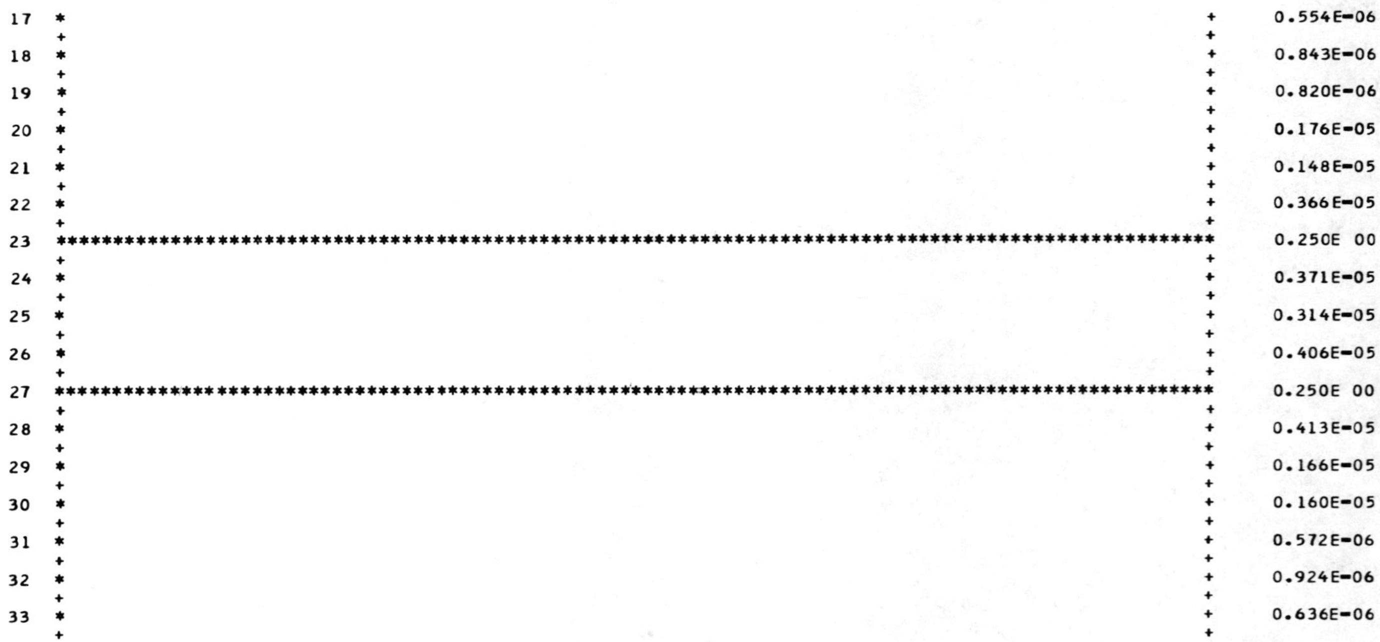
17 0.554E-06
18 0.843E-06
19 0.820E-06
20 0.176E-05
21 0.148E-05
22 0.366E-05
23 0.250E 00
24 0.371E-05
25 0.314E-05
26 0.406E-05
27 0.250E 00
28 0.413E-05
29 0.166E-05
30 0.160E-05
31 0.572E-06
32 0.924E-06
33 0.636E-06

```
34  *                                                                          +   0.160E-05
    +                                                                          +
35  *                                                                          +   0.129E-05
    +                                                                          +
36  *                                                                          +   0.608E-06
    +                                                                          +
37  *                                                                          +   0.831E-06
    +                                                                          +
38  *                                                                          +   0.471E-06
    +                                                                          +
39  *                                                                          +   0.926E-06
    +                                                                          +
40  *                                                                          +   0.673E-06
    +                                                                          +
41  *                                                                          +   0.609E-06
    +                                                                          +
42  *                                                                          +   0.340E-06
    +                                                                          +
43  *                                                                          +   0.221E-06
    +                                                                          +
44  *                                                                          +   0.256E-06
    +                                                                          +
45  *                                                                          +   0.313E-06
    +                                                                          +
46  *                                                                          +   0.643E-06
    +                                                                          +
47  *                                                                          +   0.828E-06
    +                                                                          +
48  *                                                                          +   0.385E-06
    +                                                                          +
49  *                                                                          +   0.259E-06
    +.........+.........+.........+.........+.........+.........+.........+.........+.........+.........+  TRUE VALUE
```

Figure 6-32 (Continued)

FM MODULATED SINE WAVE FM=2 FC=25 B = 1/2

M A G N I T U D E

0.0 0.1 0.2 0.3 0.4 0.5 0.6 0.7 0.8 0.9 1.

	TRUE VALUE
0	0.699E-06
1	0.102E-05
2	0.134E-05
3	0.134E-05
4	0.101E-05
5	0.148E-05
6	0.357E-06
7	0.677E-06
8	0.108E-05
9	0.108E-05
10	0.969E-06
11	0.897E-06
12	.0.111E-05
13	0.149E-05
14	0.702E-06
15	0.310E-05
16	0.107E-05
17	0.786E-04
18	0.295E-05

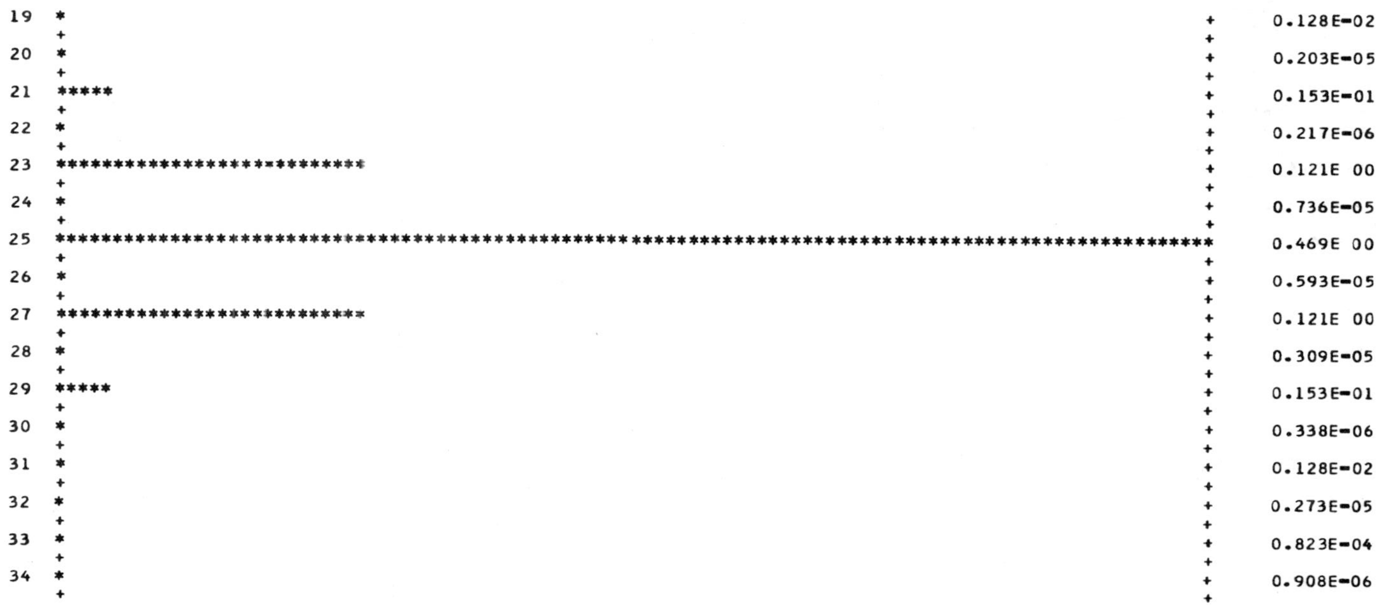

Figure 6-33. Narrow-band FM (Communication Experiment).

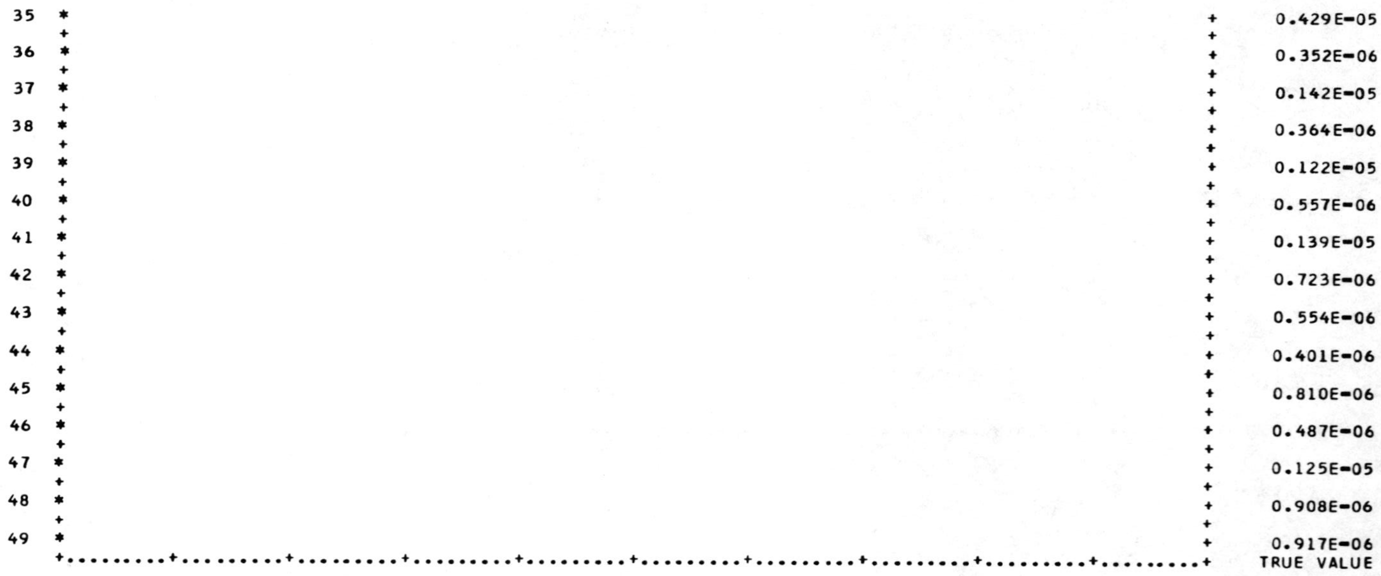

Figure 6-33 (Continued)

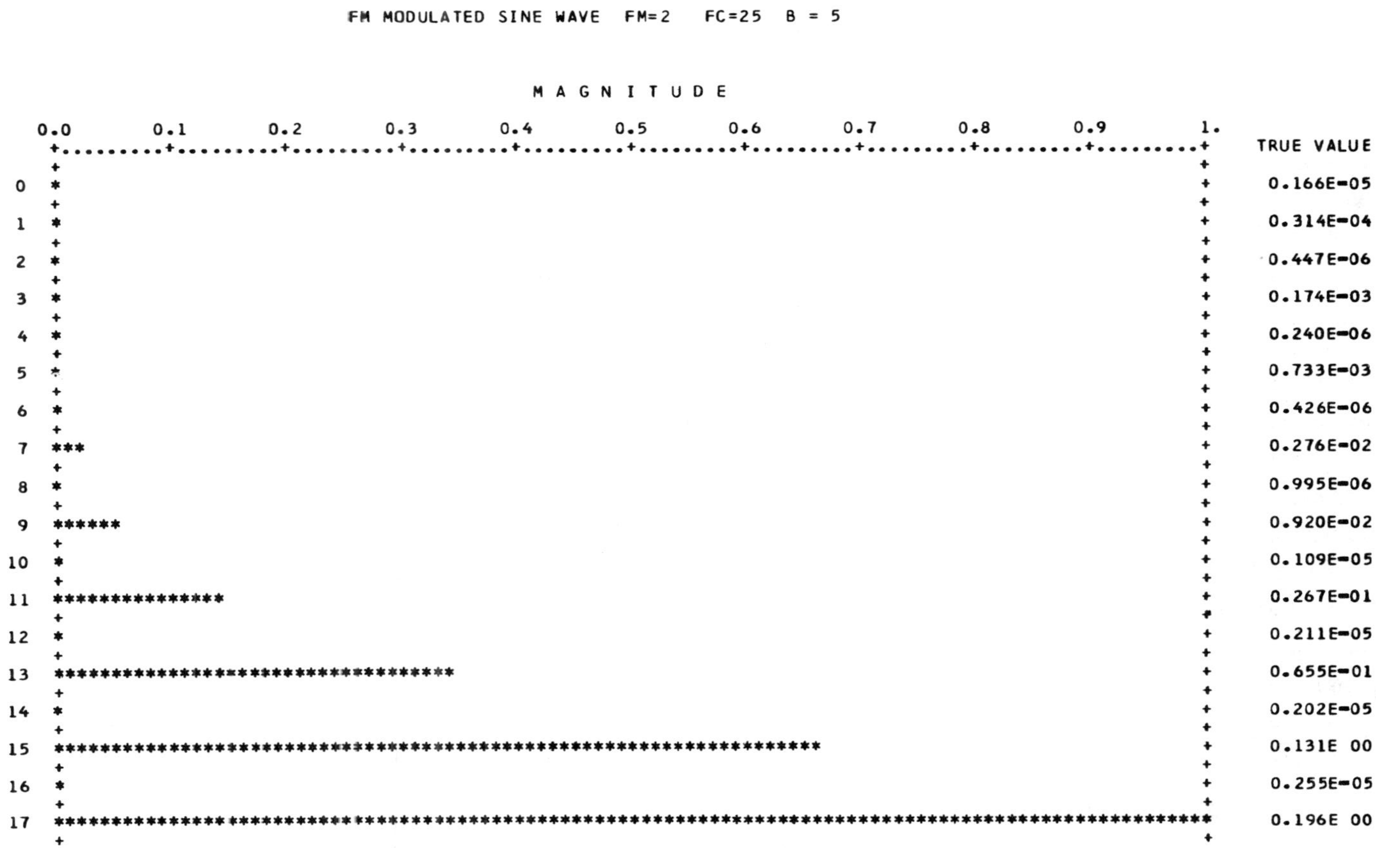

Figure 6-34. Wide-band FM (Communication Experiment).

18 0.387E-05
19 0.182E 00
20 0.178E-05
21 0.233E-01
22 0.241E-05
23 0.164E 00
24 0.167E-05
25 0.888E-01
26 0.269E-05
27 0.164E 00
28 0.460E-05
29 0.233E-01
30 0.344E-05
31 0.182E 00
32 0.362E-05
33 0.196E 00
34 0.432E-05

```
35  ********************************************************************                                +     0.131E 00
    +                                                                                                   +
36  *                                                                                                   +     0.346E-05
    +                                                                                                   +
37  ************************************                                                                +     0.655E-01
    +                                                                                                   +
38  *                                                                                                   +     0.165E-05
    +                                                                                                   +
39  ***************                                                                                     +     0.267E-01
    +                                                                                                   +
40  *                                                                                                   +     0.207E-05
    +                                                                                                   +
41  ******                                                                                              +     0.920E-02
    +                                                                                                   +
42  *                                                                                                   +     0.268E-05
    +                                                                                                   +
43  ***                                                                                                 +     0.276E-02
    +                                                                                                   +
44  *                                                                                                   +     0.186E-05
    +                                                                                                   +
45  *                                                                                                   +     0.737E-03
    +                                                                                                   +
46  *                                                                                                   +     0.627E-06
    +                                                                                                   +
47  *                                                                                                   +     0.177E-03
    +                                                                                                   +
48  *                                                                                                   +     0.367E-06
    +                                                                                                   +
49  *                                                                                                   +     0.480E-04
    +.........+.........+.........+.........+.........+.........+.........+.........+.........+.........+    TRUE VALUE
```

Figure 6-34 (Continued)

F. Status Dump

The following example will assist the user in interpreting the contents of a STATUS dump. The problem considered is contrived, and it is designed to induce a recognized SPECTRUM IV error. The problem is as follows:

1. A FREQ-AVG program is initiated. The program is to average 10 data records consisting of 16 data points each. The sample rate associated with each record is 10.1 Hz.
2. For data set 1, nine intermediate operations are to be performed. They are:
   READ IN
   SWITCH
   SWITCH
   LIBRARY
   FFT
   SWITCH
   SWITCH
   SYSTEM
   SWITCH
3. The eighth operation attempts to place data into the array reserved for ensemble averaging. This operation will be recognized as a SPECTRUM IV error. The resulting error declaration will initiate a STATUS dump since the program has been "armed" with a STATUS call initially.

The card control sequence associated with this example can be found in Figure 6-35; the result of a STATUS dump can be found in Figure 6-36. The material herein is interpreted as follows:

1. Supervisor information

   Array A was empty.

   Arrays B and C held 16 data points. Both arrays were in the FREQ domain.

2. Control parameters[a]

   7—10 data sets were to be averaged in the FREQ-AVG routine.

   8—each data set was to contain 16 data points.

   9—9 intermediate operations are to be performed on data set 1.

   10—accumulator for ensemble average is A=1.

   11—first data set would be entered from array C=3.

   12—8 intermediate operations have been performed at time of termination.

---

[a]For a listing of control parameters, see Appendix D.

```
CARD      COLUMN                                                                        8Ø
          123456789Ø12       .         .         .         .         .         .         .
------------------------------------------------------------------------------------------
1         STATUS
2         FREQ-AVG
3            1Ø   16      1Ø.1
4          9  C
5         READ IN       C           FREQ                   E        16       1Ø.
6                          E      FREQ
7                    1.ØØØE-23 1.ØØØE-23 1.ØØØE-23 1.ØØØE-23 1.ØØØE-23 1.ØØØE-23
8                    1.ØØØE-23 1.ØØØE-23 1.ØØØE-23 1.ØØØE-23 1.ØØØE-23 1.ØØØE-23
9                    1.ØØØE-23 1.ØØØE-23 1.ØØØE-23 1.ØØØE-23 1.ØØØE-23 1.ØØØE-23
1Ø                   1.ØØØE-23 1.ØØØE-23 1.ØØØE-23 1.ØØØE-23 1.ØØØE-23 1.ØØØE-23
11                   1.ØØØE-23 1.ØØØE-23 1.ØØØE-23 1.ØØØE-23 1.ØØØE-23 1.ØØØE-23
12                   1.ØØØE-23 1.ØØØE-23
13        EEEEEEEE
14        SWITCH        A    C
15        SWITCH        A    B
16        LIBRARY       A           TIME                            16       1Ø.
17        PULSE                                       2  1.Ø  Ø.Ø      .25Ø
18        FFT
19        SWITCH        A    B
2Ø        SWITCH        A    C
21        SYSTEM        B    C
22        TERM
                   .         .         .         .         .         .         .         .
```

Figure 6-35. Card Control Sequence for Debugging Example.

```
SUPERVISOR AND CONTROL STATUS READOUT FUNCTIONAL TASK

    ARRAY               A                         B                          C          ARRAY

NUMBER OF POINTS        0                        16                         16          NUMBER OF POINTS

DOMAIN               NONE                      FREQ                       FREQ          DOMAIN

SAMPLE FREQUENCY      0.0                      10.0                       10.0          SAMPLE FREQUENCY


CONTROL PARAMETER       1        2        3        4        5        6        7        8        9       10

STATUS                  1        0        0        0        0        0       10       16        9        1

CONTROL PARAMETER      11       12       13       14       15       16       17       18       19       20

STATUS                  3        8        0        0        0        0        0        0        0        1

                  THESE ARE THE PRESENT CONTENTS OF ALL WORKING ARRAYS FOR   16 POINTS

      ARRAY A                   ARRAY B                   ARRAY C              TEMPORARY ARRAY
  REAL       COMPLEX       REAL        COMPLEX        REAL       COMPLEX        REAL       COMPLEX     POINT

  0.0        0.0        0.250E 00   0.0          0.100E-22  0.100E-22     0.100E-22  0.100E-22       1
  0.0        0.0        0.222E 00  -0.442E-01    0.100E-22  0.100E-22     0.100E-22  0.100E-22       2
  0.0        0.0        0.151E 00  -0.625E-01    0.100E-22  0.100E-22     0.100E-22  0.100E-22       3
  0.0        0.0        0.661E-01  -0.442E-01    0.100E-22  0.100E-22     0.100E-22  0.100E-22       4
  0.0        0.0        0.0         0.0          0.100E-22  0.100E-22     0.100E-22  0.100E-22       5
  0.0        0.0       -0.295E-01   0.442E-01    0.100E-22  0.100E-22     0.100E-22  0.100E-22       6
  0.0        0.0       -0.259E-01   0.625E-01    0.100E-22  0.100E-22     0.100E-22  0.100E-22       7
  0.0        0.0       -0.879E-02   0.442E-01    0.100E-22  0.100E-22     0.100E-22  0.100E-22       8
  0.0        0.0        0.0         0.0          0.100E-22  0.100E-22     0.100E-22  0.100E-22       9
  0.0        0.0       -0.879E-02  -0.442E-01    0.100E-22  0.100E-22     0.100E-22  0.100E-22      10
  0.0        0.0       -0.259E-01  -0.625E-01    0.100E-22  0.100E-22     0.100E-22  0.100E-22      11
  0.0        0.0       -0.295E-01  -0.442E-01    0.100E-22  0.100E-22     0.100E-22  0.100E-22      12
  0.0        0.0        0.0         0.0          0.100E-22  0.100E-22     0.100E-22  0.100E-22      13
  0.0        0.0        0.661E-01   0.442E-01    0.100E-22  0.100E-22     0.100E-22  0.100E-22      14
  0.0        0.0        0.151E 00   0.625E-01    0.100E-22  0.100E-22     0.100E-22  0.100E-22      15
  0.0        0.0        0.222E 00   0.442E-01    0.100E-22  0.100E-22     0.100E-22  0.100E-22      16

********* ABNORMAL TERMINATION HAS HAPPENED **********
```

Figure 6-36. Status Dump (Debugging Example).

13—0 data sets were averaged at time of termination.

15—no disk activity.

19—no printing was suppressed by FREQ-AVG options.

G. Cosmetic Operations

SPECTRUM IV contains several cosmetic routines that will assist the user in presenting data in an interpretable format. The following example problem is presented to exhibit only the cosmetic capabilities of SPECTRUM IV. The problem can be briefly stated as follows:

1. Create a 5-Hz sine wave.
2. Scale the results by 12.0.
3. Plot the scaled sine wave.
4. Normalize the sine wave.
5. Plot the normalized sine wave.
6. Print the normalized sine wave in tabular form.
7. Punch the normalized sine wave on data cards.
8. Perform an FFT of the normalized sine wave.
9. Plot the magnitude spectra.
10. Print the complex spectra in tabular form.
11. Punch the complex spectra on data cards.
12. Remove trivial spectral components through a FUZZ OUT operation.
13. Plot the results.

The card control sequence of this experiment can be found in Figure 6-37. Note the many required parameters in the card sequence. Refer to the section associated with each unique operation for a detailed discussion of their meaning. Figures 6-38 through 6-44 document the experiment and supply requested graphic and tabular data displays.

```
CARD      COLUMN                                                                           8Ø
          123456789Ø12      .         .         .         .         .         .         .
-------------------------------------------------------------------------------------------
1         LIBRARY       A                                                 5Ø        5Ø.
2         THIS IS A SINE WAVE                               1  1.Ø        5.Ø
3         SCALE         A
4         MULT        .12ØE 2
5         PLOTTER       A                                                 5Ø
6         TIME                1   5Ø    THIS IS A SINE WAVE SCALED BY 12
7         NORMAL        A
8         PLOTTER       A                                                 5Ø
9         TIME                1   5Ø    THIS IS A NORMALIZED SINE WAVE
1Ø        PRINT         A          TIME                      F            5Ø
11                            F    TIME
12        PUNCH         A          TIME                      E            5Ø
13                            E    TIME
14        FFT
15        PLOTTER       A                                                 25
16        FREQ   MAG          1   25    SPECTRA OF SINE WAVE + LEAKAGE
17        PRINT         A          FREQ                      E            5Ø
18                            E    FREQ
19        PUNCH         A          FREQ                      F            5Ø
2Ø                            F    FREQ
21        FUZZ OUT      A
22                      1.ØE-2
23        PLOTTER       A                                                 25
24        FREQ   MAG          1   25    REMOVAL OF LEAKAGE
25        TERM
                    .         .         .         .         .         .
```

Figure 6-37. Card Control Sequence for Cosmetic Example.

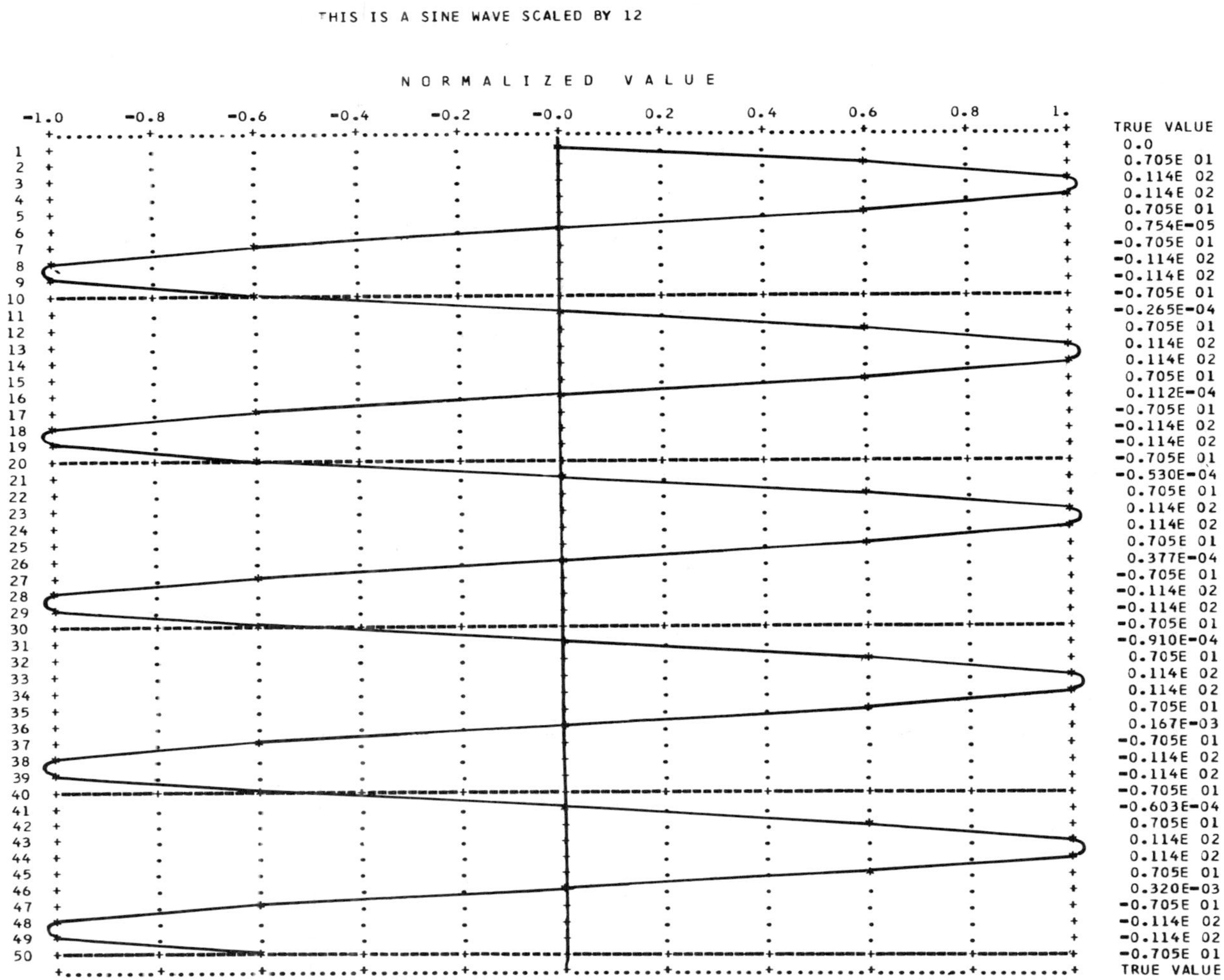

Figure 6-38. Scaled Sine Wave (Cosmetic Example).

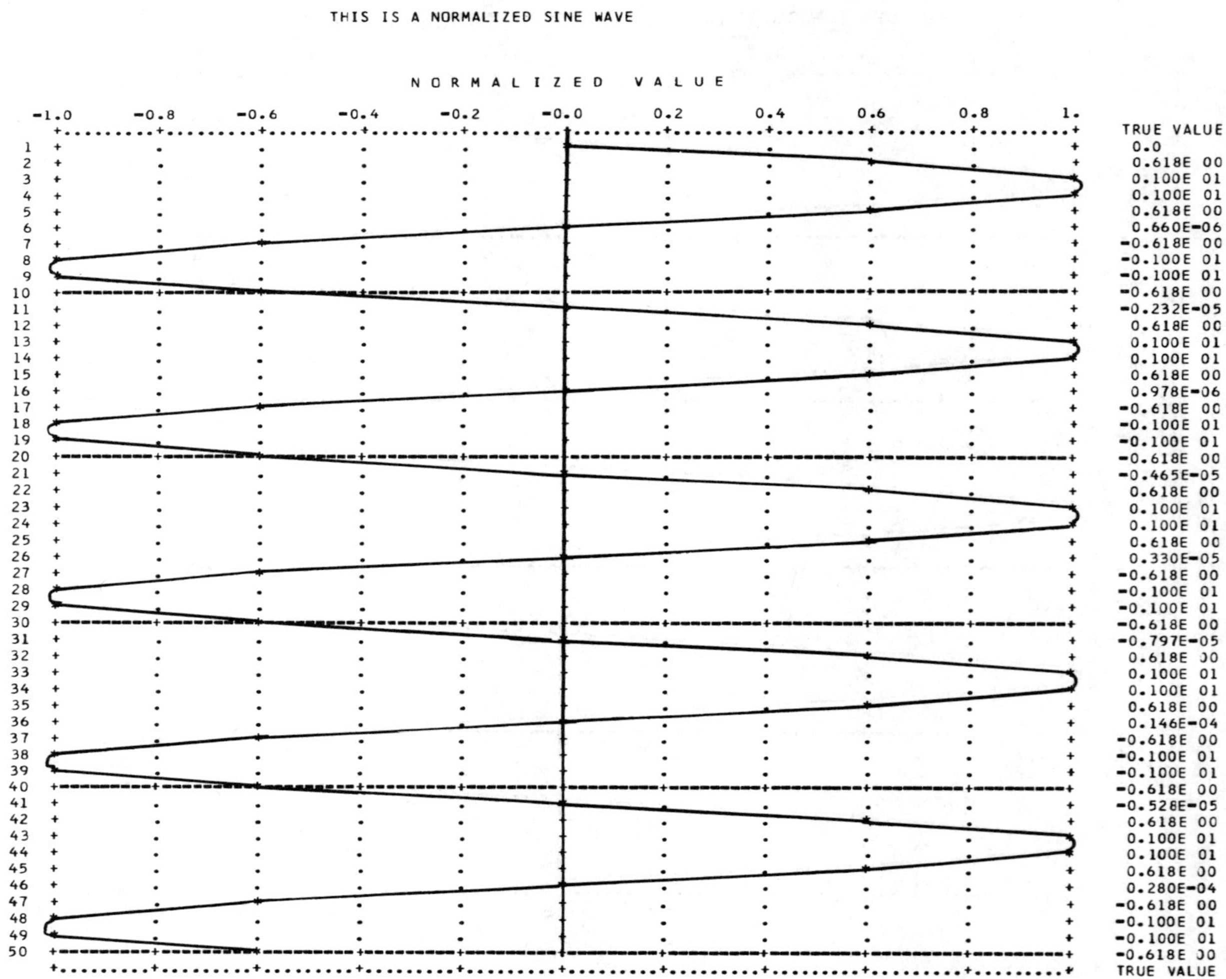

Figure 6-39. Normalized Sine Wave (Cosmetic Example).

LINE PRINTER FUNCTIONAL TASK

OUTPUT FROM ARRAY A

INFORMATION IS IN THE TIME DOMAIN

NUMBER OF SAMPLE POINTS IS 50

SAMPLING FREQUENCY OF THE DATA WAS 50.0 HZ

TIME INTERVAL BETWEEN SAMPLE POINTS IS 0.02000 SECONDS

SAMPLE POINT	REAL VALUE	COMPLEX VALUE
1	0.0	
2	0.618	
3	1.000	
4	1.000	
5	0.618	
6	0.000	
7	-0.618	
8	-1.000	
9	-1.000	
10	-0.618	
11	-0.000	
12	0.618	
13	1.000	
14	1.000	
15	0.618	
16	0.000	
17	-0.618	
18	-1.000	
19	-1.000	
20	-0.618	
21	-0.000	
22	0.618	
23	1.000	
24	1.000	
25	0.618	
26	0.000	
27	-0.618	
28	-1.000	
29	-1.000	
30	-0.618	
31	-0.000	
32	0.618	
33	1.000	
34	1.000	
35	0.618	
36	0.000	
37	-0.618	
38	-1.000	
39	-1.000	
40	-0.618	
41	-0.000	
42	0.618	
43	1.000	
44	1.000	
45	0.618	
46	0.000	
47	-0.618	
48	-1.000	
49	-1.000	
50	-0.618	

Figure 6-40. Tabular Listing of Test Time Series (Cosmetic Example).

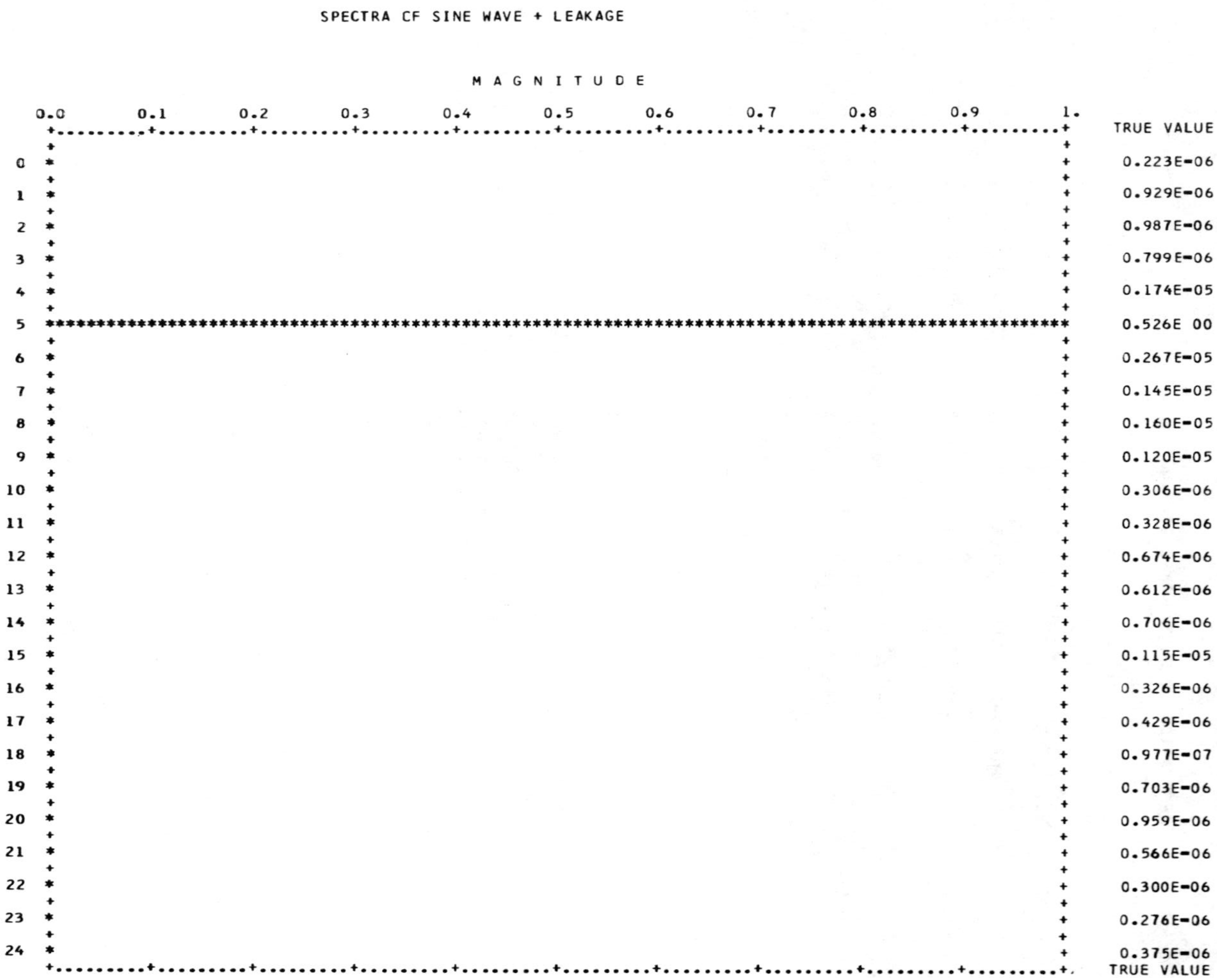

Figure 6-41. Spectra of Test Signal (Cosmetic Example).

```
LINE PRINTER FUNCTIONAL TASK

OUTPUT FROM ARRAY A

INFORMATION IN THE FREQUNCY DOMAIN

NUMBER OF FOURIER COEFFICIENTS   50

SAMPLING FREQUENCY OF THE DATA WAS       50.0 HZ

HIGHEST FREQUENCY COMPONENT OF DATA TO PREVENT ALIASING IS  0.2500E 02

FREQUENCY RESOLUTION OF THE SPECTRAL OUTPUT IS        1.0 HZ
```

HARMONIC	REAL VALUE	COMPLEX VALUE	THESE ARE THE NEGATIVE HARMONICS		
0	0.223E-06	0.0			
1	0.776E-06	-0.510E-06	-24	0.261E-06	-0.270E-06
2	0.414E-06	-0.896E-06	-23	0.264E-06	-0.815E-07
3	0.523E-08	-0.799E-06	-22	-0.254E-06	-0.160E-06
4	-0.497E-06	-0.166E-05	-21	0.130E-06	0.550E-06
5	-0.443E-05	0.526E 00	-20	0.959E-06	0.320E-07
6	-0.327E-06	0.251E-05	-19	0.254E-06	-0.656E-06
7	-0.332E-06	0.142E-05	-18	0.493E-07	-0.844E-07
8	0.508E-06	0.152E-05	-17	0.409E-06	-0.129E-06
9	0.113E-05	0.387E-06	-16	0.279E-06	-0.168E-06
10	0.298E-06	0.699E-07	-15	0.745E-06	-0.191E-07
11	-0.413E-09	-0.328E-06	-14	0.164E-06	-0.686E-06
12	-0.540E-06	0.403E-06	-13	-0.725E-07	-0.608E-06
13	-0.725E-07	0.608E-06	-12	-0.540E-06	-0.403E-06
14	0.164E-06	0.686E-06	-11	-0.413E-09	0.328E-06
15	0.715E-06	0.896E-06	-10	0.298E-06	-0.699E-07
16	0.279E-06	0.168E-06	-9	0.113E-05	-0.387E-06
17	0.409E-06	0.129E-06	-8	0.508E-06	-0.152E-05
18	0.493E-07	0.844E-07	-7	-0.332E-06	-0.142E-05
19	0.254E-06	0.656E-06	-6	-0.927E-06	-0.251E-05
20	0.959E-06	-0.320E-07	-5	-0.443E-05	-0.526E 00
21	0.130E-06	-0.550E-06	-4	-0.497E-06	0.166E-05
22	-0.254E-06	0.160E-06	-3	0.523E-08	0.799E-06
23	0.264E-06	0.815E-07	-2	0.414E-06	0.896E-06
24	0.261E-06	0.270E-06	-1	0.776E-06	0.510E-06

Figure 6-42. Tabular Listing of Complex Spectra (Cosmetic Example).

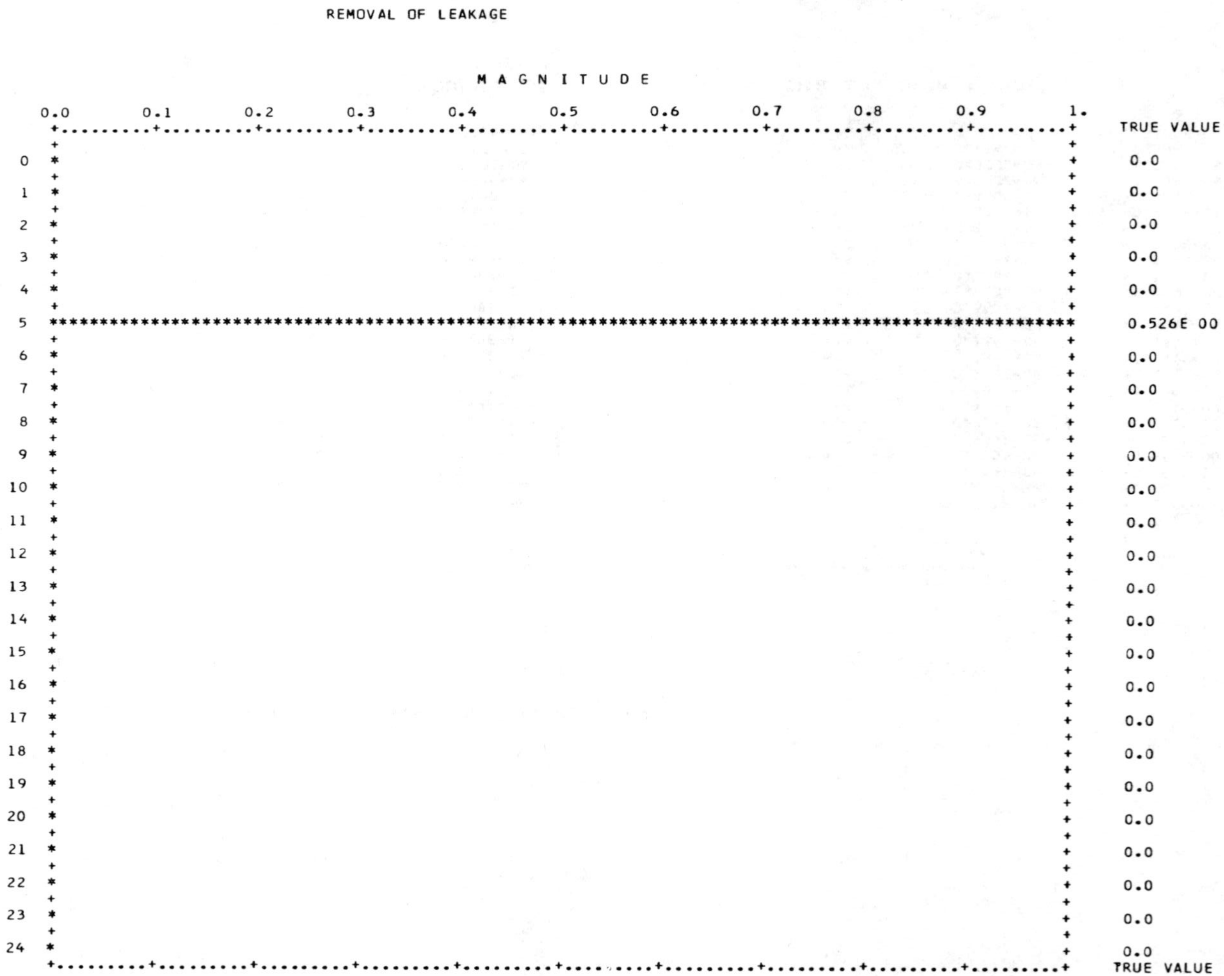

Figure 6-43. Defuzzed Spectra (Cosmetic Example).

```
CARD        COLUMN                                                                      8Ø
            123456789Ø12       .         .         .         .         .         .         .
------------------------------------------------------------------------------------------
1           IDENTIFICATION     F         FREQ
2               1          Ø.ØØØ      Ø.ØØØ      Ø.ØØØ     -Ø.ØØØ      Ø.Ø        -Ø.ØØØ
3               2          Ø.ØØØ     -Ø.ØØØ     -Ø.ØØØ     -Ø.ØØØ     -Ø.ØØØ       Ø.526
4               3         -Ø.ØØØ      Ø.ØØØ     -Ø.ØØØ      Ø.ØØØ      Ø.ØØØ       Ø.ØØØ

                           (CONTINUE)

16              15         Ø.ØØØ     -Ø.ØØØ     -Ø.ØØØ     -Ø.ØØØ     -Ø.ØØØ      -Ø.ØØØ
17              16        -Ø.ØØØ     -Ø.526     -Ø.ØØØ      Ø.ØØØ      Ø.ØØØ       Ø.ØØØ
18              17         Ø.ØØØ      Ø.ØØØ      Ø.ØØØ      Ø.ØØØ
19          FFFFFFFFFFFFFFFFFFFFFFFFFFFFFFFFFFFFFFFFFFFFFFFFFFFFFFFFFFFFFFFFFFFFFFFFFFFFFFFF
```

Figure 6-44. Punch Card Data (Cosmetic Example).

Appendixes

Appendix A
Summary of Programs

Define S to be a SPECTRUM IV operation such that it transforms an input data record, say, x and/or y into an output data record z. That is,

$$S(x,y) \rightarrow z$$

Data records x, y, and z are to be stored in working arrays A, B, or C. Then

N = None　F = Frequency　T = Time　WR = Wrap-Around
NA = Not applicable　P = Parameters　TR = Temporary register

Operation S(x, y) Mnemonic	*Domain of Input*	*Domain of Output*	*Admissible Location of Input Record*	*Admissible Location of Output Record*	*Memory-Protected Data Record*	*Option*
AUTO-C	T,F	T	A,B,C	A,B,C	A	WR
CLEAR-AL	NA	NA	A,B,C	A,B,C	NA	N
COHERNCE	F	F	A,B,C	TR	A	N
CONVOLVE	T,F	T	B,C	A	N	WR
CORRECT	T,F	T,F	A,B,C	A,B,C	NA	N
CROSS-C	T,F	T,F	B,C	A	A	WR
DB-SCALE	T,F	T,F	A,B,C	A,B,C	NA	N
D-FILTER	T,F	F,T	A,B,C	A,B,C	A,B,C	several
DIRECTRY	NA	NA	NA	NA	NA	N
DISCRETE	P	T,F	A,B,C	B,C,A	A,B,C	several
DISK IN	NA	T,F	NA	A,B,C,TR	NA	N
DISK OUT	T,F	NA	A,B,C	NA	NA	N
EDITOR	T	NA	A,B,C	NA	NA	N
ERR-LIST	NA	NA	NA	NA	NA	N
FFT	T	F	A	A	A	N
FREQ-AVG	F	F	B,C	A	A	N
FUZZ OUT	T,F	T,F	A,B,C	A,B,C	NA	N
HANNING	T,F	T,F	A,B,C	A,B,C	N	N
IFFT	F	T	A	A	A	N
INITIAL	NA	NA	NA	NA	NA	N
LIBRARY	T	T	NA	A,B,C	N	several
MATCH	T,F	F	A,B,C	A,B,C	A,B,C	N
NORMAL	T,F	T,F	A,B,C	A,B,C	NA	N
PLOTTER	T,F	T,F	A,B,C	A,B,C	NA	several
PSD	T,F	F	A,B,C	A	A	N
PUNCH	T,F	T,F	A,B,C	A,B,C	NA	N
READ IN	T,F	T,F	A,B,C	A,B,C	NA	N
SCALE	T,F	A,B,C	A,B,C	A,B,C	NA	N
STATUS	NA	NA	NA	NA	NA	N
SWITCH	T,F	T,F	A,B,C	B,C,A	N	N

Operation S(x, y) Mnemonic	*Domain of Input*	*Domain of Output*	*Admissible Location of Input Record*	*Admissible Location of Output Record*	*Memory-Protected Data Record*	*Option*
SYSTEM	F	F	C,B	A	A	N
TRANSFER	P	F	NA	A,B,C	A,B,C	N
USER-LIB	NA	T,F	A,B,C	A,B,C	NA	several
WIENER	F	F	B,C	A	A	N
ZERO-OUT	T,F	T,F	A,B,C	A,B,C	NA	N

Appendix B
Table of z Transforms

Table B-1
Properties of the z Transform

Property	*Discrete Sequence*	*z-Transform*
1. Linearity	$af(k) + bg(k)$	$aF(z) + bG(z)$
2. Right-Shifting	$f(k - m)$	$z^{-m}F(z)$
3. Convolution	$\sum_{i=0}^{k} f_1(k - i)f_2(i)$	$F_1(z)F_2(z)$
4. Left-Shifting	$f(k + m)$	$z^mF(z) - \sum_{i=0}^{m-1} f(i)z^{m-i}$
5. Summation	$\sum_{i=0}^{k} f(i)$	$\frac{z}{z - 1}F(z)$
6. Multiplication by a^k	$a^kf(k)$	$F(a^{-1}z)$
7. Initial-Value Theorem	$f(0) = \lim_{\lvert z\rvert \to \infty} F(z)$	
8. Final-Value Theorem	$f(\infty) = \lim_{z \to 1} (z - 1)F(z)$ If $(z - 1)F(z)$ is analytic for $\lvert z\rvert \geq 1$.	
9. Periodic Sequences	$f(k) = f(k + N)$	$F(z) = \frac{z^N}{z^N - 1}F_1(z)$
10. Differentiating	$kf(k)$	$-z\frac{dF(z)}{dz}$

Table B-2
Sampled z-Transform Pairs

	$f(t)$ $t \geq 0$	$f(kT)$ $k \geq 0$	$F(z)$ $F(z) = \sum_{k=0}^{\infty} f(kT)z^{-k}$	*Radius of Convergence* $\|z\| > R$
1	1	1	$\dfrac{z}{z-1}$	1
2	t	kT	$\dfrac{Tz}{(z-1)^2}$	1
3	t^2	$(kT)^2$	$\dfrac{T^2z(z+1)}{(z-1)^3}$	1
4	t^3	$(kT)^3$	$\dfrac{T^3z(z^2+4z+1)}{(z-1)^4}$	1
5	e^{-at}	e^{-akT}	$\dfrac{z}{z-e^{-aT}}$	e^{-aT}
6	te^{-at}	kTe^{-akT}	$\dfrac{zTe^{-aT}}{(z-e^{-aT})^2}$	e^{-aT}
7	t^2e^{-at}	$(kT)^2e^{-akT}$	$\dfrac{T^2e^{-aT}z(z+e^{-aT})}{(z-e^{-aT})^3}$	e^{-aT}
8	$\sin \omega t$	$\sin k\omega T$	$\dfrac{z \sin \omega T}{z^2 - 2z \cos \omega T + 1}$	1
9	$\cos \omega t$	$\cos k\omega T$	$\dfrac{z(z - \cos \omega T)}{z^2 - 2z \cos \omega T + 1}$	1

Table B-3
z Transform Pairs

	Discrete-Time Function $f(k)$ for $k = 0, 1, 2, \ldots$	*z-Transform* $F(z) = \sum_{k=0}^{\infty} f(k)z^{-k}$ for $\lvert z\rvert > R$
1.	$\delta(k)$	1
2.	$\delta(k - m)$	z^{-m}
3.	1	$\frac{z}{z - 1}$
4.	k	$\frac{z}{(z - 1)^2}$
5.	k^2	$\frac{z(z + 1)}{(z - 1)^3}$
6.	k^3	$\frac{z(z^2 + 4z + 1)}{(z - 1)^4}$
7.	k^4	$\frac{z(z^3 + 11z^2 + 11z + 1)}{(z - 1)^5}$
8.	k^5	$\frac{z(z^4 + 26z^3 + 66z^2 + 26z + 1)}{(z - 1)^6}$
9.	a^k	$\frac{z}{z - a}$
10.	ka^k	$\frac{az}{(z - a)^2}$
11.	k^2a^k	$\frac{az(z + a)}{(z - a)^3}$
12.	k^3a^k	$\frac{az(z^2 + 4az + a^2)}{(z - a)^4}$
13.	k^4a^k	$\frac{az(z^3 + 11az^2 + 11a^2z + a^3)}{(z - a)^5}$
14.	k^5a^k	$\frac{az(z^4 + 26az^3 + 66a^2z^2 + 26a^3z + a^4)}{(z - a)^6}$
15.	$(k + 1)a^k$	$\frac{z^2}{(z - a)^2}$
16.	$\frac{(k + 1)(k + 2)a^k}{2!}$	$\frac{z^3}{(z - a)^3}$
17.	$\frac{(k + 1)(k + 2((k + 3)a^k}{3!}$	$\frac{z^4}{(z - a)^4}$
18.	$\frac{(k + 1)(k + 2)\ldots(k + m)a^k}{m!}$	$\frac{z^{m+1}}{(z - a)^{m+1}}$

Table B-3 (Continued)
z Transform Pairs

	Discrete-Time Function $f(k)$ for $k = 0, 1, 2, \ldots$	*z-Transform* $F(z) = \sum_{k=0}^{\infty} f(k)z^{-k}$ for $\|z\| > R$
19.	$\sin k\omega T$	$\dfrac{z \sin \omega T}{z^2 - 2z \cos \omega T + 1}$
20.	$\cos k\omega T$	$\dfrac{z(z - \cos \omega T)}{z^2 - 2z \cos \omega T + 1}$
21.	$a^k \sin k\omega T$	$\dfrac{az \sin \omega T}{z^2 - 2az \cos \omega T + a^2}$
22.	$a^k \cos k\omega T$	$\dfrac{z(z - a \cos \omega T)}{z^2 - 2az \cos \omega T + a^2}$
23.	$\sin (k\omega T + \theta)$	$\dfrac{z[z \sin \theta + \sin(\omega T - \theta)]}{z^2 - 2z \cos \omega T + 1}$
24.	$\cos (k\omega T + \theta)$	$\dfrac{z[z \cos \theta - \cos(\omega T - \theta)]}{z^2 - 2z \cos \omega T + 1}$
25.	$ka^k \sin k\omega T$	$\dfrac{z(z - a)(z + a)a \sin \omega T}{[z^2 - 2az \cos \omega T + a^2)^2}$
26.	$ka^k \cos k\omega T$	$\dfrac{az[z^2 \cos \omega T - 2az + a^2 \cos \omega T]}{[z^2 - 2az \cos \omega T + a^2]^2}$
27.	$\sinh k\omega T$	$\dfrac{z \sinh \omega T}{z^2 - 2z \cosh \omega T + 1}$
28.	$\cosh k\omega T$	$\dfrac{z(z - \cosh \omega T)}{z^2 - 2z \cosh \omega T + 1}$
29.	$\dfrac{a^k}{k!}$	$e^{a/z}$
30.	$\dfrac{(\ln a)^k}{k!}$	$a^{1/z}$
31.	$\dfrac{n!}{(n - k)!k!} a^k b^{n-k}$	$\dfrac{(bz + a)^n}{z^n}$
32.	$\dfrac{1}{k}$ (for $k = 1, 2, 3, \ldots$)	$\ln\left(\dfrac{z}{z - 1}\right)$
33.	$\dfrac{k(k - 1)}{2!}$	$\dfrac{z}{(z - 1)^3}$
34.	$\dfrac{k(k - 1)(k - 2)}{3!}$	$\dfrac{z}{(z - 1)^4}$
35.	$\dfrac{k(k - 1)(k - 2) \ldots (k - m + 1)}{m!}$	$\dfrac{z}{(z - 1)^m}$

Appendix C
Error List

```
                    THIS IS A LIST OF THE ERROR DIAGNOSTICS OF SPECTRUM IV

ERROR  1

    CAN NOT IDENTIFY THE ARRAY SPECIFIED BY THE ACTION CARD

         RECOMMENDED COURSE OF ACTION - PUT THE LETTER A,B,OR C ON THE ACTION CARD IN THE PROPER FIELD
                                        TO SPECIFY WHICH ARRAY THE DESIRED OPERATION IS TO WORK WITH

ERROR  2

    CAN NOT IDENTIFY THE DOMAIN OF THE ARRAY SPECIFIED ON USER ACTION CARD

         RECOMMENDED COURSE OF ACTION - TYPE THE WORD TIME OR FREQ TO DENOTE THE PROPER DOMAIN OF THE INPUT

ERROR  3

    USER IS ATTEMPTING TO CHANGE THE CONTENTS OF THE ARRAY WHICH IS HOLDING AN ENSEMBLE AVERAGE OF SIGNALS

         RECOMMENDED COURSE OF ACTION - (1) DESIGNATE ANOTHER ARRAY FOR THIS ROUTINE

                                        (2) ANALYZE THE INTERMEDIATE  OPERATIONS INVOLVED WITH THIS ENSEMBLE AVERAGE

ERROR  4

    ARRAY SPECIFIED ON ACTION CARD FOR THIS ROUTINE CONTAINS NOTHING BUT ZEROES IN IT

         RECOMMENDED CCURSE OF ACTION - CHECK THE ARRAY SPECIFIED ON THE ACTION CARD

ERROR  5

    ERROR IN THE USE OF SECONDARY INPUT CARD CORRECTION PARAMETERS NM,NSTART,NSTOP FOR AN I/O OPERATION

         RECOMMENDED COURSE OF ACTION - (1) MAKE SURE RELATION NM = NSTOP-NSTART+1 IS SATISFIED

                                        (2) ABOVE PARAMETERS ARE GREATER THAN 0 AND LESS THAN 1025
```

```
ERROR  6

     NUMBER OF POINTS SPECIFIED FOR AN I/O OPERATION IS IN ERROR ON THE ACTION CARD FOR THIS ROUTINE

          RECOMMENDED COURSE OF ACTION - (1) NUMBER OF POINTS DOES NOT EXCEED 1024

                                         (2) NUMBER OF POINTS NOT LESS THAN 1

ERROR  7

     ARRAY SPECIFIED ON ACTION CARD CONTAINS DATA THAT IS IN MEMORY SOFTWARE PROTECTION

          RECOMMENDED COURSE OF ACTION - (1) USE OPTIONAL PARAMETERS IN SECONDARY INPUT TO OVERIDE THE PROTECTION

                                         (2) CLEAR THE ARRAY TC ZERO

                                         (3) OUTPUT THE ARRAY CONTENTS VIA PRINTER,PLOTTER,DISK,PUNCH

ERROR  8

     NO FORMAT SPECIFIED ON ACTION CARD OR SECONDARY INPUT CARD FOR I/O OPERATION

          RECOMMENDED COURSE OF ACTION - (1) CHECK ACTION CARD FOR THE E OR F FORMAT DESIGNATOR

                                         (2) MAKE SURE FORMAT DESIGNATOR IS ON AT LEAST ONE OF THE CARDS

ERROR  9

     END OF FILE CARD NOT IN PROPER LOCATION BEHIND THE LIST CARDS

          RECOMMENDED COURSE OF ACTION - (1) MAKE SURE END OF FILE MAKER EXISTS AND IS IN CORRECT FORM

                                         (2) CHECK TO SEE IF THE INPUT DECK HAS PROPER NUMBER OF CARCS

ERROR 10

     ERROR IN SECONDARY INPUT INFORMATION CARC ALPHANUMERIC FIELC

          RECOMMENDED CCURSE OF ACTION - TYPE THE PROPER CHARACTERS TO INDICATE ROUTINE OPTIONS OR INFORMATION
```

```
ERROR 11

     ERROR IN SPECIFICATION OF WHERE INPUT INFORMATION IS TC COME FROM

          RECCMMENDED COURSE CF ACTION - (1) CESIGNATE A CALL TO A USER SUPPLIED SUBROUTINE

                                         (2) PROVIDE PROPER INFORMATION FOR CARD INPUT

                                         (3) DESIGNATE A LIBRARY FUNCTION FROM THE LIBRARY ROUTINE

ERROR 12

     ERROR IN TRANSFER FUNCTICN SECONCARY INPUT INFORMATION

          RECOMMENDED COURSE OF ACTION - (1) SPECIFY FORM OF POLYNOMIAL INPUT  FACTORS OR COEFFICIENTS

                                         (2) SPECIFY CORRECT ORDER OF THE POLYNOMIAL

                                         (3) SPECIFY A NUMERATOR AND DENOMINATOR CORRECTLY


                                         (2) SPECIFY CORRECT ORDER OF THE POLYNOMIAL

                                         (3) SPECIFY A NUMERATOR AND DENOMINATOR CORRECTLY

ERROR 13

     ERROR IN TRANSFER FUNCTION DATA

          RECOMMENDED CCURSE OF ACTION - (1) MAKE SURE ALL COEFFICIENTS OF THE NUMERATOR OR THE DENOMINATOR ARE NOT ZEROES

                                         (2) EACH COMPLEX FACTOR SHOULD HAVE A CORRESPONDING COMPLEX CCNJUGATE

ERROR 14

     PARAMETER MISMATCH ON A DISK I/O OPERATION

          RECOMMENDED COURSE OF ACTION - MATCH SAMPLE FREQUENCY,DOMAIN,AND NUMBER OF POINTS ON ACTION CARD TO ACTUAL DATA
```

```
ERROR 15
      ARRAY PRESENTED TO THE FORWARD FFT ROUTINE HAS FREQUENCY DOMAIN INFORMATION OR ALL ZEROES IN IT
            RECOMMENDED COURSE OF ACTION - CHECK THE STATUS OF ARRAY A BEFORE PROGRAM COMES TO THIS ROUTINE

ERROR 16
      ARRAY PRESENTED TO THE INVERSE FFT ROUTINE CONTAINS TIME DOMAIN INFORMATION OR ALL ZEROES
            RECOMMENDED COURSE OF ACTION - CHECK THE STATUS OF ARRAY A INFORMATION BEFORE PROGRAM COMES TO THIS ROUTINE

ERROR 17
      ERROR IN FREQUNCY SPECIFICATIONS FOR DIGITAL FILTERING IN THE SECONDARY NUMERIC INPUT FIELDS
            RECOMMENDED COURSE OF ACTION - (1) FREQUENCIES MUST BE SPECIFIED IN CORRECT FIELDS
                                           (2) FREQUENCIES MUST NOT BE GREATER THAN THE FOLDING FREQUENCY OF THE SIGNAL
                                           (3) FREQUENCIES MUST BE GREATER THAN .001 HZ
                                           (4) SIGNAL MUST HAVE A NON-ZERO SAMPLING FREQUENCY

ERROR 18
      ERROR IN SECONDARY INPUT INFORMATION FOR DATA SET ENSEMBLE AVERAGING
            RECOMMENDED COURSE OF ACTION - (1) CHECK FOR PROPER NUMBER OF DATA SETS SPECIFIED
                                           (2) CHECK FOR A CONSISTANT NUMBER OF SAMPLE POINTS
                                           (3) CHECK FOR A CONSISTANT SAMPLING FREQUENCY IN ALL DATA SETS AVERAGED

ERROR 19
      ERROR IN SECONDARY INPUT INFORMATION CONCERNING INTERMEADIATE ACTIONS OF A DATA SET
            RECOMMENDED COURSE OF ACTION - (1) GIVE CORRECT NUMBER OF INTERMEDIATE OPERATIONS
                                           (2) DESIGNATE WHICH ARRAY B OR C GIVES THE NEW SIGNAL TO BE AVERAGED
```

```
ERROR 20

      ENSEMBLE AVERAGE RESULTS MUST BE IN ARRAY A WHEN NEW SIGNAL IS TO BE ADDED

            RECOMMENDED COURSE OF ACTION - CHECK INTERMEDIATE ACTIONS TO SEE WHERE ENSEMBLE RESULTS ARE

ERROR 21

      ROUTINE CALLS FOR SIGNALS WHICH HAVE THE SAME SAMPLING FREQUENCY FOR A MEANINGFUL PROBLEM

            RECOMMENDED COURSE CF ACTION - MAKE SAMPLING FREQUENCIES COMPATABLE ON INPUT OF SIGNAL INFCRMATION

ERROR 22

      ROUTINE CALLS FOR SIGNALS TO HAVE THE SAME NUMBER OF SAMPLE PCINTS FOR A CORRECT PROBLEM

            RECOMMENDED CCURSE OF ACTION - MAKE NUMBER OF SAMPLE POINTS COMPATABLE ON INPUT OF SIGNAL INFORMATION

ERROR 23

      ROUTINE CALLS FOR SIGNALS WHICH MUST ALREADY BE IN THE FREQUENCY DOMAIN

            RECOMMENDED COURSE OF ACTION - MAKE SURE ALL ARRAYS INVOLVED WITH THIS ROUTINE ARE IN FREQUENCY DOMAIN

ERROR 24

      INCORRECT SPECIFICATION CF ARRAYS ON ACTION CARD

            RECOMMENDED COURSE OF ACTION - (1) MAKE SURE LETTERS A,B,C ARE IN THE PROPER FIELDS

                                           (2) SAME ARRAY SHOULD NOT BE DESIGNATED TWICE

ERROR 25

      ROUTINE REQUIRES ARRAY A BE FREE OF MEMORY PROTECTION  IN ORDER TO PUT RESULTS THERE

            RECOMMENDED COURSE CF ACTION - (1) CUTPUT ARRAY A VIA PRINT,PUNCH,DISK,PLOTTER

                                           (2) ZERO OUT THE ARRAY
```

```
ERROR 26

     ERROR HAS OCCURRED IN THE FFT ROUTINE

          RECOMMENDED COURSE OF ACTION - (A) MAKE NUMBER OF SAMPLE POINTS SUCH THAT THE FOLLOWING CONDITIONS HOLD

                                         (B) MAXIMUM PRIME FACTOR OF NPOINT IS 23

                                         (C) NUMBER OF FACTORS OF NPOINT IS 11 AT MOST

                                         (D) PRODUCT OF THE SQUARE FREE FACTORS OF NPOINT DOES NOT EXCEED 209

ERROR 27

     ARRAY MUST BE IN THE TIME DOMAIN OR THE FREQUENCY DOMAIN AS INDICATED BY THE ACTION CARD OR SECONDARY INPUT INFORMATION

          RECOMMENDED COURSE OF ACTION - MATCH CARD INFORMATION WITH THE SIGNAL IN STORAGE

ERROR 28

     RECORD SPECIFIED BY USER DOES NOT EXIST ON DISK OR IS LESS THAN 1

          RECOMMENDED COURSE OF ACTION - CORRECT RECORD SPECIFICATION OR CONSULT THE DISK DIRECTORY

ERROR 29

     INTERPOLATION ERROR IN TRANSFER FUNCTION,COHERENCE FUNCTION,WIENER FILTER,OR TRANSFER FUNCTION SYNTHESIS ROUTINE

          RECOMMENDED COURSE OF ACTION - (1) TRY A DIFFERENT SAMPLING FREQUENCY

                                         (2) TRY A DIFFERENT NUMBER OF SAMPLING POINTS ON INPUT

                                         (3) THERE MAY EXIST NON-LINEARITIES IN THE SYSTEM

ERROR 30

     THERE HAS BEEN AN ERROR IN DATA TRANSMISSION WITH THE DISK

          RECOMMENDED COURSE OF ACTION - NOTIFY COMPUTER CENTER STAFF ABOUT THE ERROR

ERROR 31

     MISSING NUMERIC INFORMATION IN THE SECONDARY INPUT CARD

          RECOMMENDED COURSE OF ACTION - CHECK TO SEE THAT ALL NUMERIC PARAMETERS ARE IN THE PROPER FIELDS
```

```
ERROR 32
        ERROR IN THE RECCURSIVE DIGITAL FILTER
                RECOMMENDED COURSE OF ACTION - (1) SPECIFY THE CORRECT ORDER OF THE FILTER
                                               (2) ALL INITIAL CONDITIONS MAY NOT BE ZERO
                                               (3) ALL COEFFICIENTS OF THE FILTER MAY NOT BE ZERO
                                               (4) THE COEFFICIENT CORRESPONDING TO 0 MEMORY OUTPUT DELAY MUST BE ZERO
                                               (5) OUTPUT OF THE FILTER IS GREATER THAN A MAGNITUDE OF  1.0E10
ERROR 33
        ERROR IN TIME DATA EDITOR
                RECOMMENDED COURSE OF ACTION - (1) MAKE SURE THE SPECIFIED ARRAY IS IN THE TIME DOMAIN
                                               (2) USER'S LOWER LIMIT SHOULD NOT BE GREATER THAN HIS UPPER LIMIT
                                               (3) USER LIMITS SHOULD HAVE A DIFFERENCE OF AT LEAST 1.0E-3
ERROR 34
        INVALID OPTION INVOKED
                RECOMMENDED COURSE OF ACTION - (1) CHECK OPTION SPECIFICATION ON CARD
                                               (2) MAKE SURE ARRAYS ARE IN PROPER DOMAINS FOR THIS OPTION
```

Appendix D Control and Monitoring Parameters

0 = inactive; Active otherwise

Primary Control Parameters . . . MSUP	
MSUP(1)	Used as a counter to determine the current entry point in a program
MSUP(2)=1	Indicates no line printing is to be generated
MSUP(3)=1	Indicates a single-line listing is to be generated
MSUP(4) MSUP(5)*	Arrays that are being operated on by the program routine
MSUP(5)*	. . . can also hold the domain of a specific array
MSUP(6)	Intermediate counter for DIGIT, MATCH, AUTO-C . . .
MSUP(7)	Holds number of data sets to be ensemble averaged
MSUP(8)	Number of points in each ensemble-averaged array
MSUP(9)	Number of intermediate operations for a current ensemble-averaging task
MSUP(10)=1,2,3	Indicated array is the ensemble-average accumulator
MSUP(11)=2,3	Array that enters new data into an ensemble average
MSUP(12)	Counter for intermediate operations 1,2,. . . , MSUP(9)
MSUP(13)	Counter for the number of data sets 1,2, . . ., MSUP(7)
MSUP(15)	First record of disk has been read . . . DISK READY
MSUP(17)	Holds the maximum order of the filter then holds intermediate counter
MSUP(18)	Interpolation is occurring or starting
MSUP(19)	No printing control for FREQ-AVG
MSUP(20)	Status memory dump request

Monitoring System

NFLAG(1)	Informs system that another routine is in control	
DSO(3,2)	3 Arrays	A,B,C
	2 DOMAINS	TIME=1, FREQ=2
	VALUES	0=NULL ARRAY 1=PROTECTED ARRAY 2=UNPROTECTED ARRAY
NORIA(3)	Number of points in each array	
SAMPLE(3)	Sampling frequency of each array	
MPRINT	Controls print and page eject	
NERROR	Records current error status	
NFLAG(2)-NFLAG(22) NFLAG(35)-NFLAG(50)	Selects current routine	
NFLAG(23,25,27)	First array of the program	
NFLAG(24,26,28)	Second array of the program	
NFLAG(29),(30)	Format E=29; F=30	
NFLAG(31)	First array is in time domain	
(32)	First array is in frequency domain	
NFLAG(33)	Second array is in time domain	
(34)	Second array is in frequency domain	

Selected References

1. Athans, M., et al. *Systems, Networks, and Computation: Multivariable Methods*. New York: McGraw-Hill, 1974.
2. Bergland, G.D. "A Guided Tour of the Fast Fourier Transform." *Institute of Electrical and Electronic Engineers Spectrum*, vol, 6 (July 1969): pp. 41-52.
3. Brigham, O.E. *The Fast Fourier Transform*. Englewood Cliffs, N.J.: Prentice-Hall, 1974.
4. Burrus, C.S. and T.W. Parks. "Time Domain Design of Recursive Filters." *Institute of Electrical and Electronic Engineers Transactions on Audio Electroacoust*, vol. AU-18 (June 1970): pp. 137-141.
5. Cadzow, J.A. *Discrete-Time Systems*. Englewood Cliffs, N.J.: Prentice-Hall, 1973.
6. Cochran, W.T., et al. "What is the Fast Fourier Transform?" *Institute of Electrical and Electronic Engineers Transactions on Audio Electroacoust*, vol. AU-15 (June 1967): pp. 45-55.
7. Constatinides, A.G. "Spectral Transformations for Digital Filters." *Proceedings of the Institute of Electrical Engineers*, vol. 117 (August 1970): pp. 1585-1590.
8. Cooley, J.W., P.A.W. Lewis, and P.D. Welch. "Historical Notes on the Fast Fourier Transform." *Institute of Electrical and Electronic Engineers Transactions on Audio Electroacoustics*, vol. AU-15 (June 1967): pp. 79-84.
9. Cooley, J.W., P.A.W. Lewis, and P.D. Welch. "The Finite Fourier Transform." *Institute of Electrical and Electronic Engineers Transactions on Audio Electroacoustics*. vol. AU-17 (June 1969): pp. 77-86.
10. Cooley, J.W., and J.W. Tukey. "An Algorithm for the Machine Calculation of Complex Fourier Series." *Mathematics of Computation*, vol. 19, no. 90 (1965) Published by the American Mathematical Society.
11. Forrester, J.W. *World Dynamics*. Cambridge, Mass.: Wright Allen Press, 1971.
12. Gable, R.A. and R.A. Roberts. *Signal and Linear Systems*. New York: John Wiley, 1973.
13. Gold, B. and C.M. Rader. *Digital Processing of Signals*. New York: McGraw-Hill, 1967.
14. Oppenheim, A.V. and R.W. Schafer. *Digital Signal Processing*. Englewood Cliffs, N.J.: Prentice-Hall, 1975.
15. Papoulis, A. *Probability, Random Variables, and Stochastic Processes*. New York: McGraw-Hill, 1965.

16. Rabiner, L.R., and B. Gold. *Theory and Application of Digital Signal Processing*. Englewood Cliffs, N.J.: Prentice-Hall, 1975.
17. Rabiner, L.R. and C.M. Rader, eds. *Digital Signal Processing*. New York: IEEE Press, 1972.
18. Rader, C.M. and B. Gold. "Digital Filter Design Techniques in the Frequency Domain." *Proc. Institute of Electrical and Electronic Engineers*, vol. 55 (February 1967):
19. Schwartz, M. and L. Shaw. *Signal Processing: Discrete Spectral Analysis, Detection and Estimation*. New York: McGraw-Hill, 1975.
20. Singleton, R.C. "An Algorithm for Computing the Mixed Radix Fast Fourier Transform. *Institute of Electrical and Electronic Engineers Transactions on Audio Electroacoustics*. vol. AU-17 (June 1969): pp. 93-103.
21. Stanley, W.D. *Digital Signal Processing*. Reston, Va.: Reston Publishing Co., 1975.
22. Hewlett Packard. *Hewlett Packard Journal* vol 21, no. 10 (June 1970).
23. Hewlett Packard. *Fourier Analyzer Training Manual 140-0*, Hewlett Packard 1501 G Page Mill Rd, Palo Alto, CA 94304.
24. Tectronix. *An Introduction to . . . Time and Frequency Domain Modulation and Waveform Analysis with Lab Experiments*, Tektronic Inc., Dept. a, PO Box 500, Beaverton, OR 97077.
25. Time/Date. "TSL-Time Series Language," Time/Data 1050 Meadow Circle, Palo Alto, CA 94303.

Index

Index

About the Authors

Fred Taylor has been involved in research in the areas of information and control since graduating with the Ph.D. degree from the University of Colorado in 1969. His experience has ranged from applied industrial to abstract research. At Texas Instruments Inc., he led an effort to develop techniques applicable to optical character and speech recognition. He was awarded several patents for his work in this area. While at Texas Instruments he was a visiting industrial professor at Southern Methodist University. From 1970 until 1975 he was on the faculty of the Electrical Engineering Department at The University of Texas at El Paso, and is Associate Professor of Electrical Engineering at the University of Cincinnati. His academic responsibilities include instruction in control, communication, and computer system theory. In addition to his academic duties, he has served as a consultant to a number of research laboratories. Dr. Taylor has over thirty publications in the area of modeling, signal processing, adaptive systems, parameter identification, and optimal computational algorithms of systems theory.

Steve L. Smith received the B.S. and M.S. degrees in Electrical Engineering from the University of Texas at El Paso in 1973 and 1974, respectively. During the period 1973-1974, he served as a teaching assistant and computer programmer for the Department of Electrical Engineering. Professor Smith is a member of the Bioengineering Group at Rice University. At the present time he is conducting research in cardiac electrophysiology at the Baylor College of Medicine. His other research interests lie in the application of digital filtering techniques to biomedical data.

AS A SERVICE TO THE READER OF *DIGITAL SIGNAL PROCESSING IN FORTRAN,* TAYLOR AND SMITH, THE COMPUTER CENTER OF THE UNIVERSITY OF TEXAS AT EL PASO WILL SUPPLY TO A SUBSCRIBER, SPECTRUM IV IN SOURCE FORM ON CARDS, TAPE, OR AS A LISTING ONLY:

****

PLEASE SEND ME IN FORTRAN IV SOURCE FORM THE FOLLOWING SPECTRUM IV ITEMS:

☐ PUNCH CARDS ($30.00)

☐ 9 TRACK, 800 BPI TAPE ($10.00)

☐ LISTING ONLY ($10.00)

ORDERS ARE TO BE MADE PAYABLE TO THE UNIVERSITY OF TEXAS AT EL PASO

☐ PAYMENT ENCLOSED

☐ PURCHASE ORDER ENCLOSED

NAME ______________________________

COMPANY OR
ORGANIZATION ______________________

MAIL STATION ______________________

ADDRESS ___________________________

CITY ____________ STATE ________ ZIP ______

MAIL TO:

THE COMPUTER CENTER
BELL HALL
THE UNIVERSITY OF TEXAS AT EL PASO
EL PASO, TEXAS 79968